"THEREFORE REPENT! IF YOU DO NOT,
I WILL COME TO YOU SOON AND FIGHT
AGAINST THEM WITH THE SWORD
OF MY MOUTH."

REVELATIONS 2:16

IDW Publishing
4411 Morena Blvd. Ste 106
San Diego, CA 92117
www.idwpublishing.com

Therefore Repent! : a post-Rapture graphic novel /
Jim Munroe ; illustrations by Salgood Sam.

ISBN 978-1-60010-146-5
10 09 08 07 1 2 3 4

An excerpt from this book appeared in Taddle Creek Vol. 10, No. 1.

Published by No Media Kings <www.nomediakings.org> in Canada.
Published by IDW <www.idwpublishing.com> in the United States.

IDW Publishing is:
Ted Adams, President
Robbie Robbins, EVP/Sr. Graphic Artist
Chris Ryall, Publisher/Editor-in-Chief
Clifford Meth, EVP of Strategies/Editorial
Alan Payne, VP of Sales
Neil Uyetake, Art Director
Tom Waltz, Editor
Andrew Steven Harris, Editor
Chris Mowry, Graphic Artist
Amauri Osorio, Graphic Artist
Dene Nee, Graphic Artist/Editor
Matthew Ruzicka, CPA, Controller
Alonzo Simon, Shipping Manager
Kris Oprisko, Editor/Foreign Lic. Rep.

We can publish a novel independently, but we can't do it alone. Thanks to our editing team: Suzanne Andrew, Carol Borden, Susan Bustos, Claudia Dávila, Todd Dills, Shannon Gerard, Nancy Johnston, Carma Jolly, Guy Leshinski, Hamish MacDonald, Craig Macnaughton, Joe Meno, Marc Ngui, Matthew Shepherd, Jef Smith, Conan Tobias, Scott Waters, & Jessica Westhead. Thanks also to Peter Birkemoe, Chris Butcher, Terry Grogan, Michel Lacombe, Terry Lau, Mike O'Connor, & Cassandra Witteman.

We acknowledge the support of the Canada Council for the Arts which last year invested $20.1 million in writing and publishing throughout Canada.

CHAPTER 1

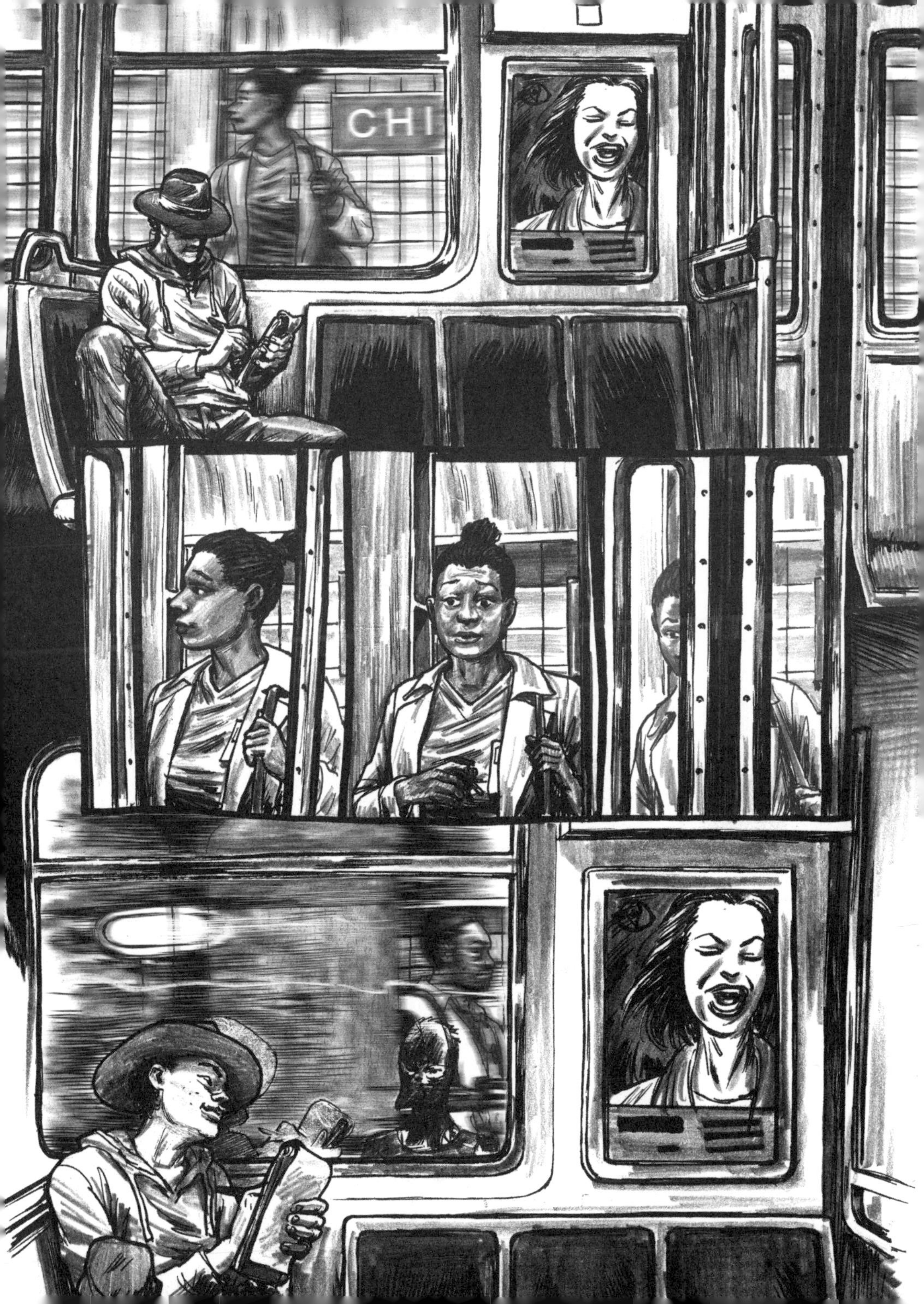
CHI

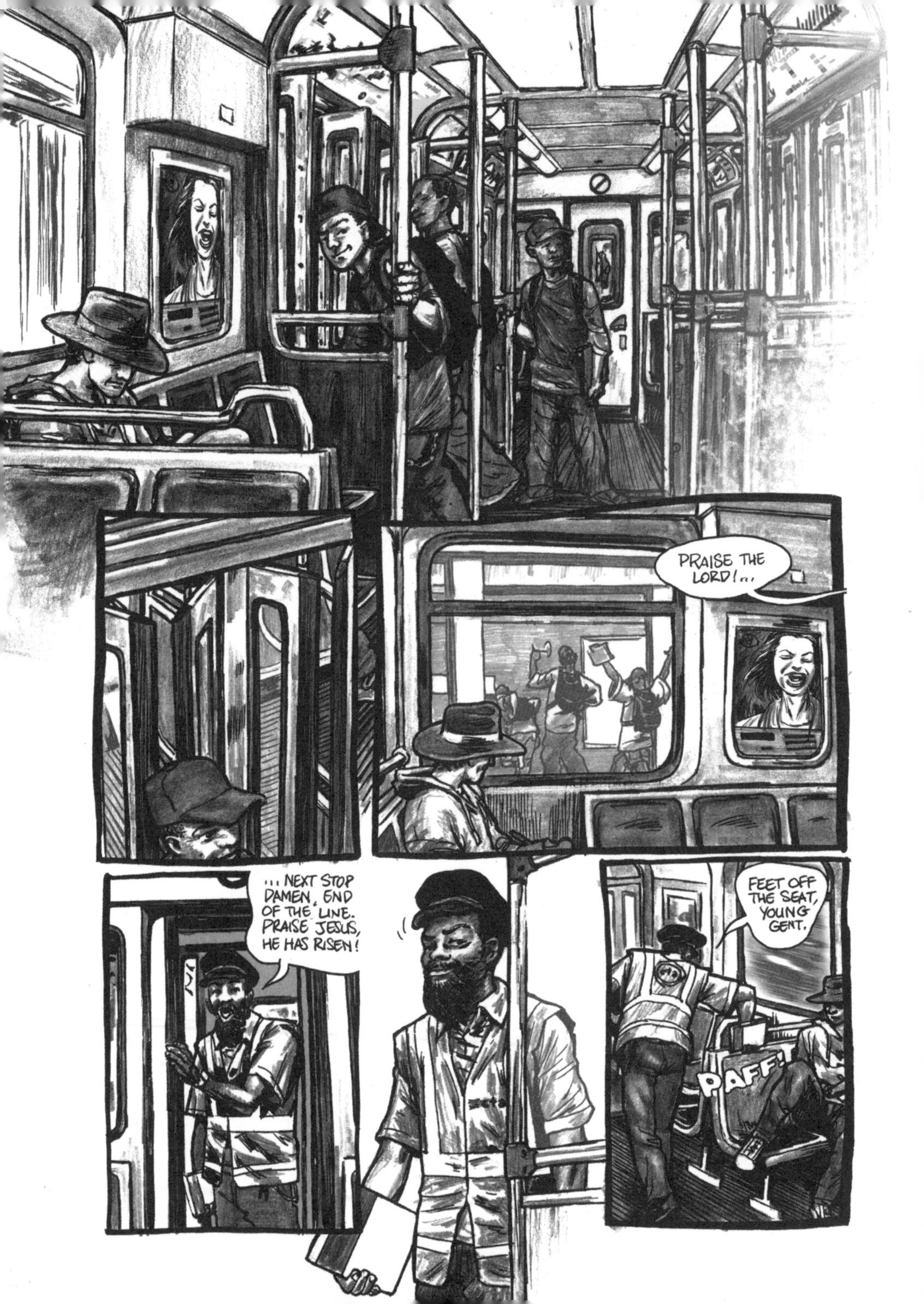
PRAISE THE LORD!...
...NEXT STOP DAMEN, END OF THE LINE. PRAISE JESUS, HE HAS RISEN!
FEET OFF THE SEAT, YOUNG GENT.
PAFF!

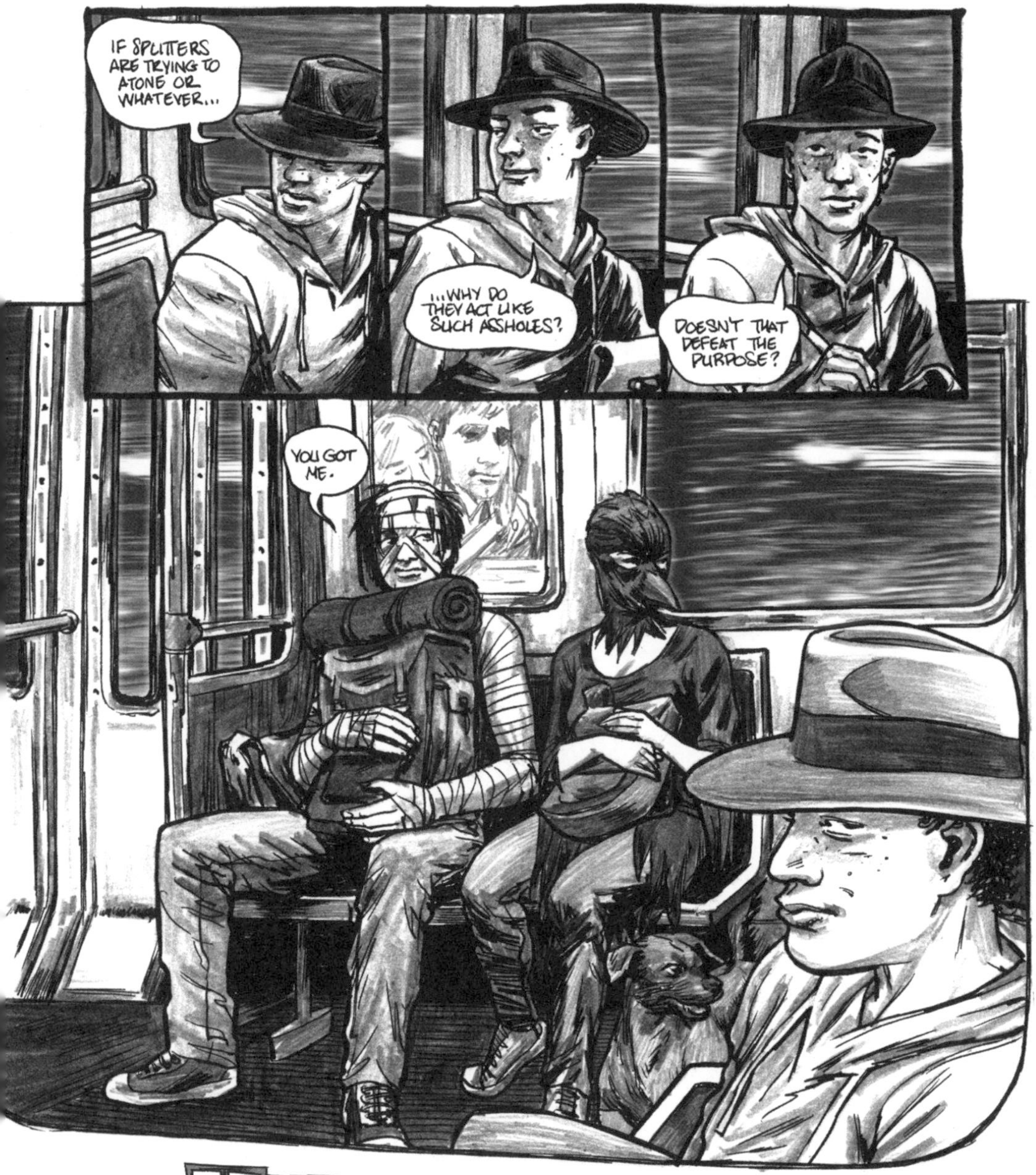
IF SPLITTERS ARE TRYING TO ATONE OR WHATEVER...
...WHY DO THEY ACT LIKE SUCH ASSHOLES?
DOESN'T THAT DEFEAT THE PURPOSE?
YOU GOT ME.

THEREFORE REPENT!

Story by Jim Munroe
Art by Salgood Sam

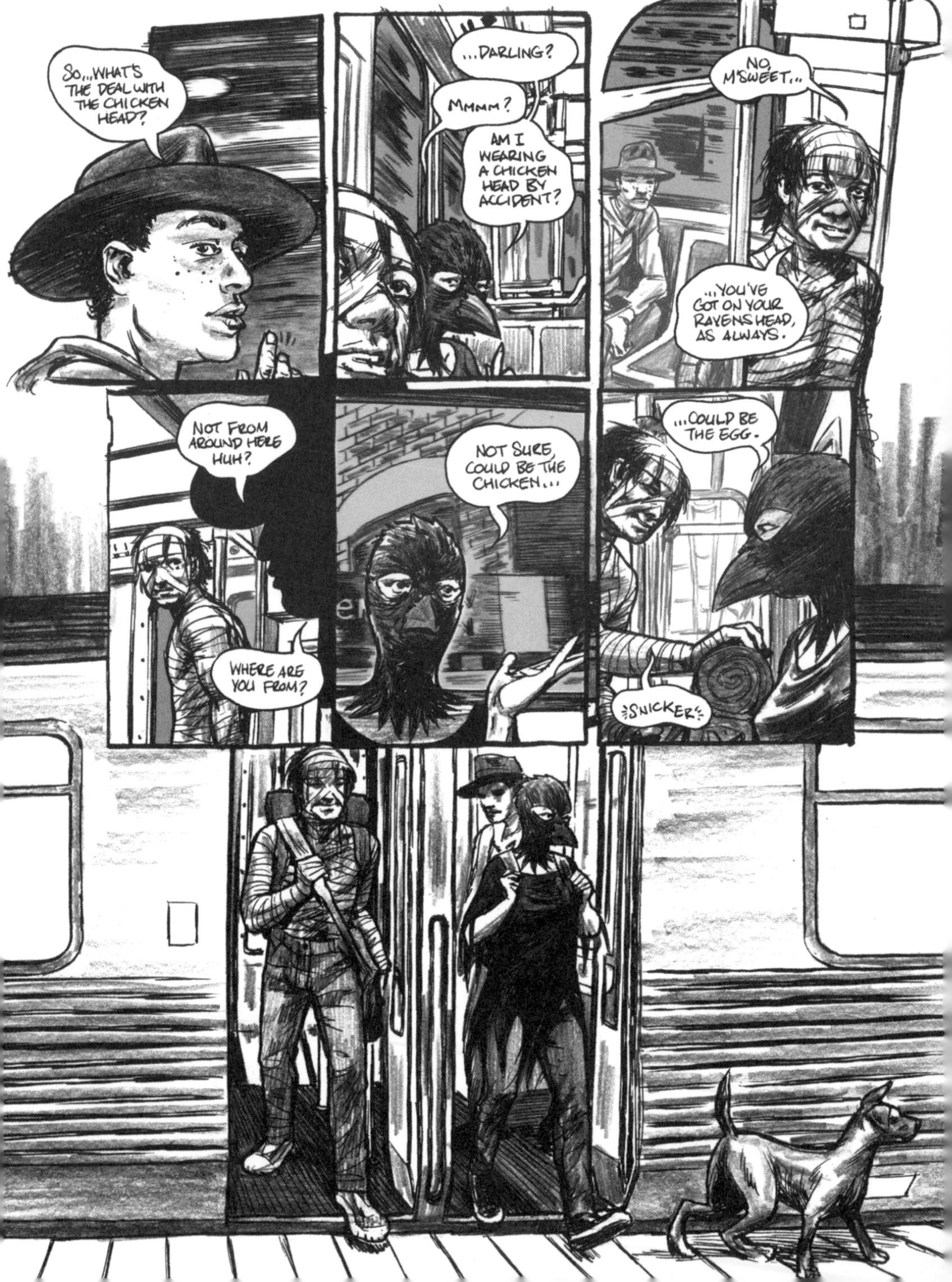
So,.. WHAT'S THE DEAL WITH THE CHICKEN HEAD?
...DARLING?
MMMM?
AM I WEARING A CHICKEN HEAD BY ACCIDENT?
NO, M'SWEET,..
..YOU'VE GOT ON YOUR RAVENS HEAD, AS ALWAYS.
NOT FROM AROUND HERE HUH?
WHERE ARE YOU FROM?
NOT SURE, COULD BE THE CHICKEN...
...COULD BE THE EGG.
SNICKER

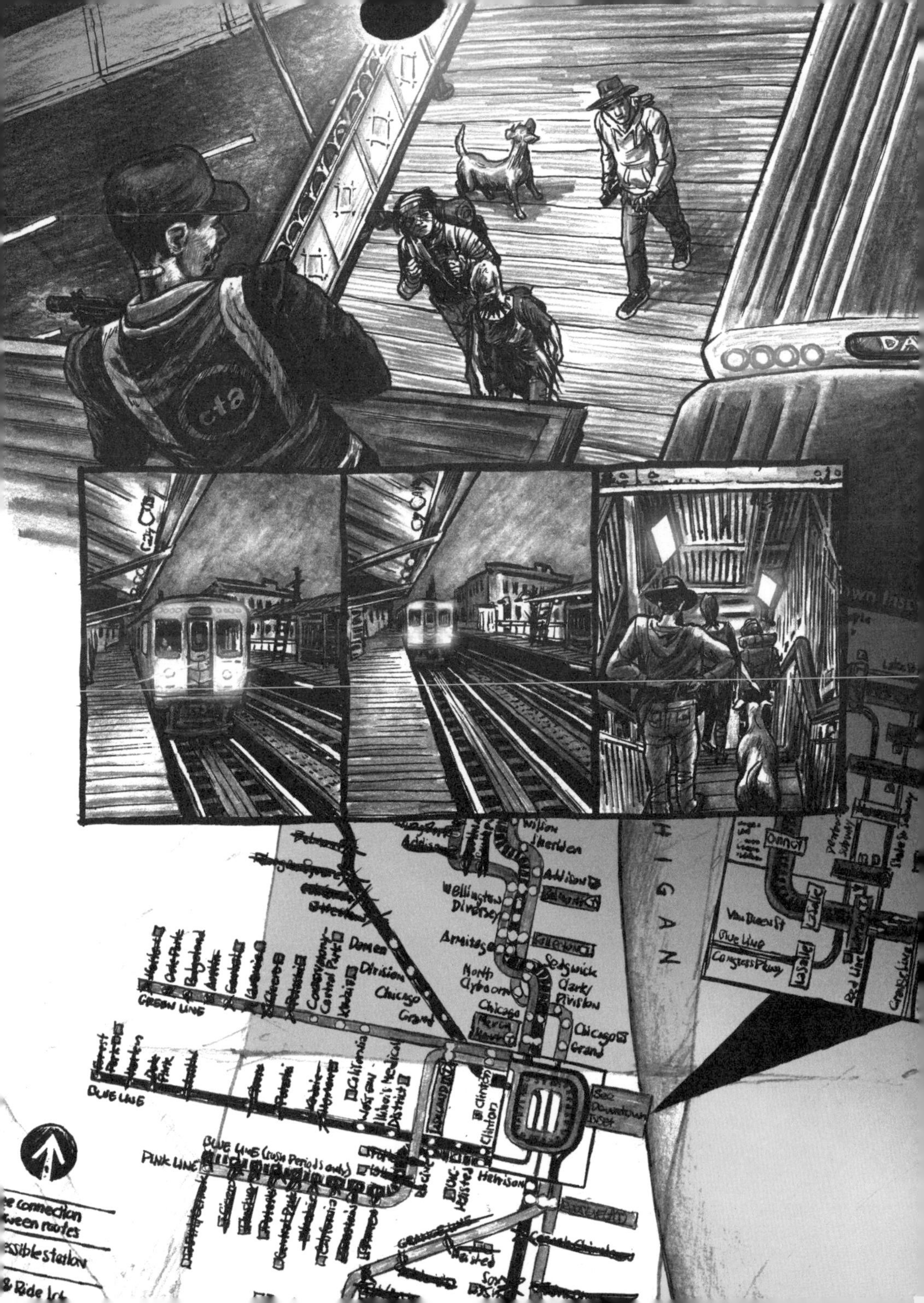
cta
Wilson
Sheridan
Addison
Wellington
Diversey
Armitage
Sedgwick
North
Clybourn
Clark/
Division
Chicago
Grand
Damen
Division
Chicago
Grand
GREEN LINE
BLUE LINE
Illinois Medical
District
Clinton
Clinton
BLUE LINE (rush Periods only)
PINK LINE
UIC
Halsted
Harrison
See
Downtown
Inset
H
I
G
A
N
Quincy
Van Buren St
Blue Line
Congress Pkwy
LaSalle
Red Line
ee connection
tween routes
ssible station
& Ride lot

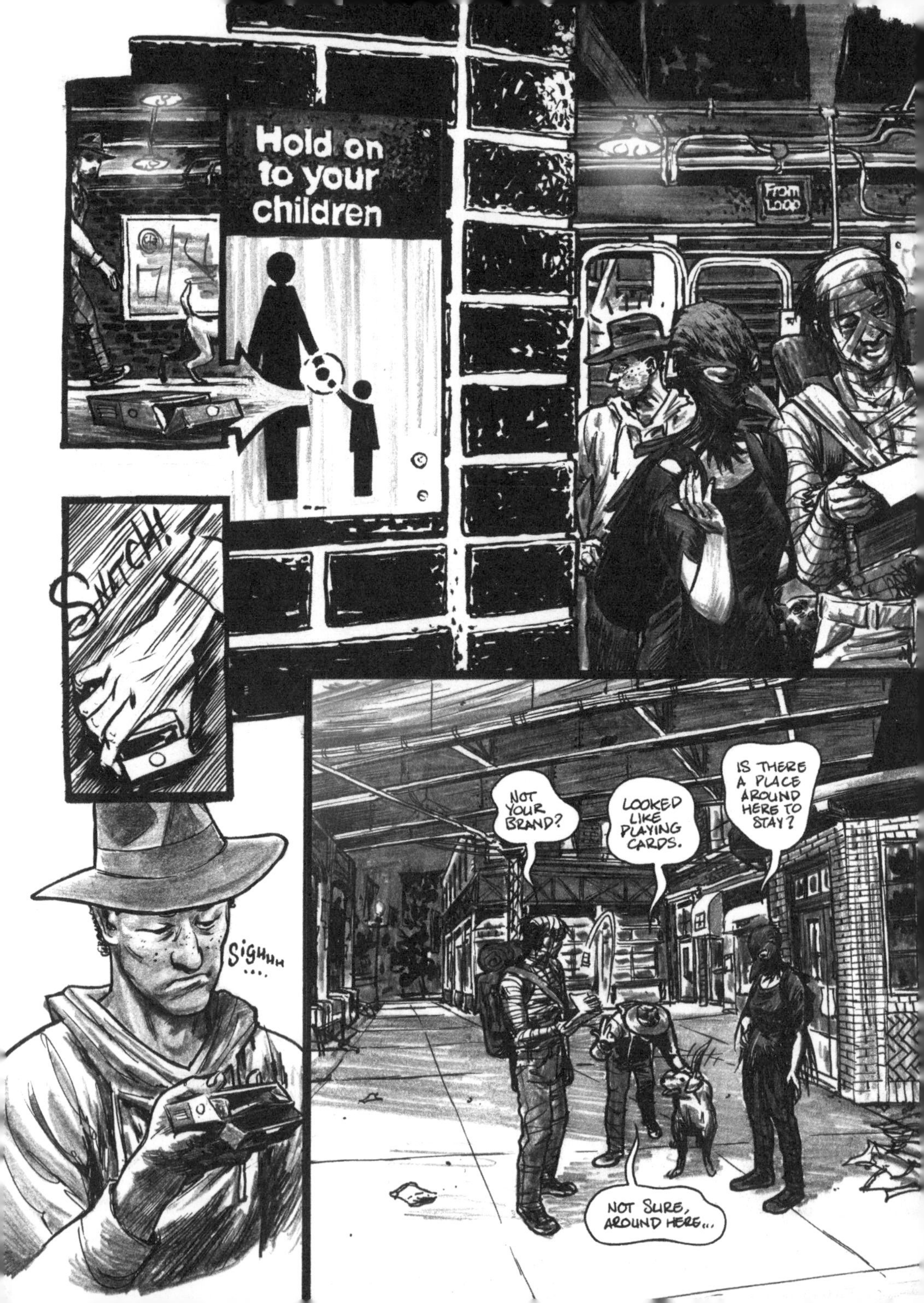
Hold on to your children
From Loop
SNATCH!
Sighhh....
NOT YOUR BRAND?
LOOKED LIKE PLAYING CARDS.
IS THERE A PLACE AROUND HERE TO STAY?
NOT SURE, AROUND HERE...

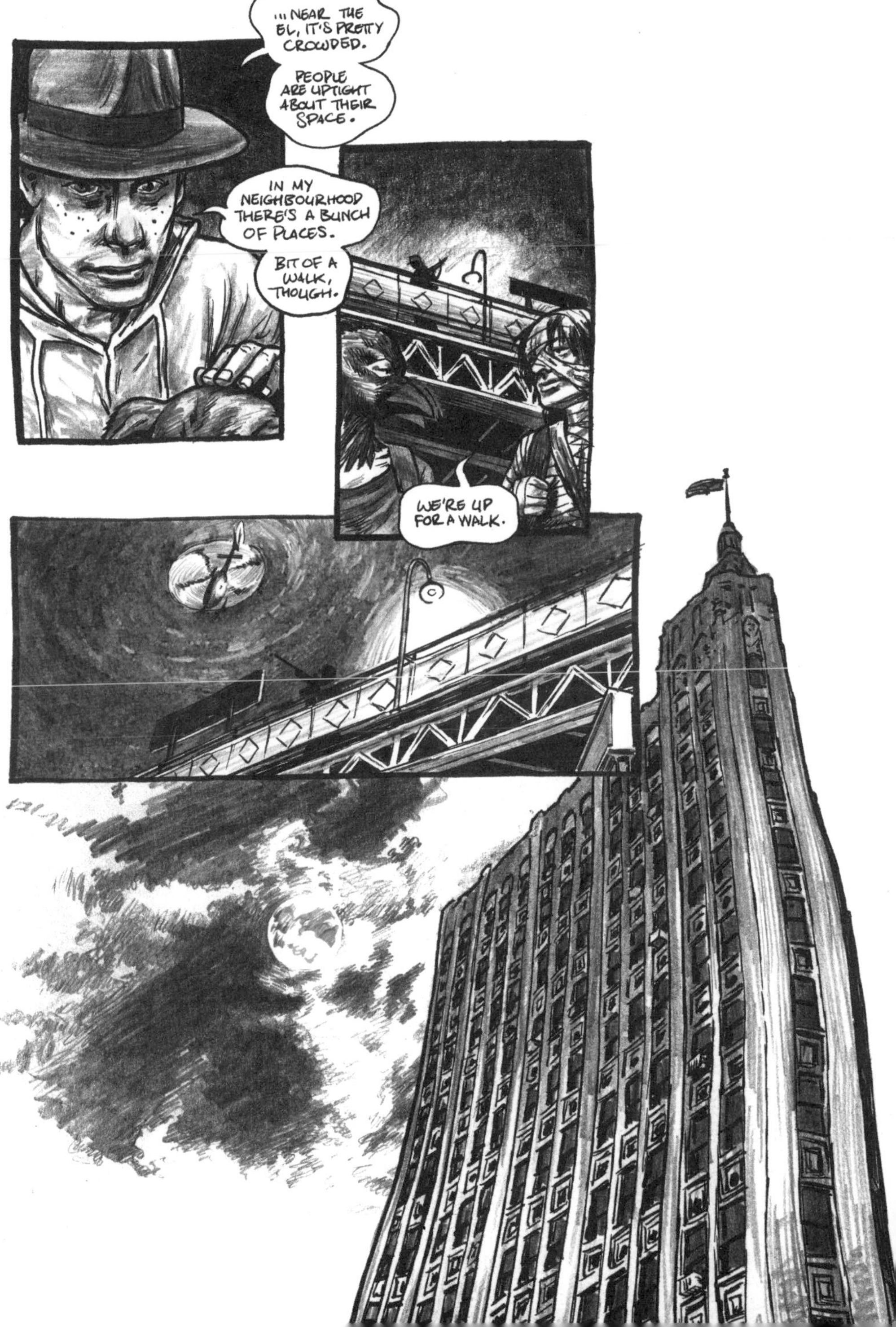
...NEAR THE EL, IT'S PRETTY CROWDED.
PEOPLE ARE UPTIGHT ABOUT THEIR SPACE.
IN MY NEIGHBOURHOOD THERE'S A BUNCH OF PLACES.
BIT OF A WALK, THOUGH.
WE'RE UP FOR A WALK.

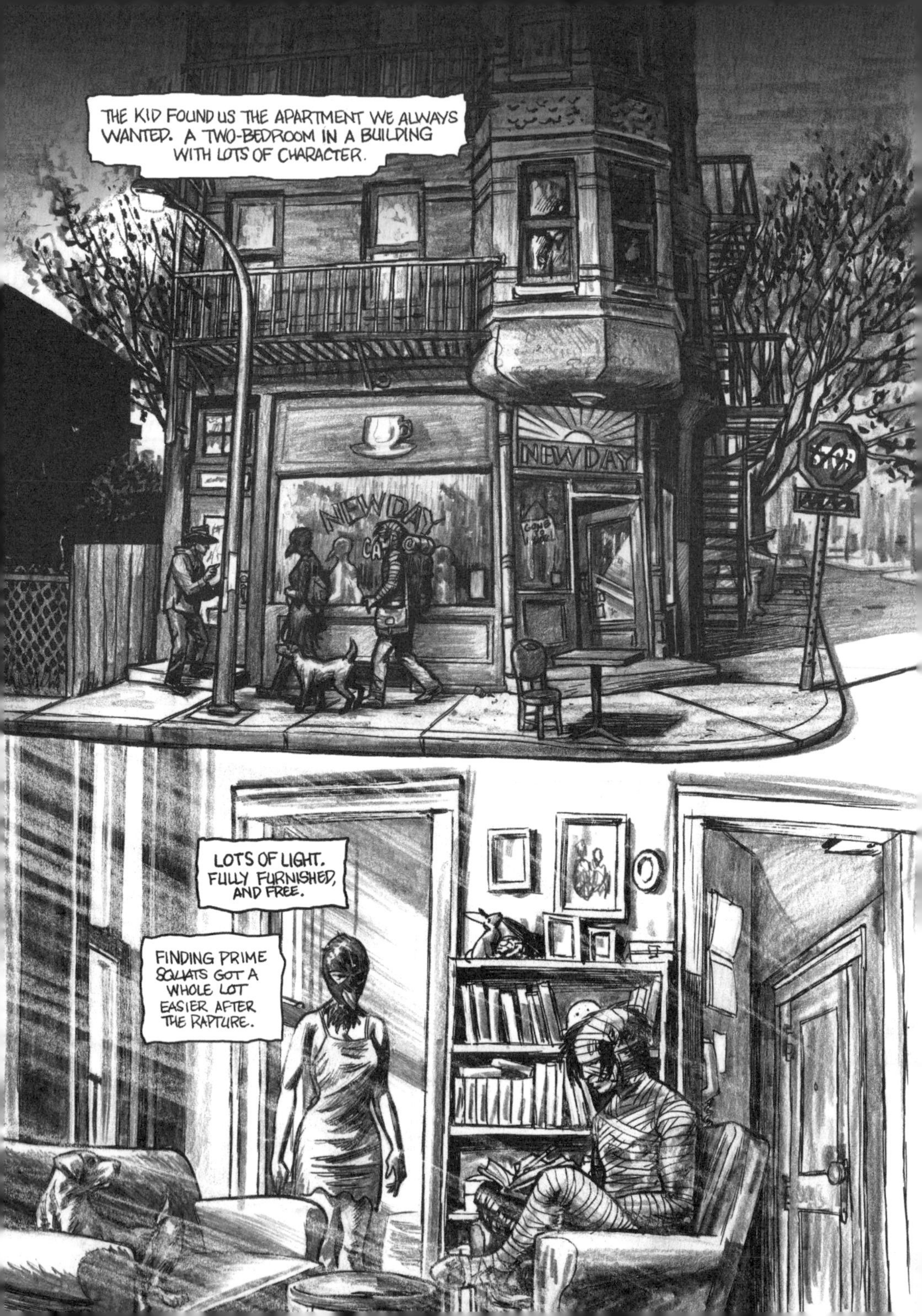
THE KID FOUND US THE APARTMENT WE ALWAYS WANTED. A TWO-BEDROOM IN A BUILDING WITH LOTS OF CHARACTER.
NEW DAY
NEW DAY
LOTS OF LIGHT. FULLY FURNISHED, AND FREE.
FINDING PRIME SQUATS GOT A WHOLE LOT EASIER AFTER THE RAPTURE.

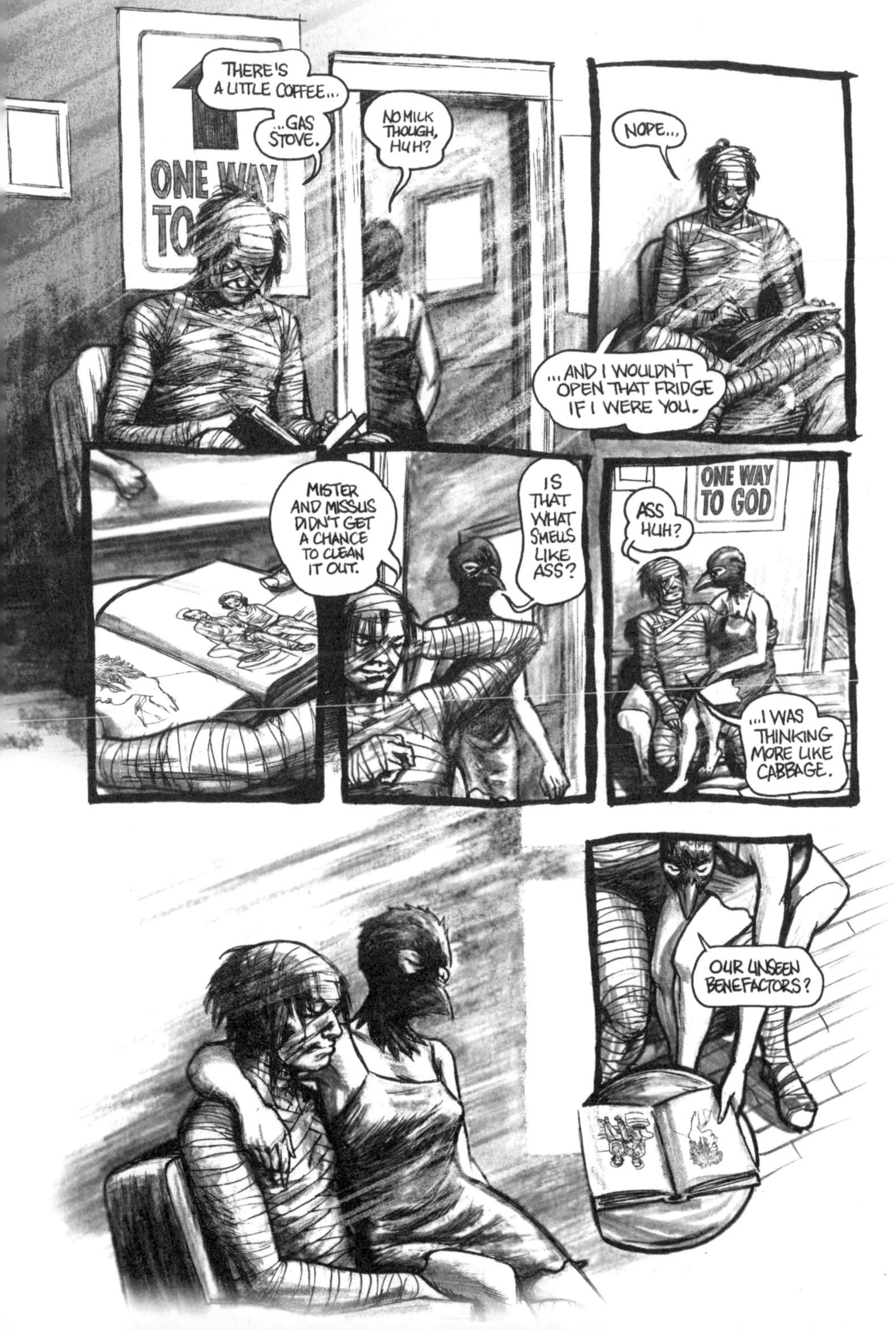
THERE'S A LITTLE COFFEE...
...GAS STOVE.
NO MILK THOUGH, HUH?
NOPE...
...AND I WOULDN'T OPEN THAT FRIDGE IF I WERE YOU.
MISTER AND MISSUS DIDN'T GET A CHANCE TO CLEAN IT OUT.
IS THAT WHAT SMELLS LIKE ASS?
ONE WAY TO GOD
ASS HUH?
...I WAS THINKING MORE LIKE CABBAGE.
OUR UNSEEN BENEFACTORS?

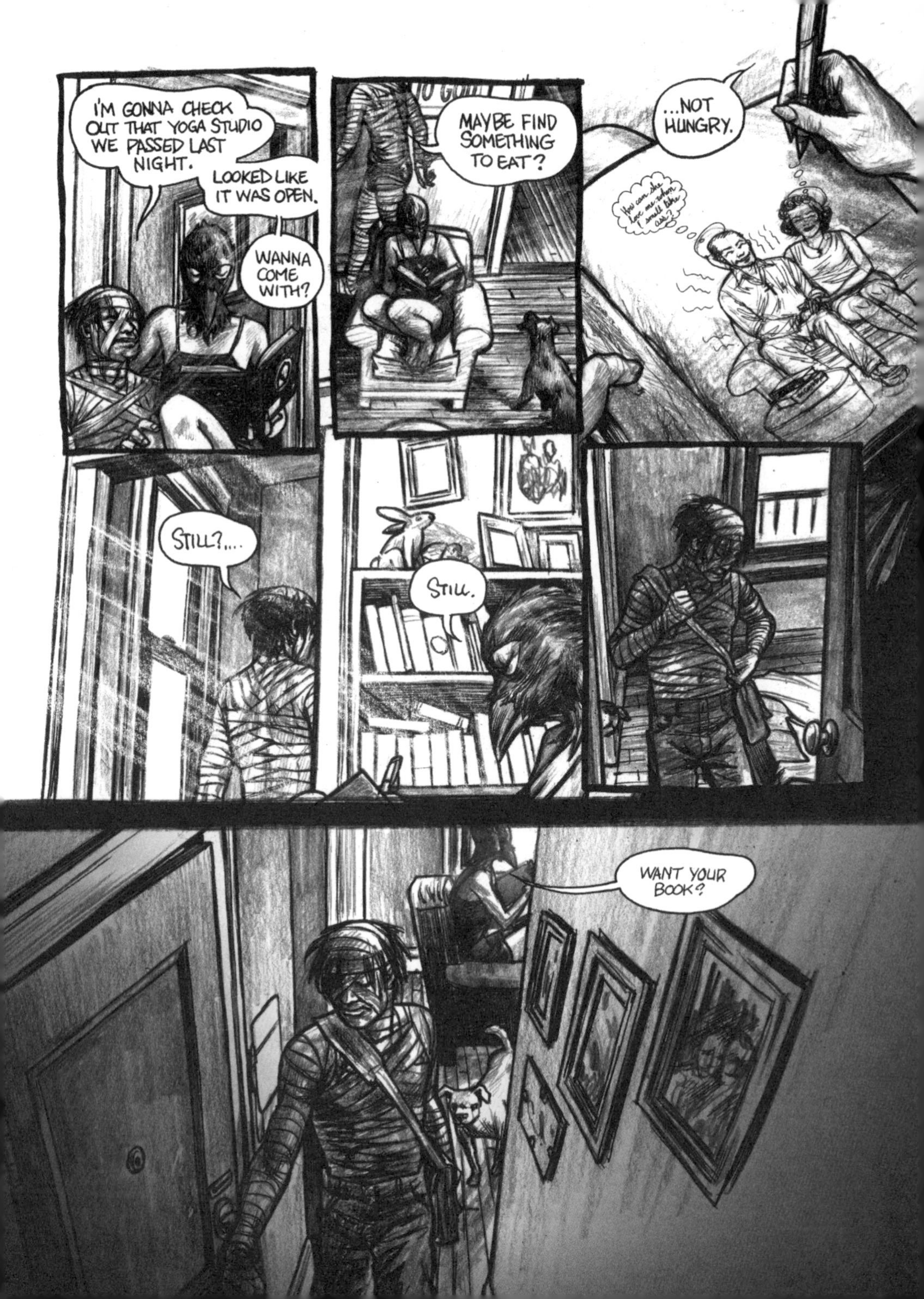
I'M GONNA CHECK OUT THAT YOGA STUDIO WE PASSED LAST NIGHT.
LOOKED LIKE IT WAS OPEN.
WANNA COME WITH?
MAYBE FIND SOMETHING TO EAT?
...NOT HUNGRY.
How can she love me when I smell like ass?
STILL?....
STILL.
WANT YOUR BOOK?

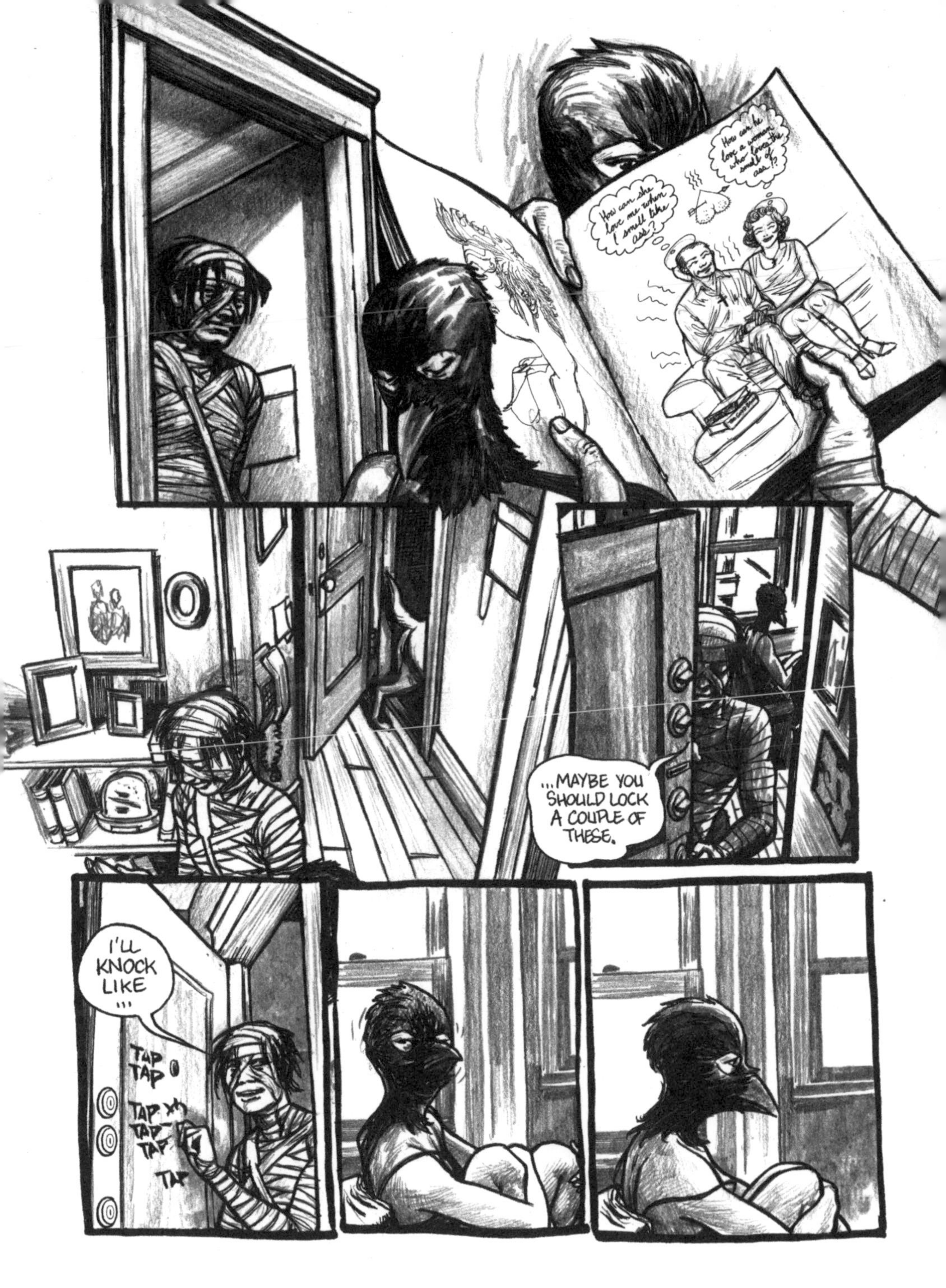

How can she love me when I smell like ass?
How can he love a woman who loves the smell of ass!?
...MAYBE YOU SHOULD LOCK A COUPLE OF THESE.
I'LL KNOCK LIKE ...
TAP TAP
TAP TAP TAP
TAP

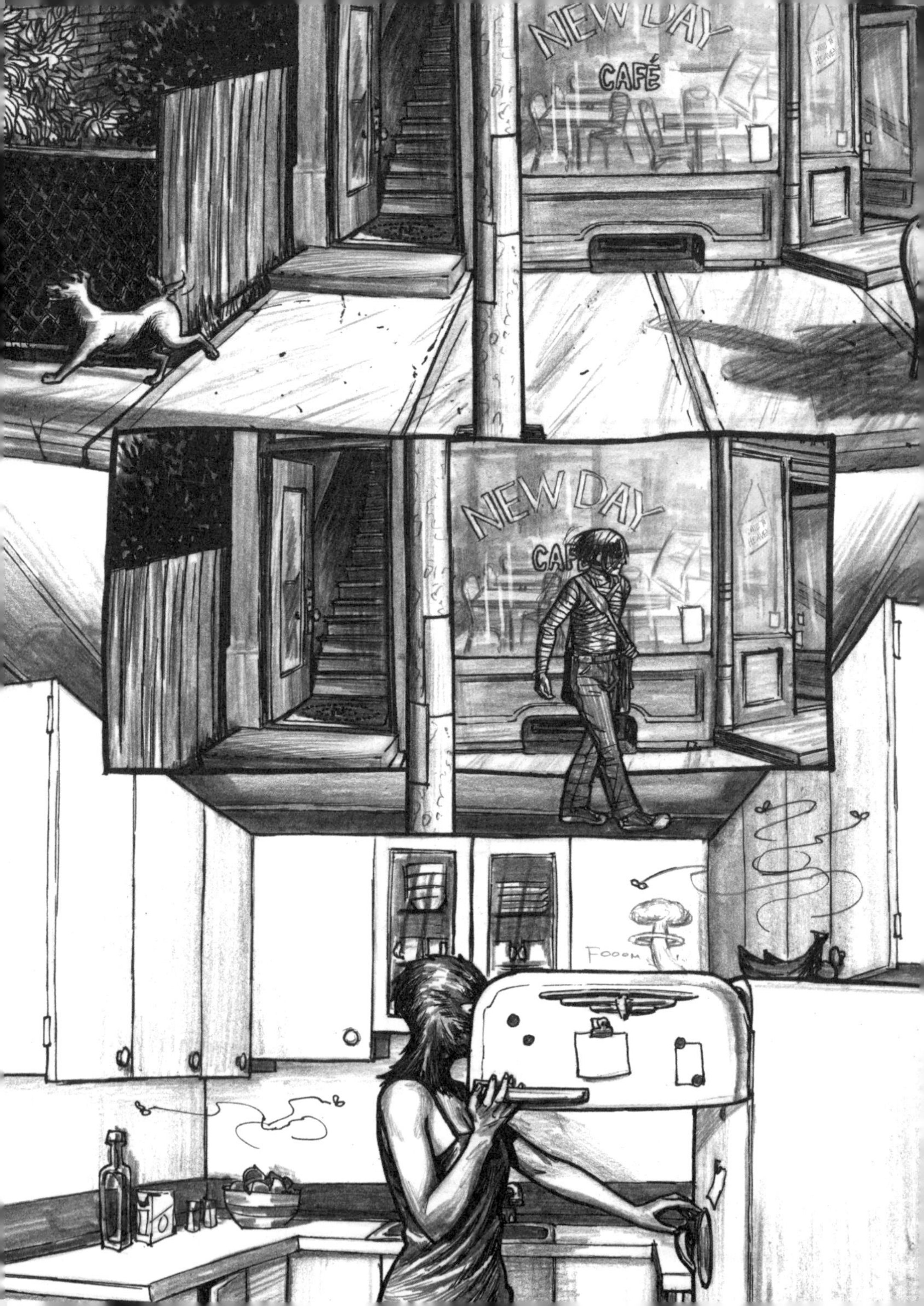
NEW DAY
CAFÉ
NEW DAY
CAF
FOOOM

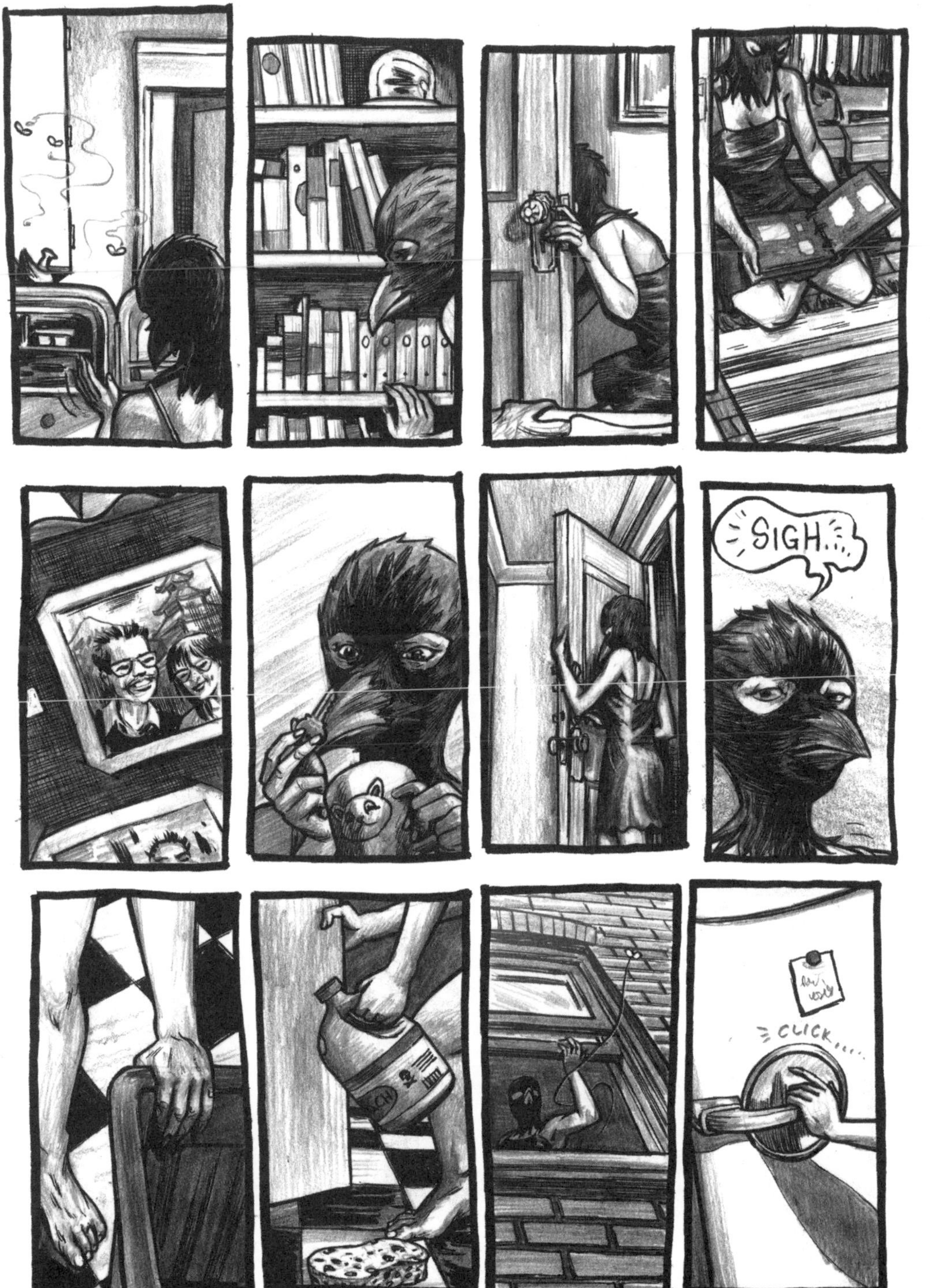
SIGH...
CLICK.....

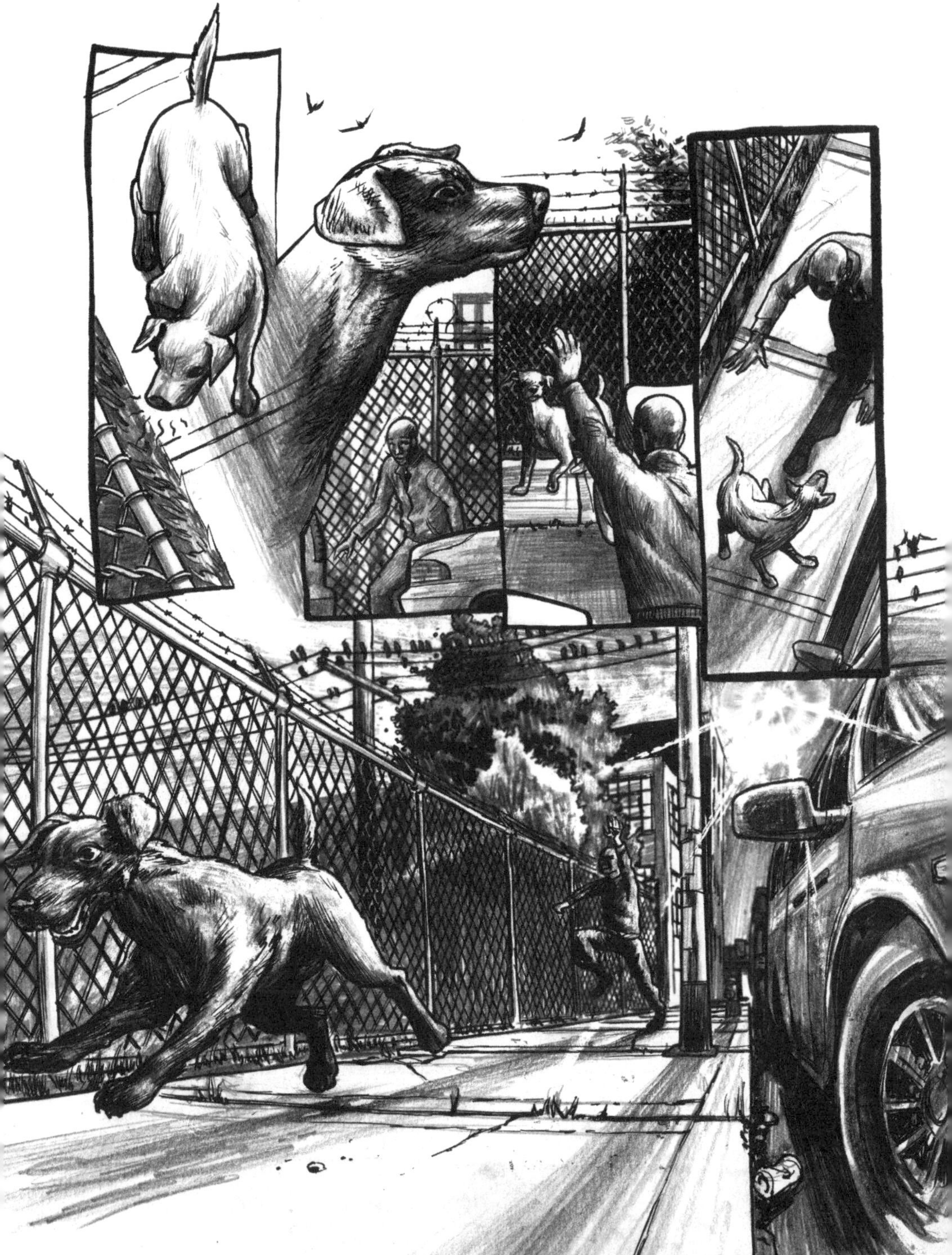

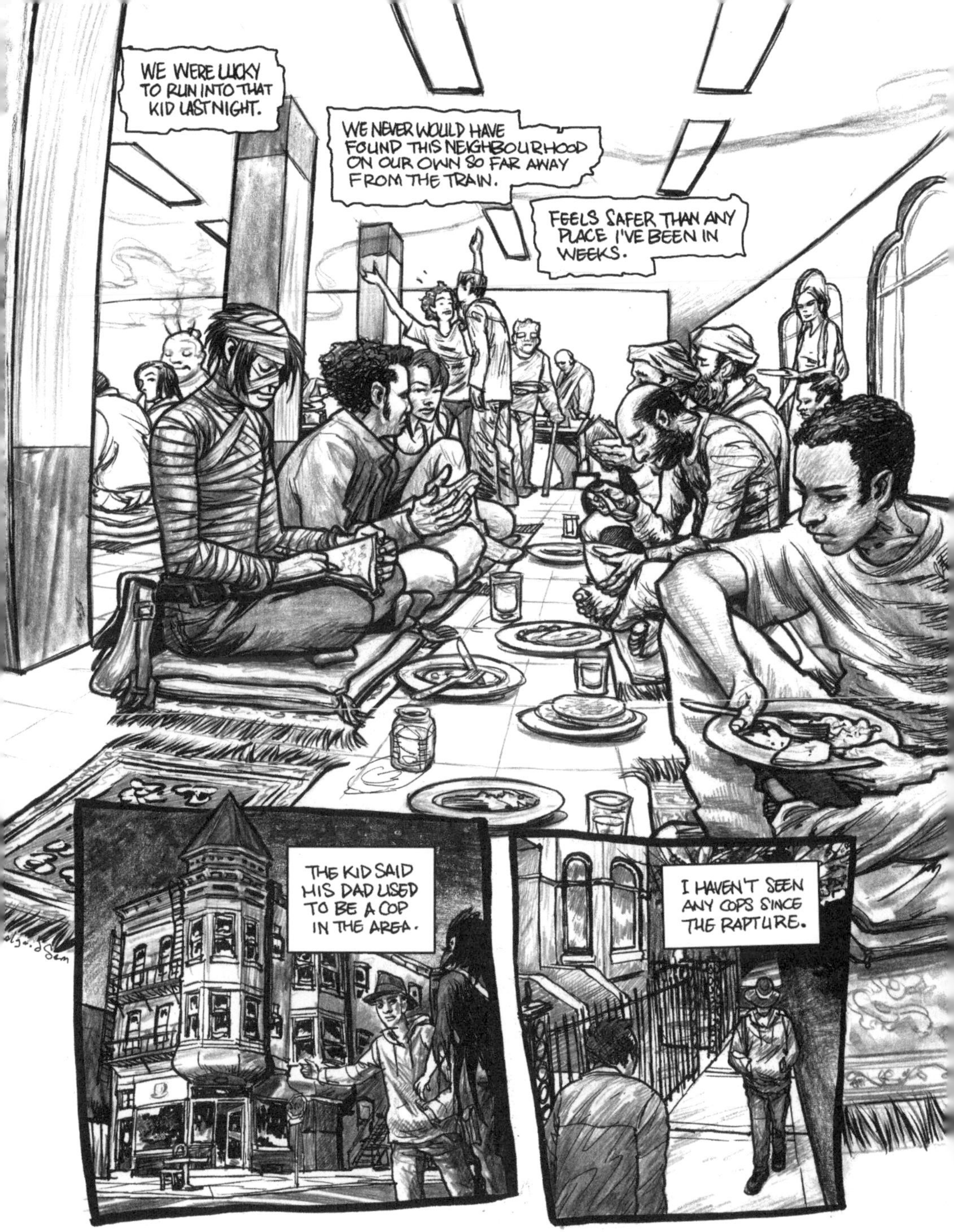
WE WERE LUCKY TO RUN INTO THAT KID LAST NIGHT.
WE NEVER WOULD HAVE FOUND THIS NEIGHBOURHOOD ON OUR OWN SO FAR AWAY FROM THE TRAIN.
FEELS SAFER THAN ANY PLACE I'VE BEEN IN WEEKS.
THE KID SAID HIS DAD USED TO BE A COP IN THE AREA.
I HAVEN'T SEEN ANY COPS SINCE THE RAPTURE.

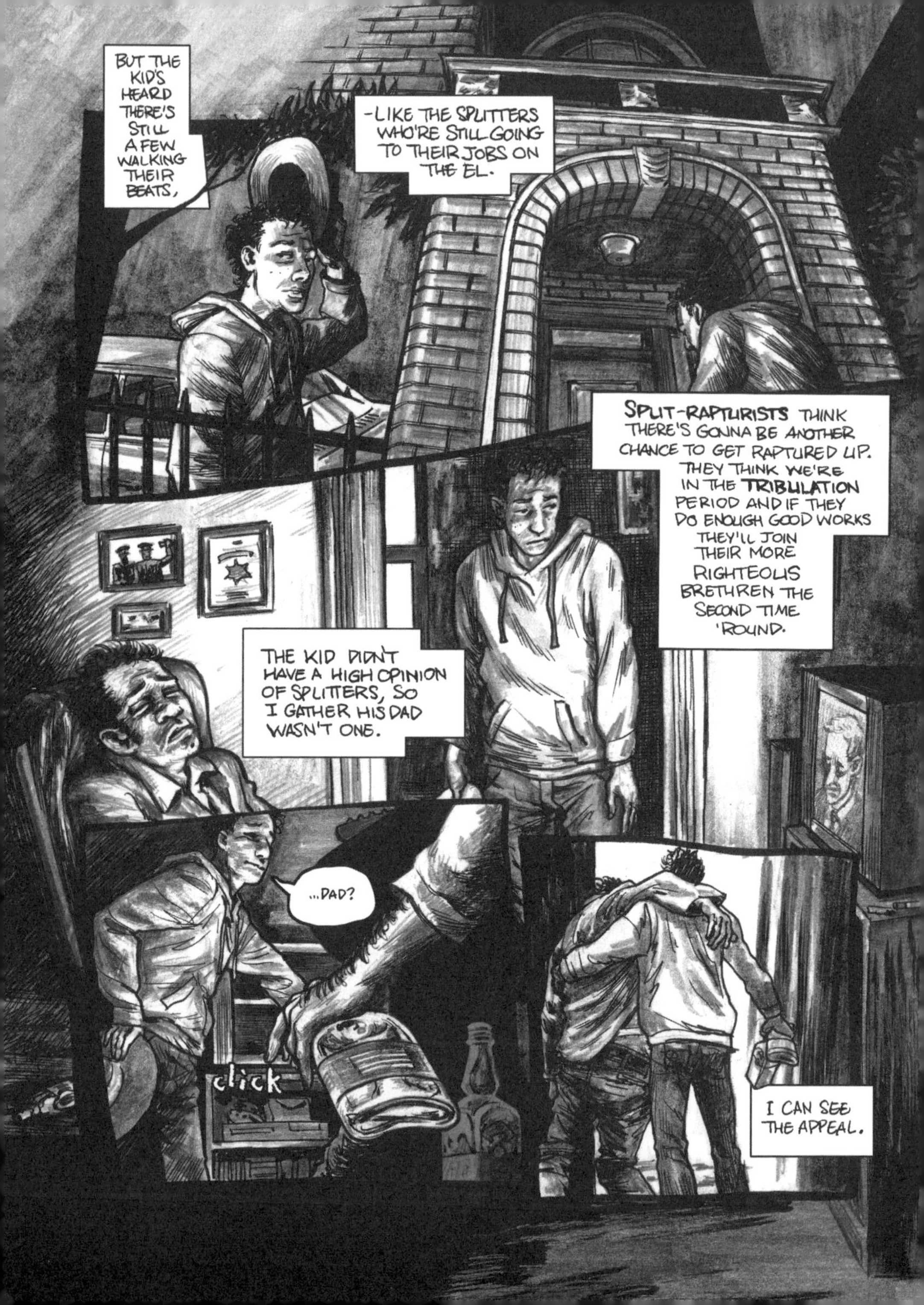
BUT THE KID'S HEARD THERE'S STILL A FEW WALKING THEIR BEATS,
-LIKE THE SPLITTERS WHO'RE STILL GOING TO THEIR JOBS ON THE EL.
SPLIT-RAPTURISTS THINK THERE'S GONNA BE ANOTHER CHANCE TO GET RAPTURED UP. THEY THINK WE'RE IN THE TRIBULATION PERIOD AND IF THEY DO ENOUGH GOOD WORKS THEY'LL JOIN THEIR MORE RIGHTEOUS BRETHREN THE SECOND TIME 'ROUND.
THE KID DIDN'T HAVE A HIGH OPINION OF SPLITTERS, SO I GATHER HIS DAD WASN'T ONE.
...DAD?
click
I CAN SEE THE APPEAL.

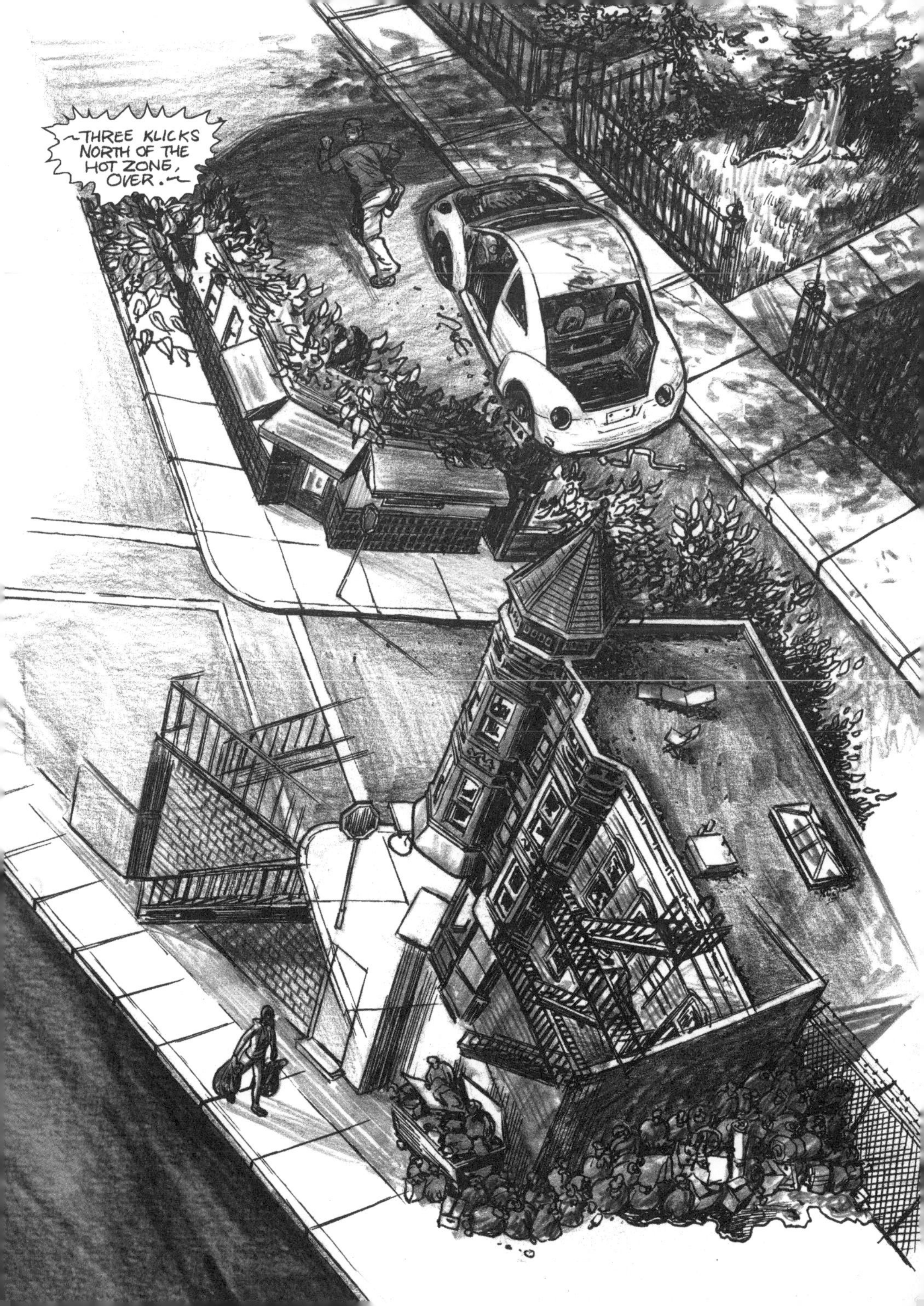
~THREE KLICKS NORTH OF THE HOT ZONE, OVER.~

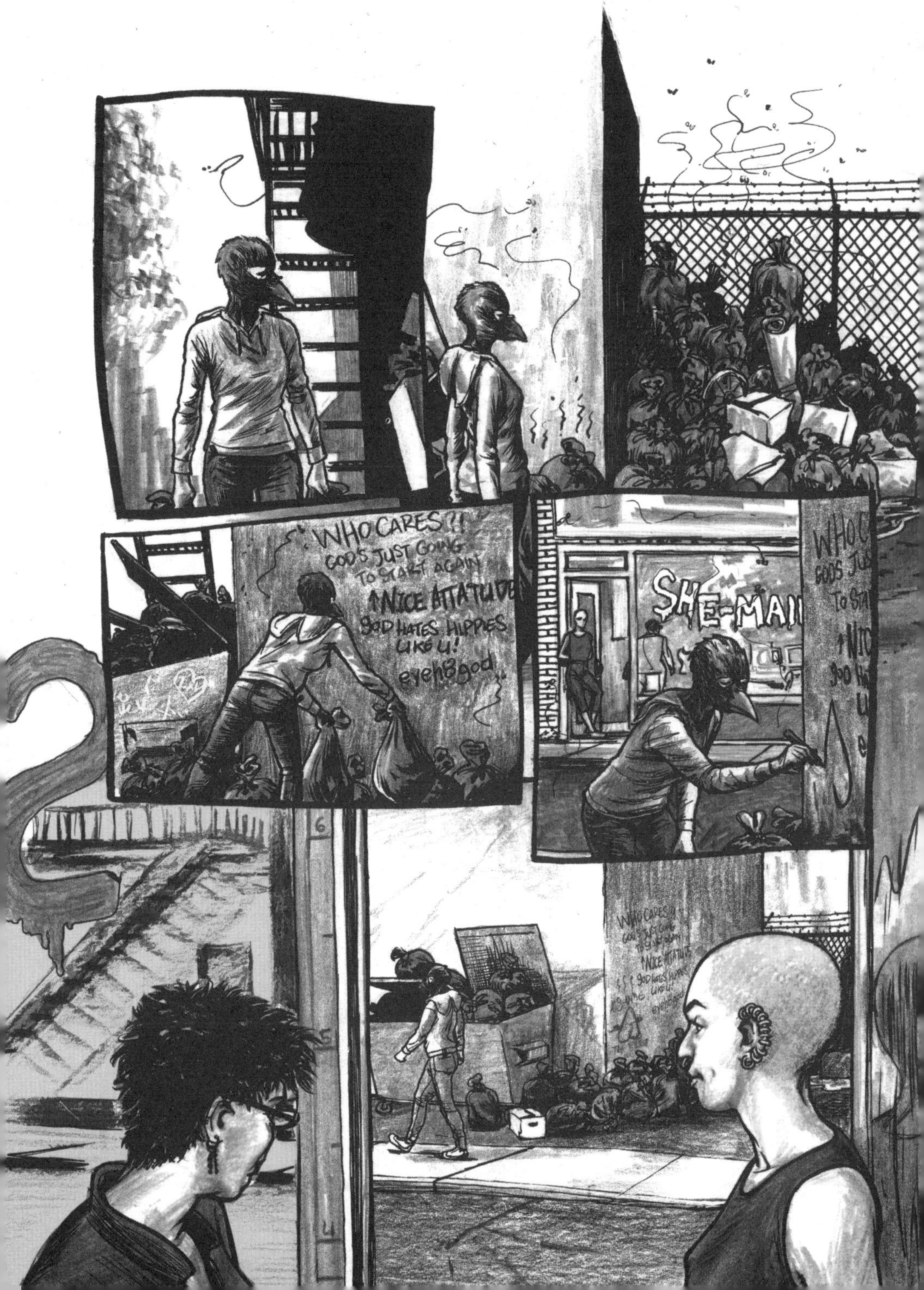
WHO CARES?!
GOD'S JUST GOING TO START AGAIN
↑NICE ATTATUDE
GOD HATES HIPPIES LIKE U!
eyeh8god
SHE-MAI

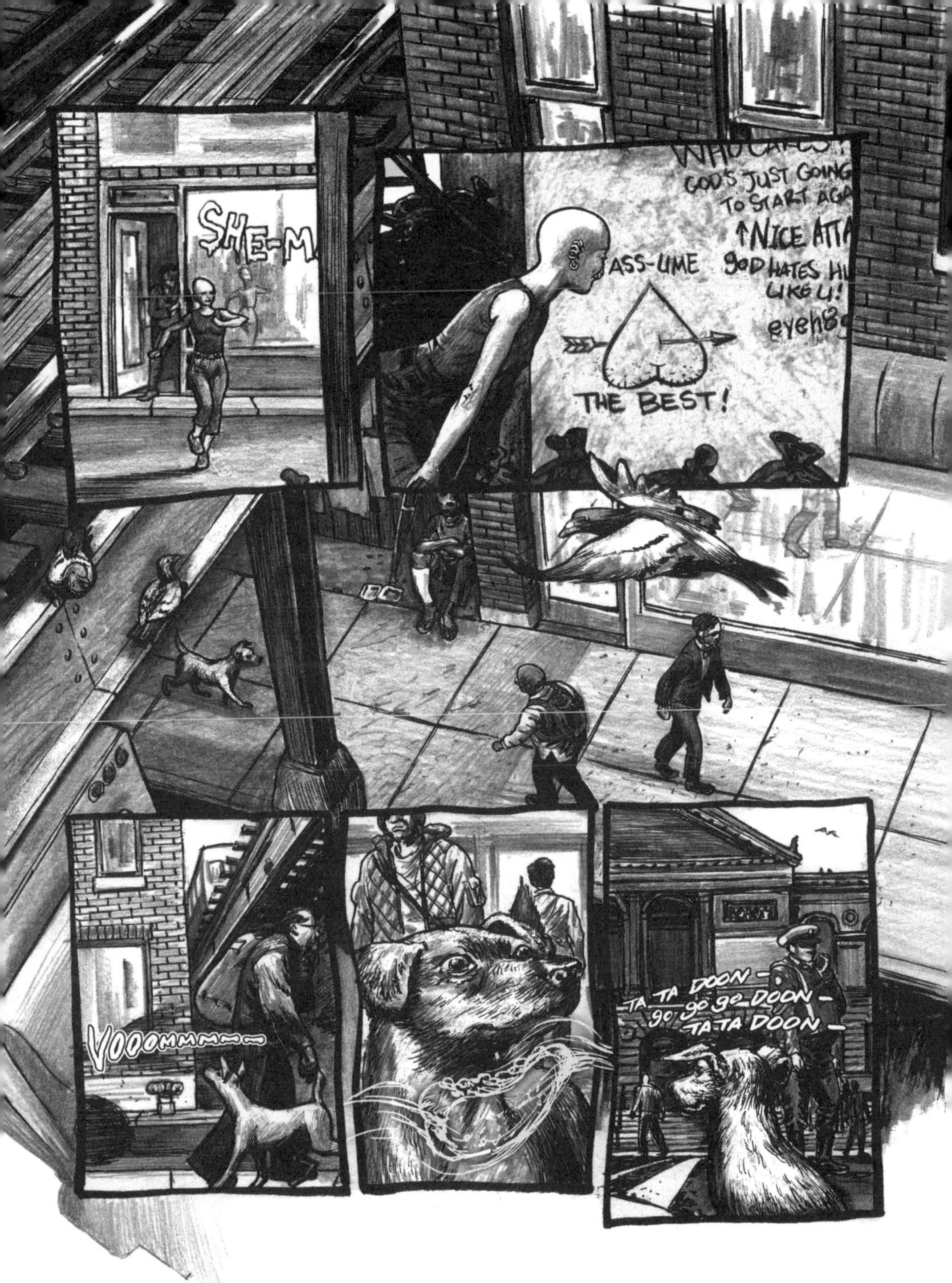
SHE-M
GOD'S JUST GOING
TO START AGA
↑NICE ATTA
ASS-UME
THE BEST!
god HATES HU
LIKE U!
eyeh8
VOOOMMM
TA TA DOON –
go go go DOON –
TA TA DOON –

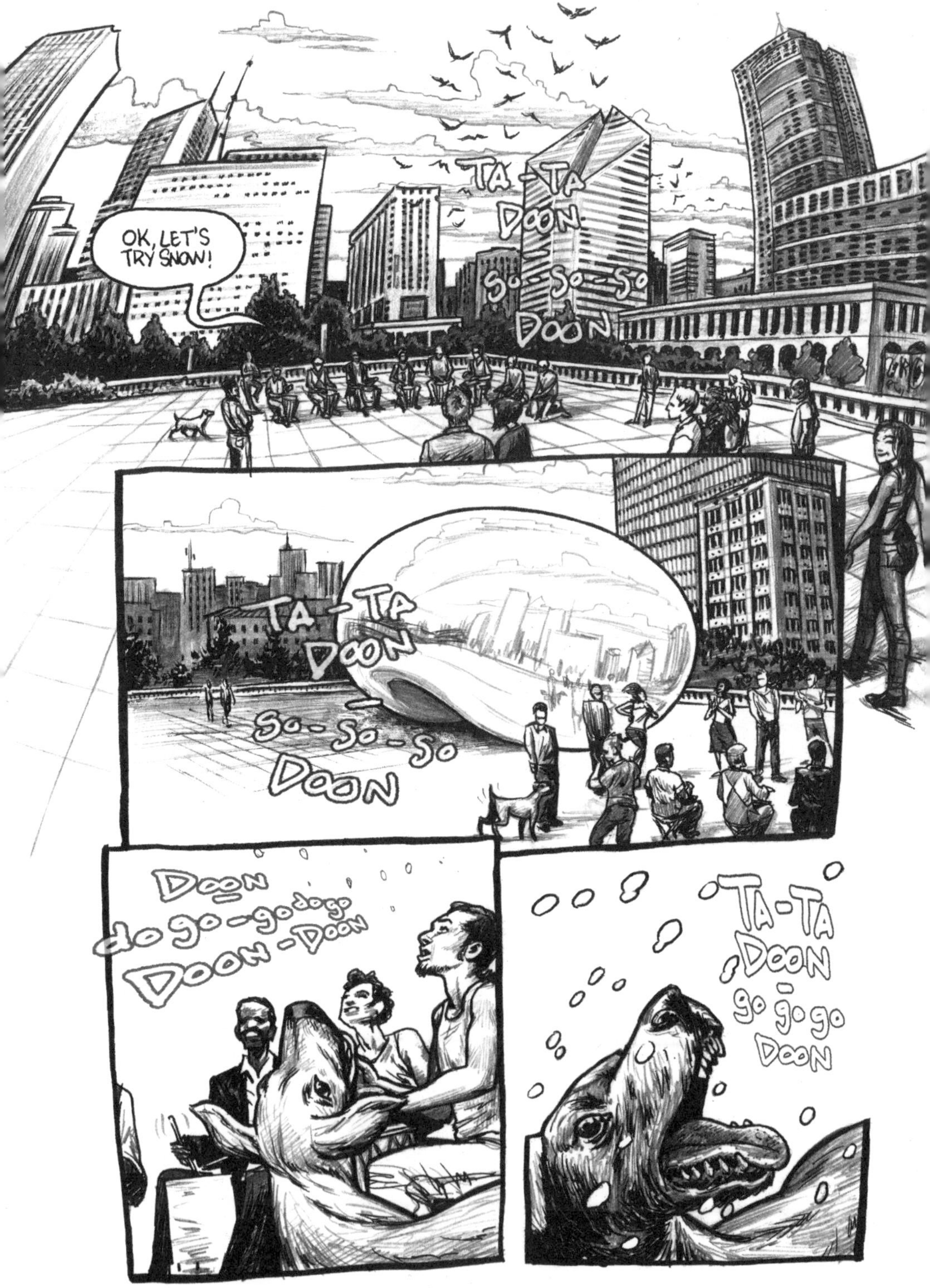
OK, LET'S TRY SNOW!
TA-TA DOON - SO-SO-SO DOON
TA-TA DOON - SO-SO-SO DOON
DOON - DO GO-GO DO GO DOON-DOON DOON
TA-TA DOON - GO GO GO DOON

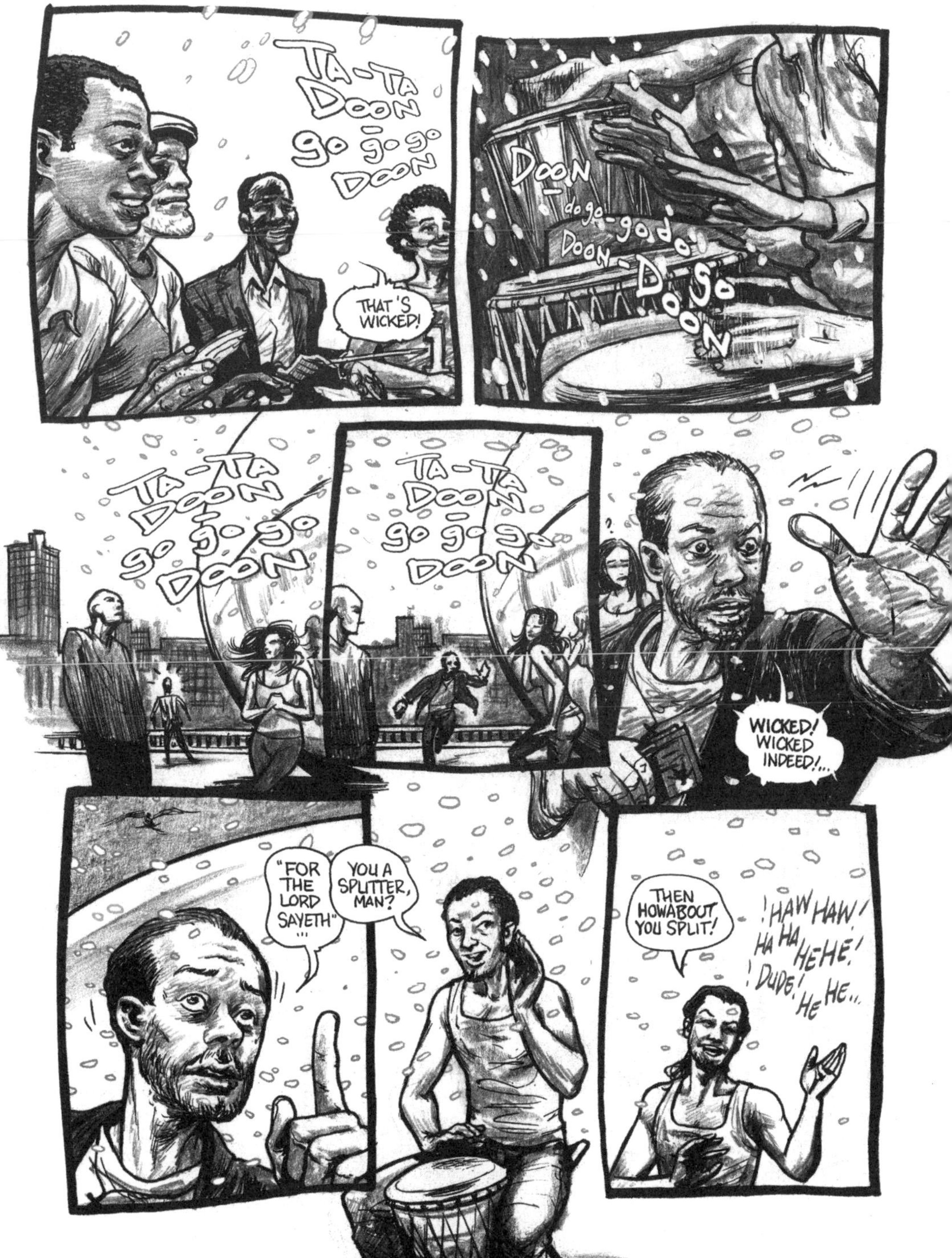
TA-TA DOON - GO GO GO DOON
THAT'S WICKED!
DOON - DOGO - GODO DOON - DOON SO
TA-TA DOON - GO GO GO DOON
TA-TA DOON - GO GO GO DOON
WICKED! WICKED INDEED!...
"FOR THE LORD SAYETH"...
YOU A SPLUTTER, MAN?
THEN HOWABOUT YOU SPLIT!
HAW HAW! HA HA HE HE! DUDE! HE HE...

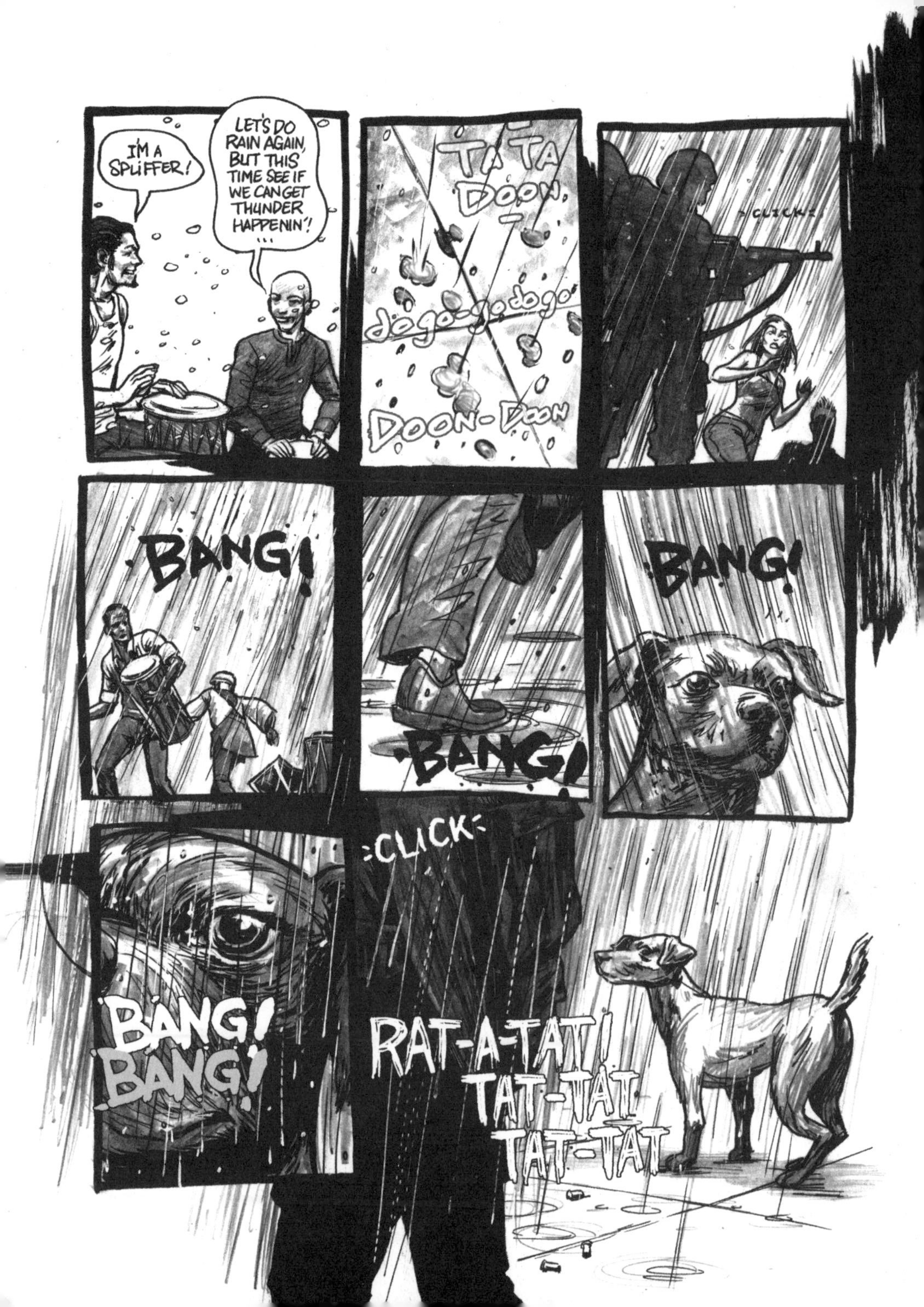
I'M A SPLIFFER!
LET'S DO RAIN AGAIN, BUT THIS TIME SEE IF WE CAN GET THUNDER HAPPENIN'! ...
TA TA DOON
dogo-go-dogo
DOON-DOON
CLICK
BANG!
BANG!
BANG!
CLICK
BANG! BANG!
RAT-A-TAT! TAT-TAT TAT-TAT

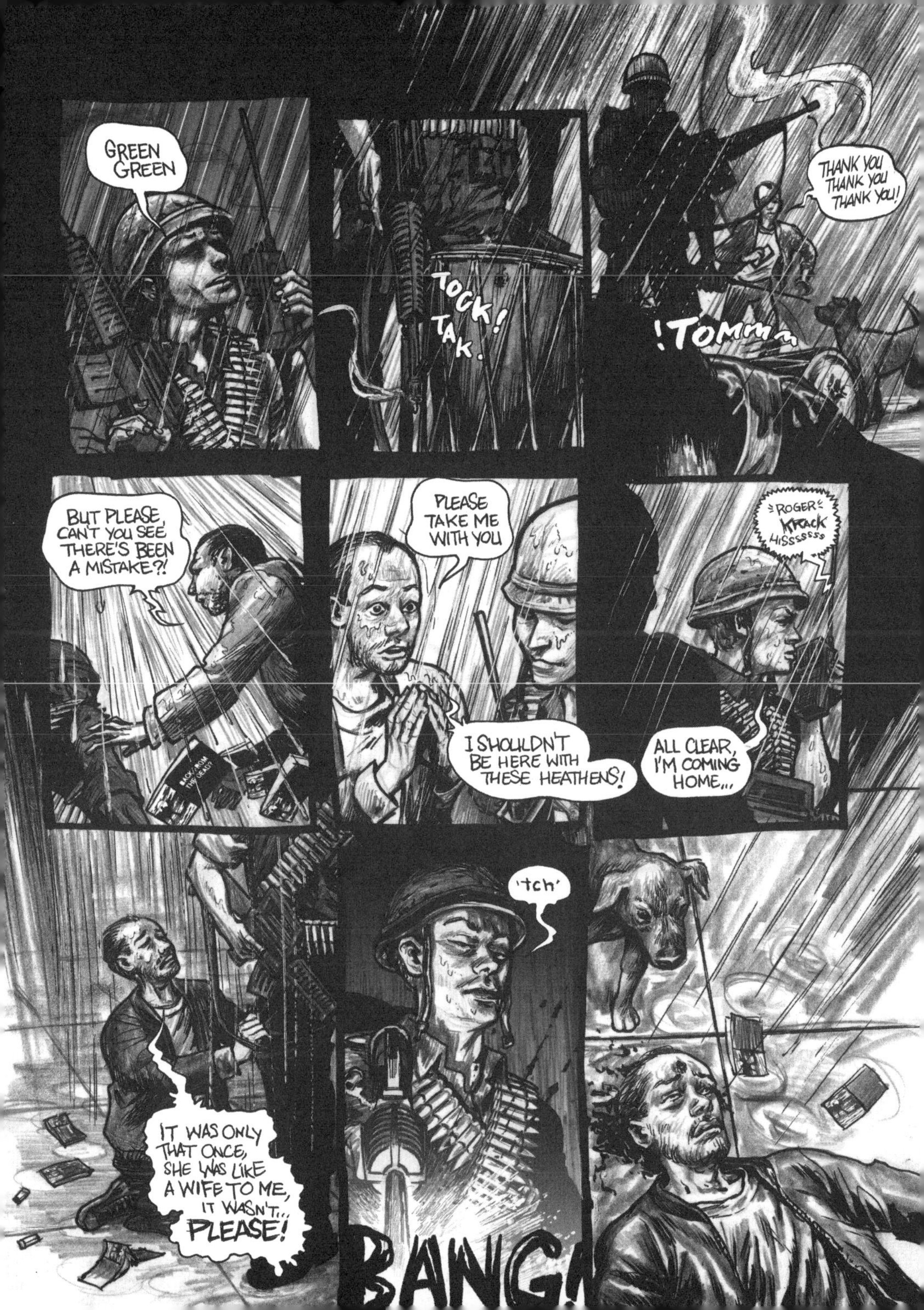
GREEN GREEN
TOCK! TAK.
THANK YOU THANK YOU THANK YOU!
!TOMM
BUT PLEASE, CAN'T YOU SEE THERE'S BEEN A MISTAKE?!
PLEASE TAKE ME WITH YOU
I SHOULDN'T BE HERE WITH THESE HEATHENS!
ROGER
KRACK
HISSSSSSS
ALL CLEAR, I'M COMING HOME...
IT WAS ONLY THAT ONCE, SHE WAS LIKE A WIFE TO ME, IT WASN'T... PLEASE!
'tch'
BANG

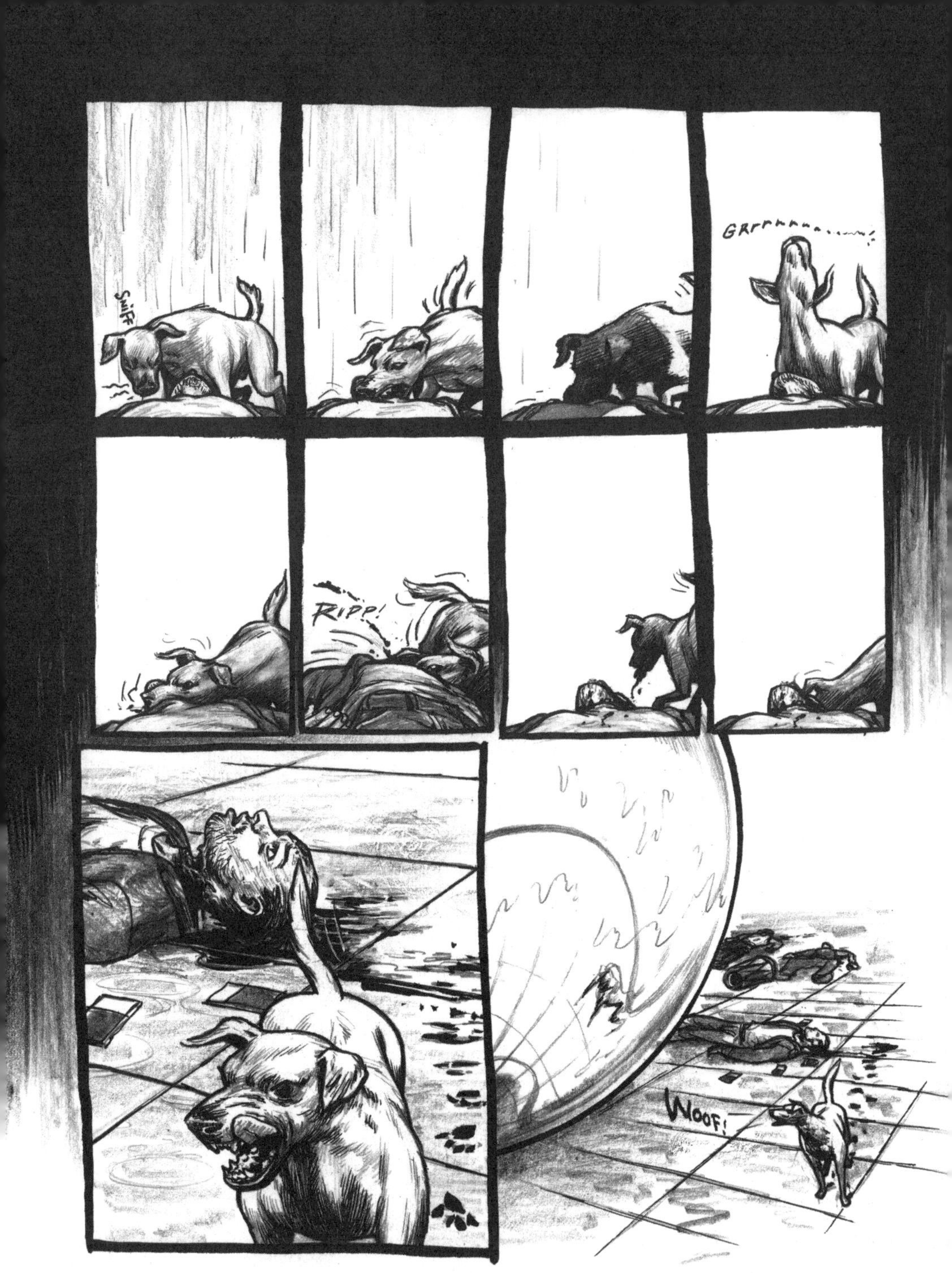
SNIFF
GRRRRRRR......!
RIPP!
WOOF!

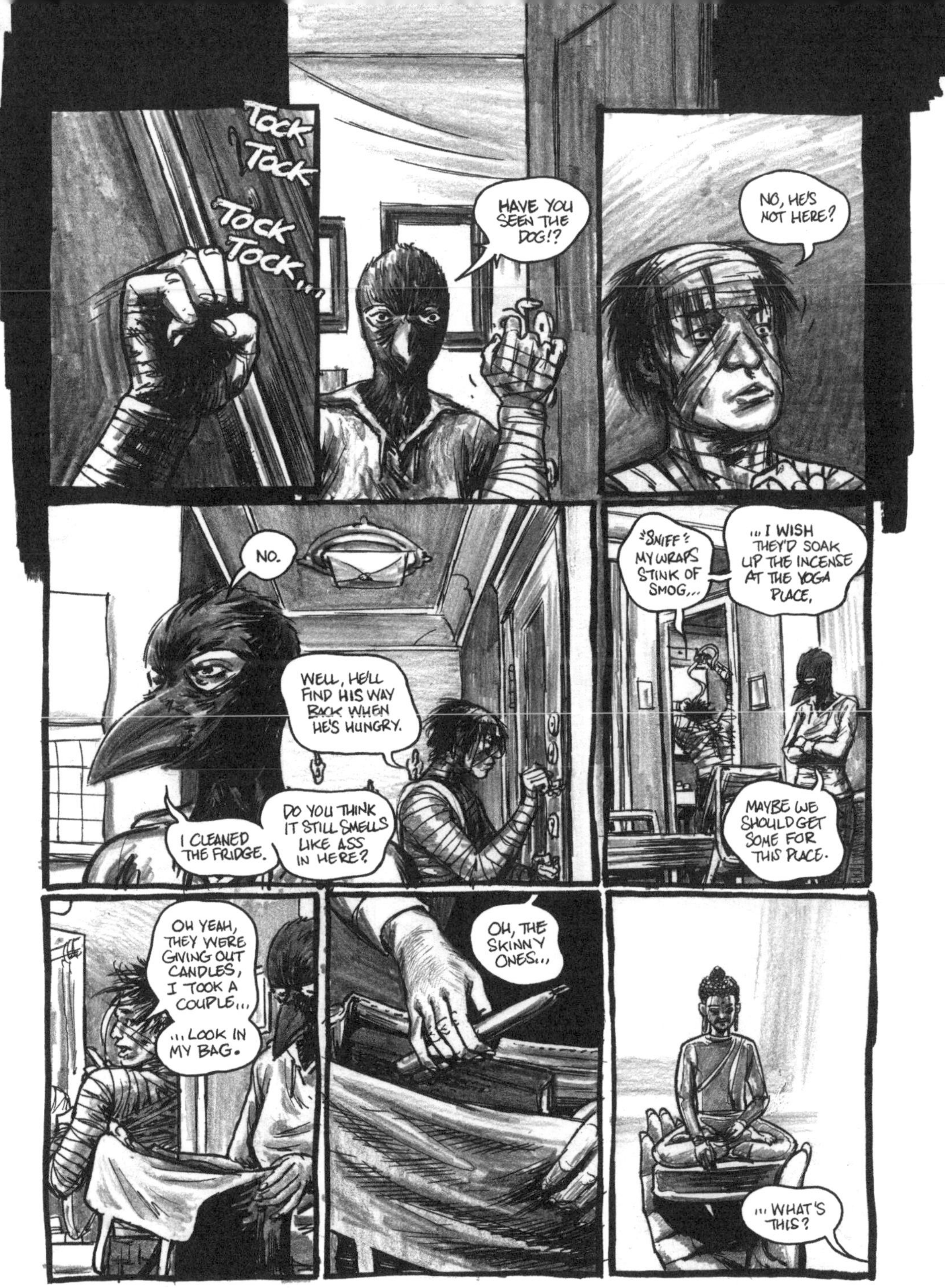
TOCK TOCK
TOCK TOCK...
HAVE YOU SEEN THE DOG!?
NO, HE'S NOT HERE?
NO.
WELL, HE'LL FIND HIS WAY BACK WHEN HE'S HUNGRY.
I CLEANED THE FRIDGE.
DO YOU THINK IT STILL SMELLS LIKE ASS IN HERE?
SNIFF MY WRAPS STINK OF SMOG...
...I WISH THEY'D SOAK UP THE INCENSE AT THE YOGA PLACE.
MAYBE WE SHOULD GET SOME FOR THIS PLACE.
OH YEAH, THEY WERE GIVING OUT CANDLES, I TOOK A COUPLE...
...LOOK IN MY BAG.
OH, THE SKINNY ONES...
...WHAT'S THIS?

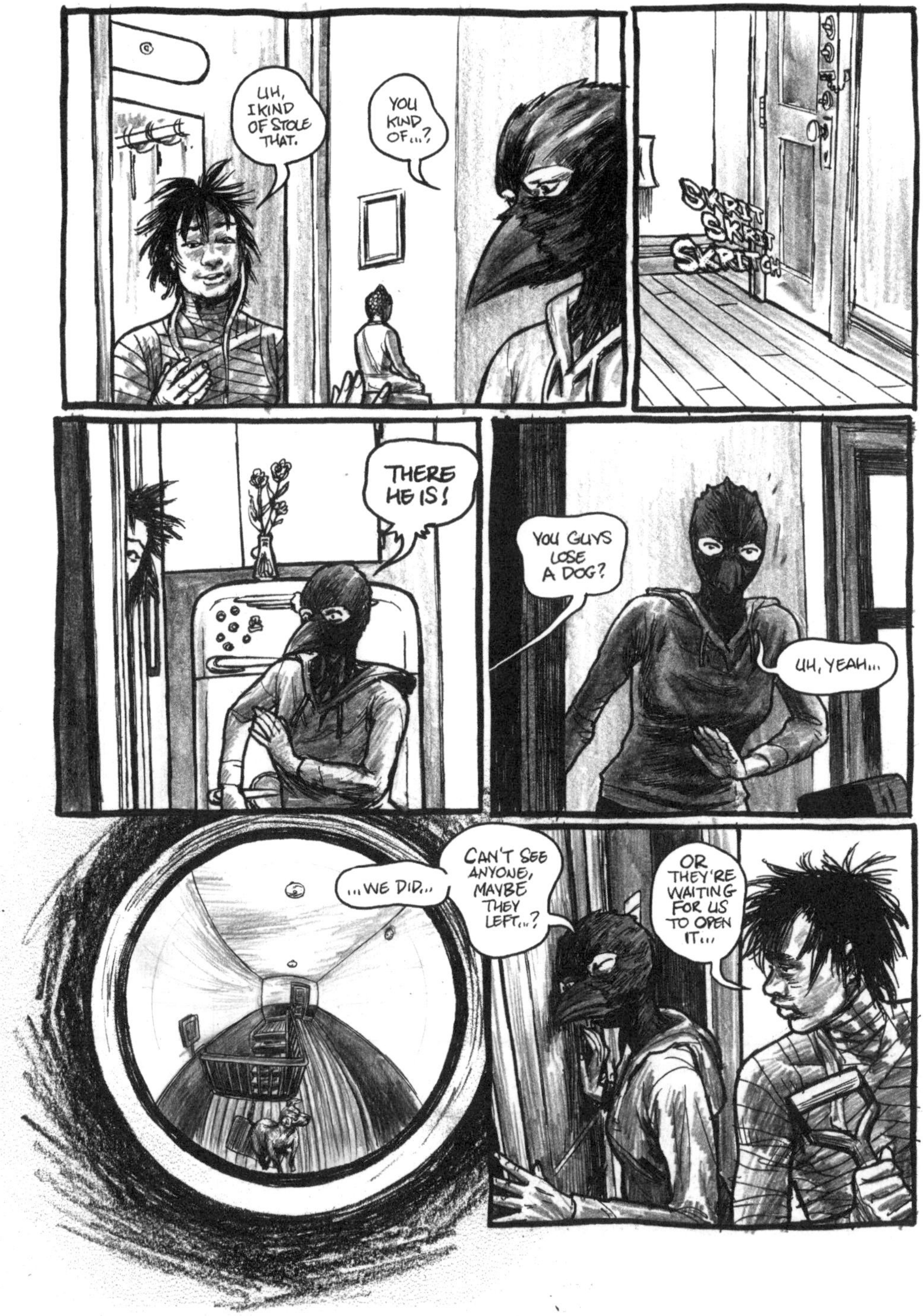
UH, I KIND OF STOLE THAT.
YOU KIND OF...?
SKRIT SKRIT SKRITCH
THERE HE IS!
YOU GUYS LOSE A DOG?
UH, YEAH...
...WE DID...
CAN'T SEE ANYONE, MAYBE THEY LEFT...?
OR THEY'RE WAITING FOR US TO OPEN IT...

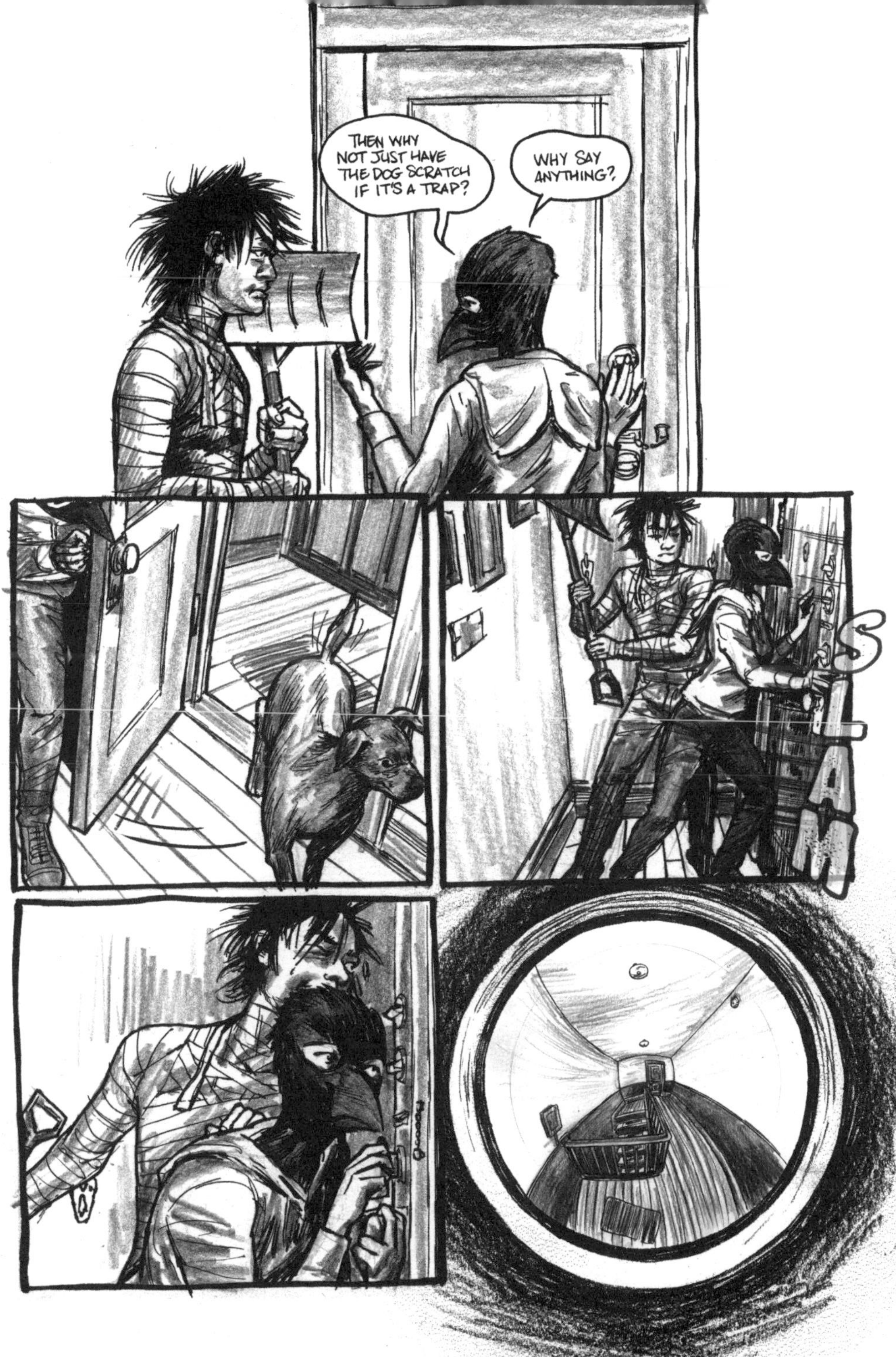
THEN WHY NOT JUST HAVE THE DOG SCRATCH IF IT'S A TRAP?
WHY SAY ANYTHING?
SLAM

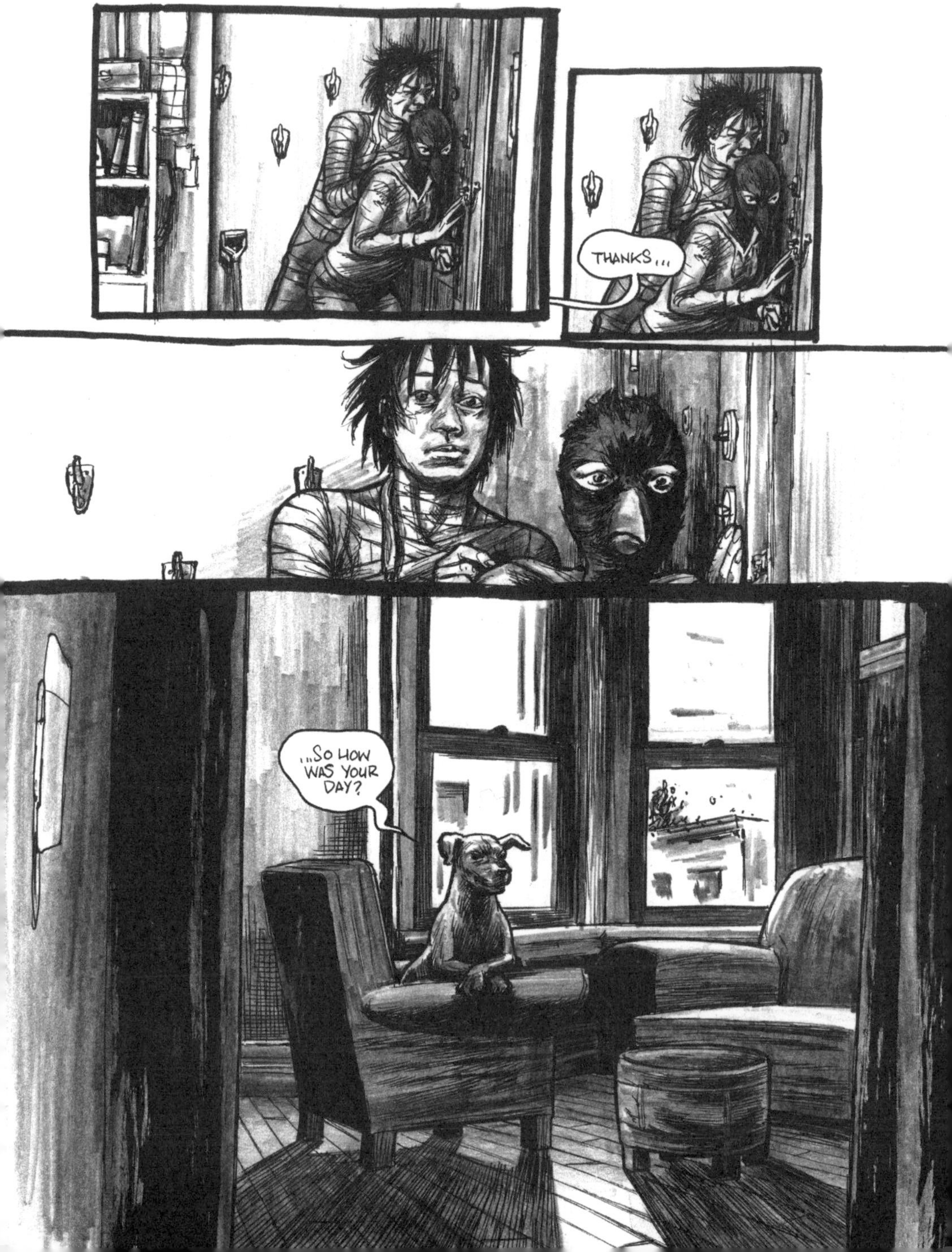
THANKS...
...SO HOW WAS YOUR DAY?

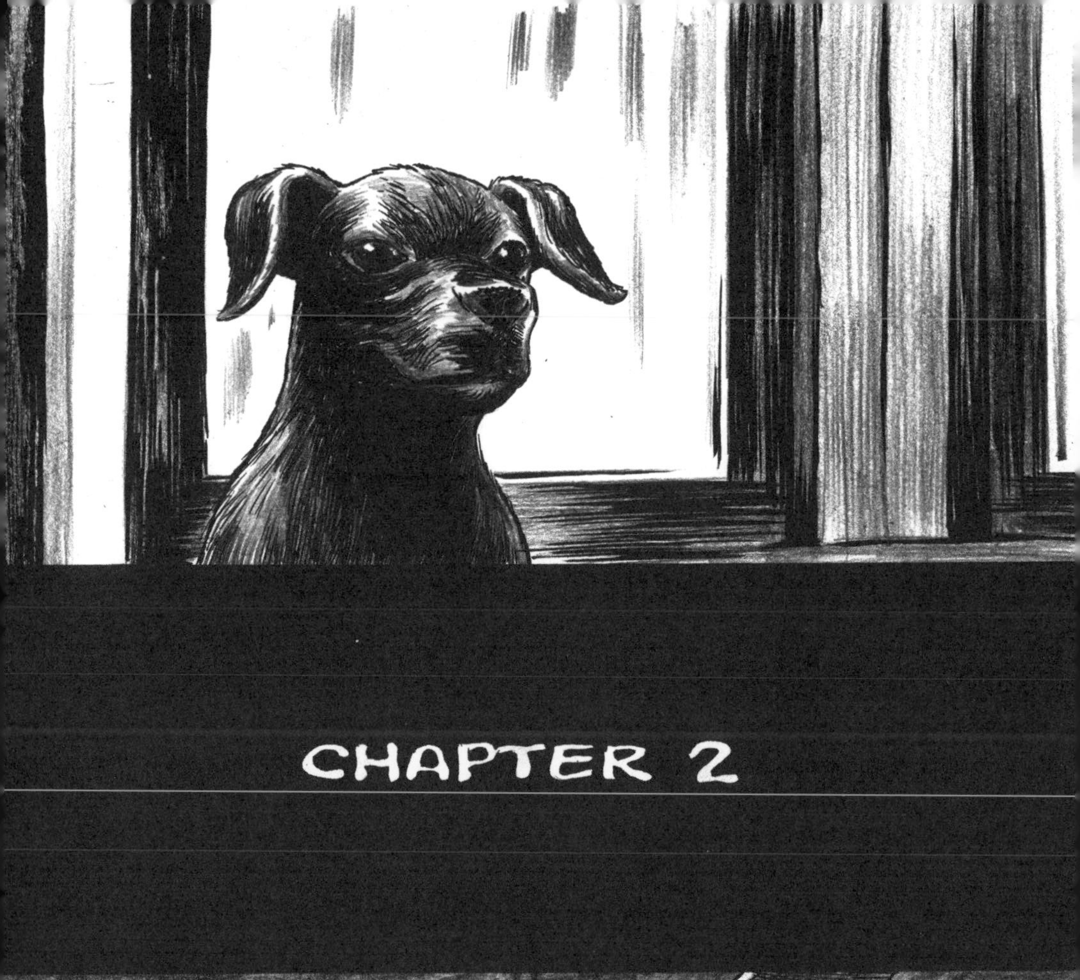

CHAPTER 2

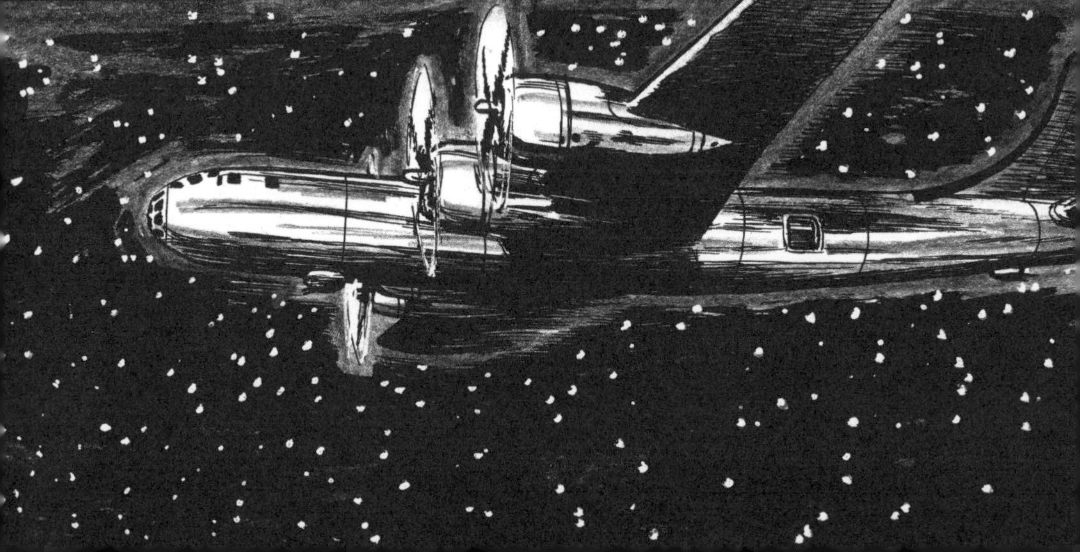

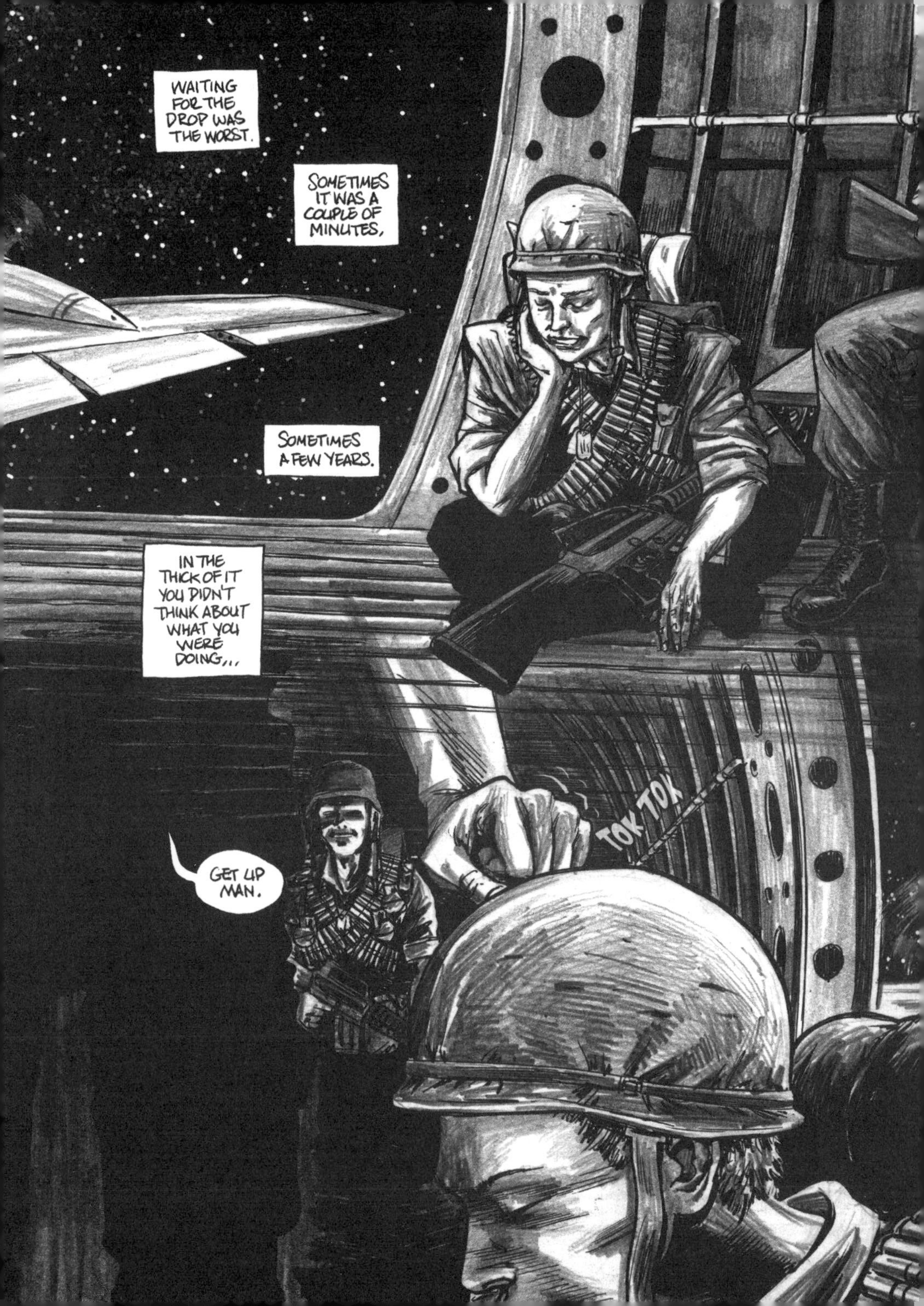
WAITING FOR THE DROP WAS THE WORST.
SOMETIMES IT WAS A COUPLE OF MINUTES,
SOMETIMES A FEW YEARS.
IN THE THICK OF IT YOU DIDN'T THINK ABOUT WHAT YOU WERE DOING...
TOK TOK
GET UP MAN.

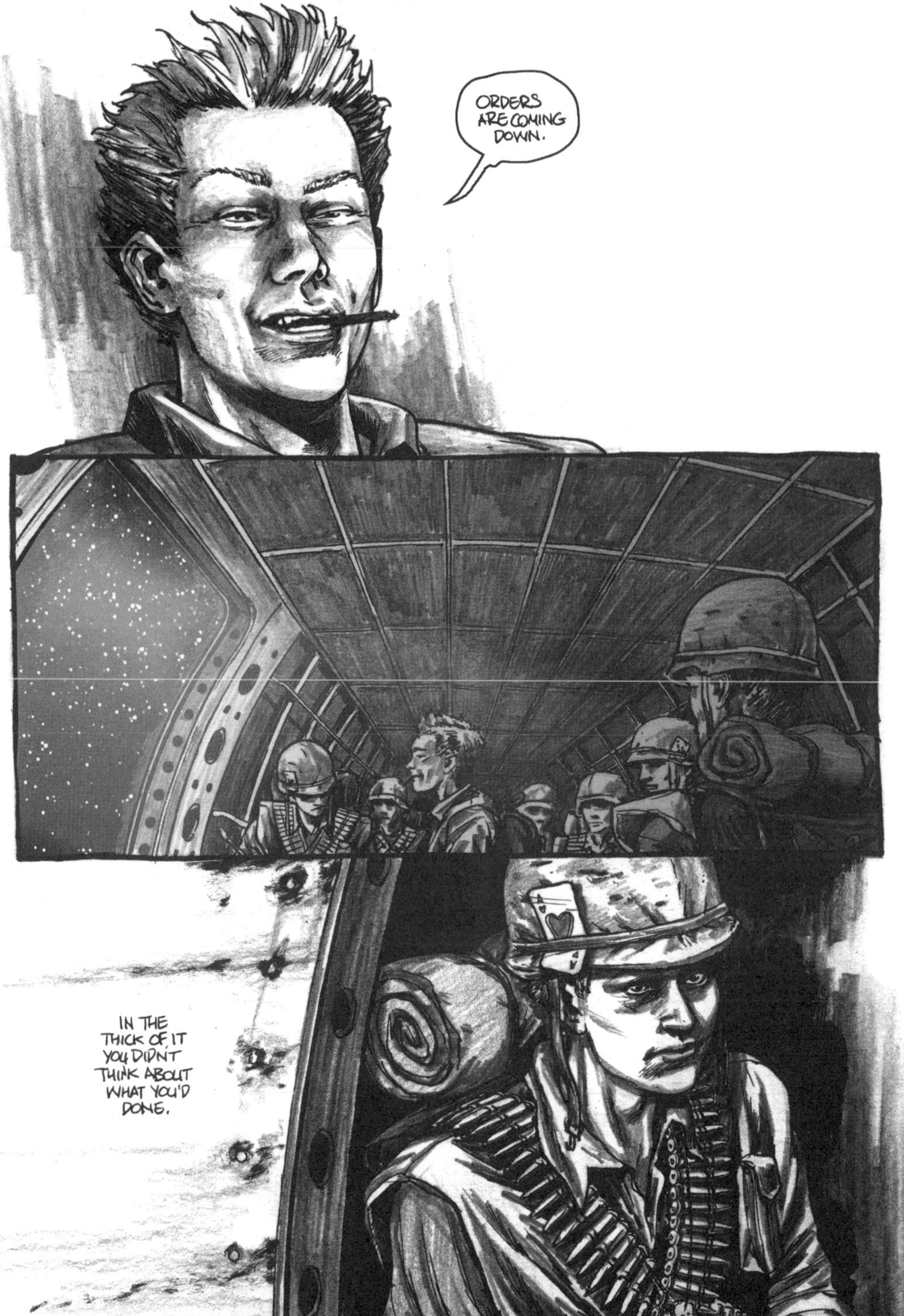
ORDERS ARE COMING DOWN.
IN THE THICK OF IT YOU DIDN'T THINK ABOUT WHAT YOU'D DONE.

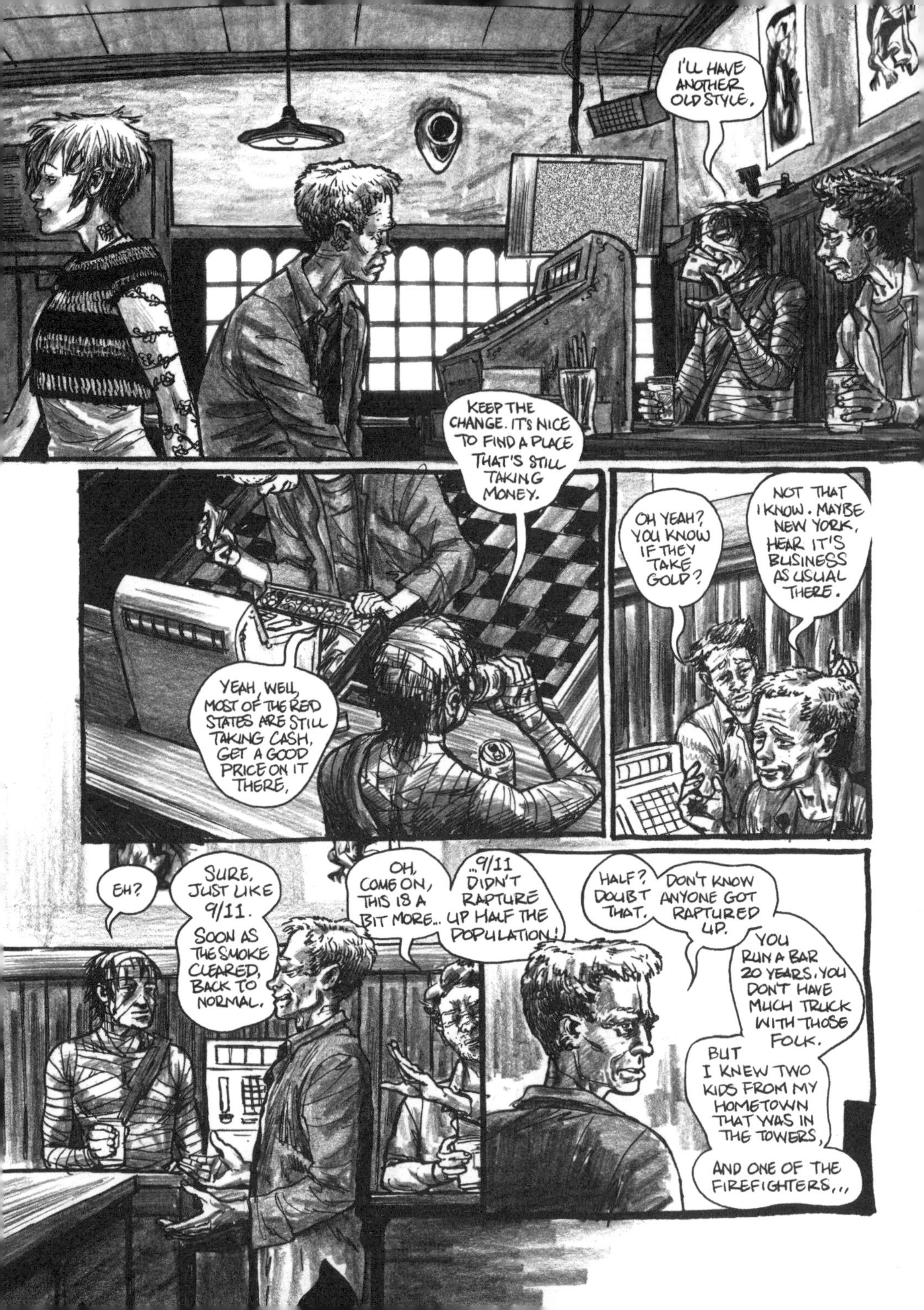
I'LL HAVE ANOTHER OLD STYLE.
KEEP THE CHANGE. IT'S NICE TO FIND A PLACE THAT'S STILL TAKING MONEY.
YEAH, WELL, MOST OF THE RED STATES ARE STILL TAKING CASH, GET A GOOD PRICE ON IT THERE.
OH YEAH? YOU KNOW IF THEY TAKE GOLD?
NOT THAT I KNOW. MAYBE NEW YORK, HEAR IT'S BUSINESS AS USUAL THERE.
EH?
SURE, JUST LIKE 9/11.
SOON AS THE SMOKE CLEARED, BACK TO NORMAL.
OH, COME ON, THIS IS A BIT MORE...
...9/11 DIDN'T RAPTURE UP HALF THE POPULATION!
HALF? DOUBT THAT.
DON'T KNOW ANYONE GOT RAPTURED UP.
YOU RUN A BAR 20 YEARS, YOU DON'T HAVE MUCH TRUCK WITH THOSE FOLK.
BUT I KNEW TWO KIDS FROM MY HOMETOWN THAT WAS IN THE TOWERS,
AND ONE OF THE FIREFIGHTERS...

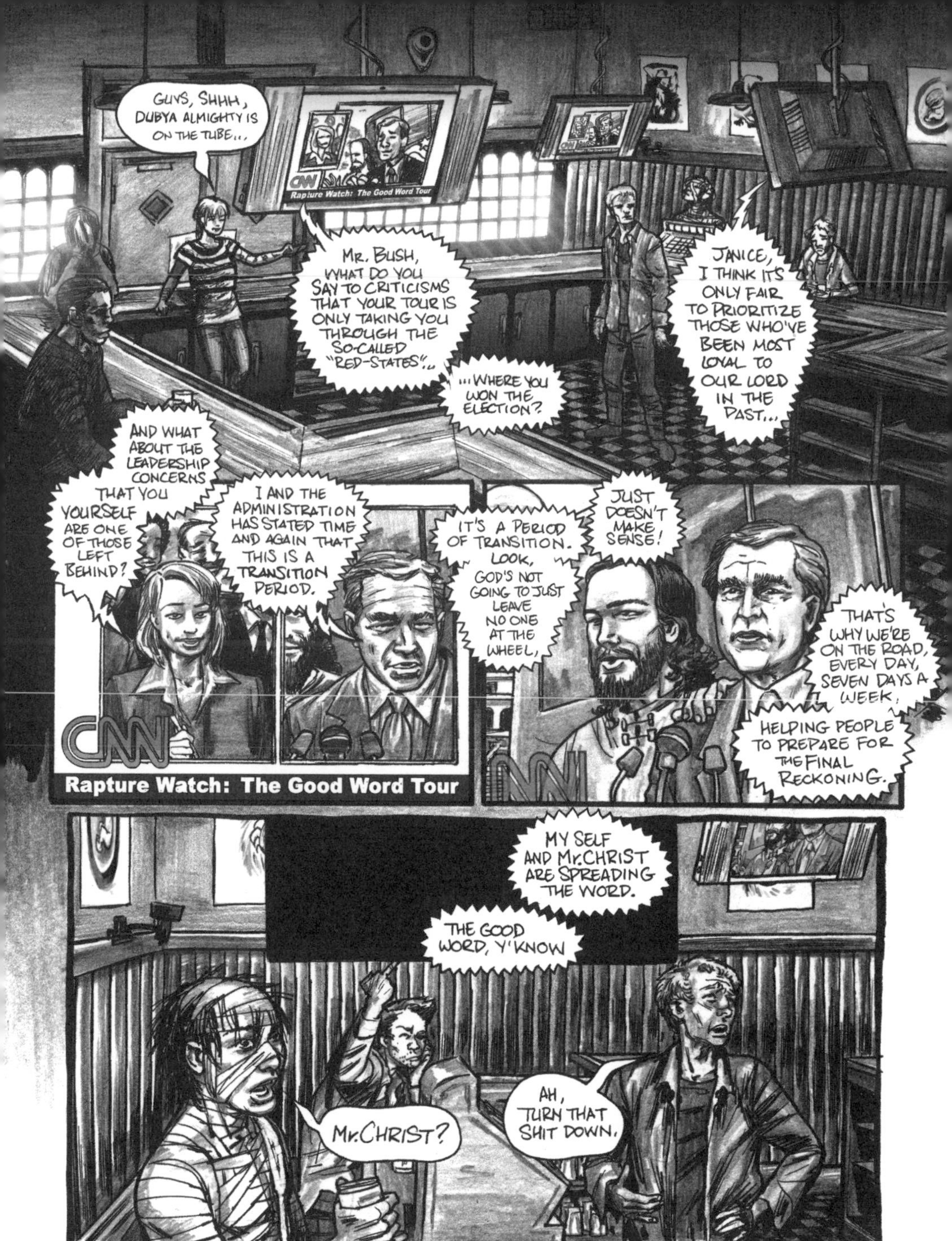
GUYS, SHHH, DUBYA ALMIGHTY IS ON THE TUBE...
Rapture Watch: The Good Word Tour
MR. BUSH, WHAT DO YOU SAY TO CRITICISMS THAT YOUR TOUR IS ONLY TAKING YOU THROUGH THE SO-CALLED "RED-STATES"...
...WHERE YOU WON THE ELECTION?
JANICE, I THINK IT'S ONLY FAIR TO PRIORITIZE THOSE WHO'VE BEEN MOST LOYAL TO OUR LORD IN THE PAST...
AND WHAT ABOUT THE LEADERSHIP CONCERNS THAT YOU YOURSELF ARE ONE OF THOSE LEFT BEHIND?
I AND THE ADMINISTRATION HAS STATED TIME AND AGAIN THAT THIS IS A TRANSITION PERIOD.
CNN
Rapture Watch: The Good Word Tour
IT'S A PERIOD OF TRANSITION. LOOK, GOD'S NOT GOING TO JUST LEAVE NO ONE AT THE WHEEL,
JUST DOESN'T MAKE SENSE!
THAT'S WHY WE'RE ON THE ROAD, EVERY DAY, SEVEN DAYS A WEEK,
HELPING PEOPLE TO PREPARE FOR THE FINAL RECKONING.
MY SELF AND Mr.CHRIST ARE SPREADING THE WORD.
THE GOOD WORD, Y'KNOW
Mr.CHRIST?
AH, TURN THAT SHIT DOWN.

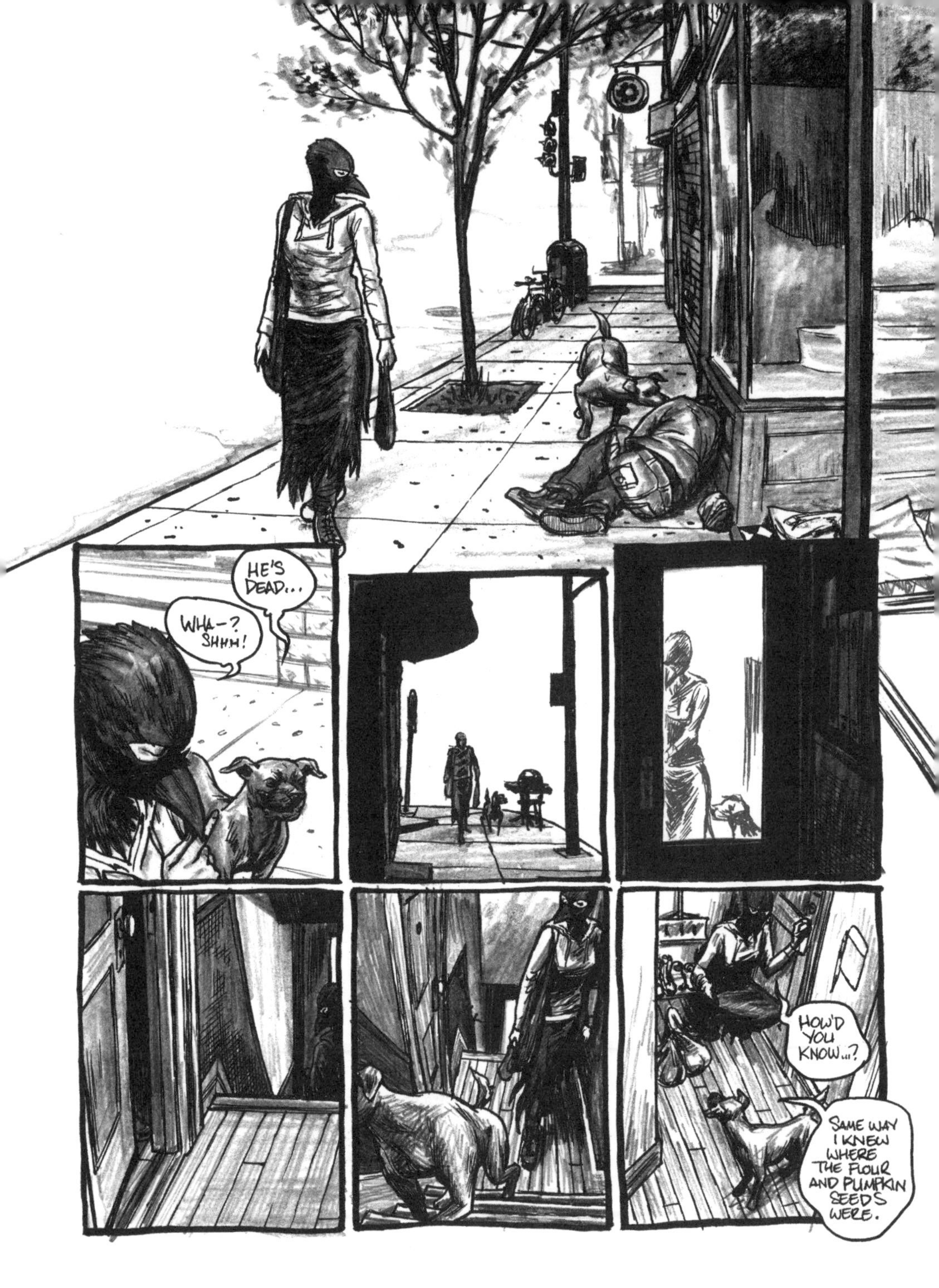
HE'S DEAD...
WHA-? SHHH!
HOW'D YOU KNOW...?
SAME WAY I KNEW WHERE THE FLOUR AND PUMPKIN SEEDS WERE.

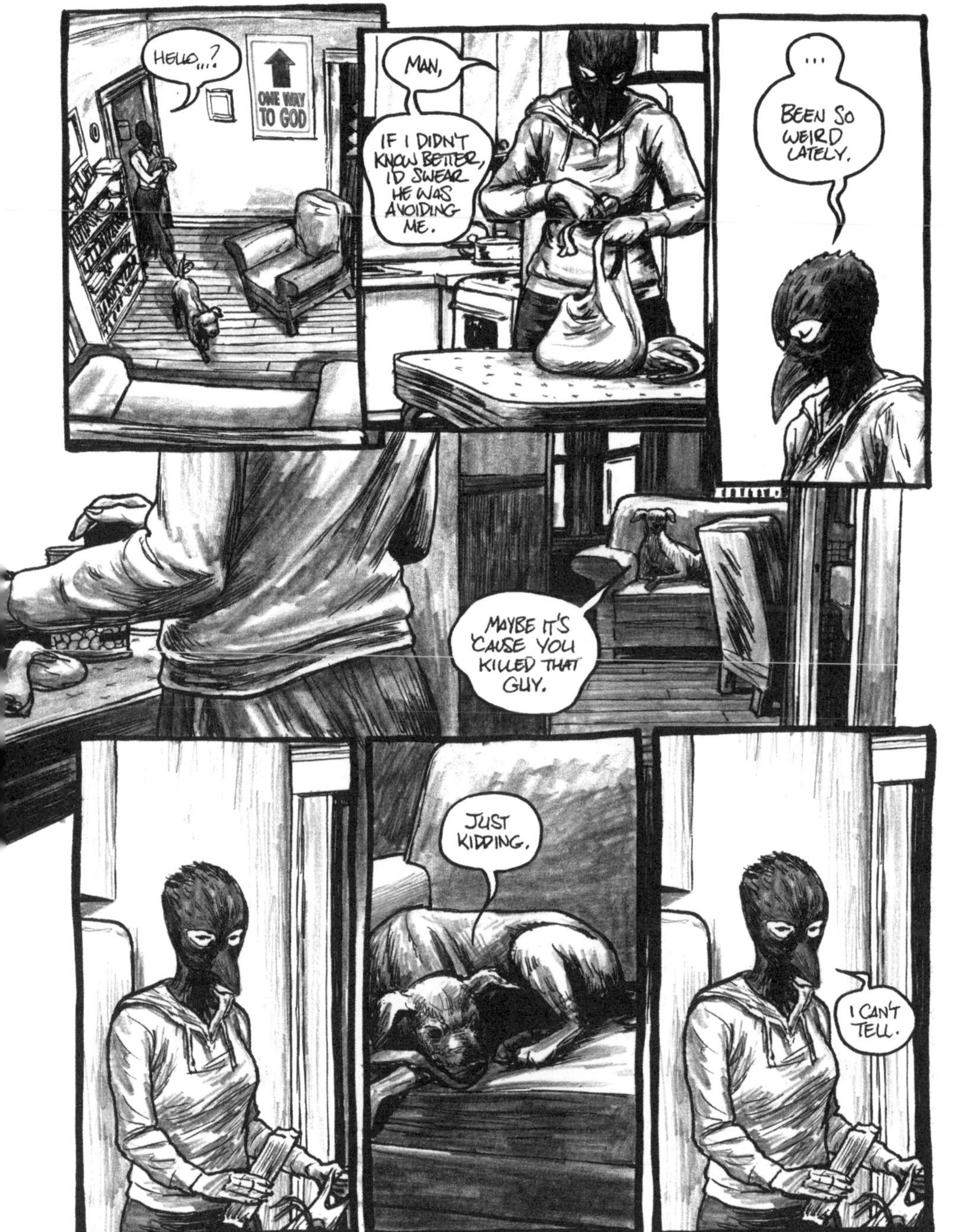
HELLO...?
ONE WAY TO GOD
MAN,
IF I DIDN'T KNOW BETTER, I'D SWEAR HE WAS AVOIDING ME.
...
BEEN SO WEIRD LATELY.
MAYBE IT'S 'CAUSE YOU KILLED THAT GUY.
JUST KIDDING.
I CAN'T TELL.

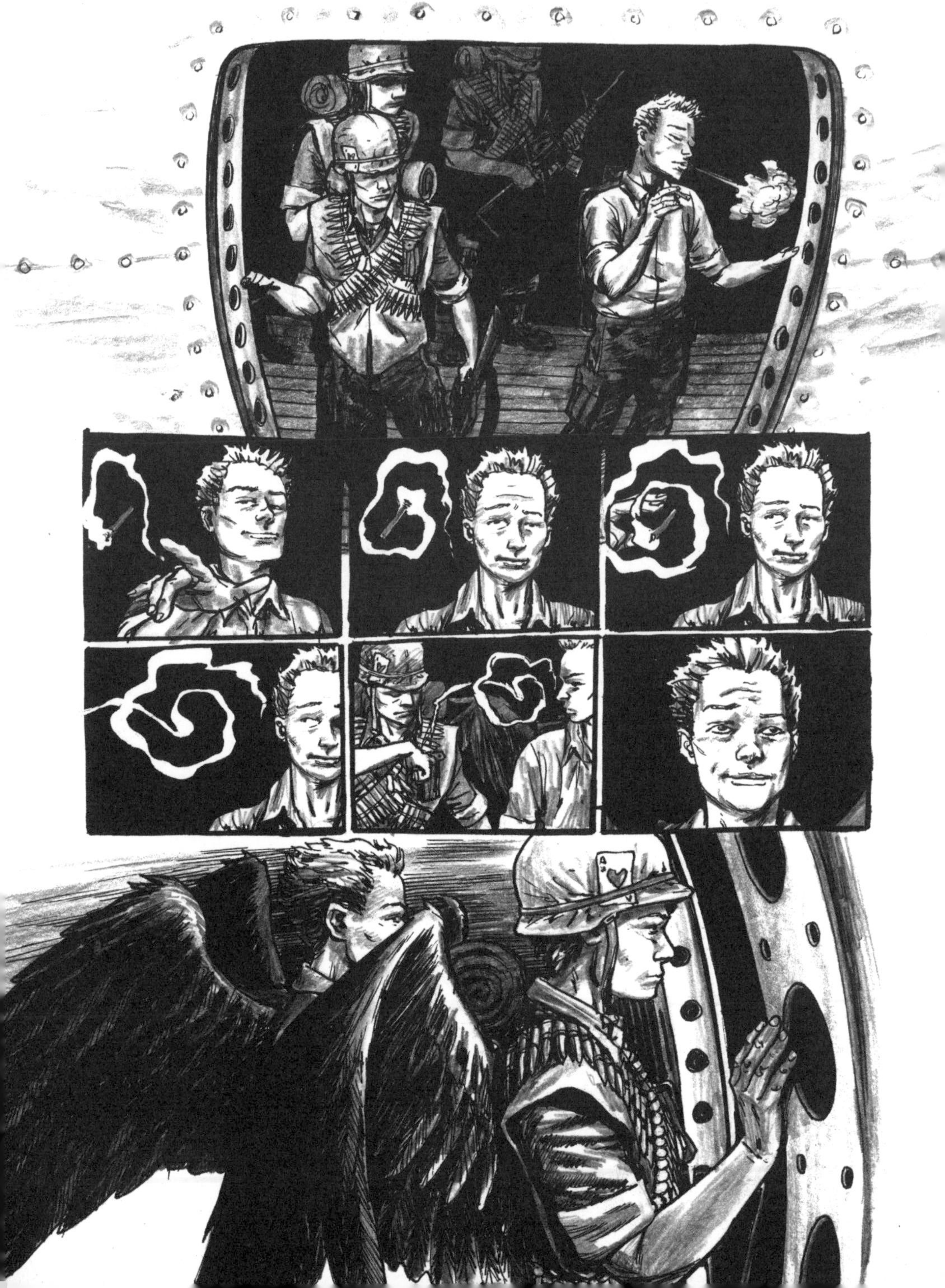

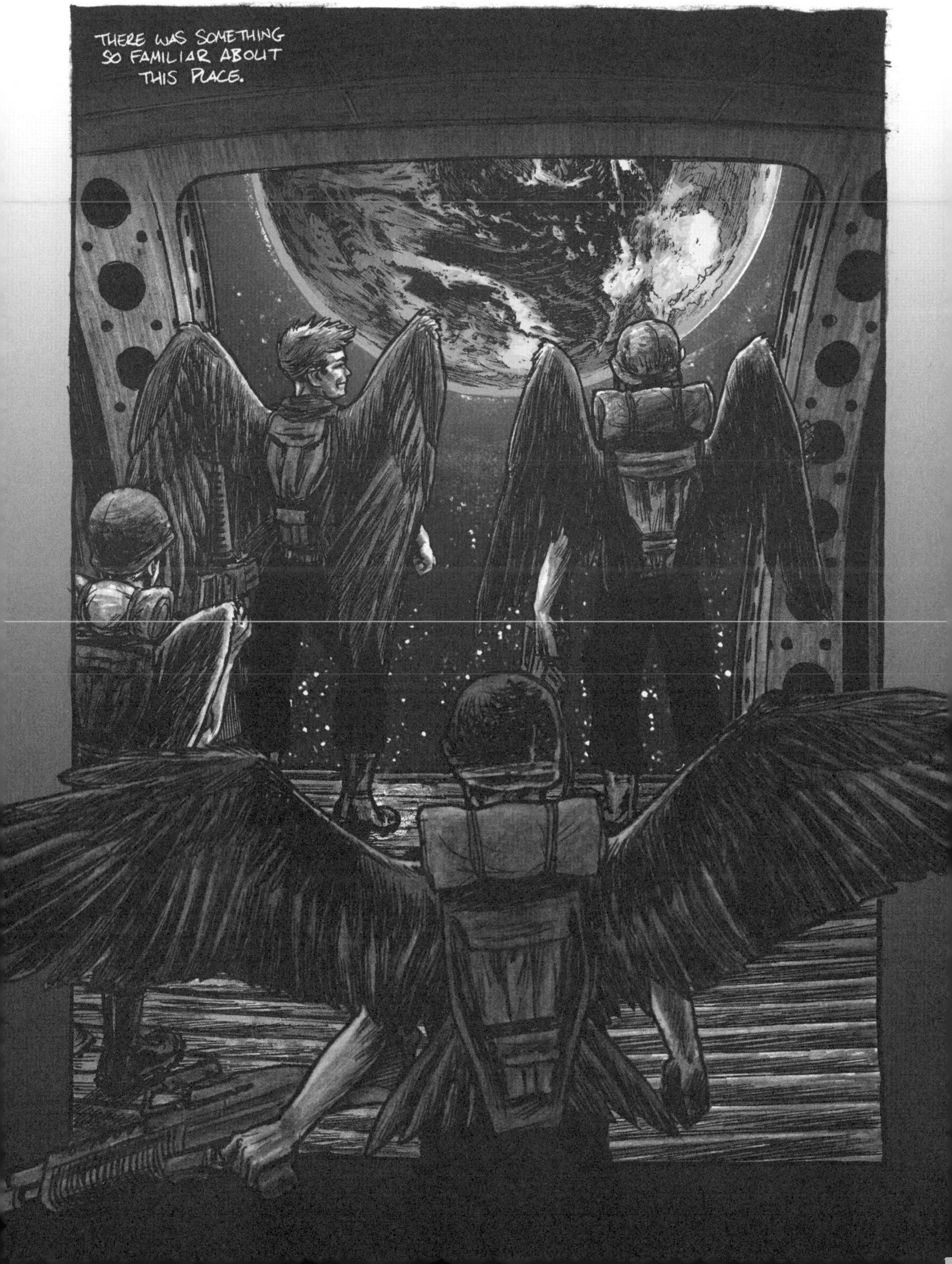
THERE WAS SOMETHING SO FAMILIAR ABOUT THIS PLACE.

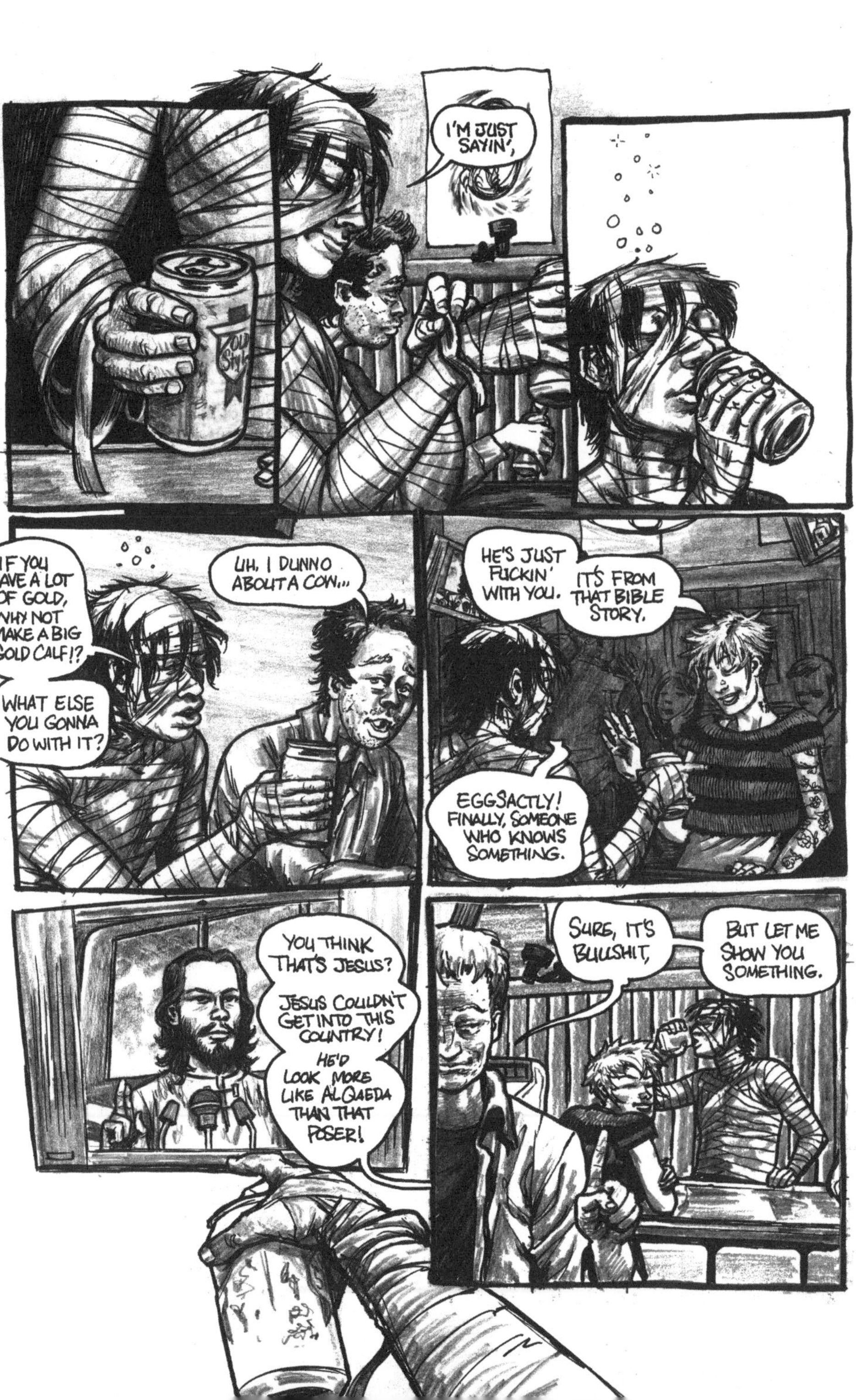
I'M JUST SAYIN',
IF YOU HAVE A LOT OF GOLD, WHY NOT MAKE A BIG GOLD CALF!?
WHAT ELSE YOU GONNA DO WITH IT?
UH, I DUNNO ABOUT A COW...
HE'S JUST FUCKIN' WITH YOU.
IT'S FROM THAT BIBLE STORY.
EGGSACTLY! FINALLY, SOMEONE WHO KNOWS SOMETHING.
YOU THINK THAT'S JESUS?
JESUS COULDN'T GET INTO THIS COUNTRY!
HE'D LOOK MORE LIKE AL QAEDA THAN THAT POSER!
SURE, IT'S BULLSHIT,
BUT LET ME SHOW YOU SOMETHING.

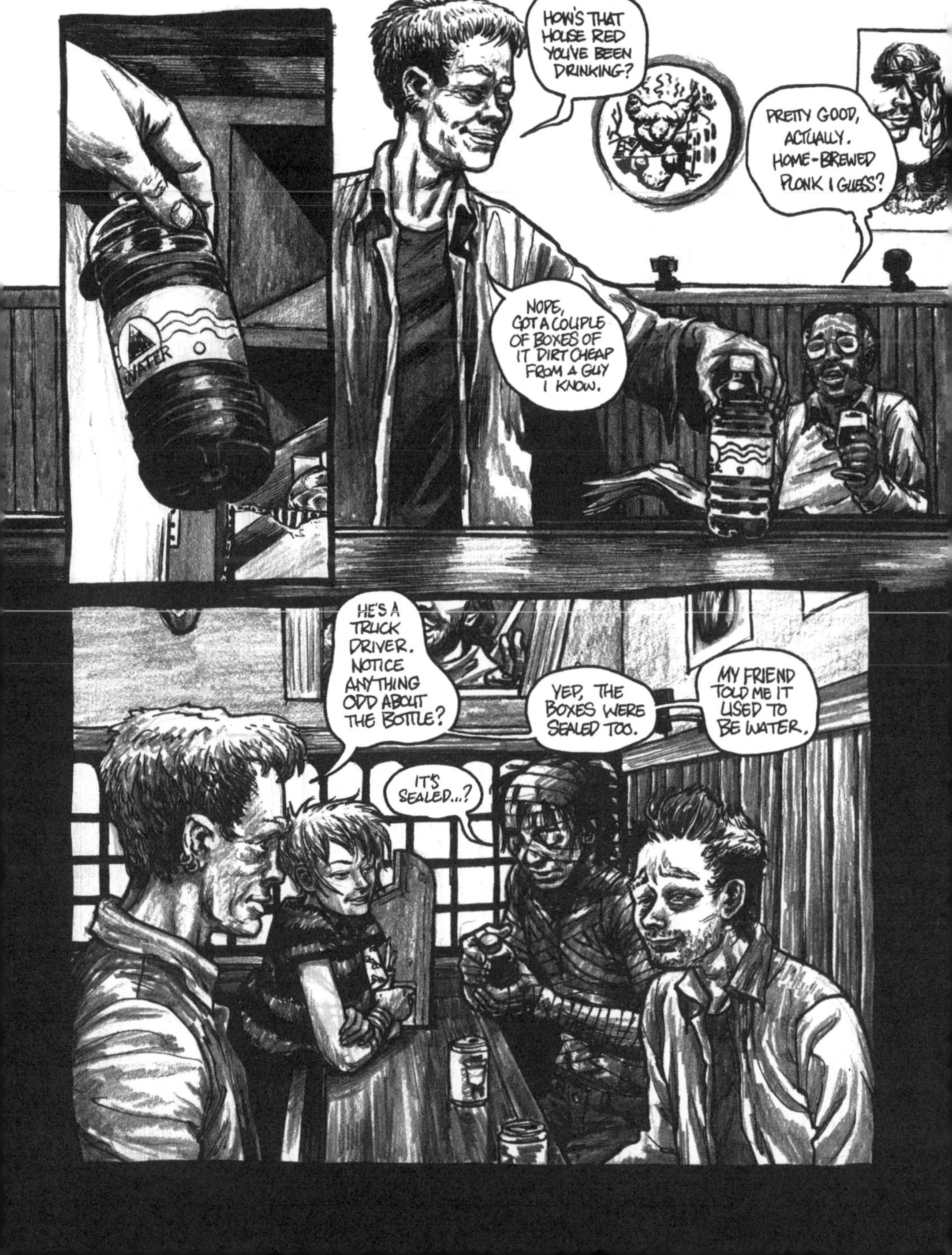
WATER
HOW'S THAT HOUSE RED YOU'VE BEEN DRINKING?
PRETTY GOOD, ACTUALLY. HOME-BREWED PLONK I GUESS?
NOPE, GOT A COUPLE OF BOXES OF IT DIRT CHEAP FROM A GUY I KNOW.
HE'S A TRUCK DRIVER. NOTICE ANYTHING ODD ABOUT THE BOTTLE?
IT'S SEALED...?
YEP, THE BOXES WERE SEALED TOO.
MY FRIEND TOLD ME IT USED TO BE WATER.

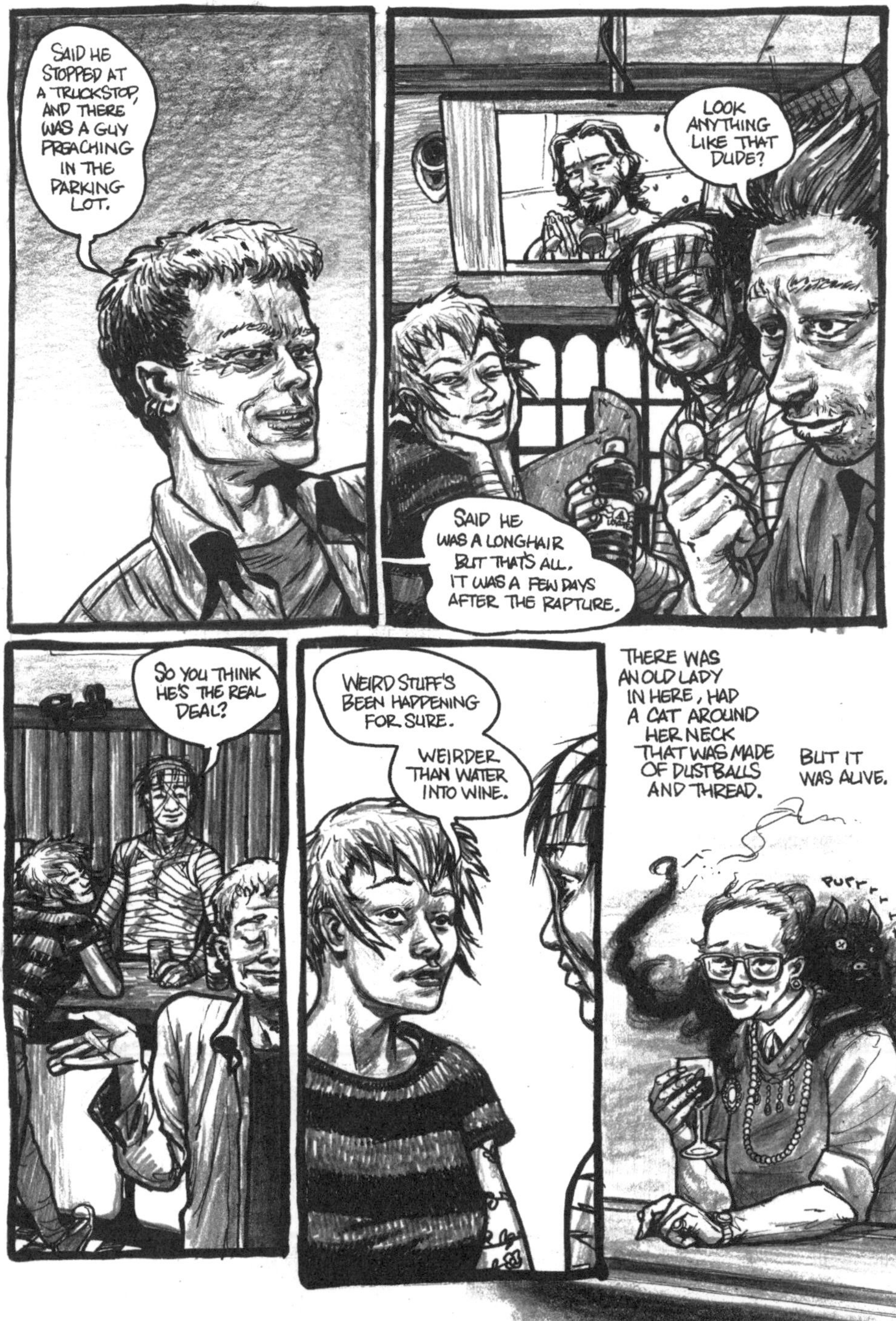
SAID HE STOPPED AT A TRUCKSTOP, AND THERE WAS A GUY PREACHING IN THE PARKING LOT.
LOOK ANYTHING LIKE THAT DUDE?
SAID HE WAS A LONGHAIR BUT THAT'S ALL. IT WAS A FEW DAYS AFTER THE RAPTURE.
SO YOU THINK HE'S THE REAL DEAL?
WEIRD STUFF'S BEEN HAPPENING FOR SURE.
WEIRDER THAN WATER INTO WINE.
THERE WAS AN OLD LADY IN HERE, HAD A CAT AROUND HER NECK THAT WAS MADE OF DUSTBALLS AND THREAD.
BUT IT WAS ALIVE.
PURRRRR

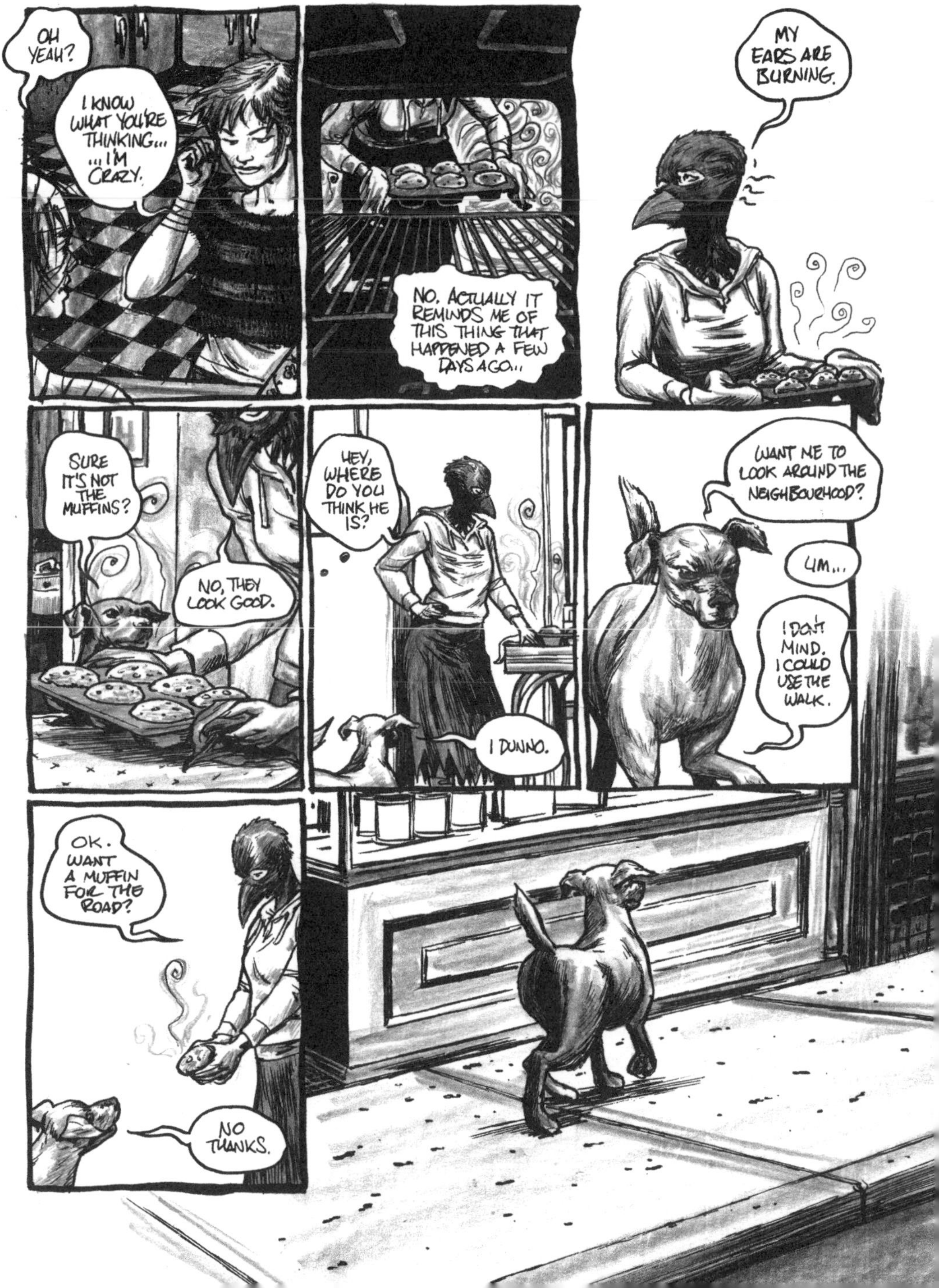
OH YEAH?
I KNOW WHAT YOU'RE THINKING... ...I'M CRAZY.
NO. ACTUALLY IT REMINDS ME OF THIS THING THAT HAPPENED A FEW DAYS AGO...
MY EARS ARE BURNING.
SURE IT'S NOT THE MUFFINS?
NO, THEY LOOK GOOD.
HEY, WHERE DO YOU THINK HE IS?
I DUNNO.
WANT ME TO LOOK AROUND THE NEIGHBOURHOOD?
UM...
I DON'T MIND. I COULD USE THE WALK.
OK. WANT A MUFFIN FOR THE ROAD?
NO THANKS.

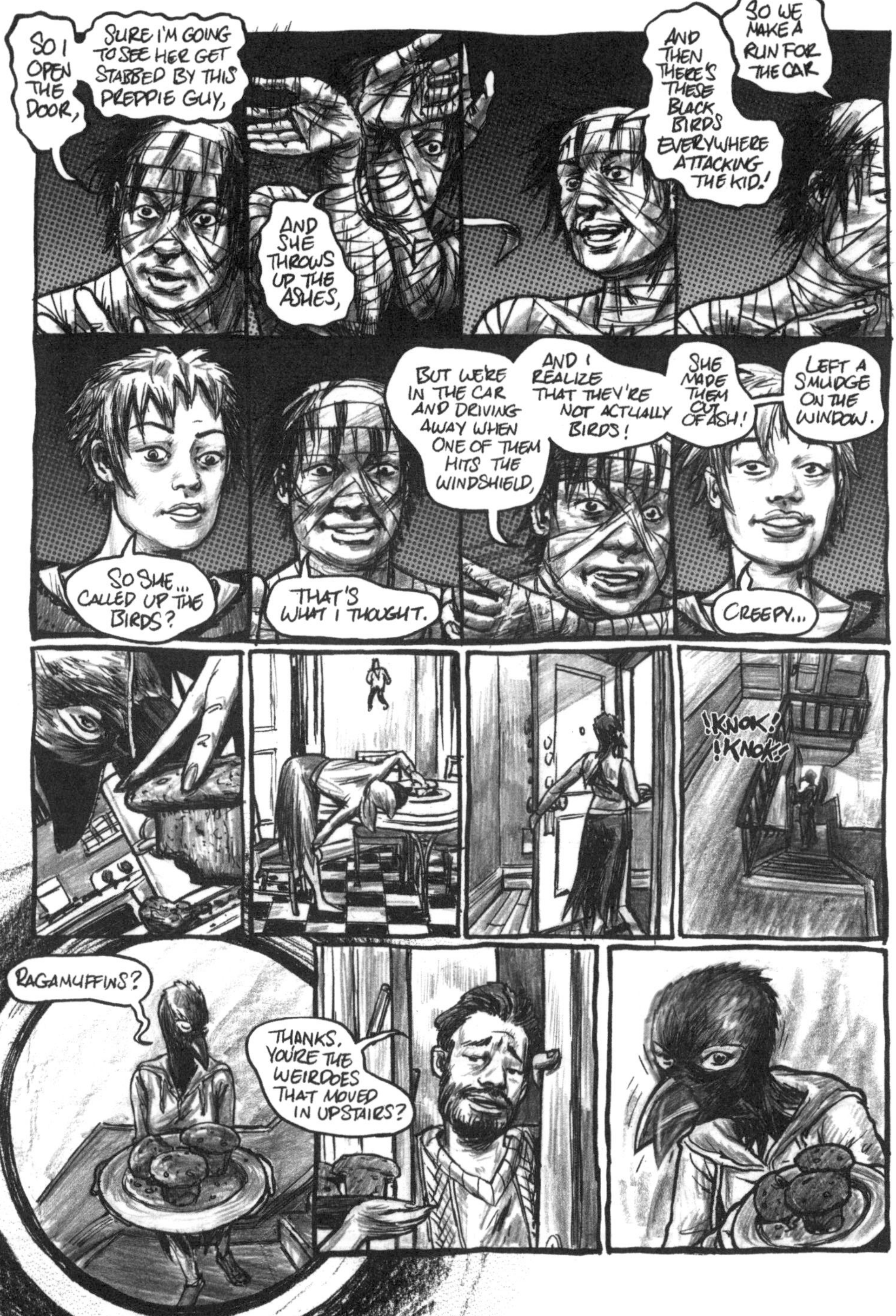
So I open the door,
Sure I'm going to see her get stabbed by this preppie guy,
And she throws up the ashes,
And then there's these black birds everywhere attacking the kid!
So we make a run for the car
So she... called up the birds?
That's what I thought.
But we're in the car and driving away when one of them hits the windshield,
And I realize that they're not actually birds!
She made them out of ash!
Left a smudge on the window.
Creepy...
!Knok! !Knok!
Ragamuffins?
Thanks. You're the weirdoes that moved in upstairs?

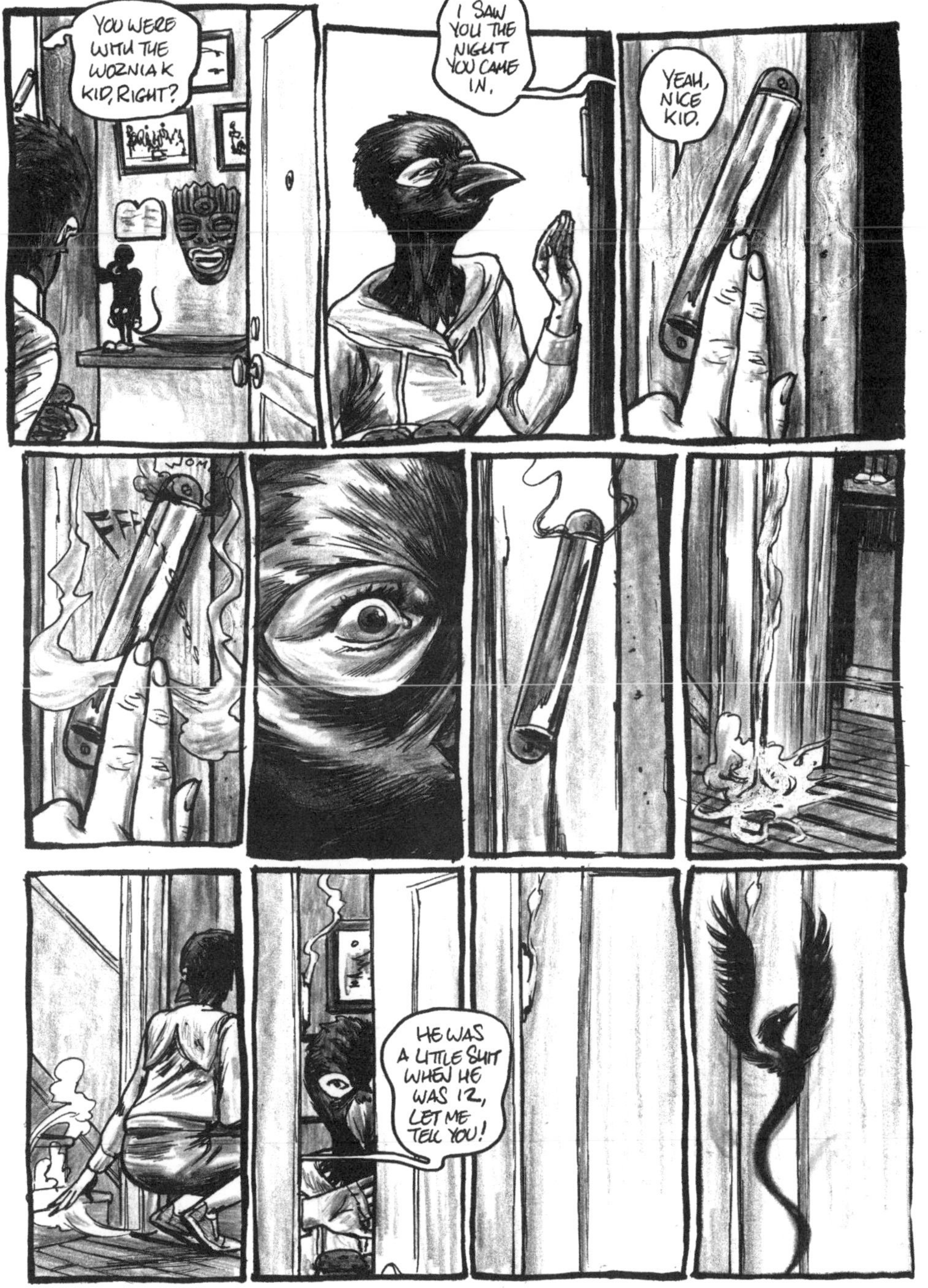
YOU WERE WITH THE WOZNIAK KID, RIGHT?
I SAW YOU THE NIGHT YOU CAME IN.
YEAH, NICE KID.
WOM
FFF
HE WAS A LITTLE SHIT WHEN HE WAS 12, LET ME TELL YOU!

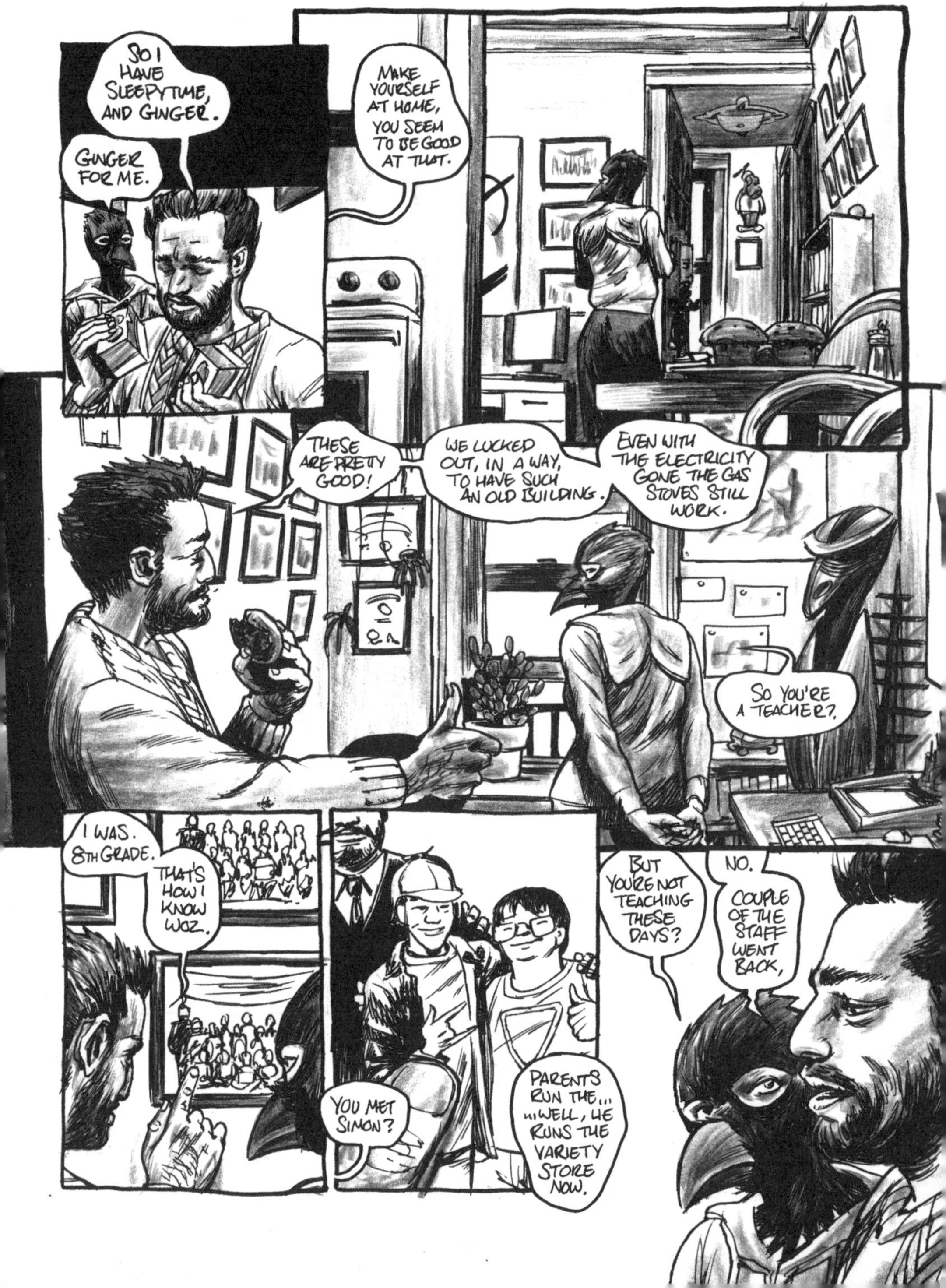
So I have Sleepytime, and Ginger.
Ginger for me.
Make yourself at home, you seem to be good at that.
These are pretty good!
We lucked out, in a way, to have such an old building.
Even with the electricity gone the gas stoves still work.
So you're a teacher?
I was. 8th grade.
That's how I know Woz.
You met Simon?
Parents run the... ...well, he runs the variety store now.
But you're not teaching these days?
No.
Couple of the staff went back,

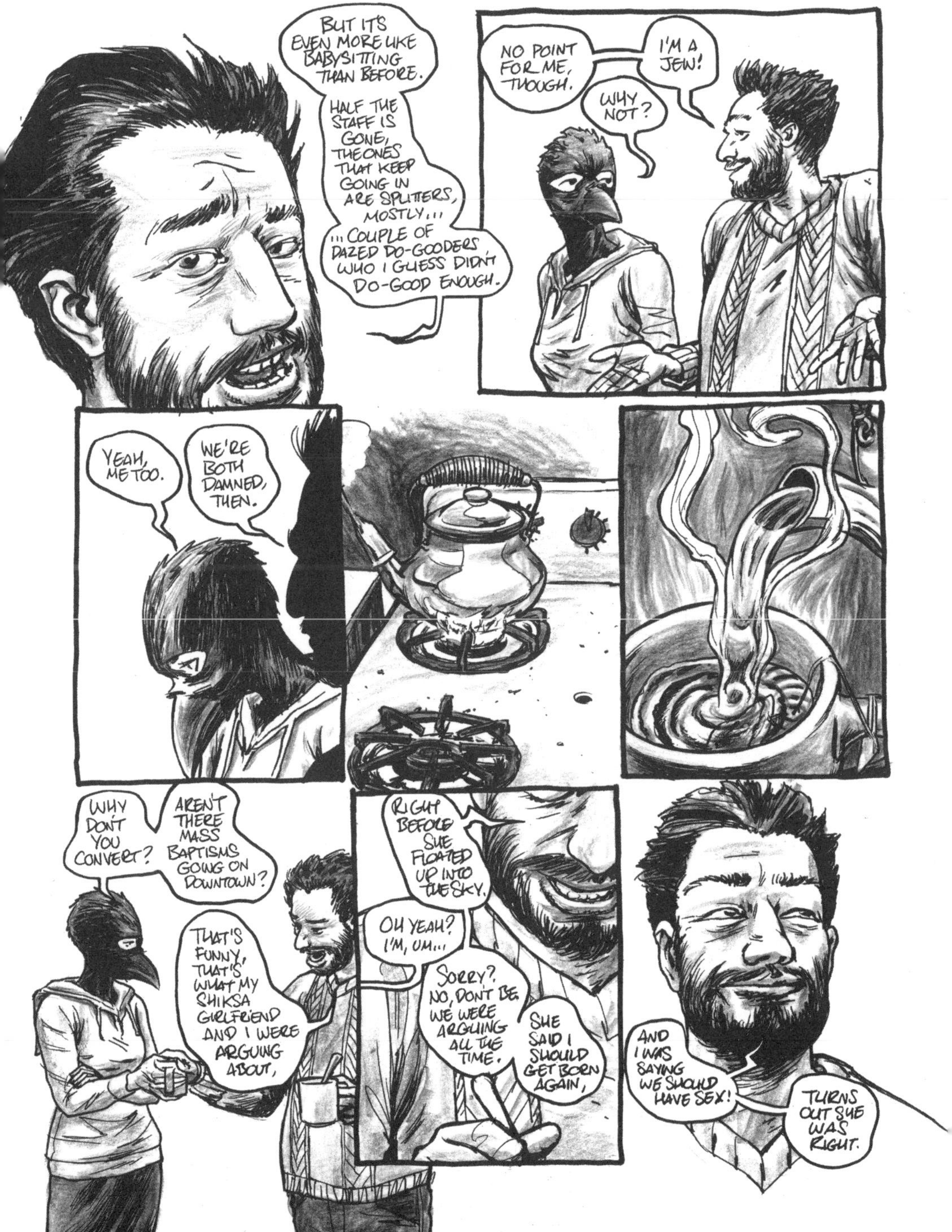
BUT IT'S EVEN MORE LIKE BABYSITTING THAN BEFORE.
HALF THE STAFF IS GONE, THE ONES THAT KEEP GOING IN ARE SPLITTERS, MOSTLY...
...COUPLE OF DAZED DO-GOODERS WHO I GUESS DIDN'T DO-GOOD ENOUGH.
NO POINT FOR ME, THOUGH.
WHY NOT?
I'M A JEW!
YEAH, ME TOO.
WE'RE BOTH DAMNED, THEN.
WHY DON'T YOU CONVERT?
AREN'T THERE MASS BAPTISMS GOING ON DOWNTOWN?
THAT'S FUNNY, THAT'S WHAT MY SHIKSA GIRLFRIEND AND I WERE ARGUING ABOUT,
RIGHT BEFORE SHE FLOATED UP INTO THE SKY.
OH YEAH? I'M, UM...
SORRY?
NO, DON'T BE, WE WERE ARGUING ALL THE TIME.
SHE SAID I SHOULD GET BORN AGAIN,
AND I WAS SAYING WE SHOULD HAVE SEX!
TURNS OUT SHE WAS RIGHT.

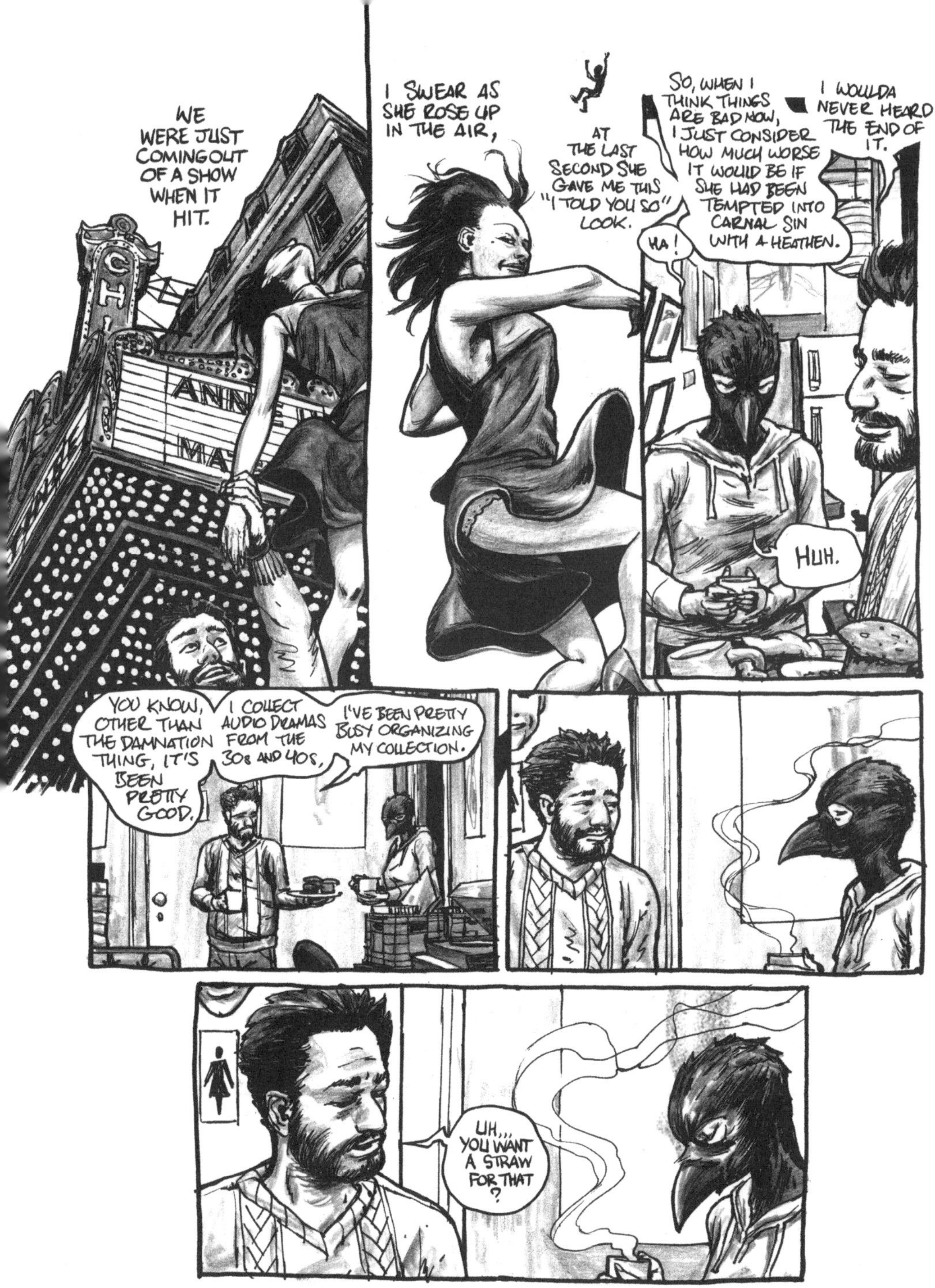
WE WERE JUST COMINGOUT OF A SHOW WHEN IT HIT.
I SWEAR AS SHE ROSE UP IN THE AIR,
AT THE LAST SECOND SHE GAVE ME THIS "I TOLD YOU SO" LOOK.
HA!
SO, WHEN I THINK THINGS ARE BAD NOW, I JUST CONSIDER HOW MUCH WORSE IT WOULD BE IF SHE HAD BEEN TEMPTED INTO CARNAL SIN WITH A HEATHEN.
I WOULDA NEVER HEARD THE END OF IT.
HUH.
YOU KNOW, OTHER THAN THE DAMNATION THING, IT'S BEEN PRETTY GOOD.
I COLLECT AUDIO DRAMAS FROM THE 30s AND 40s,
I'VE BEEN PRETTY BUSY ORGANIZING MY COLLECTION.
UH,,, YOU WANT A STRAW FOR THAT ?

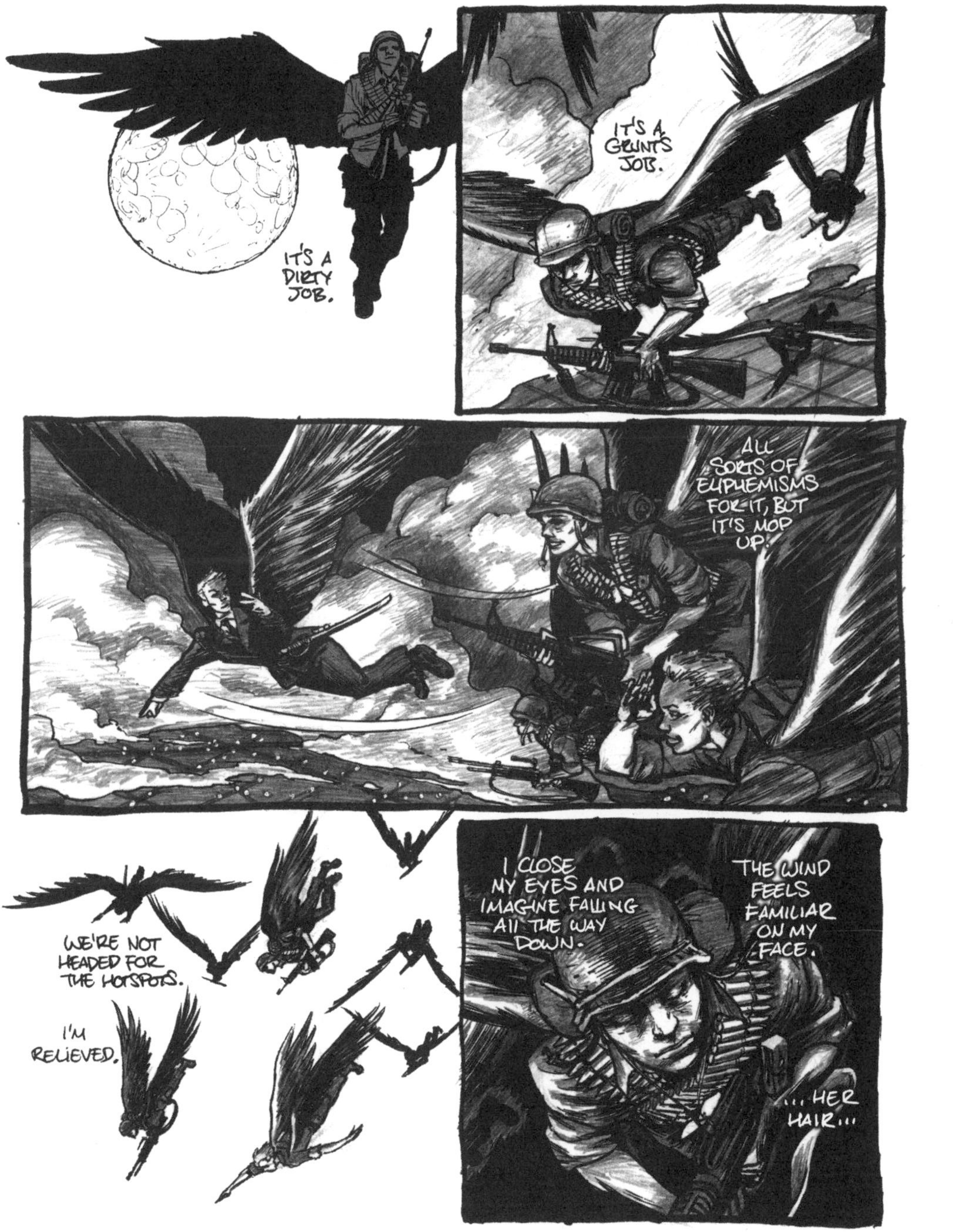
IT'S A DIRTY JOB.
IT'S A GRUNT'S JOB.
ALL SORTS OF EUPHEMISMS FOR IT, BUT IT'S MOP UP.
WE'RE NOT HEADED FOR THE HOTSPOTS.
I'M RELIEVED.
I CLOSE MY EYES AND IMAGINE FALLING ALL THE WAY DOWN.
THE WIND FEELS FAMILIAR ON MY FACE.
... HER HAIR...

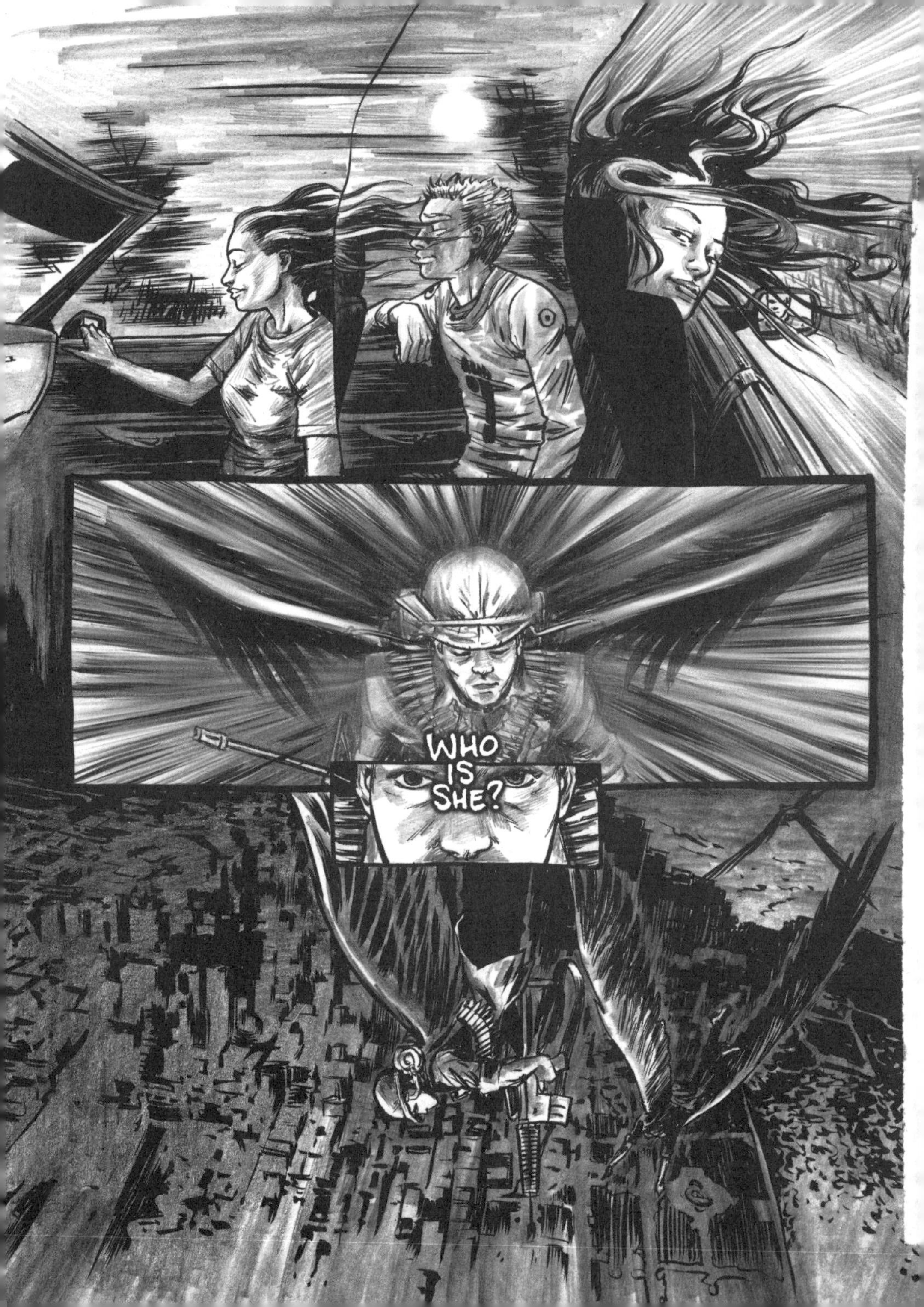
WHO IS SHE?

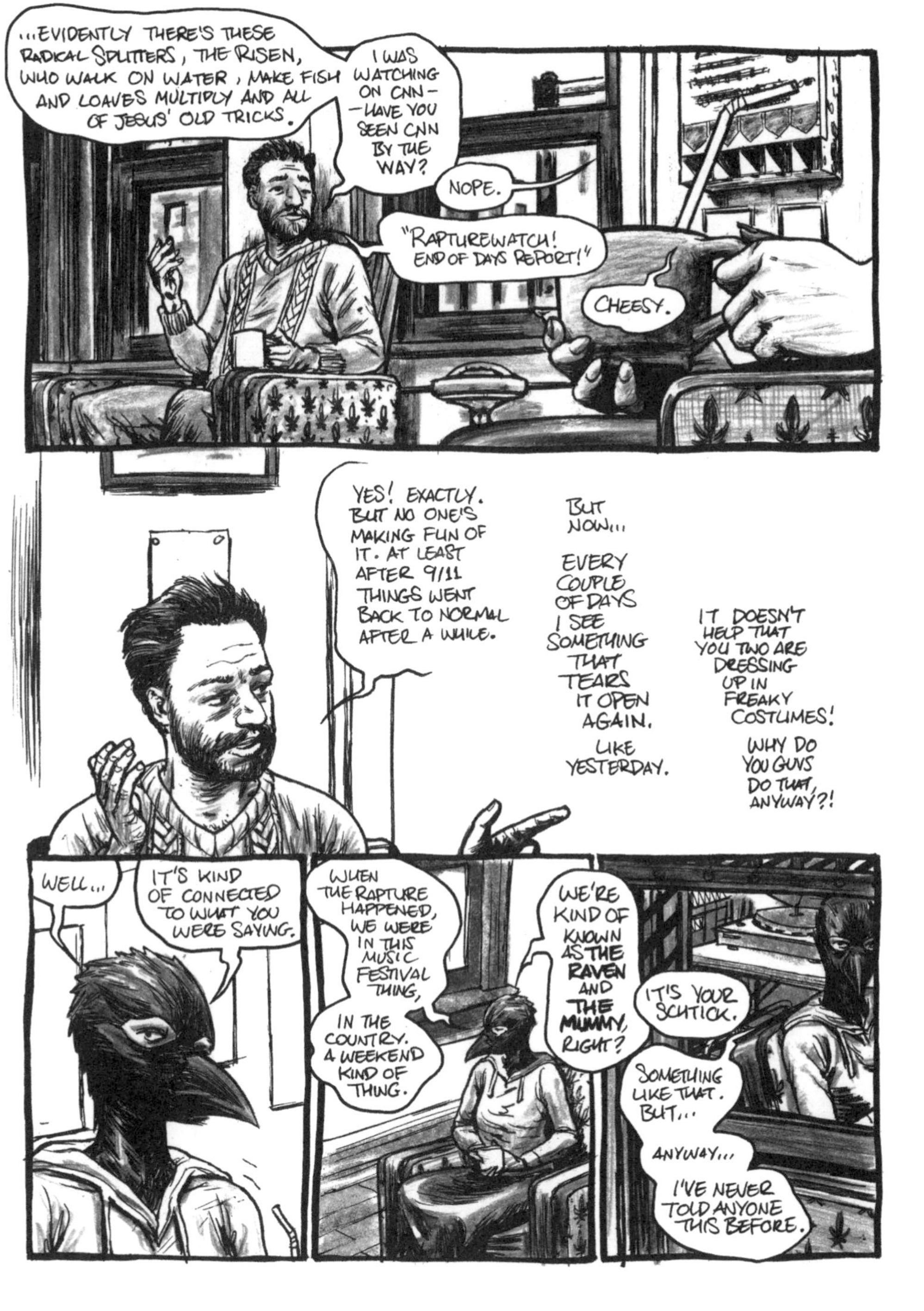
...EVIDENTLY THERE'S THESE RADICAL SPLITTERS, THE RISEN, WHO WALK ON WATER, MAKE FISH AND LOAVES MULTIPLY AND ALL OF JESUS' OLD TRICKS.
I WAS WATCHING ON CNN— —HAVE YOU SEEN CNN BY THE WAY?
NOPE.
"RAPTUREWATCH! END OF DAYS REPORT!"
CHEESY.
YES! EXACTLY. BUT NO ONE'S MAKING FUN OF IT. AT LEAST AFTER 9/11 THINGS WENT BACK TO NORMAL AFTER A WHILE.
BUT NOW...
EVERY COUPLE OF DAYS I SEE SOMETHING THAT TEARS IT OPEN AGAIN.
LIKE YESTERDAY.
IT DOESN'T HELP THAT YOU TWO ARE DRESSING UP IN FREAKY COSTUMES!
WHY DO YOU GUYS DO THAT, ANYWAY?!
WELL...
IT'S KIND OF CONNECTED TO WHAT YOU WERE SAYING.
WHEN THE RAPTURE HAPPENED, WE WERE IN THIS MUSIC FESTIVAL THING,
IN THE COUNTRY. A WEEKEND KIND OF THING.
WE'RE KIND OF KNOWN AS THE RAVEN AND THE MUMMY, RIGHT?
IT'S YOUR SCHTICK.
SOMETHING LIKE THAT. BUT...
ANYWAY...
I'VE NEVER TOLD ANYONE THIS BEFORE.

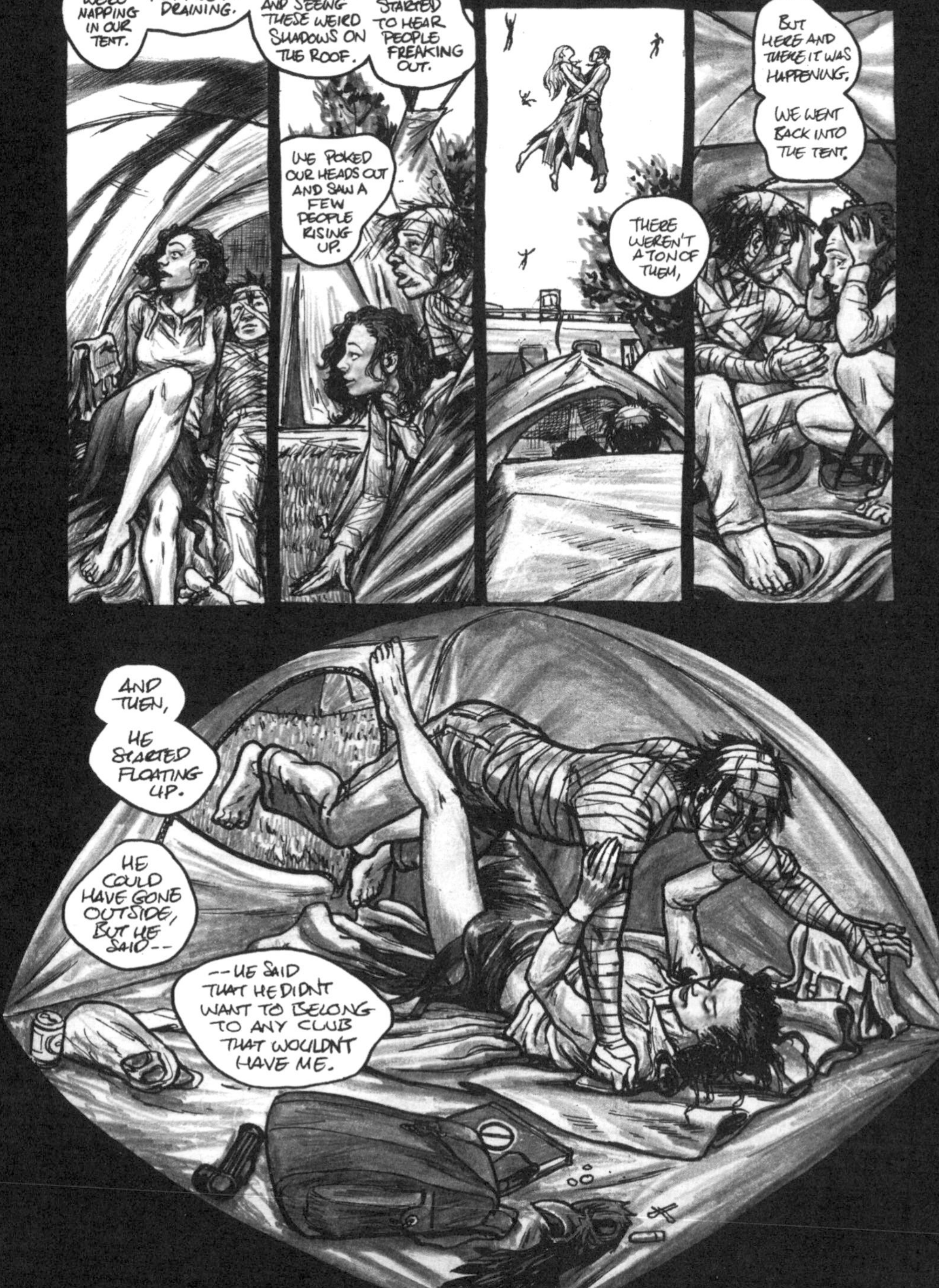
WE WERE NAPPING IN OUR TENT.
SOCIALIZING THAT MUCH IS DRAINING.
I JUST REMEMBER WAKING UP AND SEEING THESE WEIRD SHADOWS ON THE ROOF.
STARTED TO HEAR PEOPLE FREAKING OUT.
WE POKED OUR HEADS OUT AND SAW A FEW PEOPLE RISING UP.
THERE WEREN'T A TON OF THEM,
BUT HERE AND THERE IT WAS HAPPENING.
WE WENT BACK INTO THE TENT.
AND THEN,
HE STARTED FLOATING UP.
HE COULD HAVE GONE OUTSIDE, BUT HE SAID--
--HE SAID THAT HE DIDN'T WANT TO BELONG TO ANY CLUB THAT WOULDN'T HAVE ME.

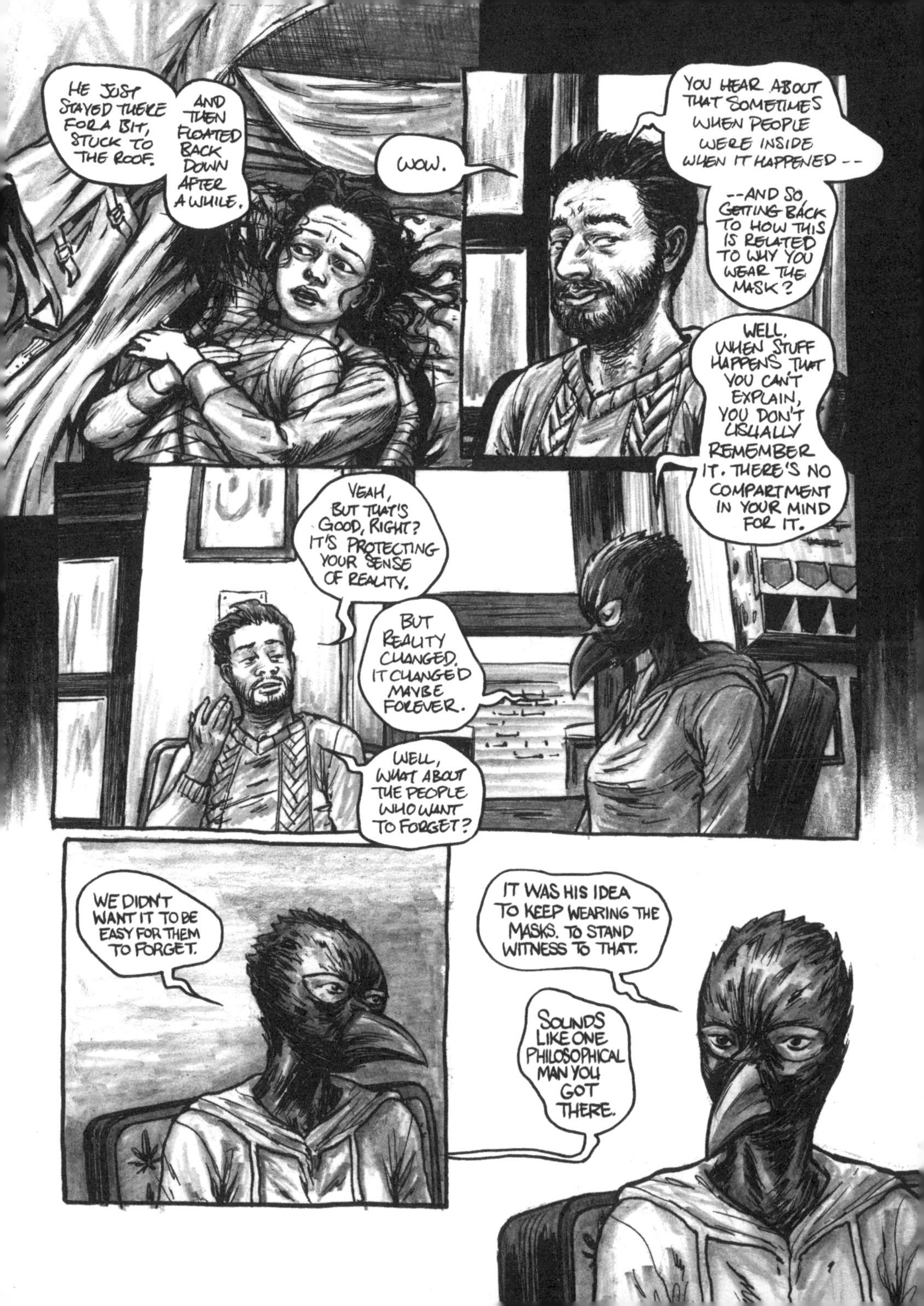
HE JUST STAYED THERE FOR A BIT, STUCK TO THE ROOF.
AND THEN FLOATED BACK DOWN AFTER A WHILE.
WOW.
YOU HEAR ABOUT THAT SOMETIMES WHEN PEOPLE WERE INSIDE WHEN IT HAPPENED --
--AND SO, GETTING BACK TO HOW THIS IS RELATED TO WHY YOU WEAR THE MASK?
WELL, WHEN STUFF HAPPENS THAT YOU CAN'T EXPLAIN, YOU DON'T USUALLY REMEMBER IT. THERE'S NO COMPARTMENT IN YOUR MIND FOR IT.
YEAH, BUT THAT'S GOOD, RIGHT? IT'S PROTECTING YOUR SENSE OF REALITY.
BUT REALITY CHANGED. IT CHANGED MAYBE FOREVER.
WELL, WHAT ABOUT THE PEOPLE WHO WANT TO FORGET?
WE DIDN'T WANT IT TO BE EASY FOR THEM TO FORGET.
IT WAS HIS IDEA TO KEEP WEARING THE MASKS. TO STAND WITNESS TO THAT.
SOUNDS LIKE ONE PHILOSOPHICAL MAN YOU GOT THERE.

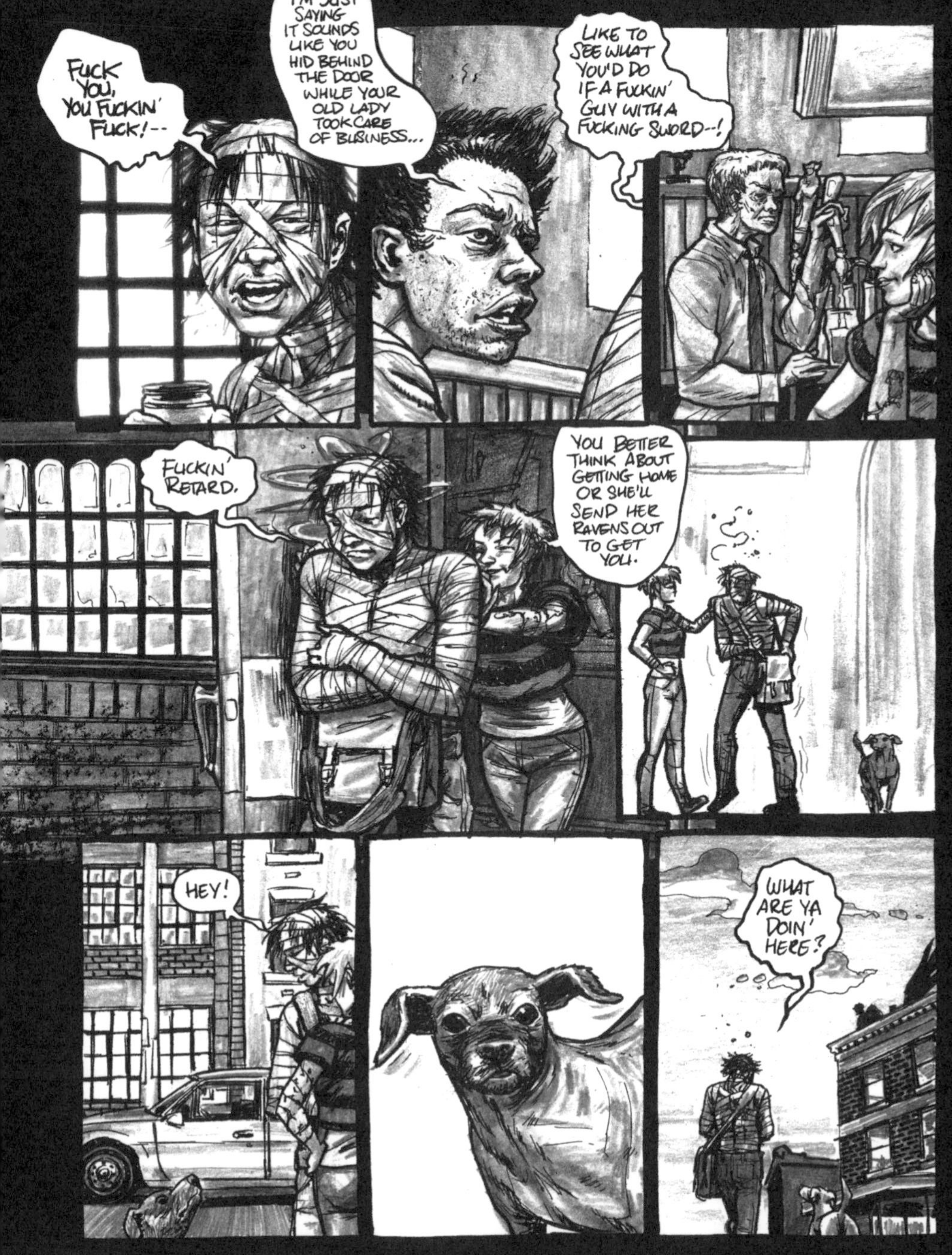
FUCK YOU, YOU FUCKIN' FUCK!--
I'M JUST SAYING IT SOUNDS LIKE YOU HID BEHIND THE DOOR WHILE YOUR OLD LADY TOOK CARE OF BUSINESS...
LIKE TO SEE WHAT YOU'D DO IF A FUCKIN' GUY WITH A FUCKING SWORD--!
FUCKIN' RETARD.
YOU BETTER THINK ABOUT GETTING HOME OR SHE'LL SEND HER RAVENS OUT TO GET YOU.
HEY!
WHAT ARE YA DOIN' HERE?

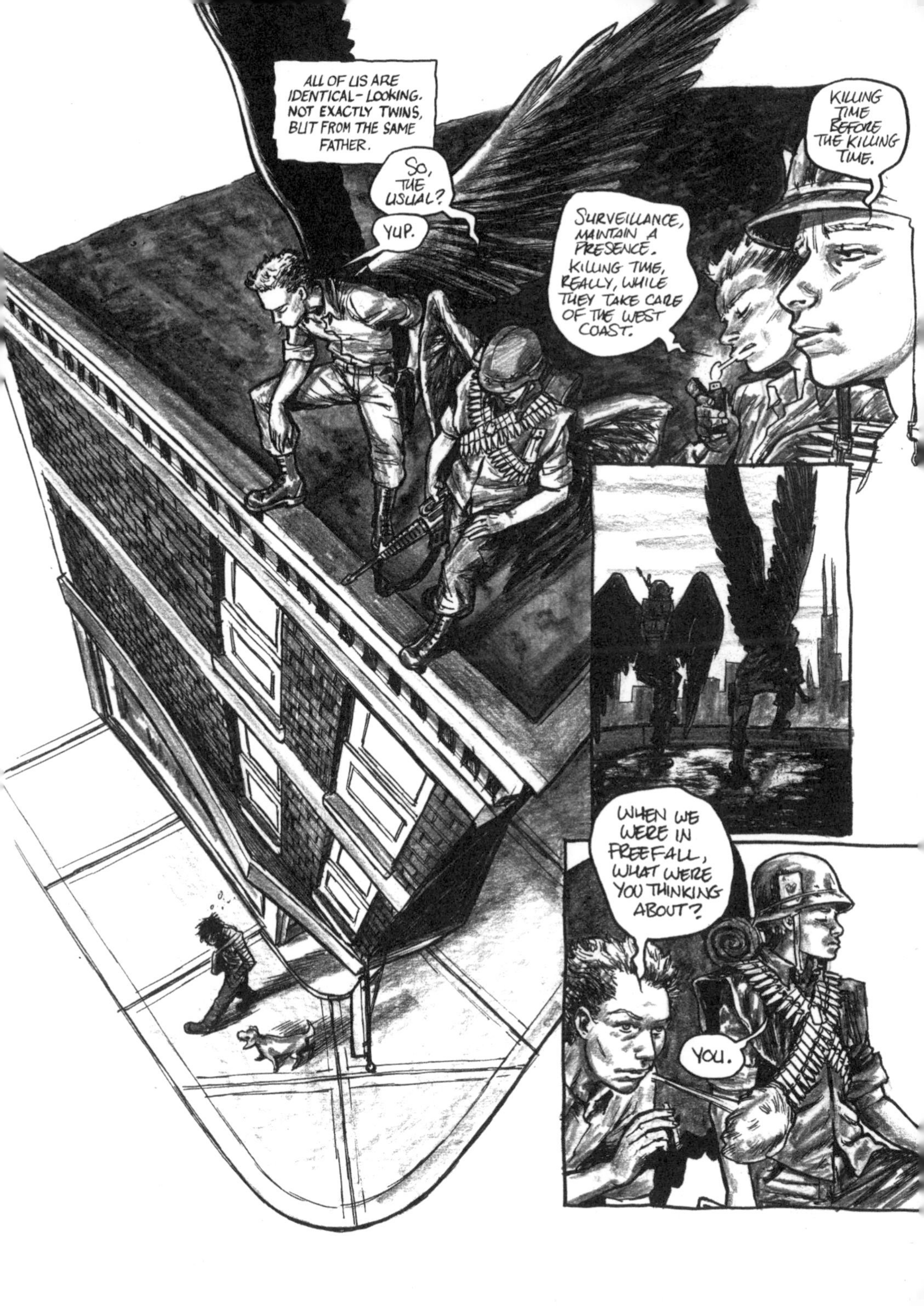
ALL OF US ARE IDENTICAL-LOOKING. NOT EXACTLY TWINS, BUT FROM THE SAME FATHER.
SO, THE USUAL?
YUP.
SURVEILLANCE, MAINTAIN A PRESENCE. KILLING TIME, REALLY, WHILE THEY TAKE CARE OF THE WEST COAST.
KILLING TIME BEFORE THE KILLING TIME.
WHEN WE WERE IN FREEFALL, WHAT WERE YOU THINKING ABOUT?
YOU.

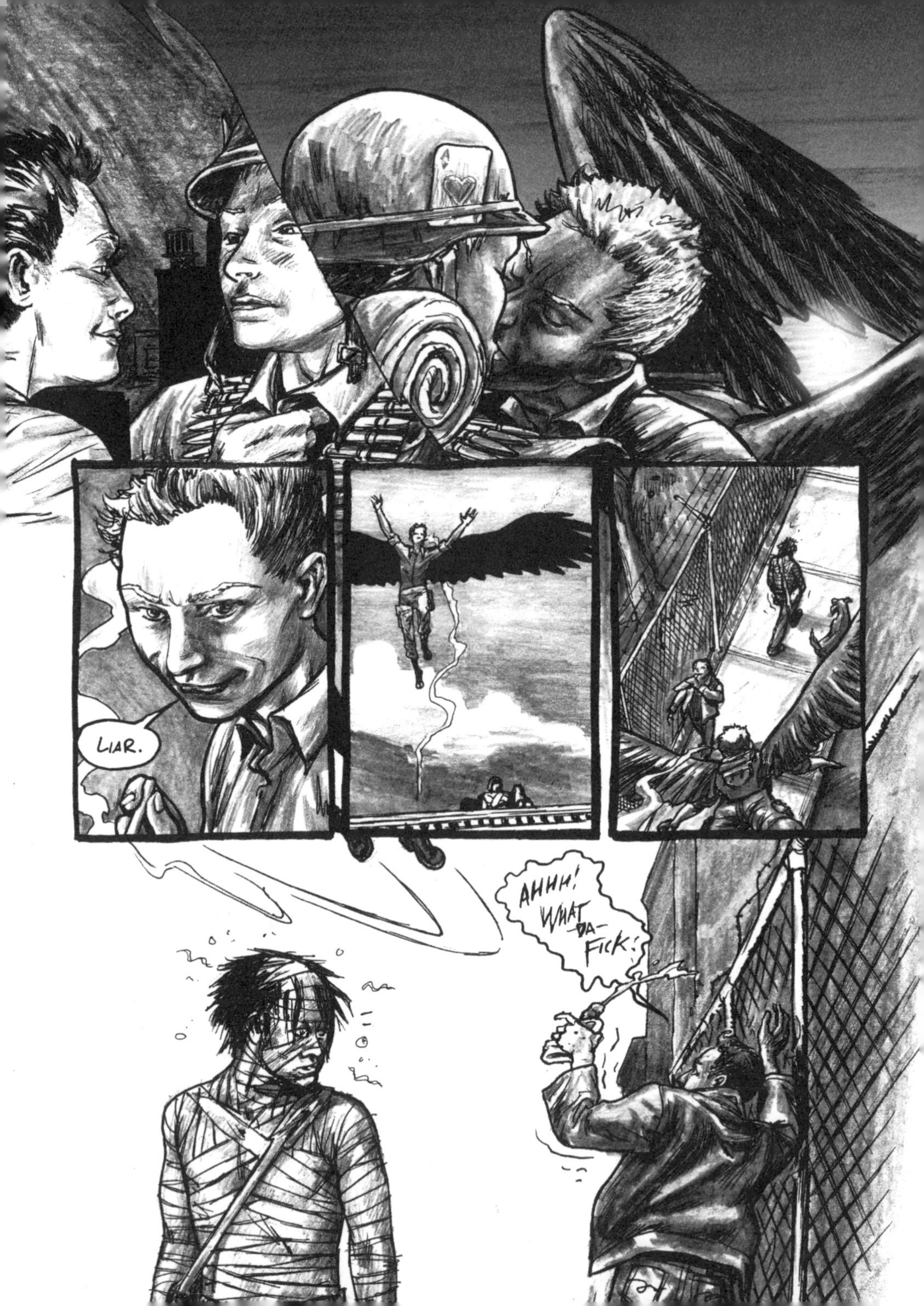
LIAR.
AHHH! WHAT DA FICK!

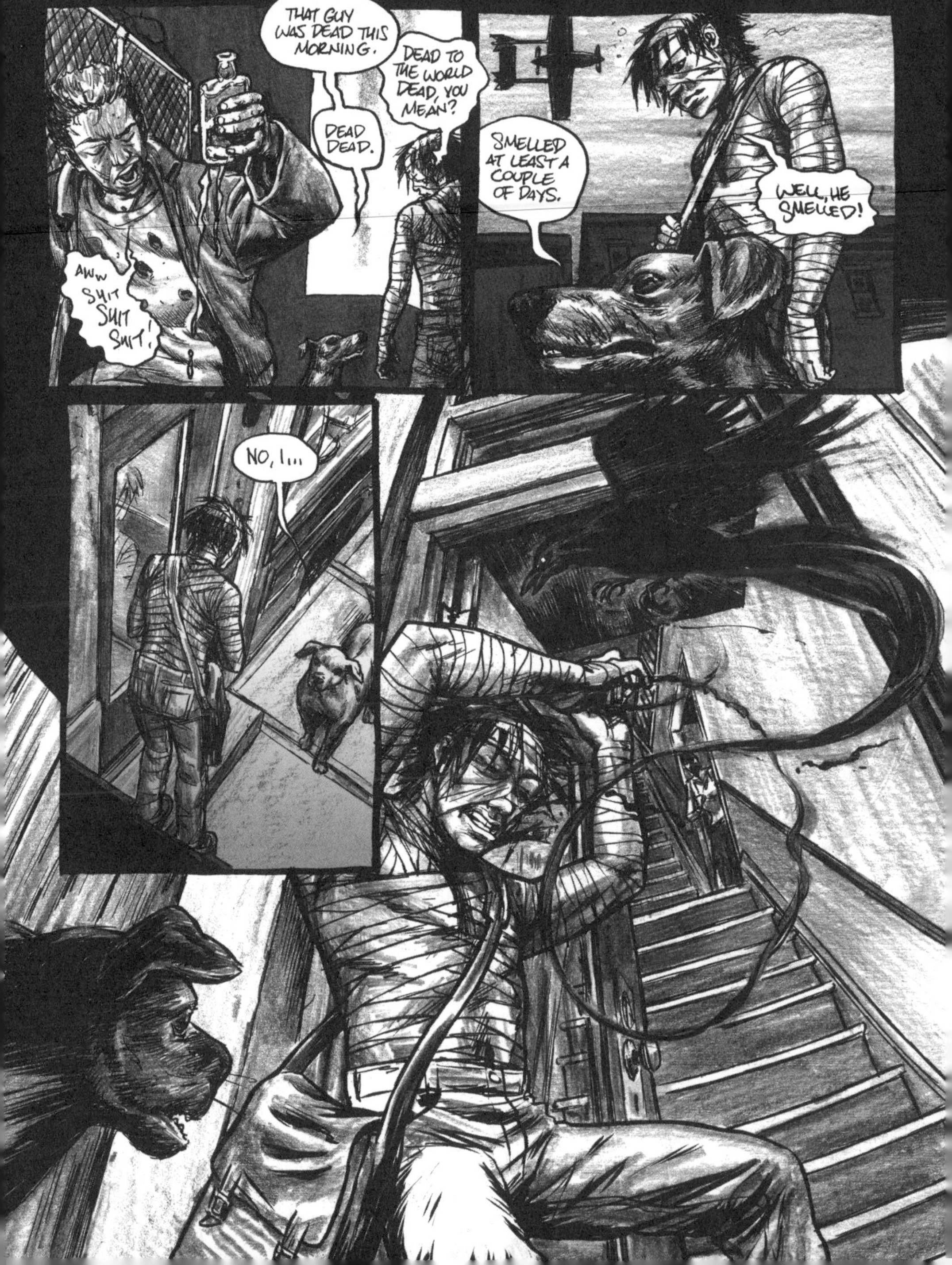
AWW SHIT SHIT SHIT!
THAT GUY WAS DEAD THIS MORNING.
DEAD DEAD.
DEAD TO THE WORLD DEAD, YOU MEAN?
SMELLED AT LEAST A COUPLE OF DAYS.
WELL, HE SMELLED!
NO, I...

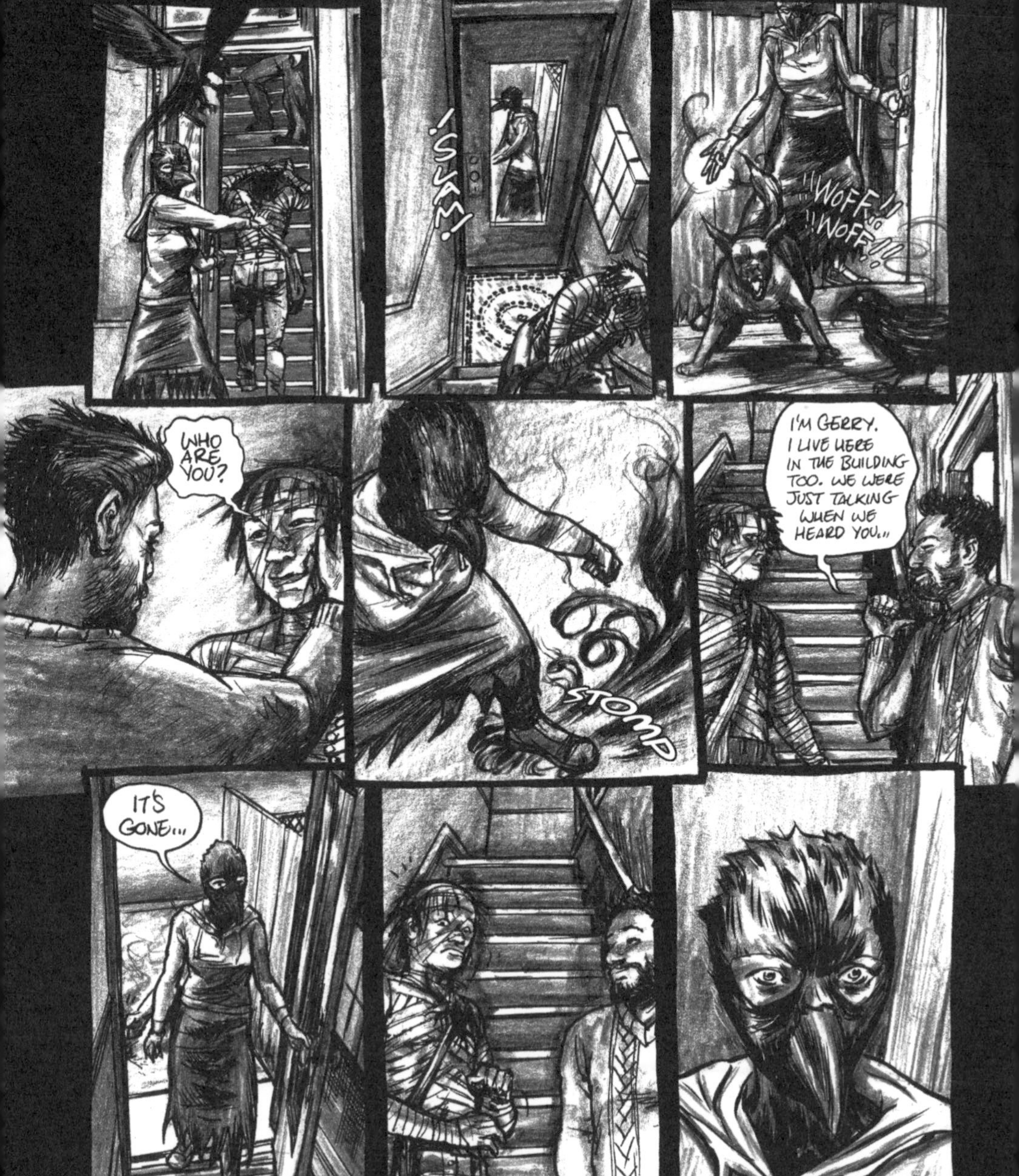
!SLAM!
!!WOFF!!
!!WOFF!!
WHO ARE YOU?
STOMP
I'M GERRY. I LIVE HERE IN THE BUILDING TOO. WE WERE JUST TALKING WHEN WE HEARD YOU...
IT'S GONE...

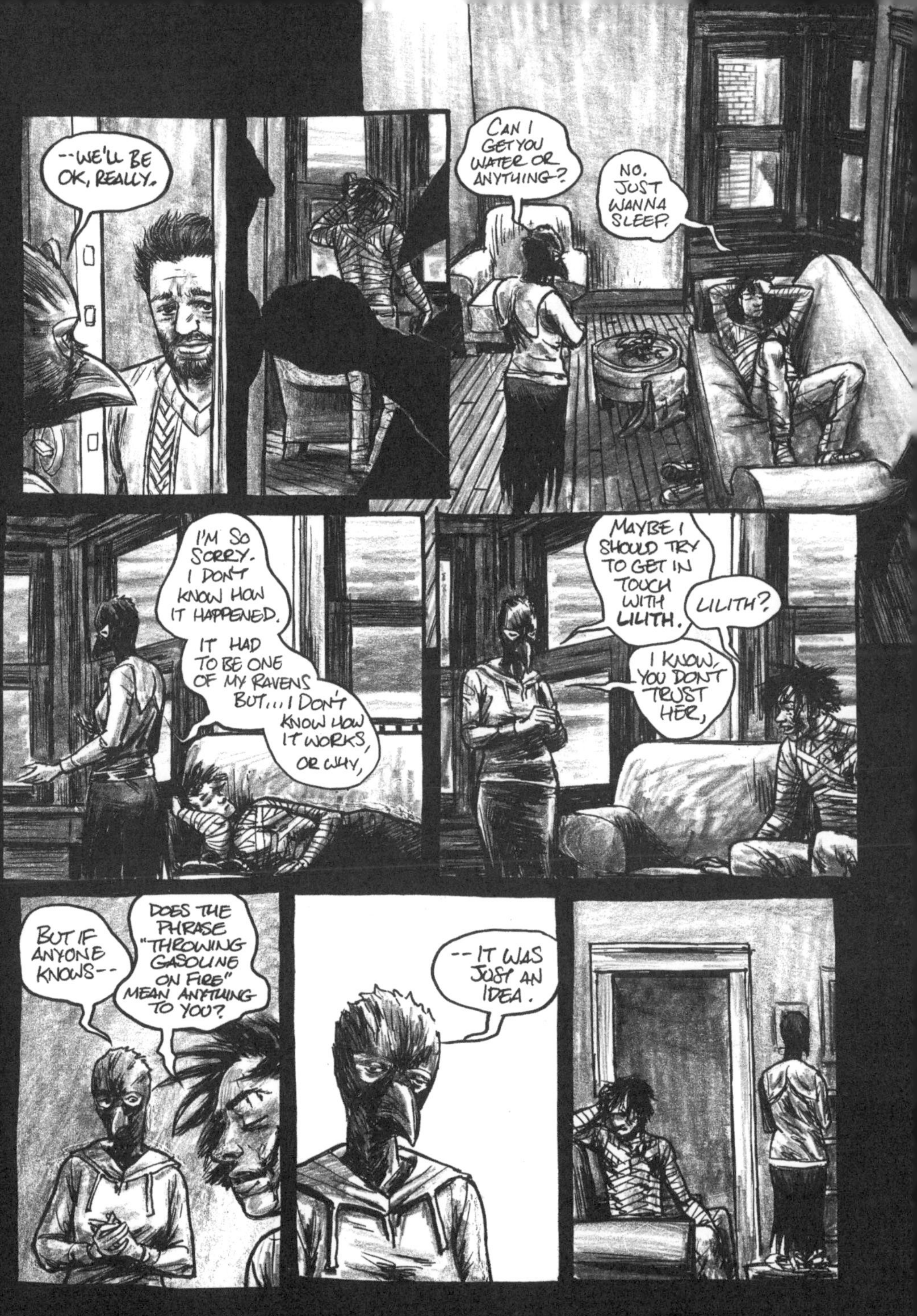
--WE'LL BE OK, REALLY.
CAN I GET YOU WATER OR ANYTHING?
NO. JUST WANNA SLEEP.
I'M SO SORRY. I DON'T KNOW HOW IT HAPPENED.
IT HAD TO BE ONE OF MY RAVENS BUT... I DON'T KNOW HOW IT WORKS, OR WHY,
MAYBE I SHOULD TRY TO GET IN TOUCH WITH LILITH.
LILITH?
I KNOW, YOU DONT TRUST HER,
BUT IF ANYONE KNOWS--
DOES THE PHRASE "THROWING GASOLINE ON FIRE" MEAN ANYTHING TO YOU?
--IT WAS JUST AN IDEA.

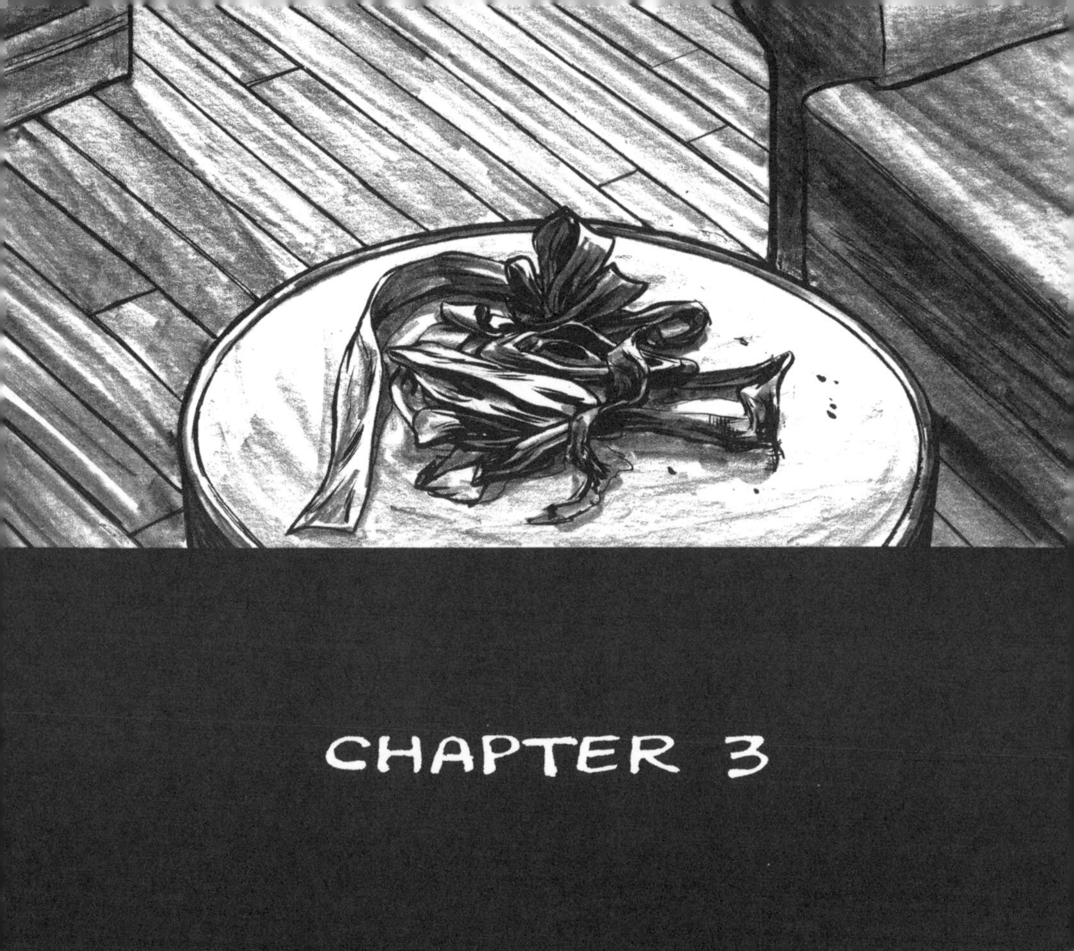

CHAPTER 3

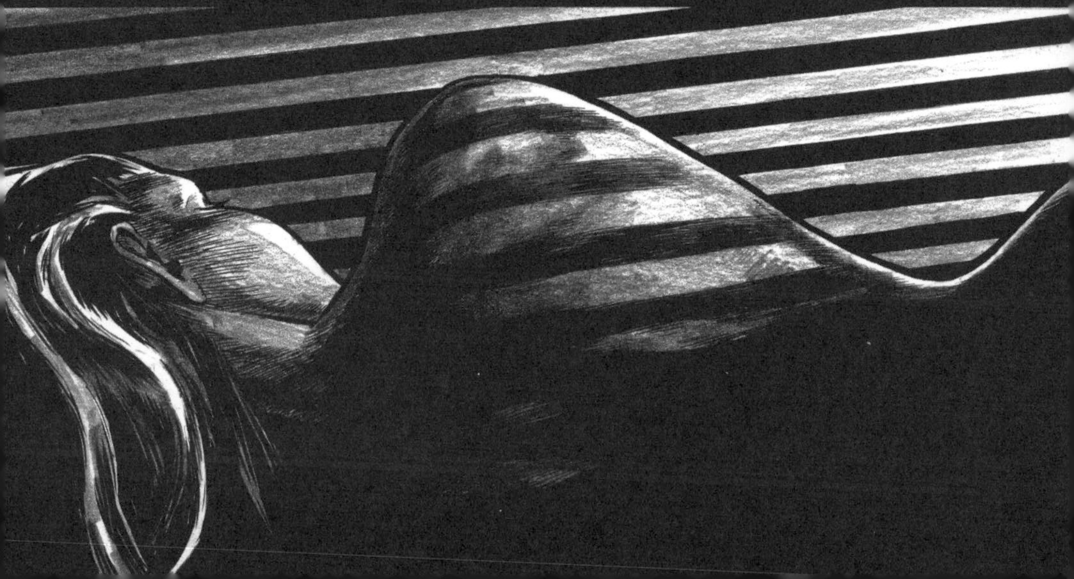

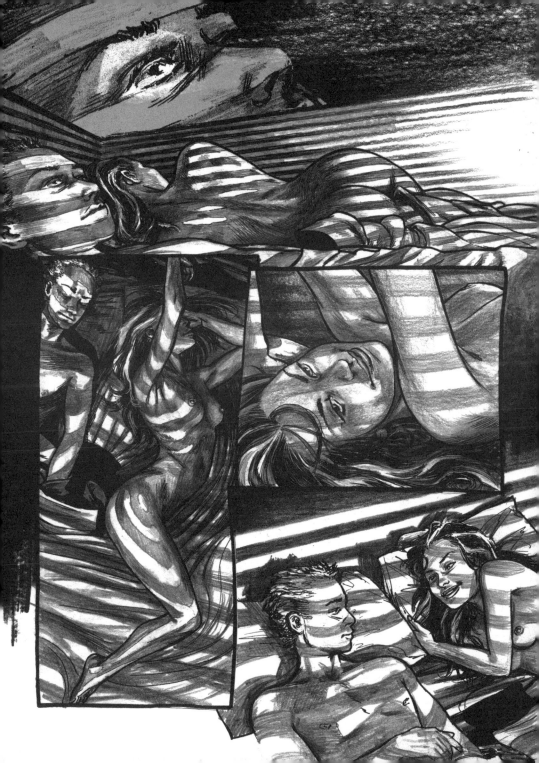

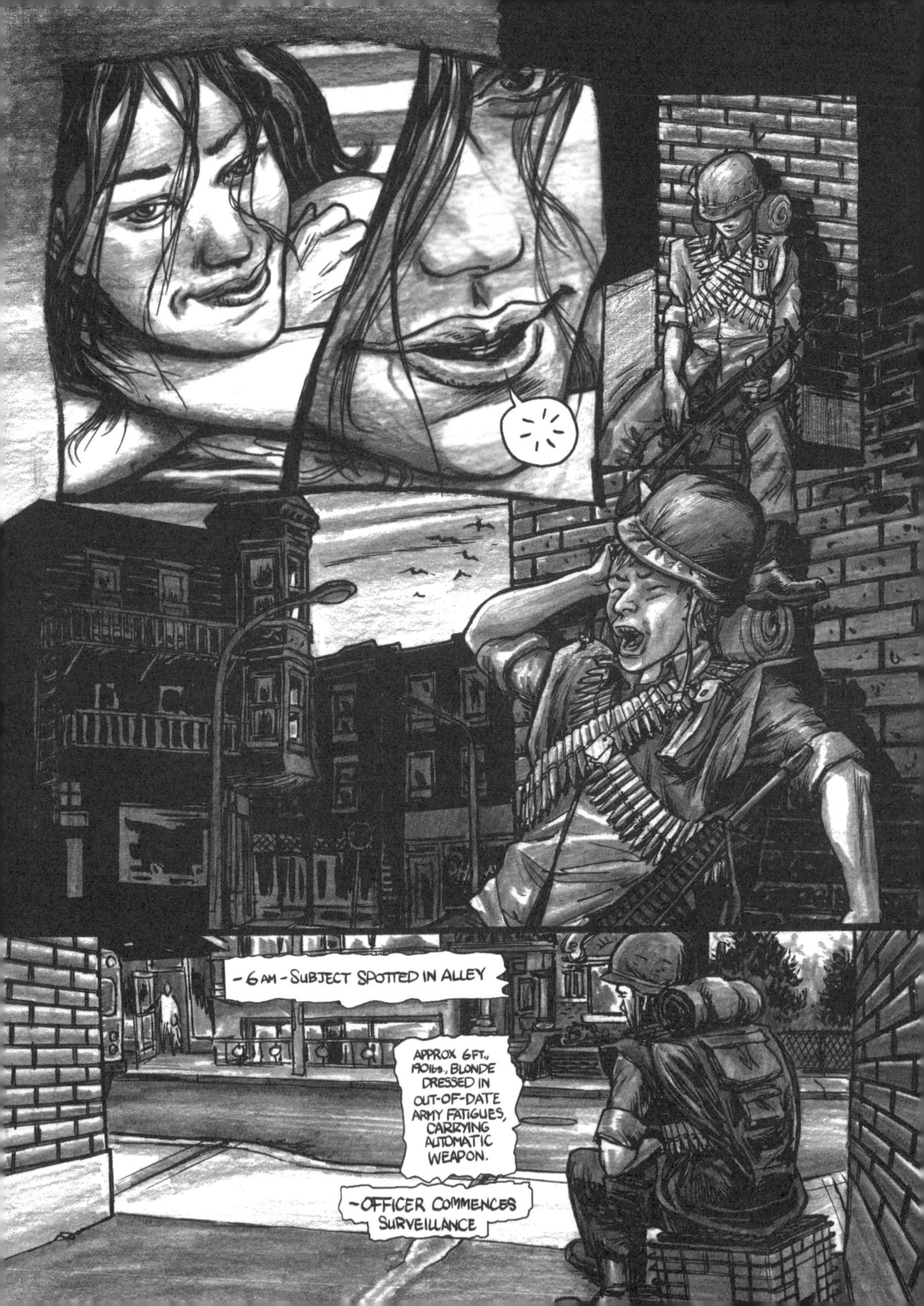
-6 AM - SUBJECT SPOTTED IN ALLEY
APPROX 6FT., 190lbs., BLONDE DRESSED IN OUT-OF-DATE ARMY FATIGUES, CARRYING AUTOMATIC WEAPON.
-OFFICER COMMENCES SURVEILLANCE

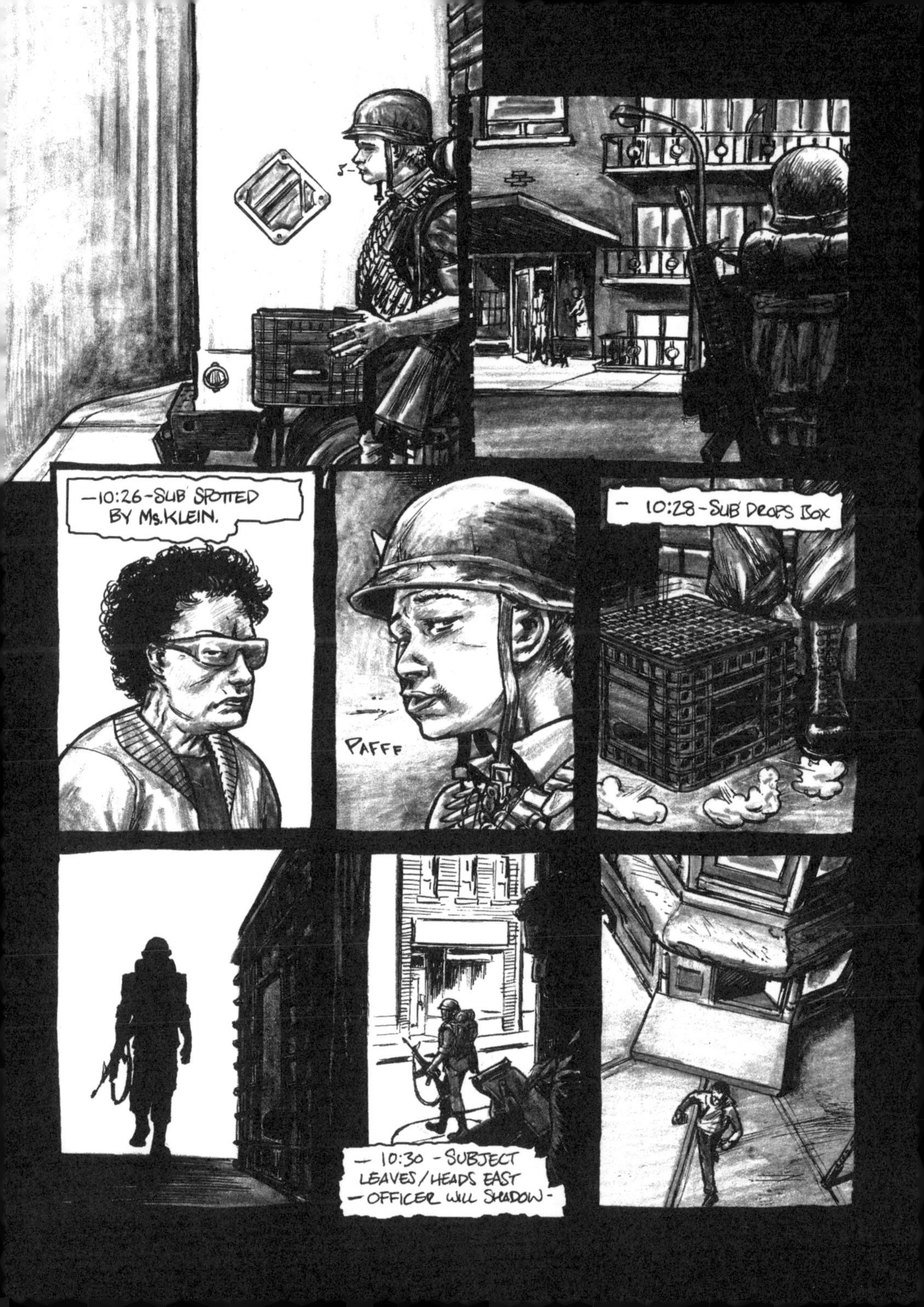

—10:26-SUB SPOTTED BY Ms.KLEIN.
PAFFF
— 10:28-SUB DROPS BOX
— 10:30 - SUBJECT LEAVES / HEADS EAST
— OFFICER WILL SHADOW -

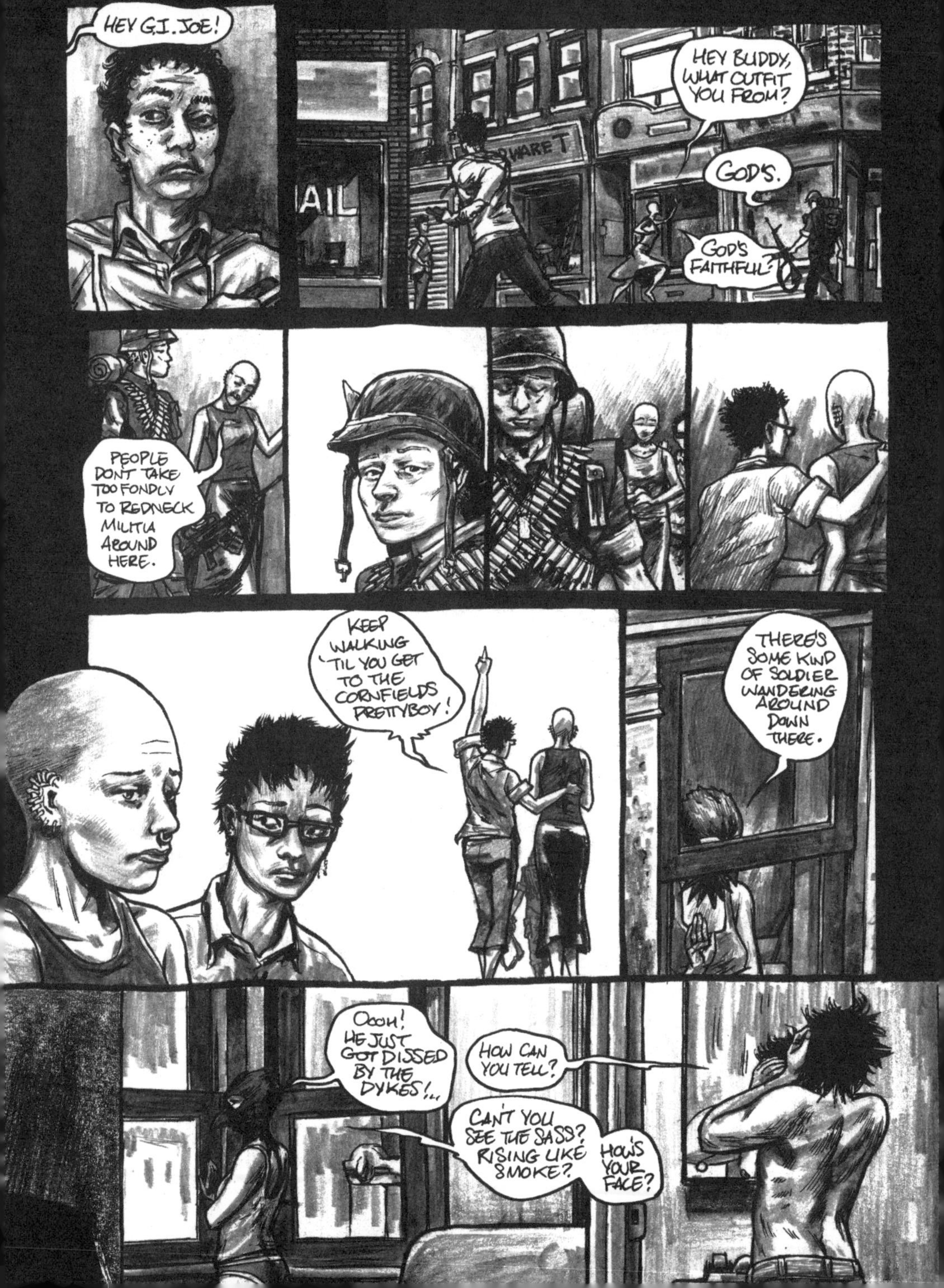
HEY G.I. JOE!
HEY BUDDY, WHAT OUTFIT YOU FROM?
GOD'S.
GOD'S FAITHFUL.
AIL
PEOPLE DONT TAKE TOO FONDLY TO REDNECK MILITIA AROUND HERE.
KEEP WALKING 'TIL YOU GET TO THE CORNFIELDS PRETTYBOY!
THERE'S SOME KIND OF SOLDIER WANDERING AROUND DOWN THERE.
OOOH! HE JUST GOT DISSED BY THE DYKES!...
HOW CAN YOU TELL?
CAN'T YOU SEE THE SASS? RISING LIKE SMOKE?
HOW'S YOUR FACE?

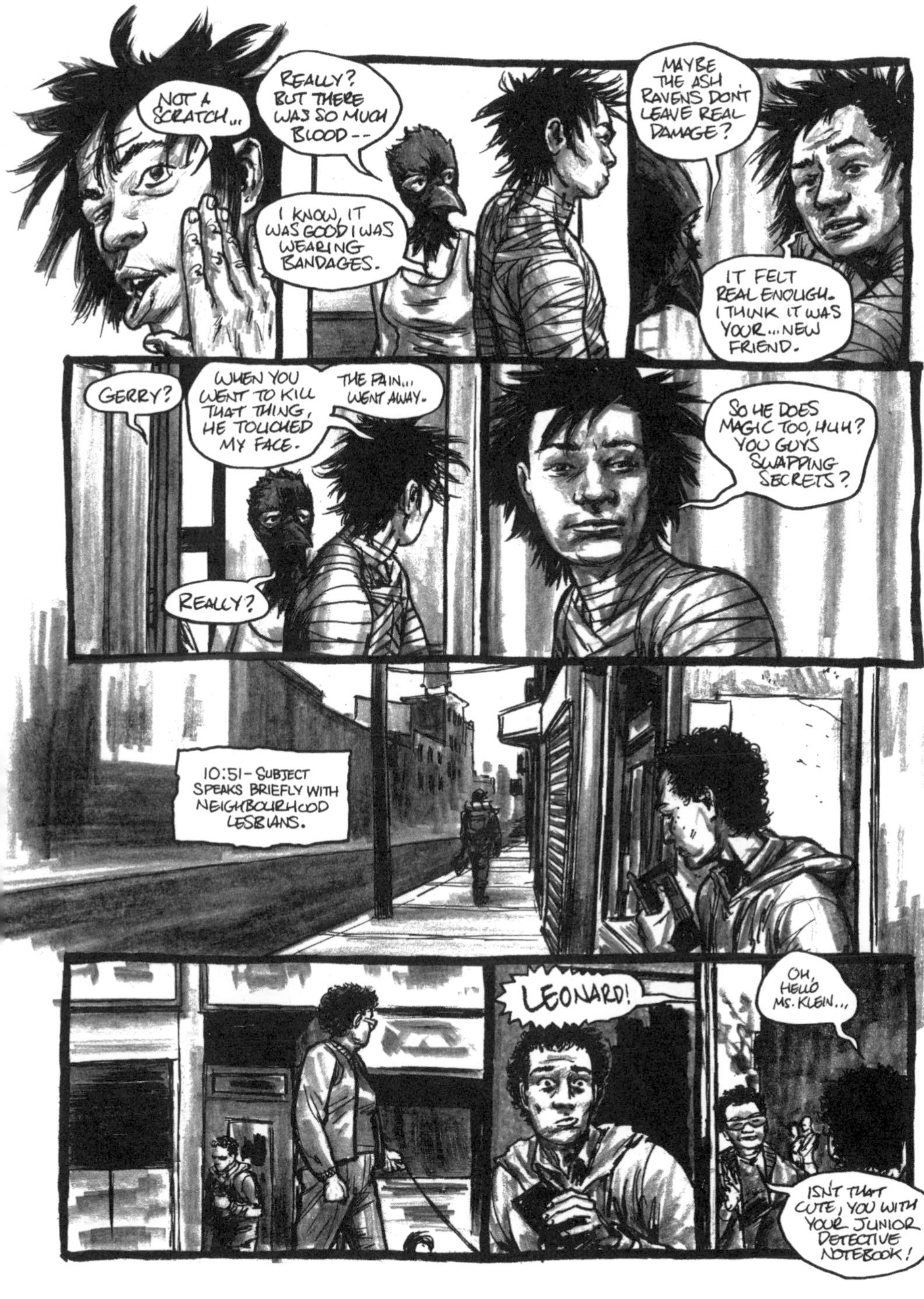
NOT A SCRATCH...
REALLY? BUT THERE WAS SO MUCH BLOOD--
I KNOW, IT WAS GOOD I WAS WEARING BANDAGES.
MAYBE THE ASH RAVENS DON'T LEAVE REAL DAMAGE?
IT FELT REAL ENOUGH. I THINK IT WAS YOUR...NEW FRIEND.
GERRY?
WHEN YOU WENT TO KILL THAT THING, HE TOUCHED MY FACE.
THE PAIN... WENT AWAY.
REALLY?
SO HE DOES MAGIC TOO, HUH? YOU GUYS SWAPPING SECRETS?
10:51- SUBJECT SPEAKS BRIEFLY WITH NEIGHBOURHOOD LESBIANS.
LEONARD!
OH, HELLO MS. KLEIN...
ISN'T THAT CUTE, YOU WITH YOUR JUNIOR DETECTIVE NOTEBOOK!

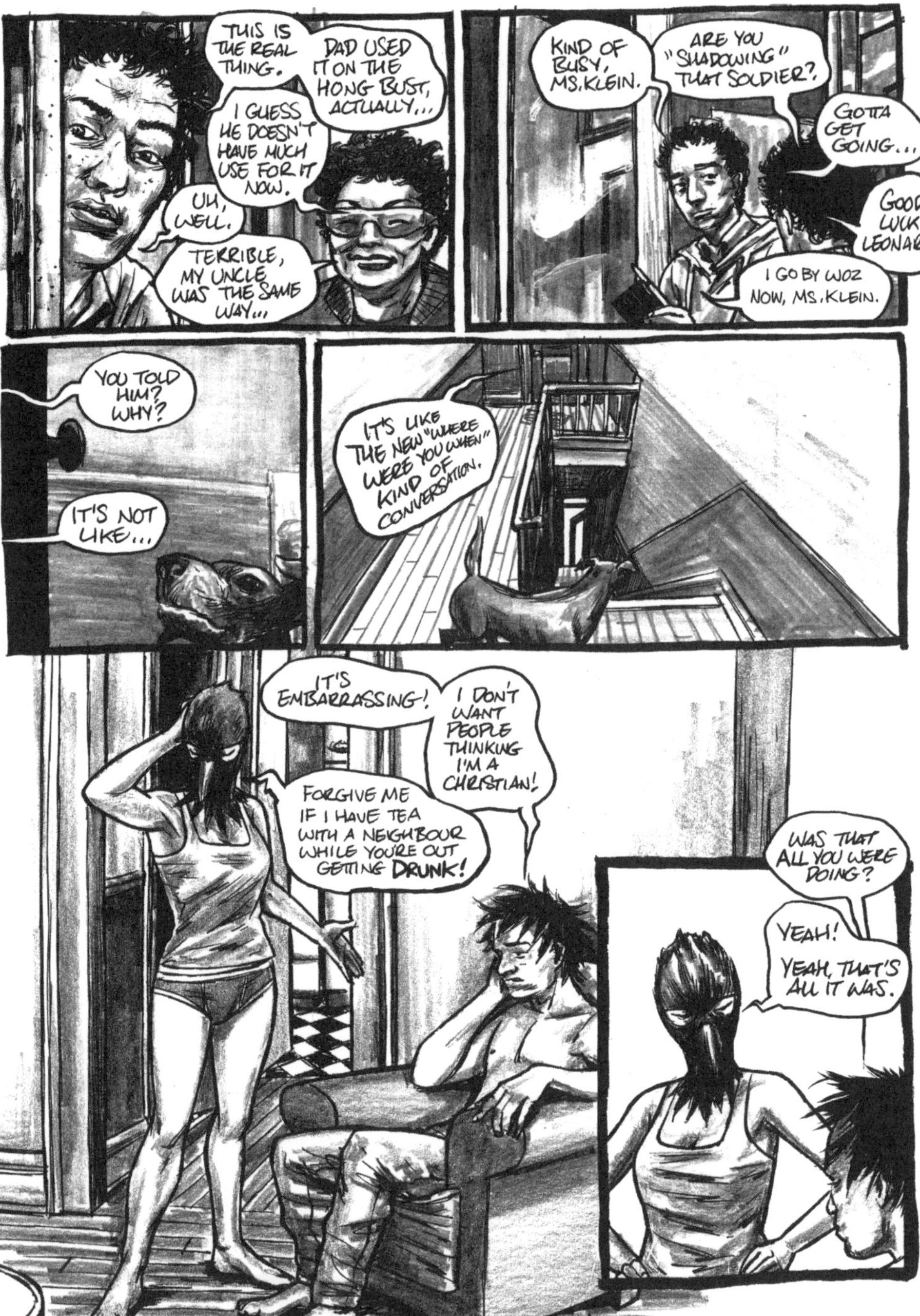
THIS IS THE REAL THING.
DAD USED IT ON THE HONG BUST, ACTUALLY...
I GUESS HE DOESN'T HAVE MUCH USE FOR IT NOW.
UH, WELL.
TERRIBLE, MY UNCLE WAS THE SAME WAY...
KIND OF BUSY, MS. KLEIN.
ARE YOU "SHADOWING" THAT SOLDIER?
GOTTA GET GOING...
GOOD LUCK LEONARD!
I GO BY WOZ NOW, MS. KLEIN.
YOU TOLD HIM? WHY?
IT'S NOT LIKE...
IT'S LIKE THE NEW "WHERE WERE YOU WHEN" KIND OF CONVERSATION.
IT'S EMBARRASSING!
I DON'T WANT PEOPLE THINKING I'M A CHRISTIAN!
FORGIVE ME IF I HAVE TEA WITH A NEIGHBOUR WHILE YOU'RE OUT GETTING DRUNK!
WAS THAT ALL YOU WERE DOING?
YEAH!
YEAH, THAT'S ALL IT WAS.

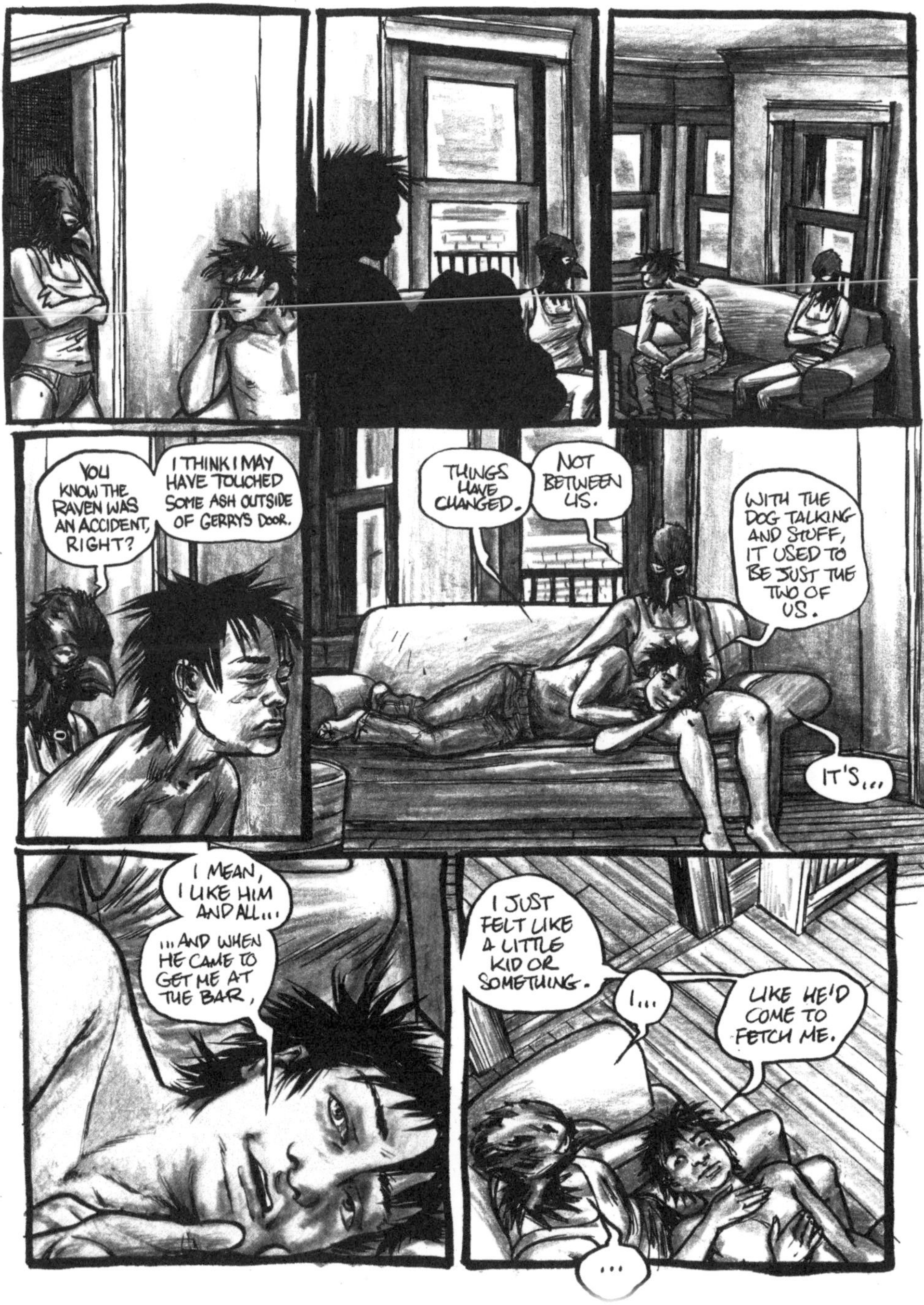

YOU KNOW THE RAVEN WAS AN ACCIDENT, RIGHT?
I THINK I MAY HAVE TOUCHED SOME ASH OUTSIDE OF GERRYS DOOR.
THINGS HAVE CHANGED.
NOT BETWEEN US.
WITH THE DOG TALKING AND STUFF, IT USED TO BE JUST THE TWO OF US.
IT'S...
I MEAN, I LIKE HIM AND ALL...
...AND WHEN HE CAME TO GET ME AT THE BAR,
I JUST FELT LIKE A LITTLE KID OR SOMETHING.
I...
LIKE HE'D COME TO FETCH ME.
...

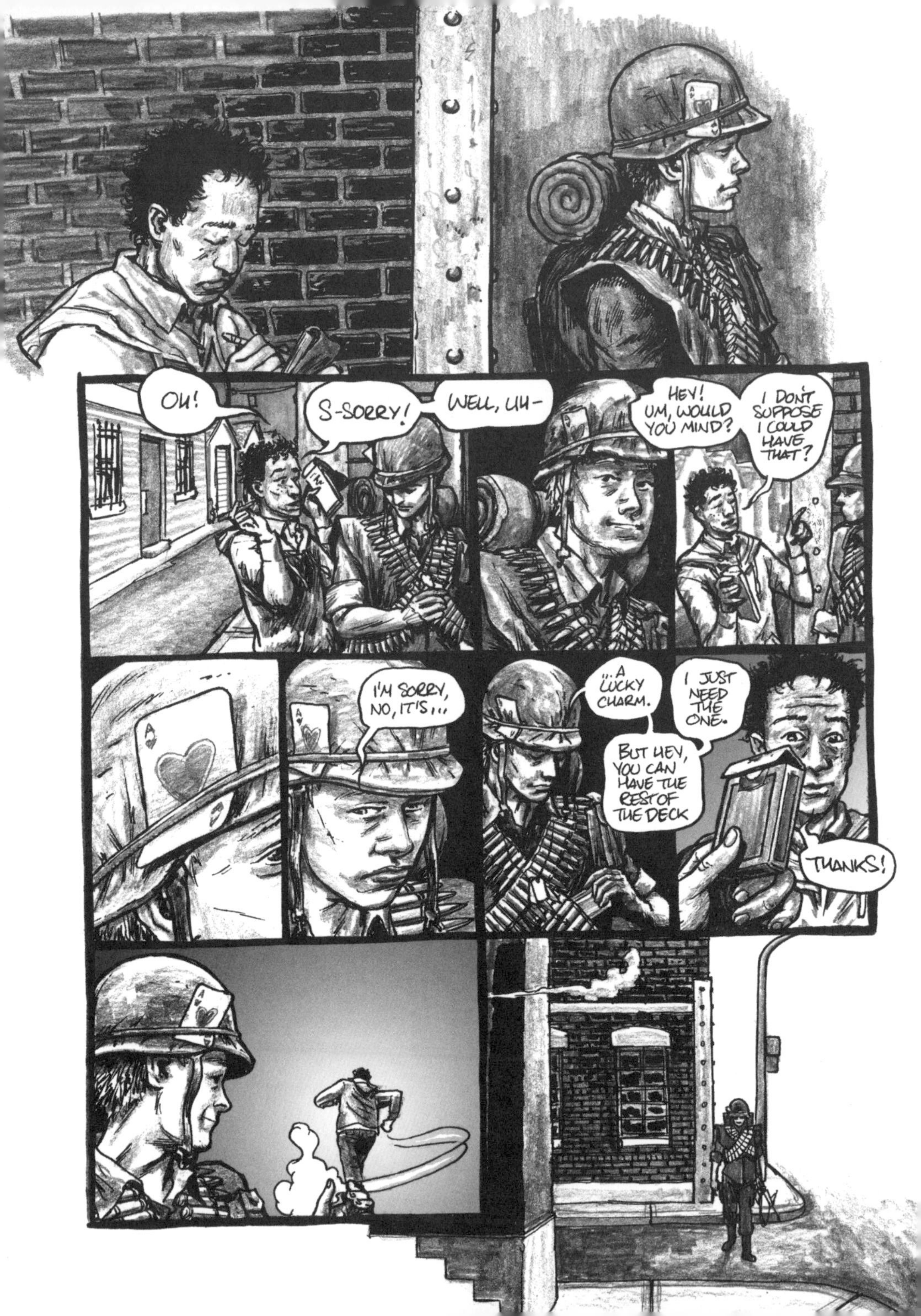
OH!
S-SORRY!
WELL, UH-
HEY! UM, WOULD YOU MIND?
I DON'T SUPPOSE I COULD HAVE THAT?
...
I'M SORRY, NO, IT'S...
...A LUCKY CHARM.
BUT HEY, YOU CAN HAVE THE REST OF THE DECK
I JUST NEED THE ONE.
THANKS!

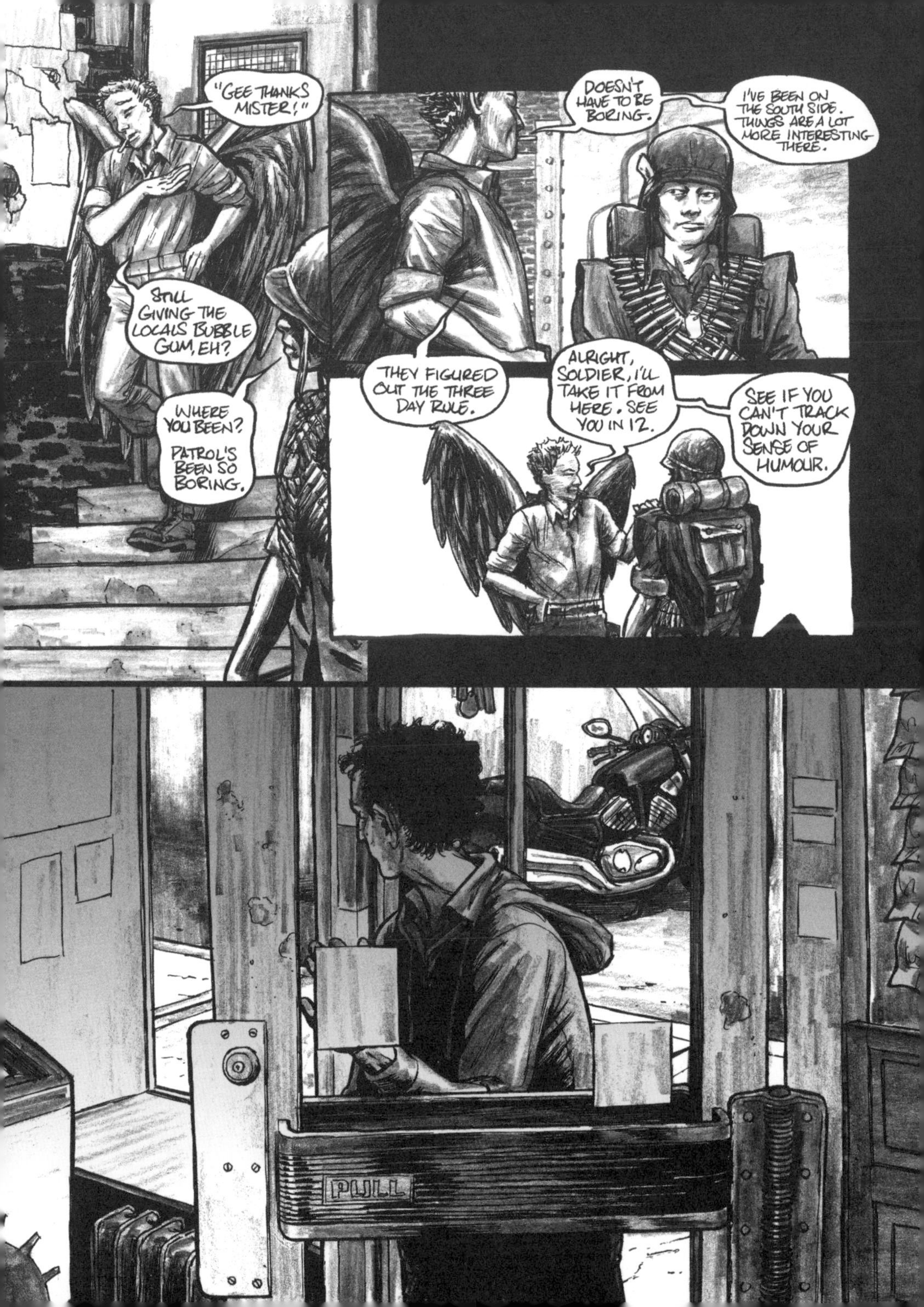
"GEE THANKS MISTER!"
STILL GIVING THE LOCALS BUBBLE GUM, EH?
WHERE YOU BEEN?
PATROL'S BEEN SO BORING.
DOESN'T HAVE TO BE BORING.
I'VE BEEN ON THE SOUTH SIDE. THINGS ARE A LOT MORE INTERESTING THERE.
THEY FIGURED OUT THE THREE DAY RULE.
ALRIGHT, SOLDIER, I'LL TAKE IT FROM HERE. SEE YOU IN 12.
SEE IF YOU CAN'T TRACK DOWN YOUR SENSE OF HUMOUR.
PULL

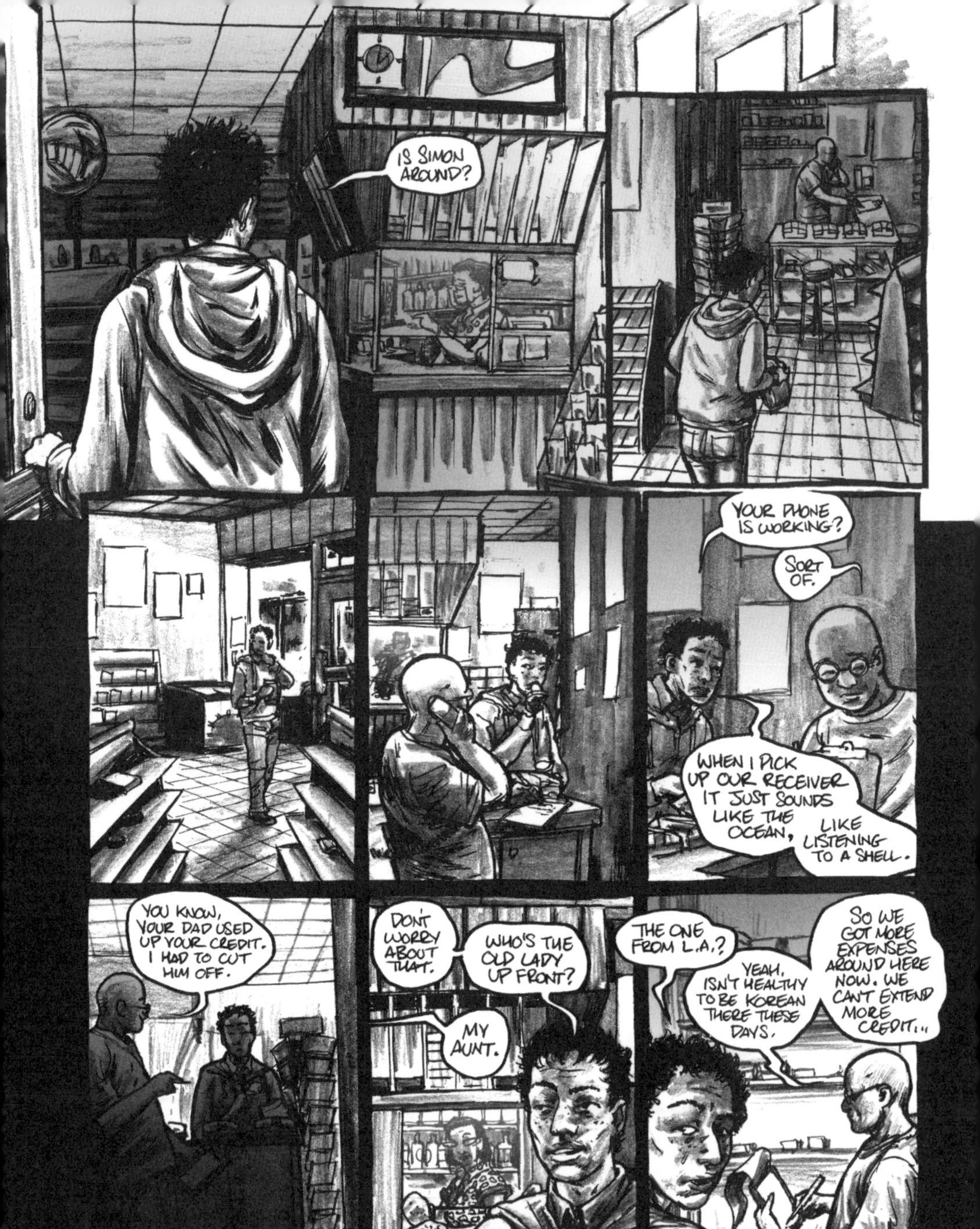

IS SIMON AROUND?
YOUR PHONE IS WORKING?
SORT OF.
WHEN I PICK UP OUR RECEIVER IT JUST SOUNDS LIKE THE OCEAN,
LIKE LISTENING TO A SHELL.
YOU KNOW, YOUR DAD USED UP YOUR CREDIT. I HAD TO CUT HIM OFF.
DON'T WORRY ABOUT THAT.
WHO'S THE OLD LADY UP FRONT?
MY AUNT.
THE ONE FROM L.A.?
YEAH, ISN'T HEALTHY TO BE KOREAN THERE THESE DAYS.
SO WE GOT MORE EXPENSES AROUND HERE NOW. WE CAN'T EXTEND MORE CREDIT...

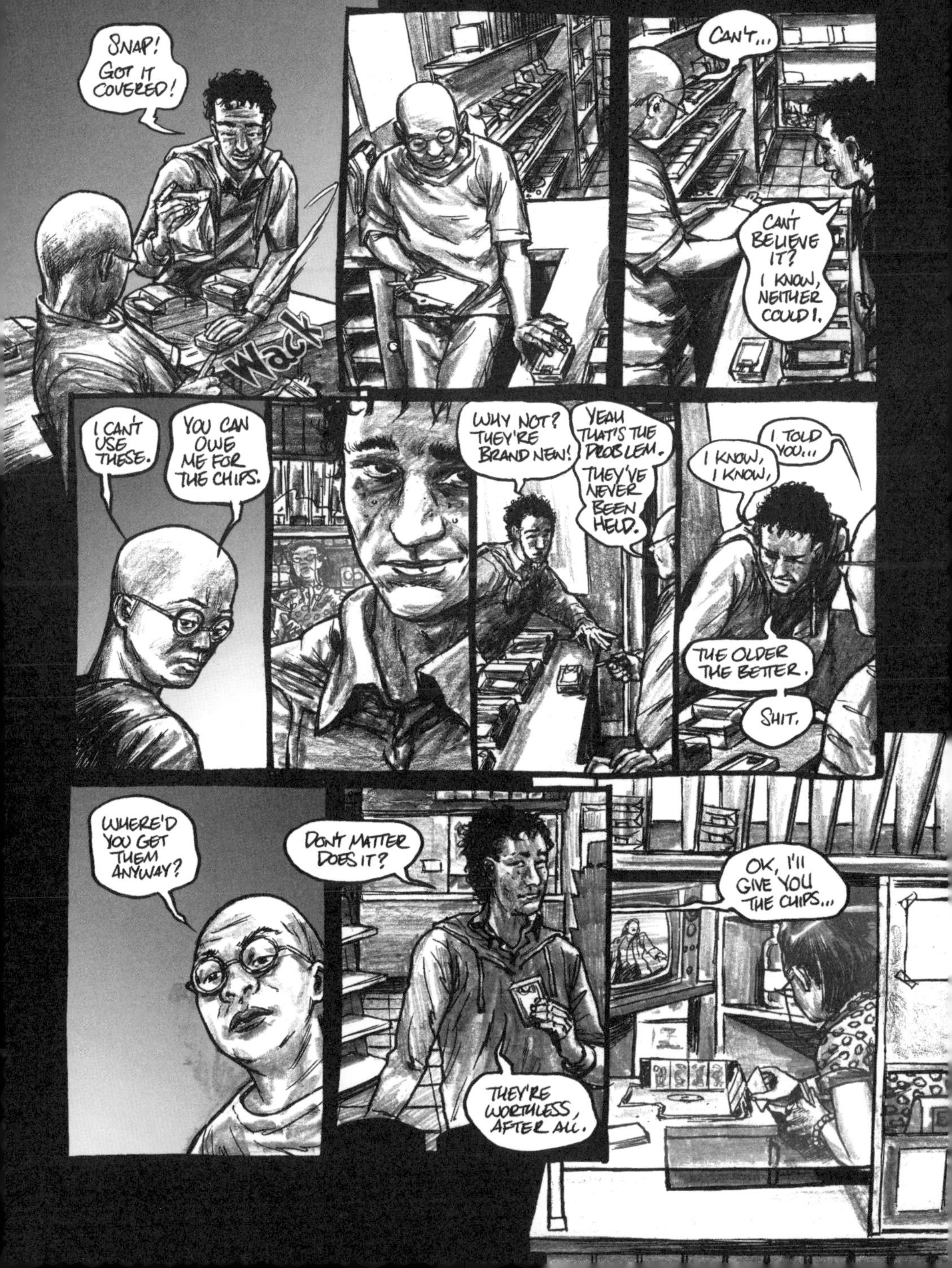
SNAP! GOT IT COVERED!
WACK
CAN'T...
CAN'T BELIEVE IT? I KNOW, NEITHER COULD I.
I CAN'T USE THESE.
YOU CAN OWE ME FOR THE CHIPS.
WHY NOT? THEY'RE BRAND NEW!
YEAH THAT'S THE PROBLEM.
THEY'VE NEVER BEEN HELD.
I TOLD YOU...
I KNOW, I KNOW,
THE OLDER THE BETTER.
SHIT.
WHERE'D YOU GET THEM ANYWAY?
DON'T MATTER DOES IT?
THEY'RE WORTHLESS, AFTER ALL.
OK, I'LL GIVE YOU THE CHIPS...

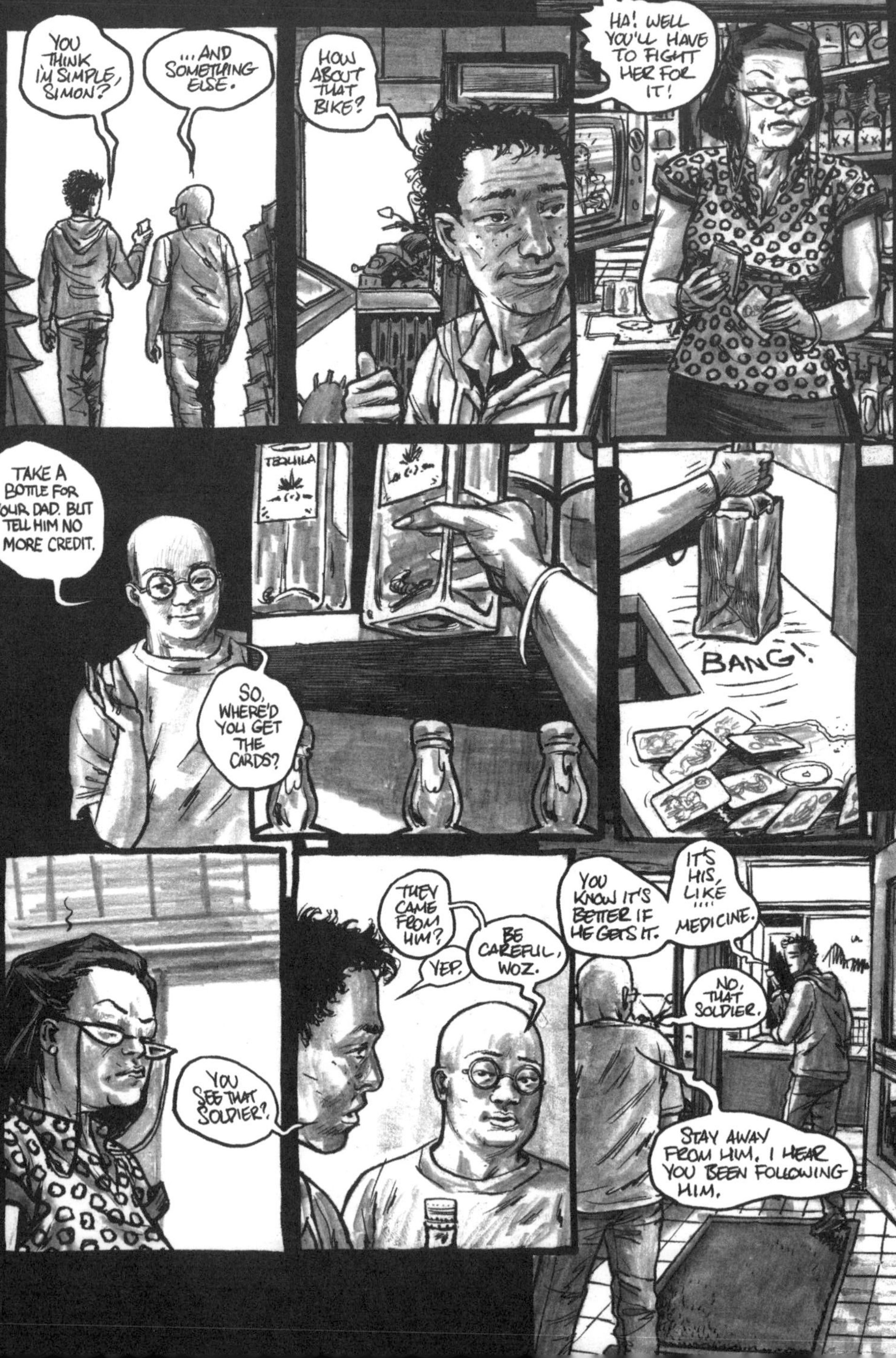
YOU THINK I'M SIMPLE, SIMON?
...AND SOMETHING ELSE.
HOW ABOUT THAT BIKE?
HA! WELL YOU'LL HAVE TO FIGHT HER FOR IT!
TAKE A BOTTLE FOR YOUR DAD. BUT TELL HIM NO MORE CREDIT.
SO, WHERE'D YOU GET THE CARDS?
TEQUILA
BANG!
YOU SEE THAT SOLDIER?
THEY CAME FROM HIM?
YEP.
BE CAREFUL, WOZ.
YOU KNOW IT'S BETTER IF HE GETS IT.
IT'S HIS, LIKE .... MEDICINE.
NO, THAT SOLDIER.
STAY AWAY FROM HIM. I HEAR YOU BEEN FOLLOWING HIM.

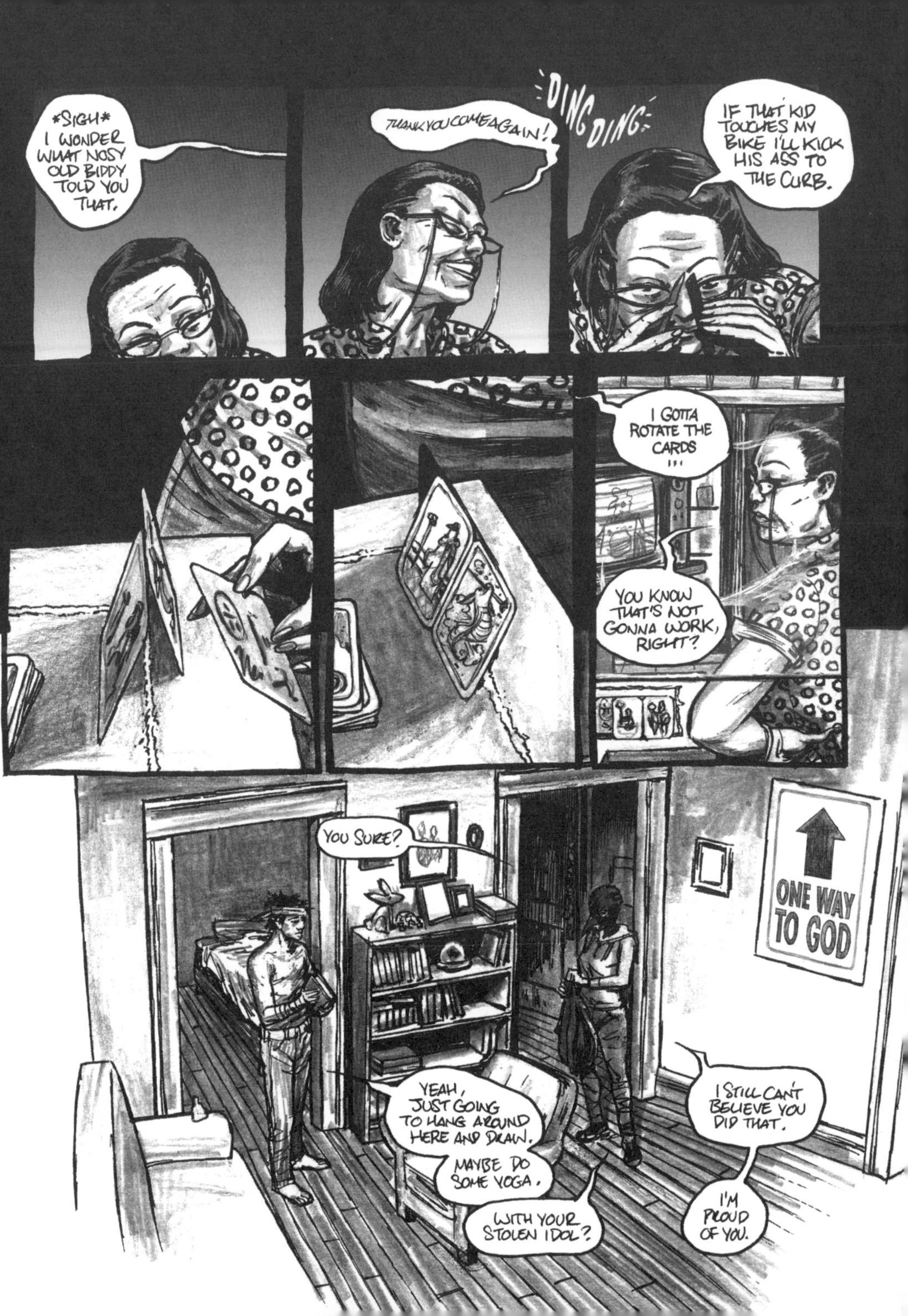
SIGH I WONDER WHAT NOSY OLD BIDDY TOLD YOU THAT.
THANK YOU COME AGAIN!
DING DING
IF THAT KID TOUCHES MY BIKE I'LL KICK HIS ASS TO THE CURB.
I GOTTA ROTATE THE CARDS ...
YOU KNOW THAT'S NOT GONNA WORK, RIGHT?
YOU SURE?
ONE WAY TO GOD
YEAH, JUST GOING TO HANG AROUND HERE AND DRAW.
MAYBE DO SOME YOGA.
WITH YOUR STOLEN IDOL?
I STILL CAN'T BELIEVE YOU DID THAT.
I'M PROUD OF YOU.

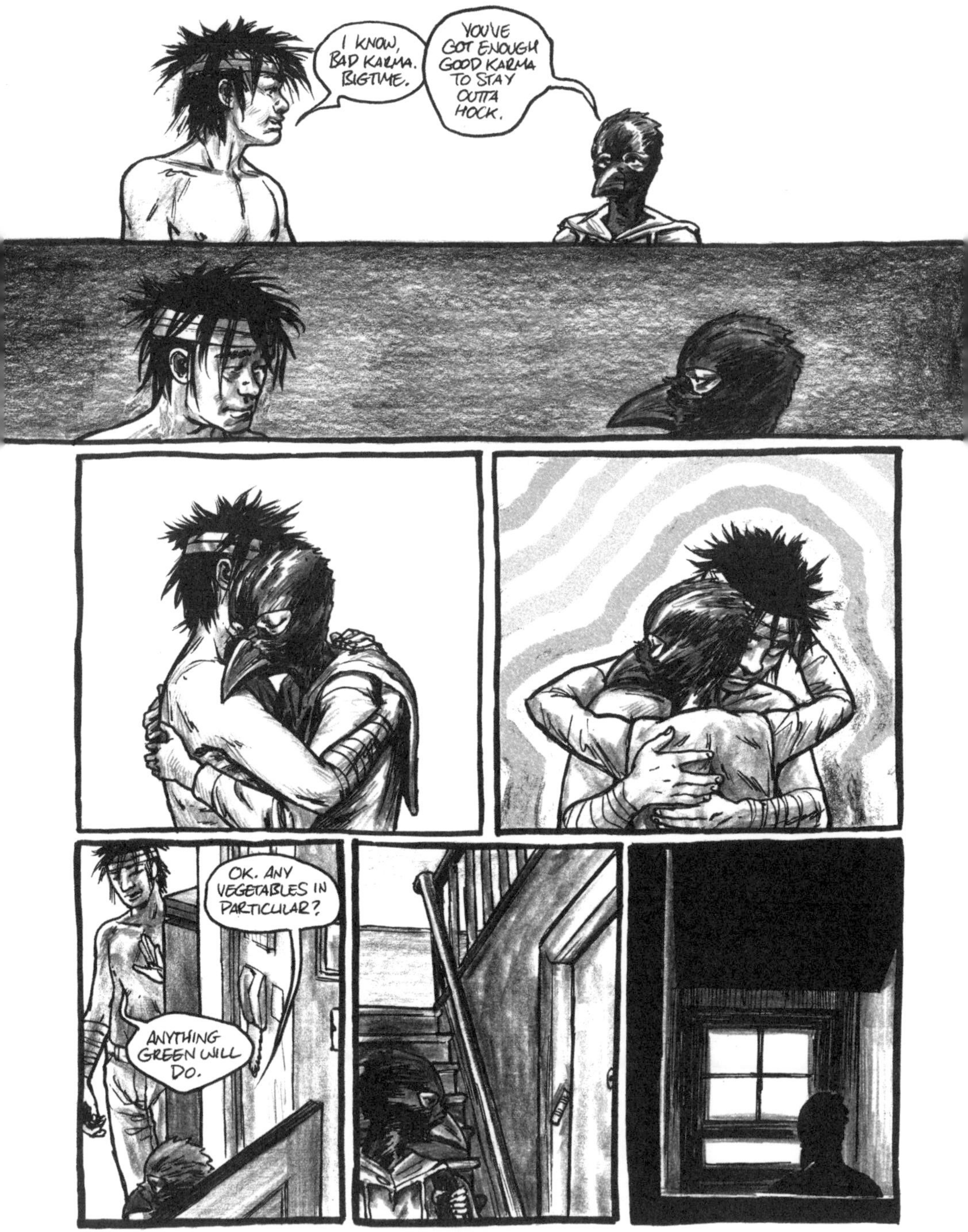
I KNOW, BAD KARMA. BIGTIME.
YOU'VE GOT ENOUGH GOOD KARMA TO STAY OUTTA HOCK.
OK. ANY VEGETABLES IN PARTICULAR?
ANYTHING GREEN WILL DO.

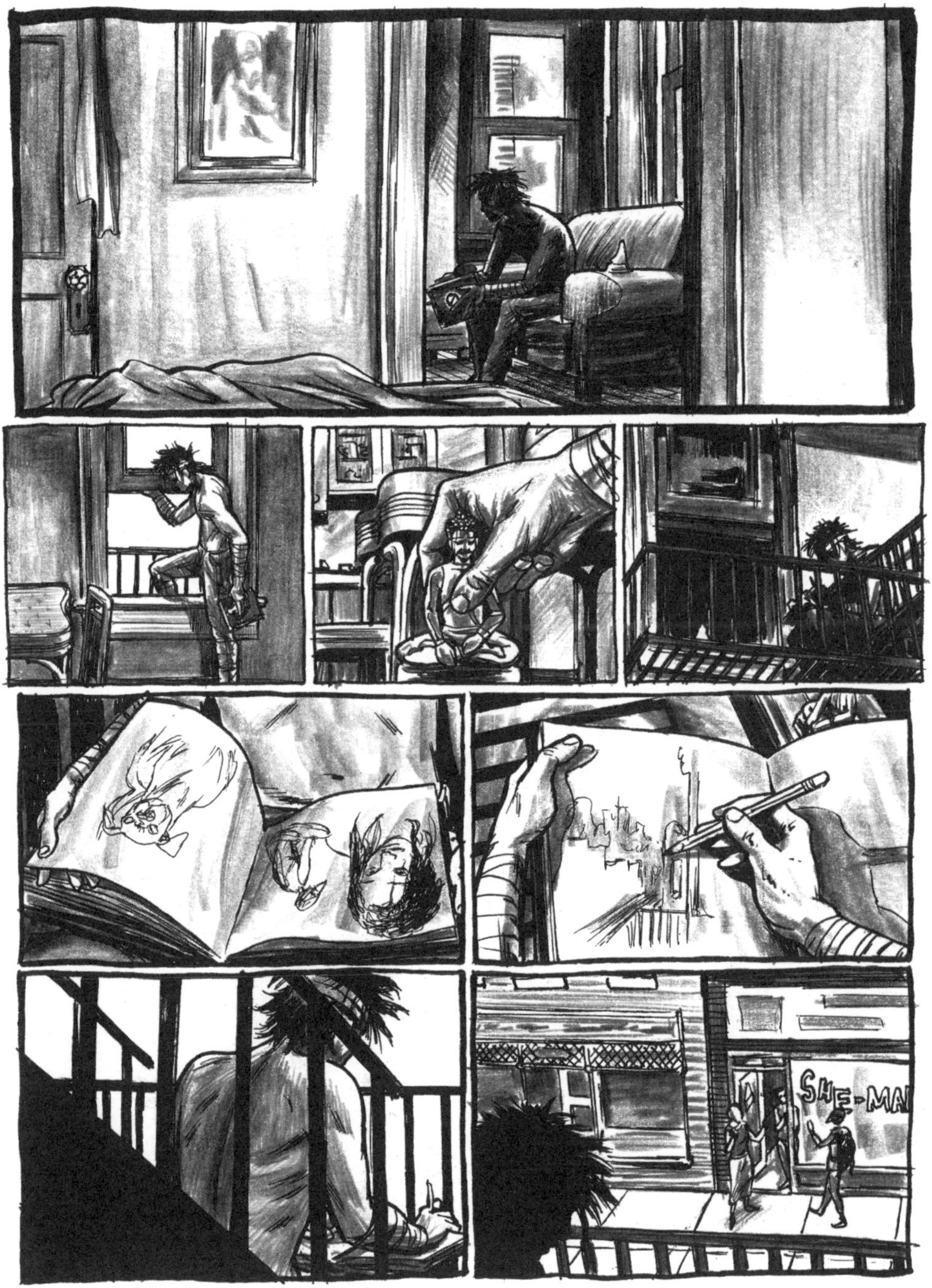
SHE-MA

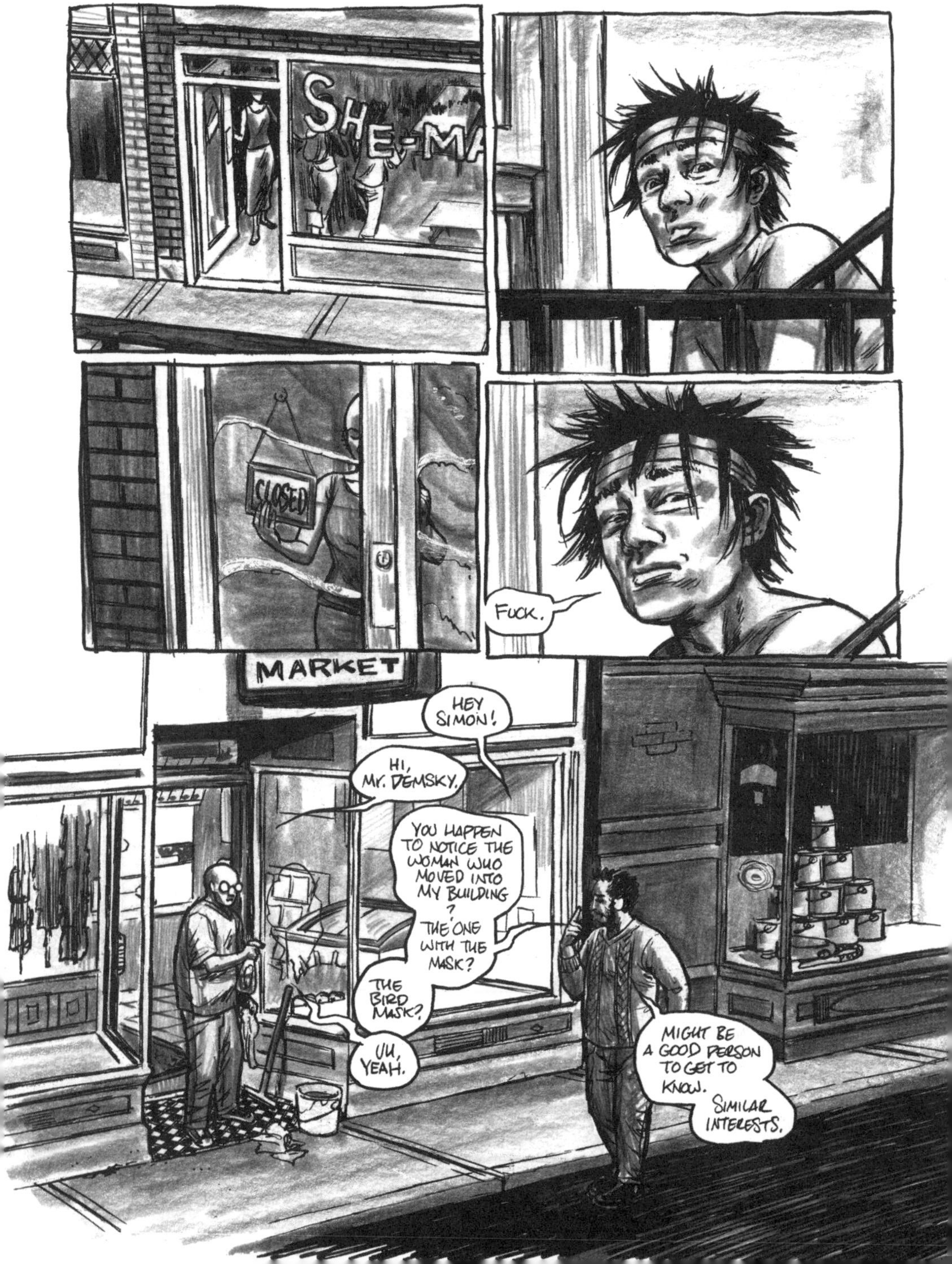
SHE-MA
CLOSED
FUCK.
MARKET
HEY SIMON!
HI, MR. DEMSKY.
YOU HAPPEN TO NOTICE THE WOMAN WHO MOVED INTO MY BUILDING?
THE ONE WITH THE MASK?
THE BIRD MASK?
UH, YEAH.
MIGHT BE A GOOD PERSON TO GET TO KNOW.
SIMILAR INTERESTS.

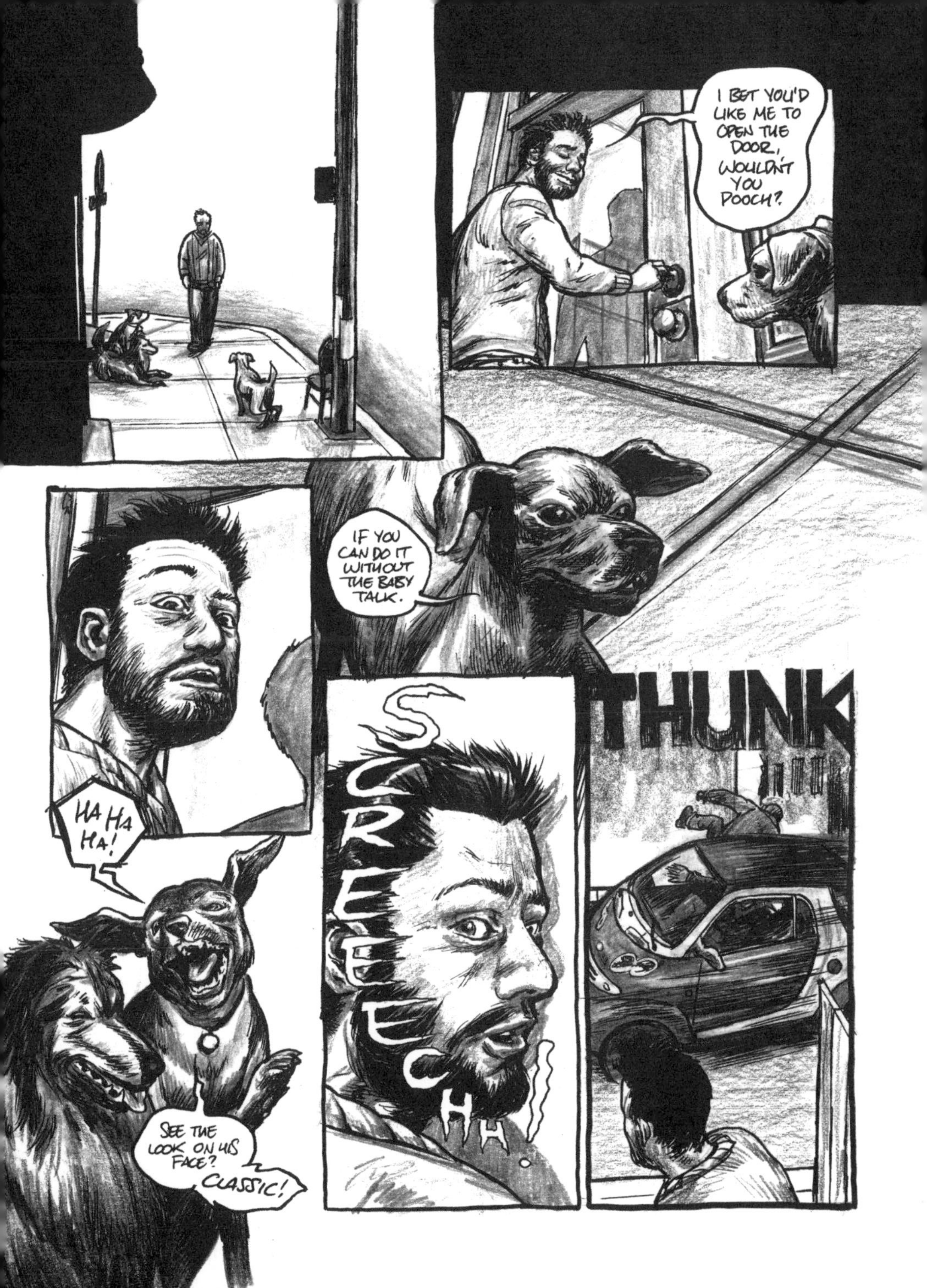
I BET YOU'D LIKE ME TO OPEN THE DOOR, WOULDN'T YOU POOCH?
IF YOU CAN DO IT WITHOUT THE BABY TALK.
THUNK
SCREEECH
HA HA HA!
SEE THE LOOK ON HIS FACE? CLASSIC!

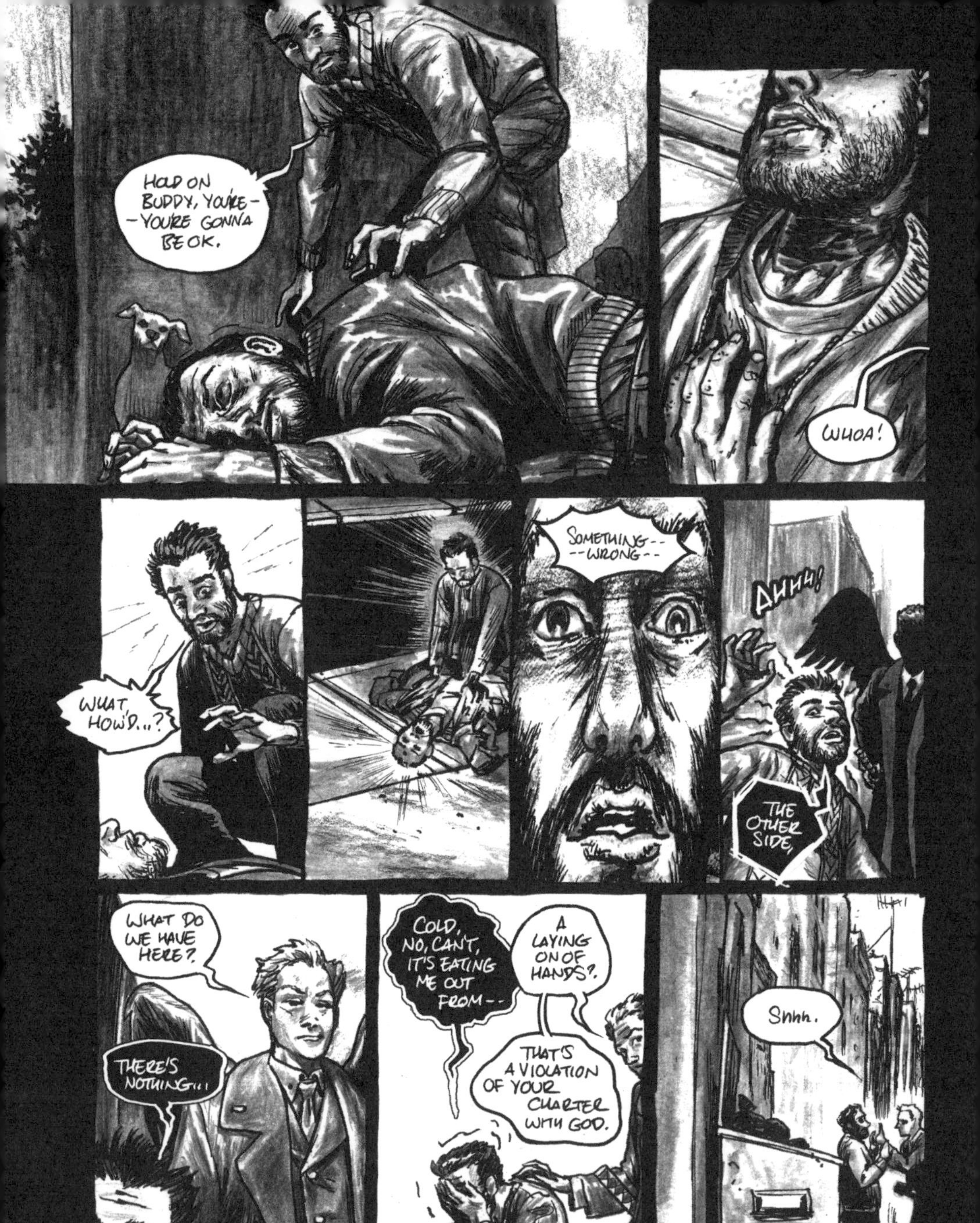
HOLD ON BUDDY, YOU'RE- -YOU'RE GONNA BE OK.
WHOA!
WHAT, HOW'D...?
SOMETHING-- --WRONG--
AHHH!
THE OTHER SIDE,
WHAT DO WE HAVE HERE?
THERE'S NOTHING...
COLD, NO, CAN'T, IT'S EATING ME OUT FROM--
A LAYING ON OF HANDS?.
THAT'S A VIOLATION OF YOUR CHARTER WITH GOD.
Shhh.

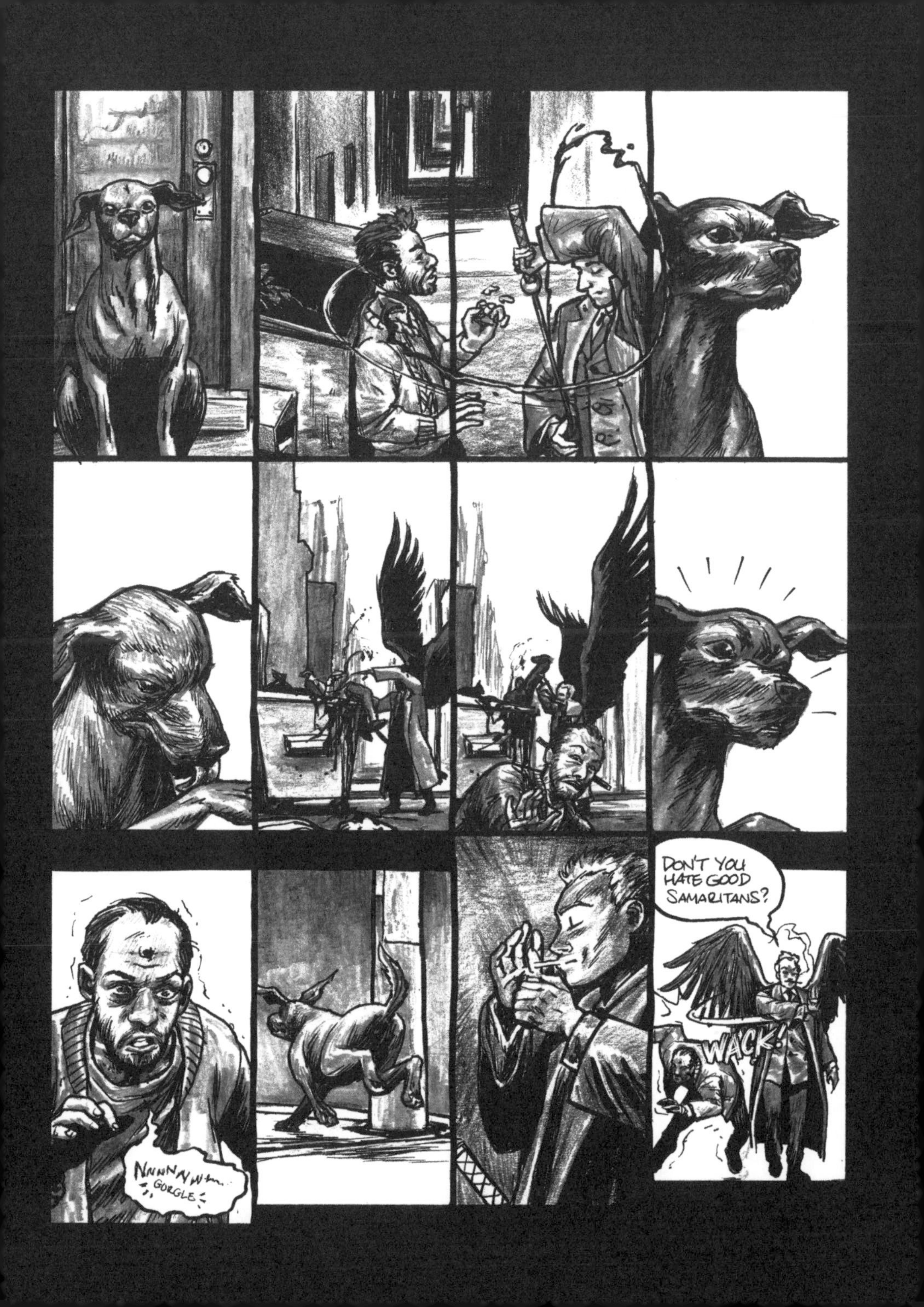
NNNNNWH...
GORGLE
DON'T YOU HATE GOOD SAMARITANS?
WACK!

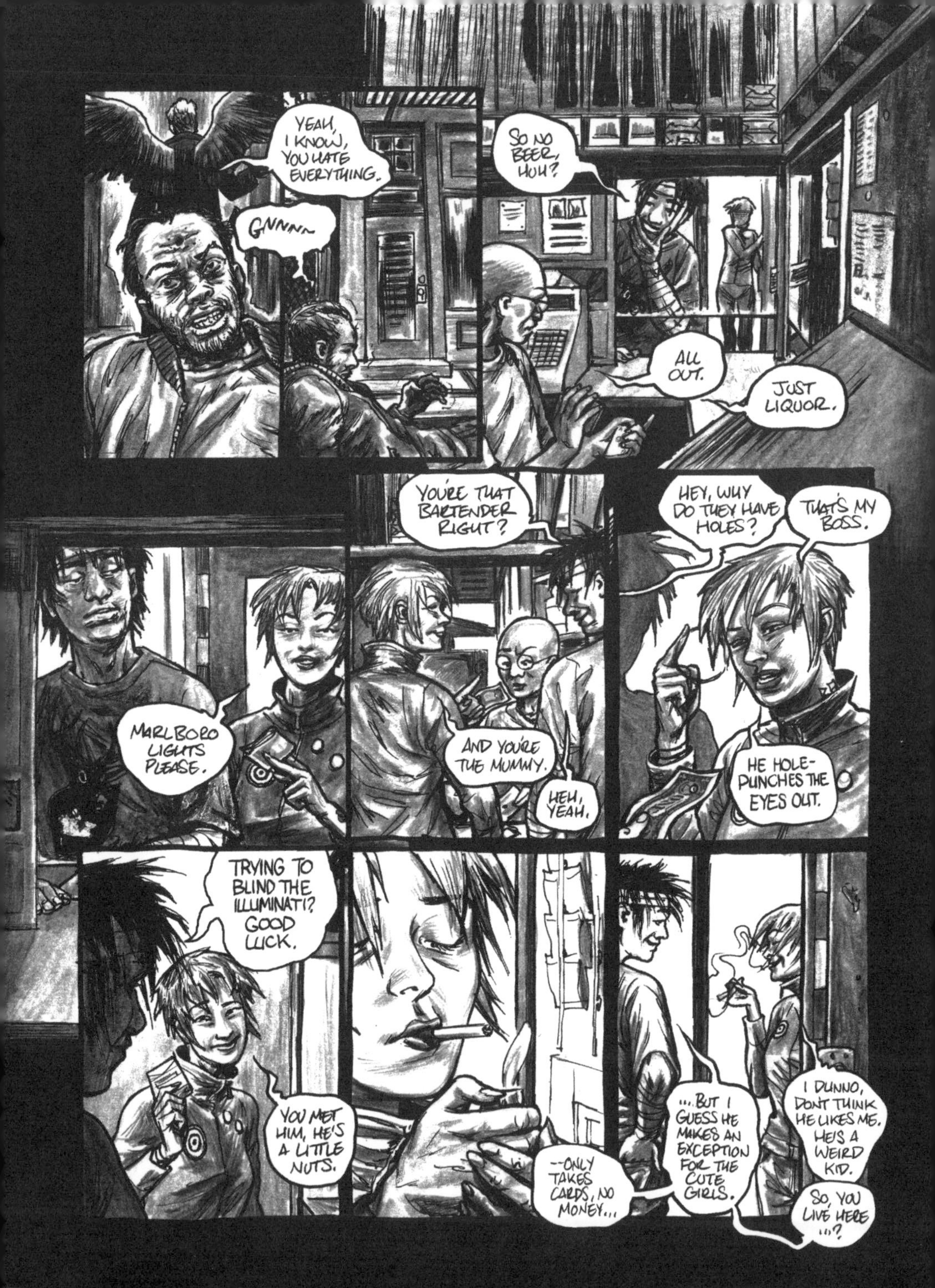
YEAH, I KNOW, YOU HATE EVERYTHING.
GNNN~
SO NO BEER, HUH?
ALL OUT.
JUST LIQUOR.
MARLBORO LIGHTS PLEASE.
YOU'RE THAT BARTENDER RIGHT?
AND YOU'RE THE MUMMY.
HEH, YEAH.
HEY, WHY DO THEY HAVE HOLES?
THAT'S MY BOSS.
HE HOLE-PUNCHES THE EYES OUT.
TRYING TO BLIND THE ILLUMINATI? GOOD LUCK.
YOU MET HIM, HE'S A LITTLE NUTS.
--ONLY TAKES CARDS, NO MONEY...
...BUT I GUESS HE MAKES AN EXCEPTION FOR THE CUTE GIRLS.
I DUNNO, DON'T THINK HE LIKES ME. HE'S A WEIRD KID.
SO, YOU LIVE HERE...?

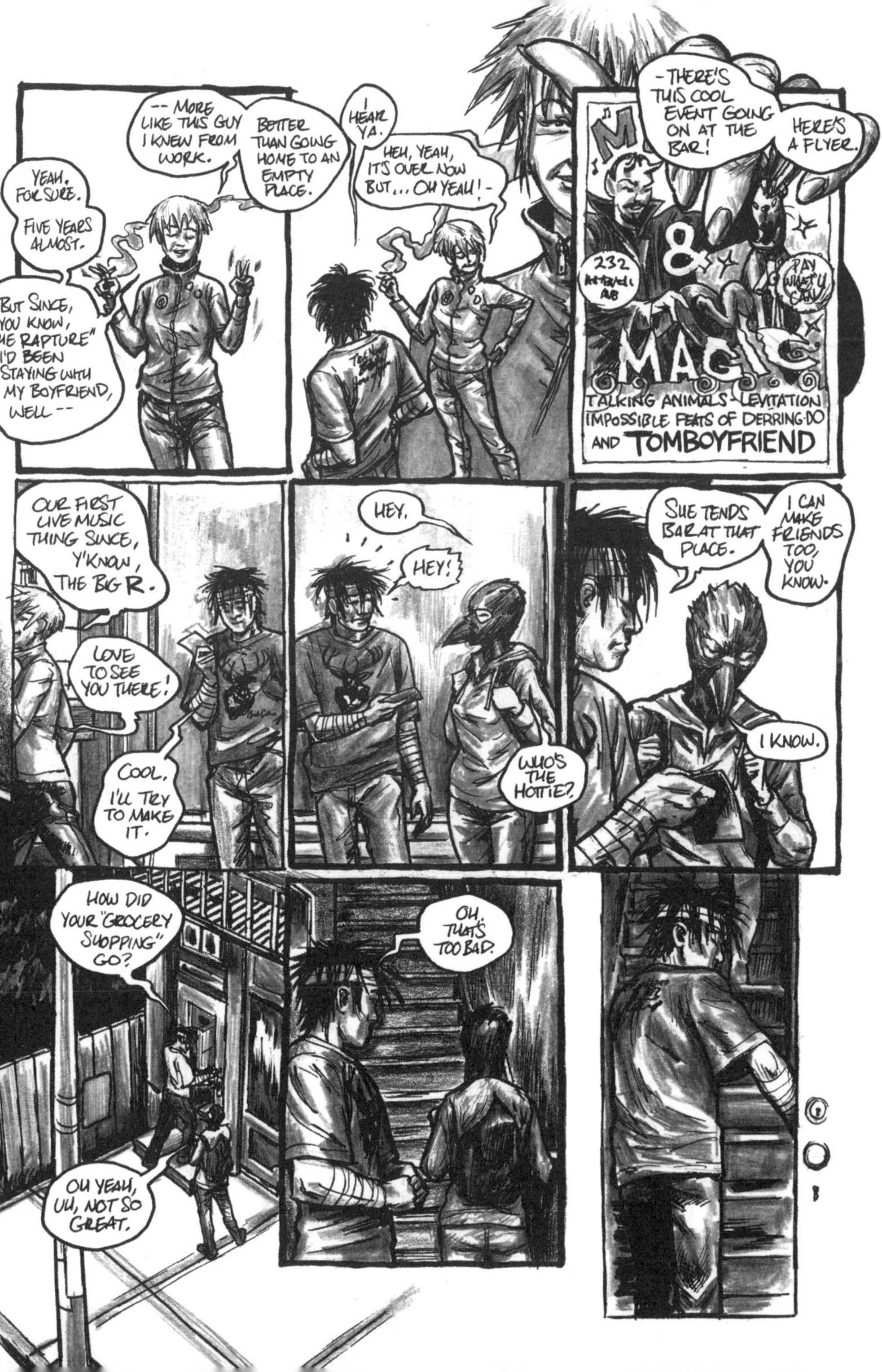
YEAH. FOR SURE.
FIVE YEARS ALMOST.
BUT SINCE, YOU KNOW, "THE RAPTURE" I'D BEEN STAYING WITH MY BOYFRIEND, WELL --
-- MORE LIKE THIS GUY I KNEW FROM WORK.
BETTER THAN GOING HOME TO AN EMPTY PLACE.
I HEAR YA.
HEH, YEAH, IT'S OVER NOW BUT... OH YEAH! -
-THERE'S THIS COOL EVENT GOING ON AT THE BAR!
HERE'S A FLYER.
&
232
PAY WHAT U CAN
MAGIC
TALKING ANIMALS - LEVITATION
IMPOSSIBLE FEATS OF DERRING-DO
AND TOMBOYFRIEND
OUR FIRST LIVE MUSIC THING SINCE, Y'KNOW, THE BIG R.
LOVE TO SEE YOU THERE!
COOL. I'LL TRY TO MAKE IT.
HEY.
HEY!
WHO'S THE HOTTIE?
SUE TENDS BAR AT THAT PLACE.
I CAN MAKE FRIENDS TOO, YOU KNOW.
I KNOW.
HOW DID YOUR "GROCERY SHOPPING" GO?
OH YEAH, UH, NOT SO GREAT.
OH. THAT'S TOO BAD.

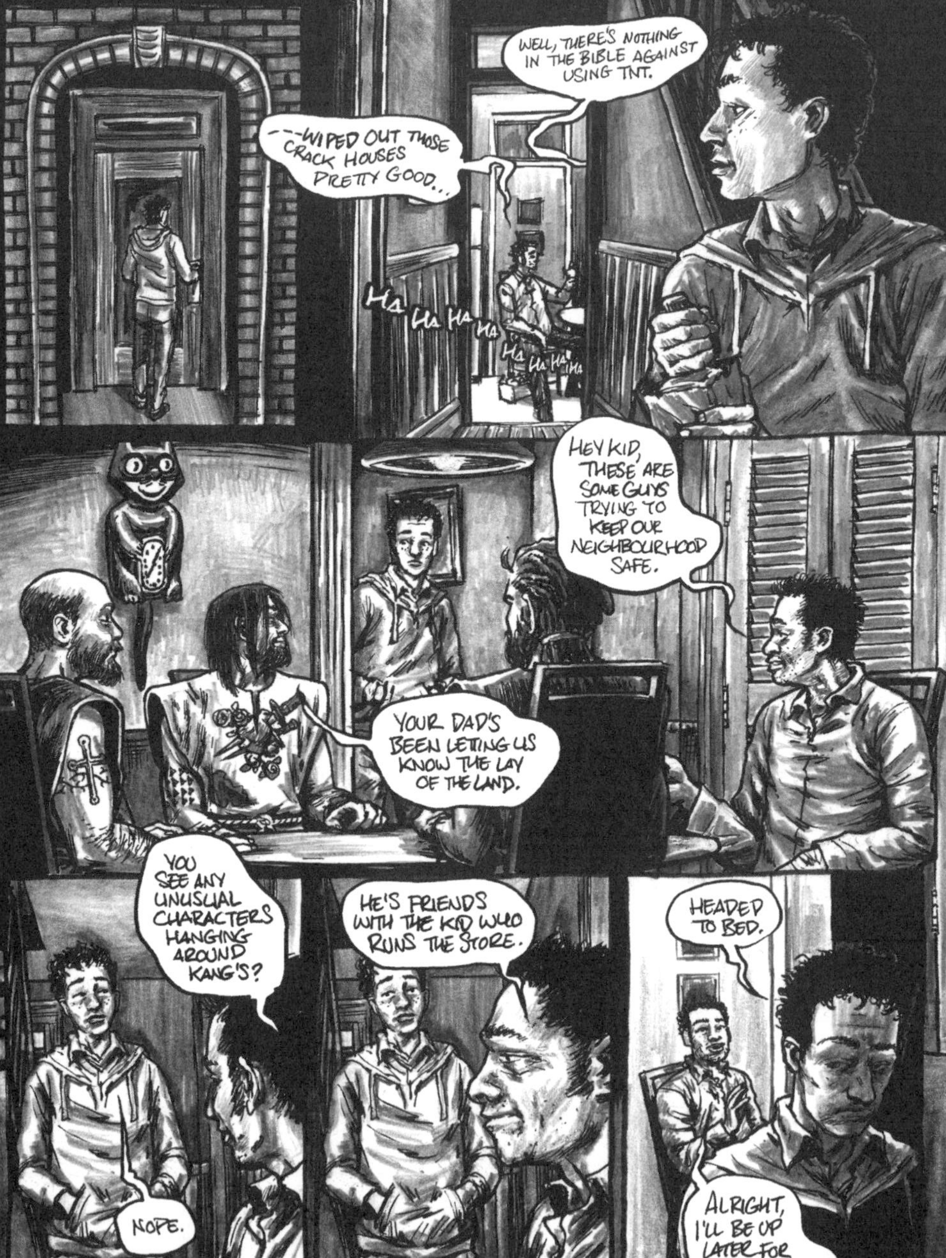

---WIPED OUT THOSE CRACK HOUSES PRETTY GOOD...
WELL, THERE'S NOTHING IN THE BIBLE AGAINST USING TNT.
HA HA HA HA HA HA HA HA
HEY KID, THESE ARE SOME GUYS TRYING TO KEEP OUR NEIGHBOURHOOD SAFE.
YOUR DAD'S BEEN LETTING US KNOW THE LAY OF THE LAND.
YOU SEE ANY UNUSUAL CHARACTERS HANGING AROUND KANG'S?
NOPE.
HE'S FRIENDS WITH THE KID WHO RUNS THE STORE.
HEADED TO BED.
ALRIGHT, I'LL BE UP LATER FOR PRAYERS...!

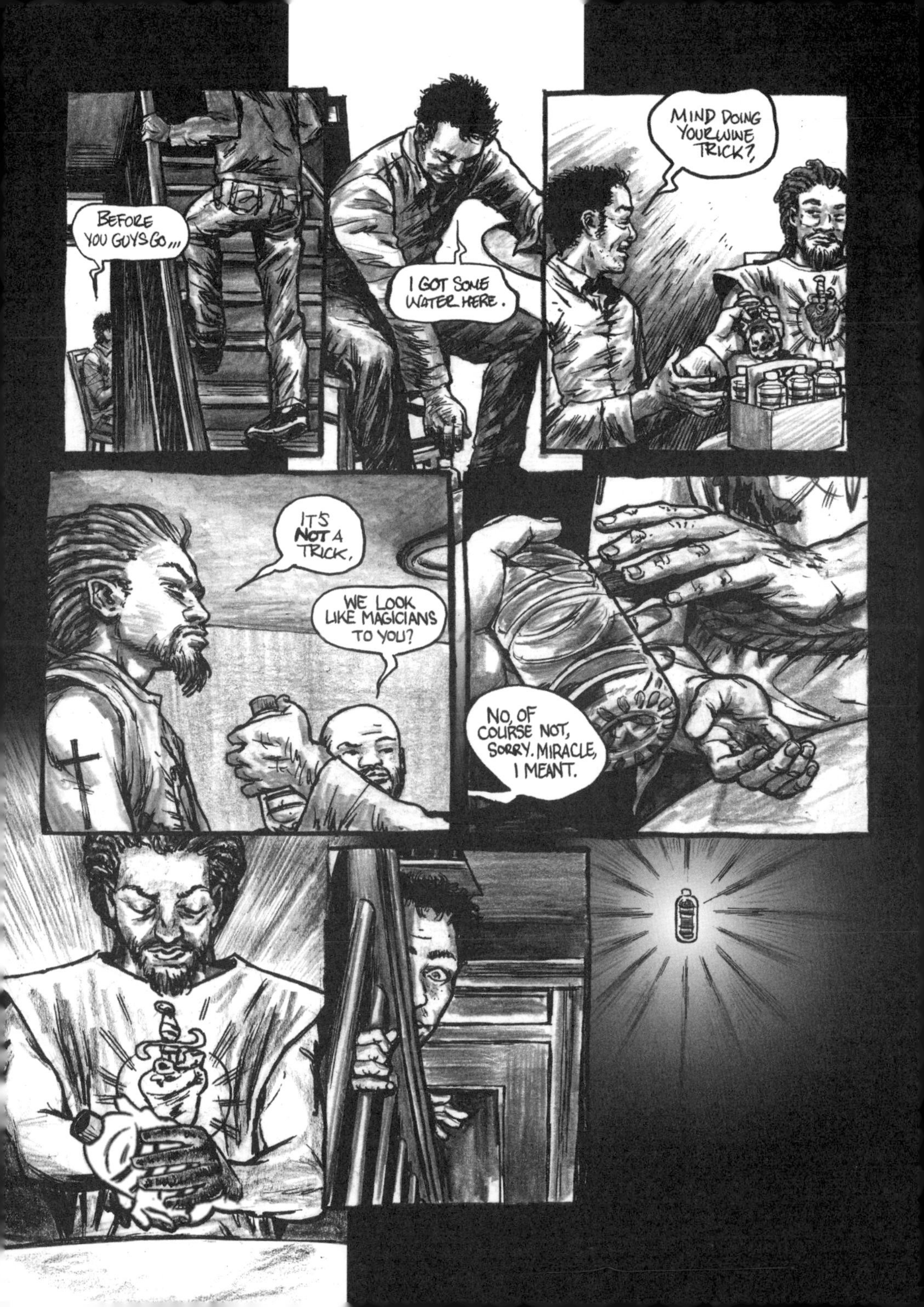
BEFORE YOU GUYS GO...
I GOT SOME WATER HERE.
MIND DOING YOUR WINE TRICK?
IT'S NOT A TRICK.
WE LOOK LIKE MAGICIANS TO YOU?
NO, OF COURSE NOT, SORRY. MIRACLE, I MEANT.

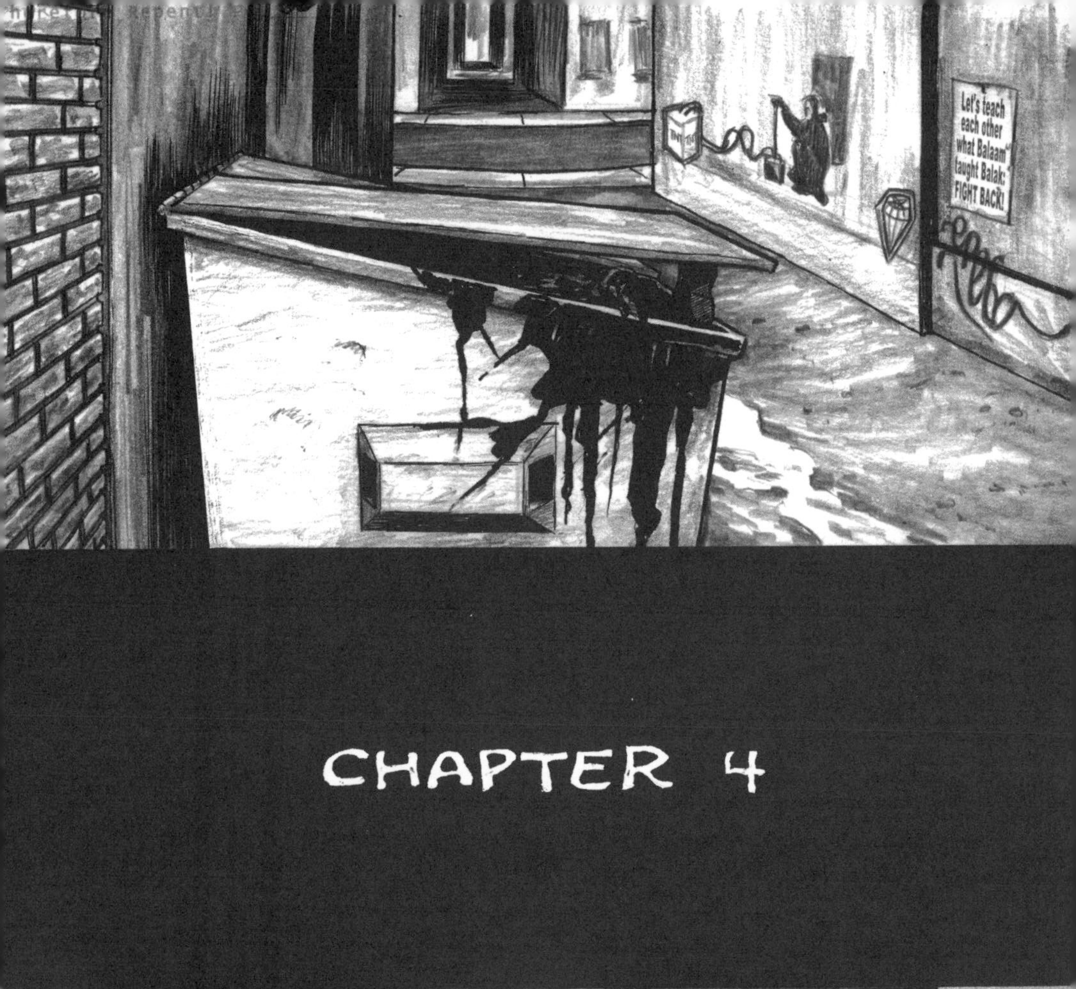
Let's teach each other what Balaam taught Balak: FIGHT BACK!

CHAPTER 4

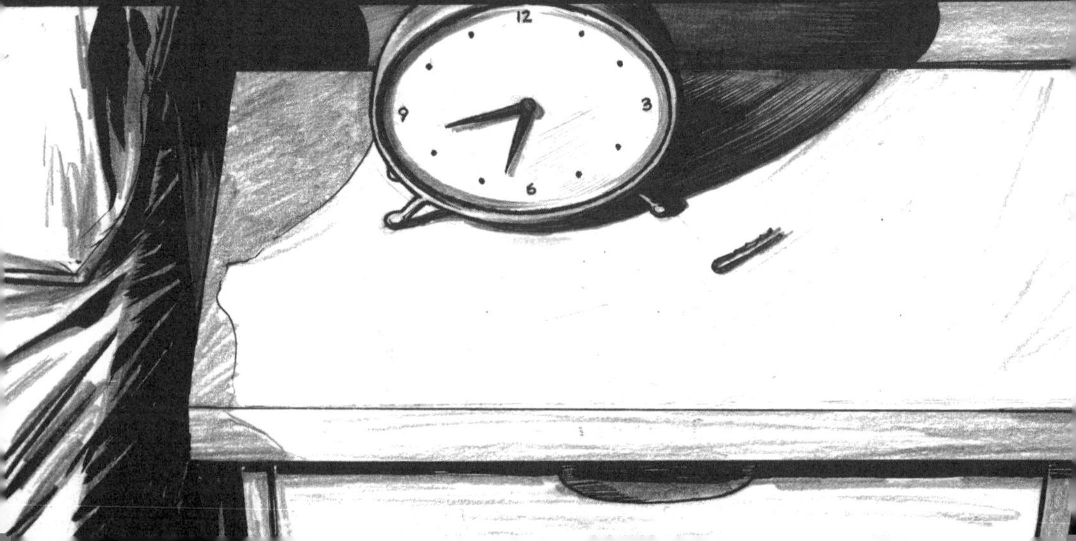

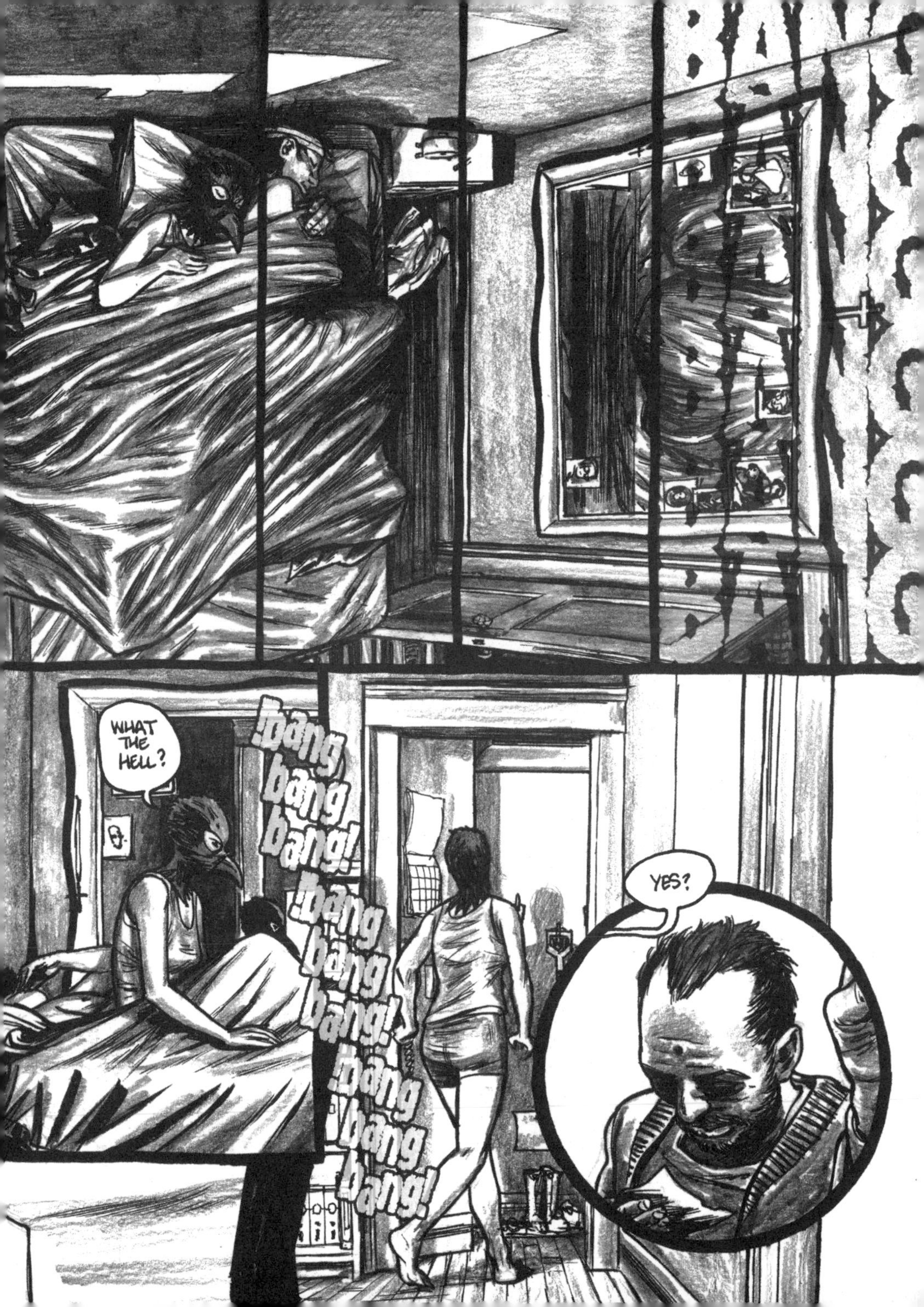
WHAT THE HELL?
bang bang bang! bang bang bang! bang bang bang!
YES?

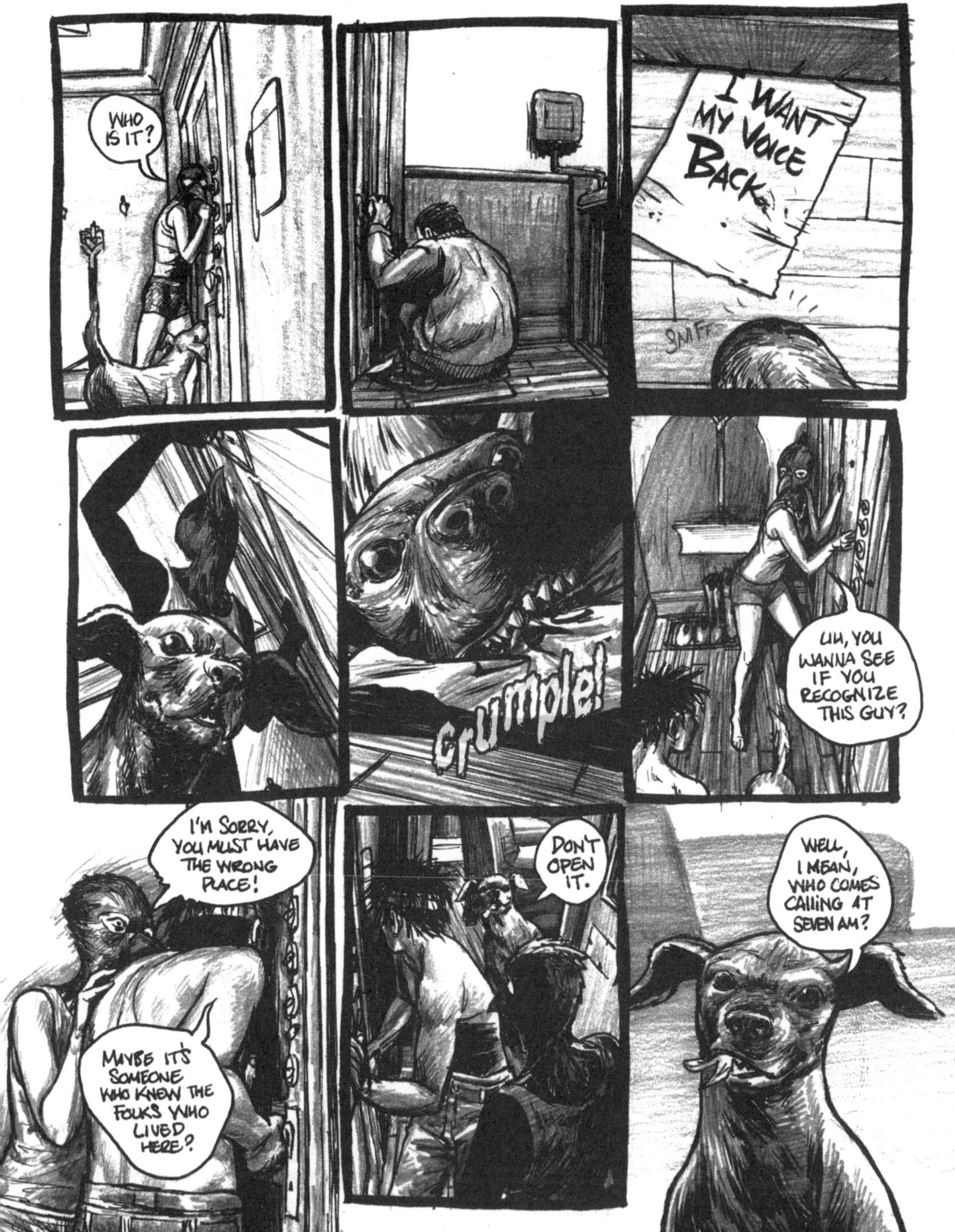
WHO IS IT?
I WANT MY VOICE BACK
SNIFF
crumple!
UH, YOU WANNA SEE IF YOU RECOGNIZE THIS GUY?
I'M SORRY, YOU MUST HAVE THE WRONG PLACE!
MAYBE IT'S SOMEONE WHO KNEW THE FOLKS WHO LIVED HERE?
DON'T OPEN IT.
WELL, I MEAN, WHO COMES CALLING AT SEVEN AM?

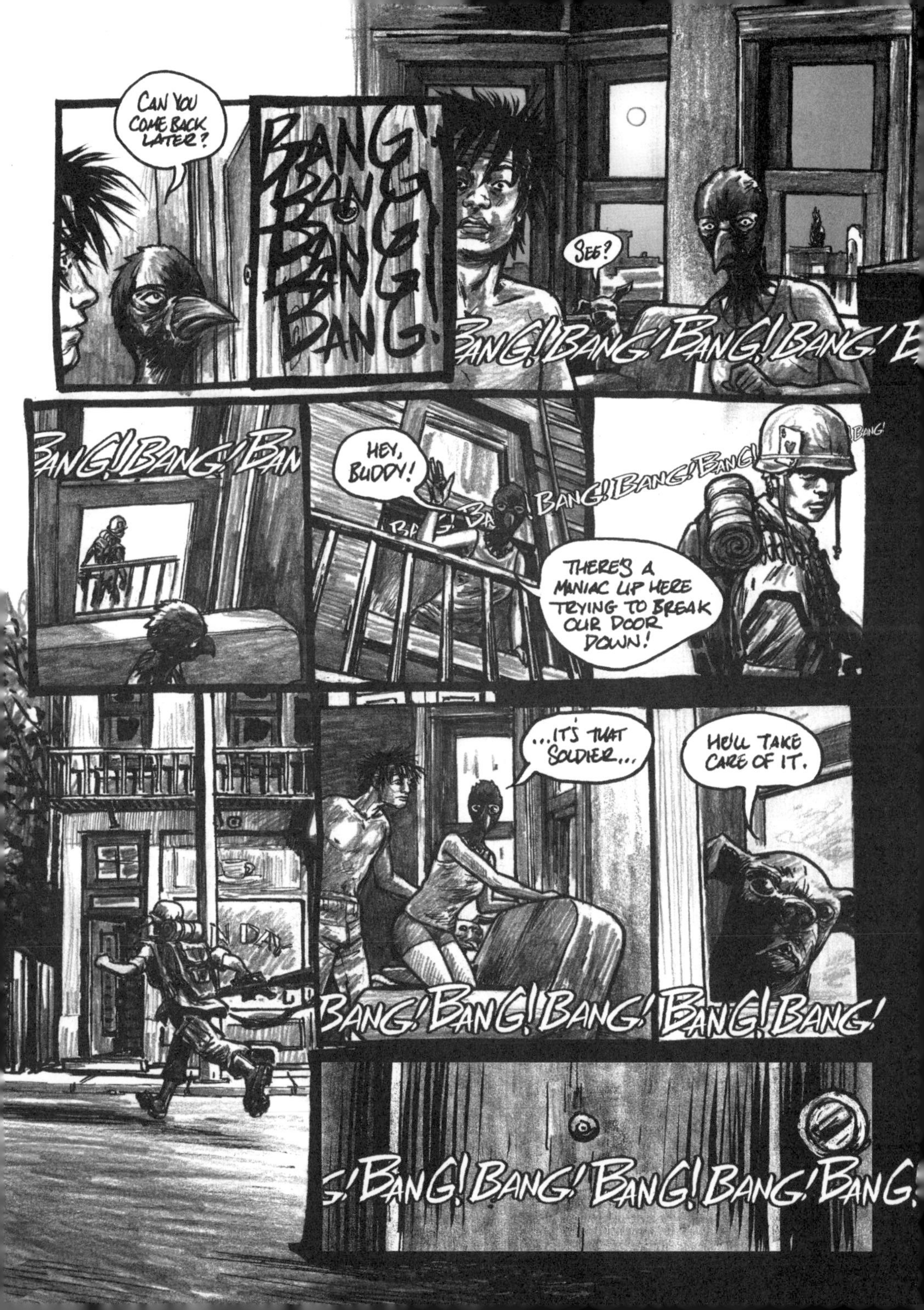

CAN YOU COME BACK LATER?
BANG! BANG! BANG! BANG! BANG!
SEE?
BANG! BANG! BANG! BANG! BA
BANG! BANG! BAN
HEY, BUDDY!
BANG! BANG! BANG! BANG!
BANG!
THERE'S A MANIAC UP HERE TRYING TO BREAK OUR DOOR DOWN!
...IT'S THAT SOLDIER...
HE'LL TAKE CARE OF IT.
BANG! BANG! BANG! BANG! BANG!
G! BANG! BANG! BANG! BANG! BANG.

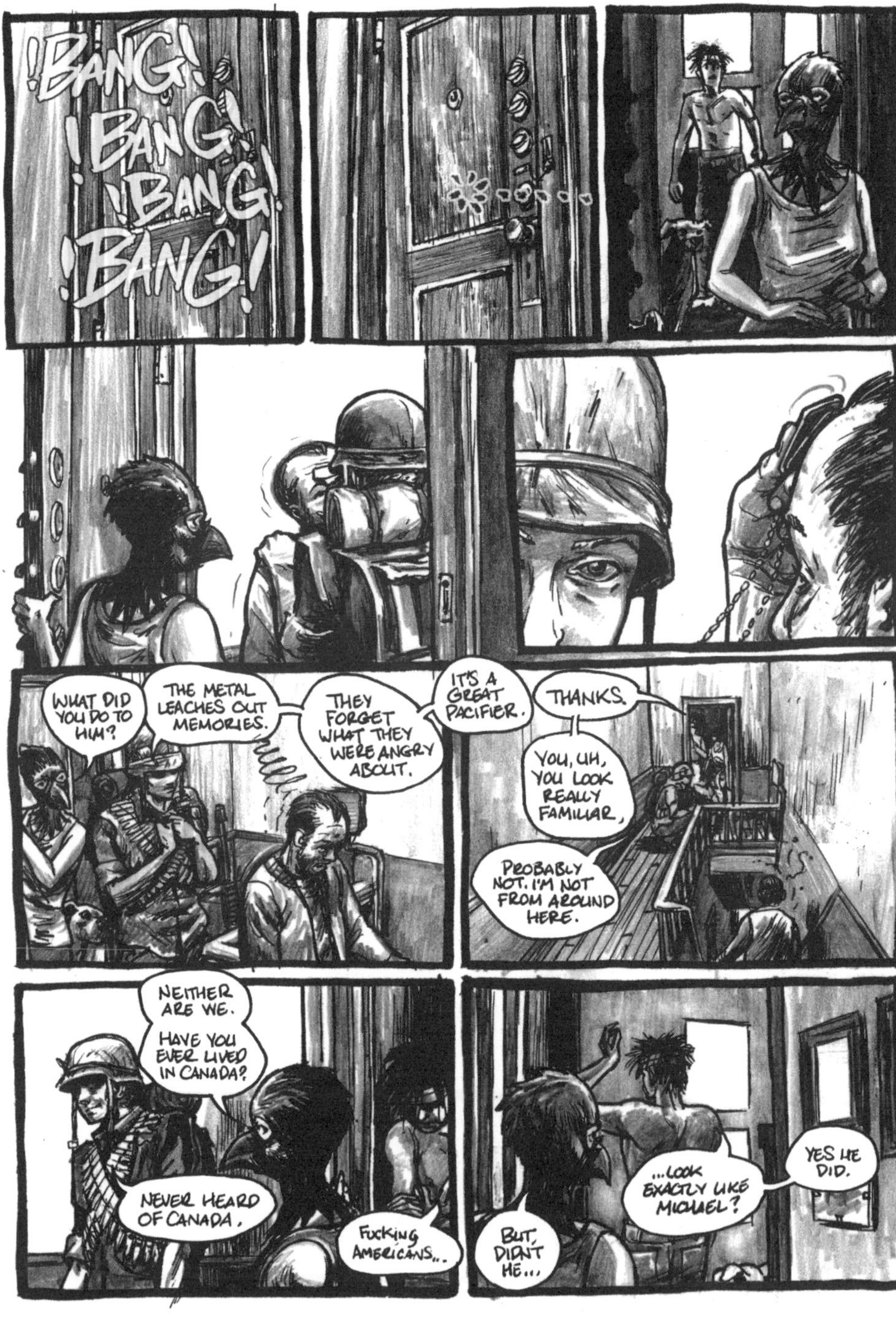
!BANG!
!BANG!
!BANG!
!BANG!
WHAT DID YOU DO TO HIM?
THE METAL LEACHES OUT MEMORIES.
THEY FORGET WHAT THEY WERE ANGRY ABOUT.
IT'S A GREAT PACIFIER.
THANKS.
YOU, UH, YOU LOOK REALLY FAMILIAR.
PROBABLY NOT. I'M NOT FROM AROUND HERE.
NEITHER ARE WE.
HAVE YOU EVER LIVED IN CANADA?
NEVER HEARD OF CANADA.
FUCKING AMERICANS...
BUT, DIDN'T HE...
...LOOK EXACTLY LIKE MICHAEL?
YES HE DID.

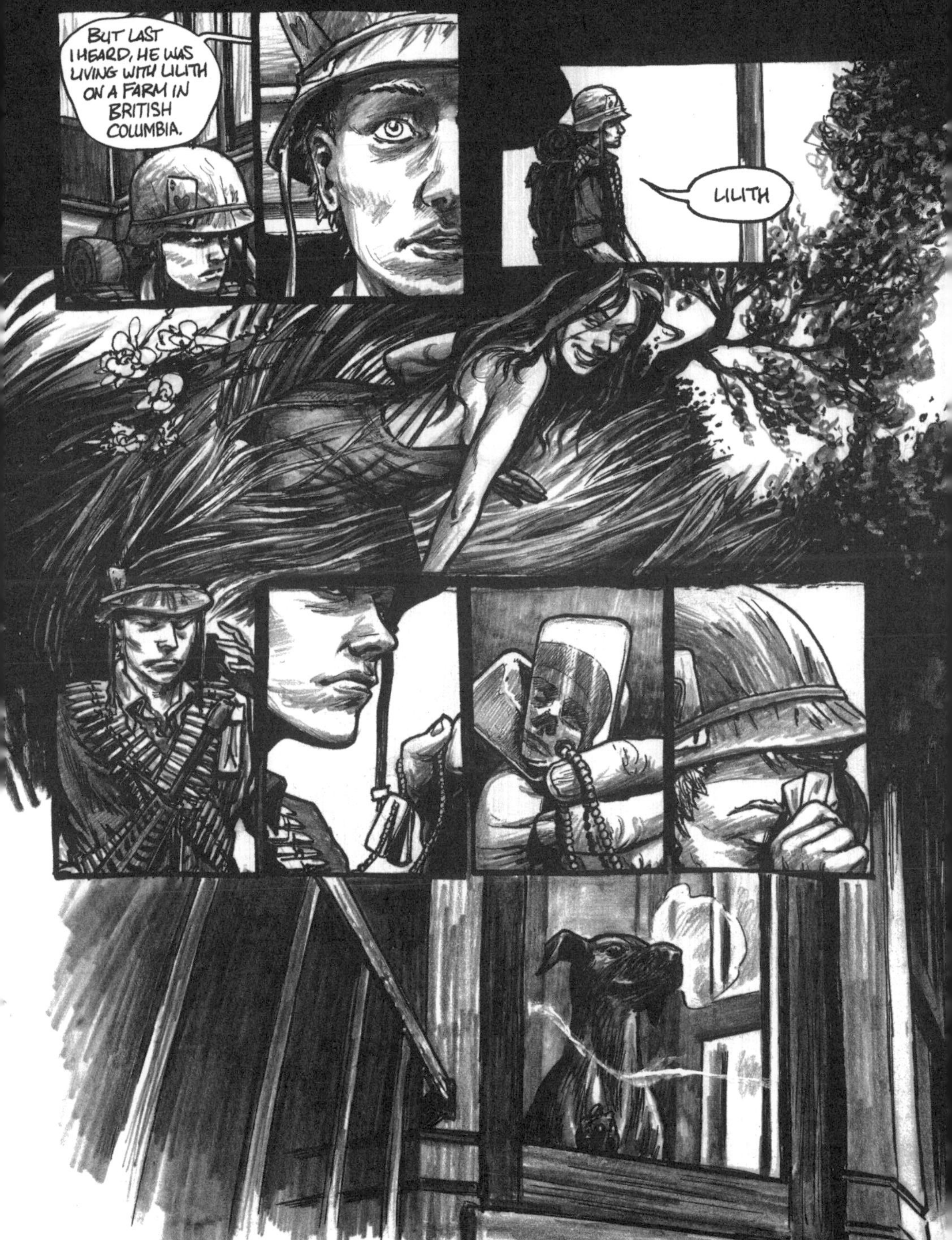
BUT LAST I HEARD, HE WAS LIVING WITH LILITH ON A FARM IN BRITISH COLUMBIA.
LILITH

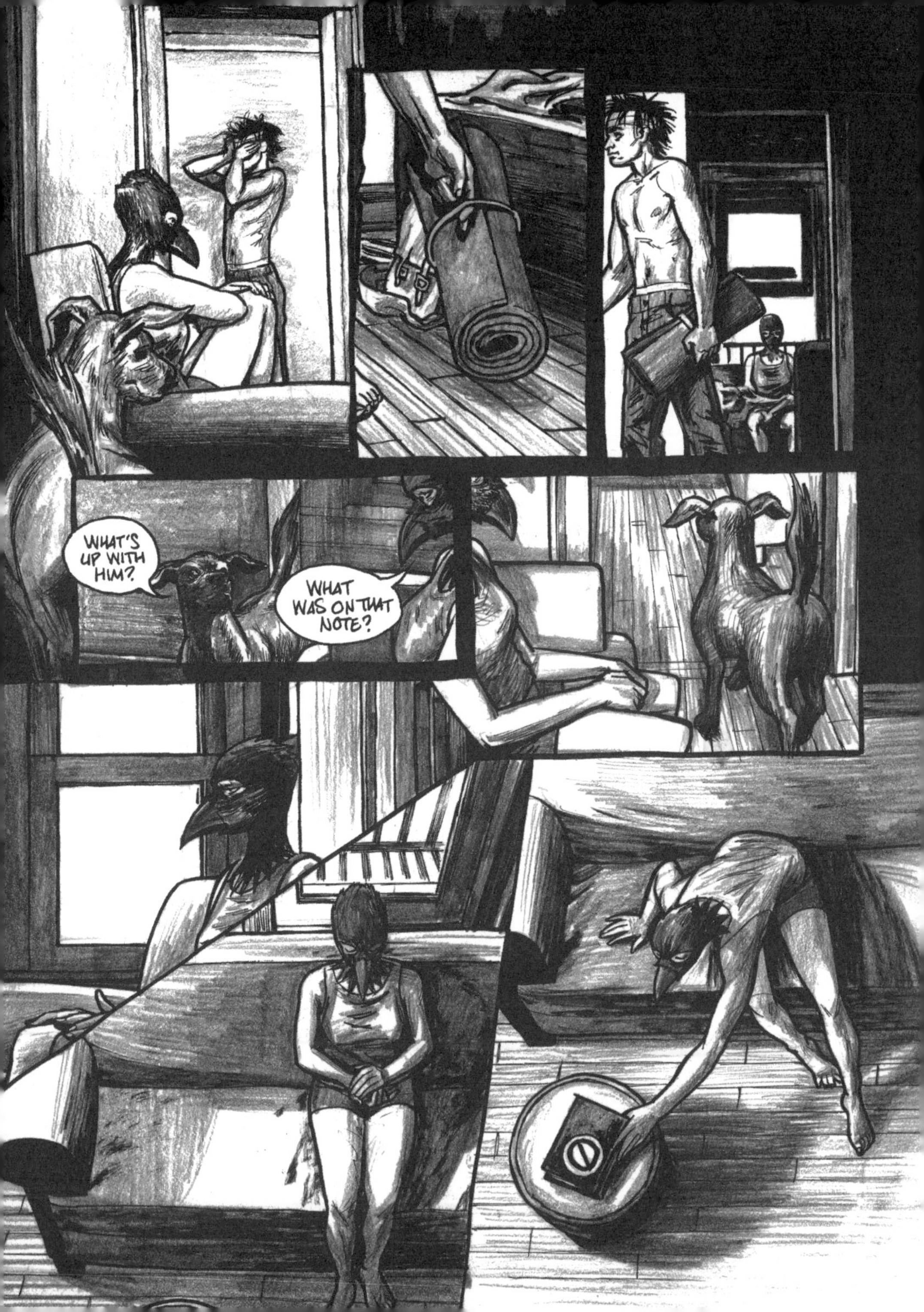
WHAT'S UP WITH HIM?
WHAT WAS ON THAT NOTE?

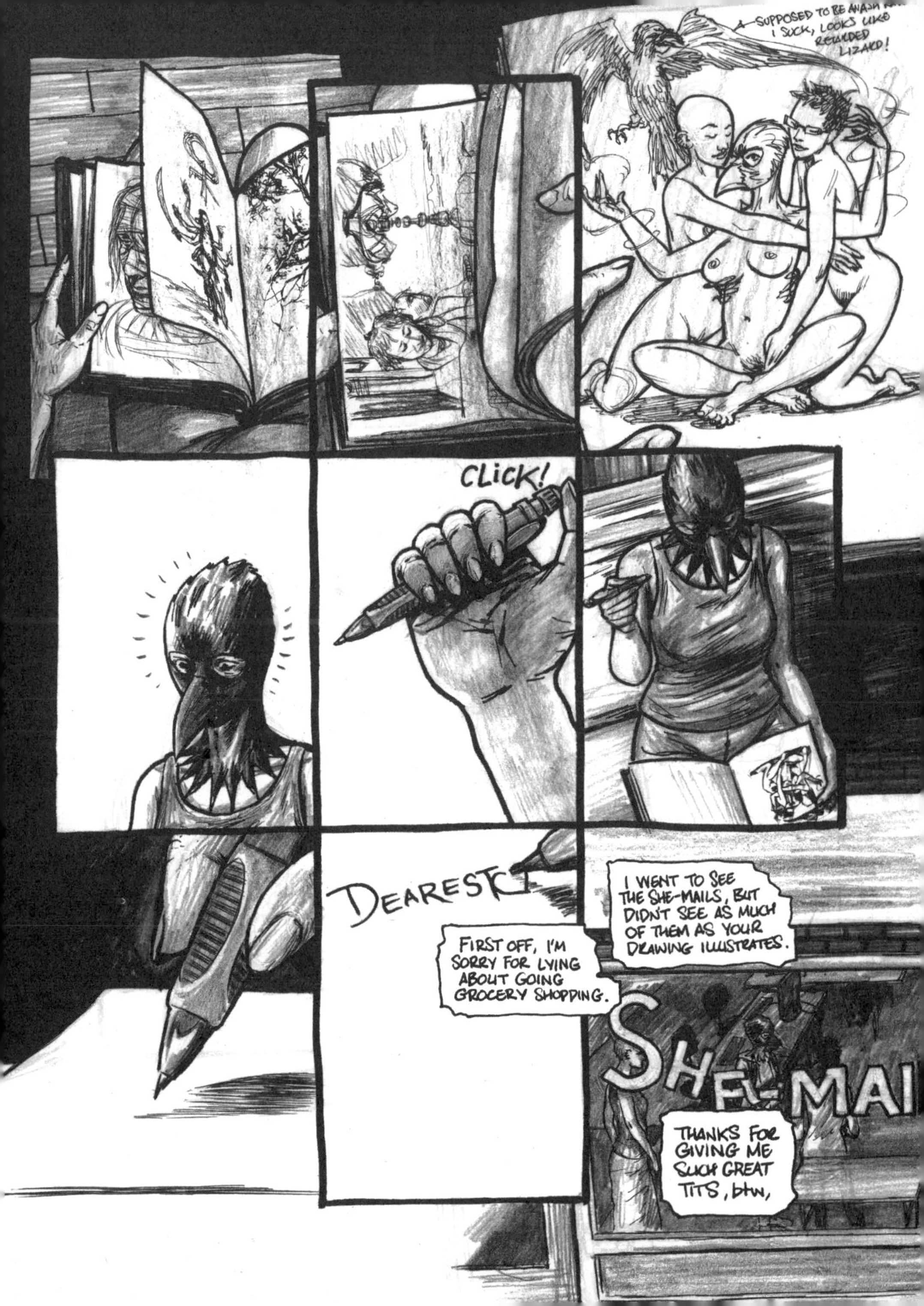
SUPPOSED TO BE ANASH
I SUCK, LOOKS LIKE RETARDED LIZARD!
CLICK!
DEAREST
FIRST OFF, I'M SORRY FOR LYING ABOUT GOING GROCERY SHOPPING.
I WENT TO SEE THE SHE-MAILS, BUT DIDN'T SEE AS MUCH OF THEM AS YOUR DRAWING ILLUSTRATES.
SHE-MAI
THANKS FOR GIVING ME SUCH GREAT TITS, btw,

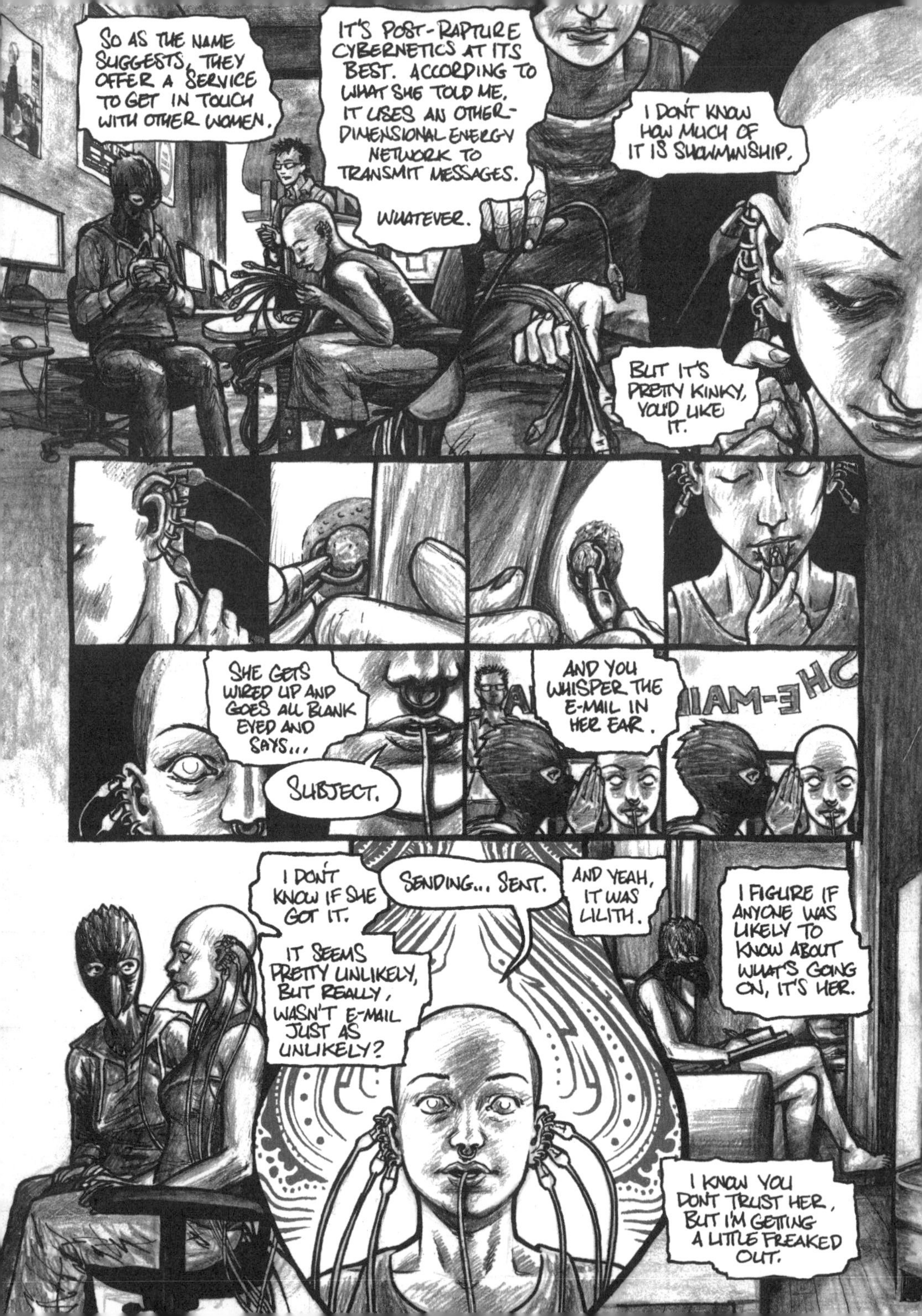
SO AS THE NAME SUGGESTS, THEY OFFER A SERVICE TO GET IN TOUCH WITH OTHER WOMEN.
IT'S POST-RAPTURE CYBERNETICS AT ITS BEST. ACCORDING TO WHAT SHE TOLD ME, IT USES AN OTHER-DIMENSIONAL ENERGY NETWORK TO TRANSMIT MESSAGES.
WHATEVER.
I DON'T KNOW HOW MUCH OF IT IS SHOWMANSHIP.
BUT IT'S PRETTY KINKY, YOU'D LIKE IT.
SHE GETS WIRED UP AND GOES ALL BLANK EYED AND SAYS...
SUBJECT.
AND YOU WHISPER THE E-MAIL IN HER EAR.
SHE-MAIL
SENDING... SENT.
I DON'T KNOW IF SHE GOT IT.
IT SEEMS PRETTY UNLIKELY, BUT REALLY, WASN'T E-MAIL JUST AS UNLIKELY?
AND YEAH, IT WAS LILITH.
I FIGURE IF ANYONE WAS LIKELY TO KNOW ABOUT WHAT'S GOING ON, IT'S HER.
I KNOW YOU DON'T TRUST HER, BUT I'M GETTING A LITTLE FREAKED OUT.

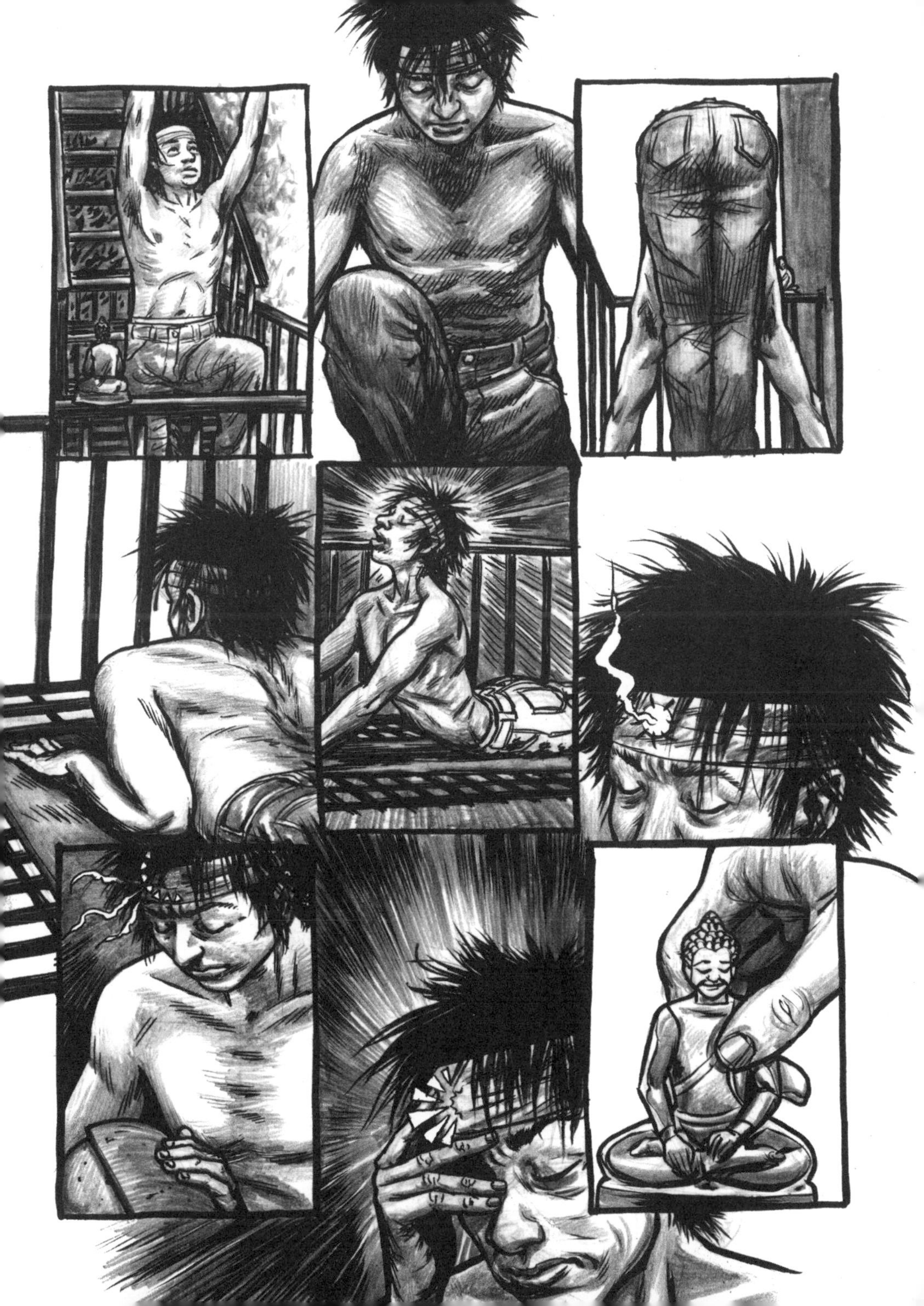

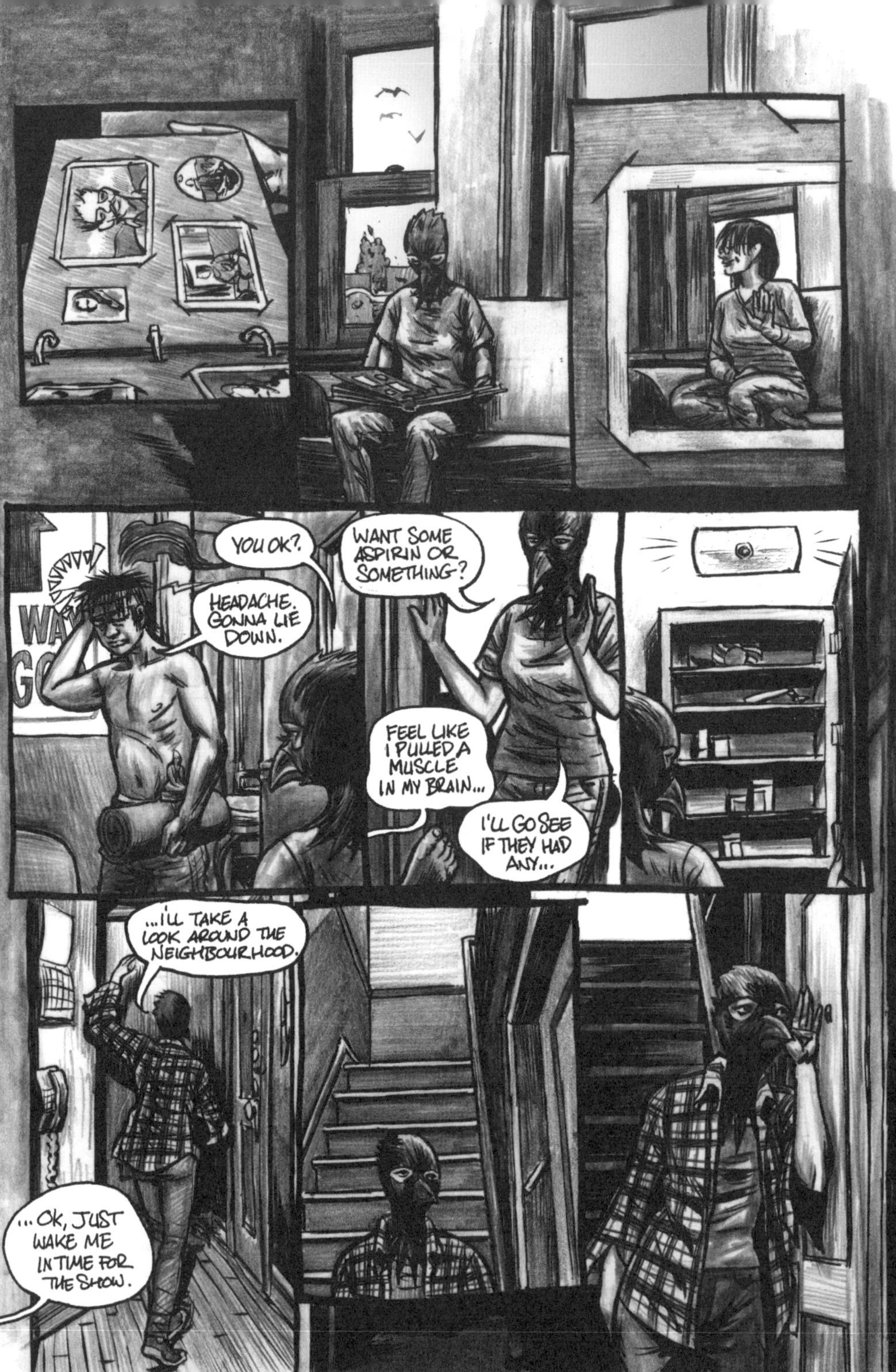
YOU OK?
HEADACHE. GONNA LIE DOWN.
WANT SOME ASPIRIN OR SOMETHING?
FEEL LIKE I PULLED A MUSCLE IN MY BRAIN...
I'LL GO SEE IF THEY HAD ANY...
...I'LL TAKE A LOOK AROUND THE NEIGHBOURHOOD.
...OK, JUST WAKE ME IN TIME FOR THE SHOW.

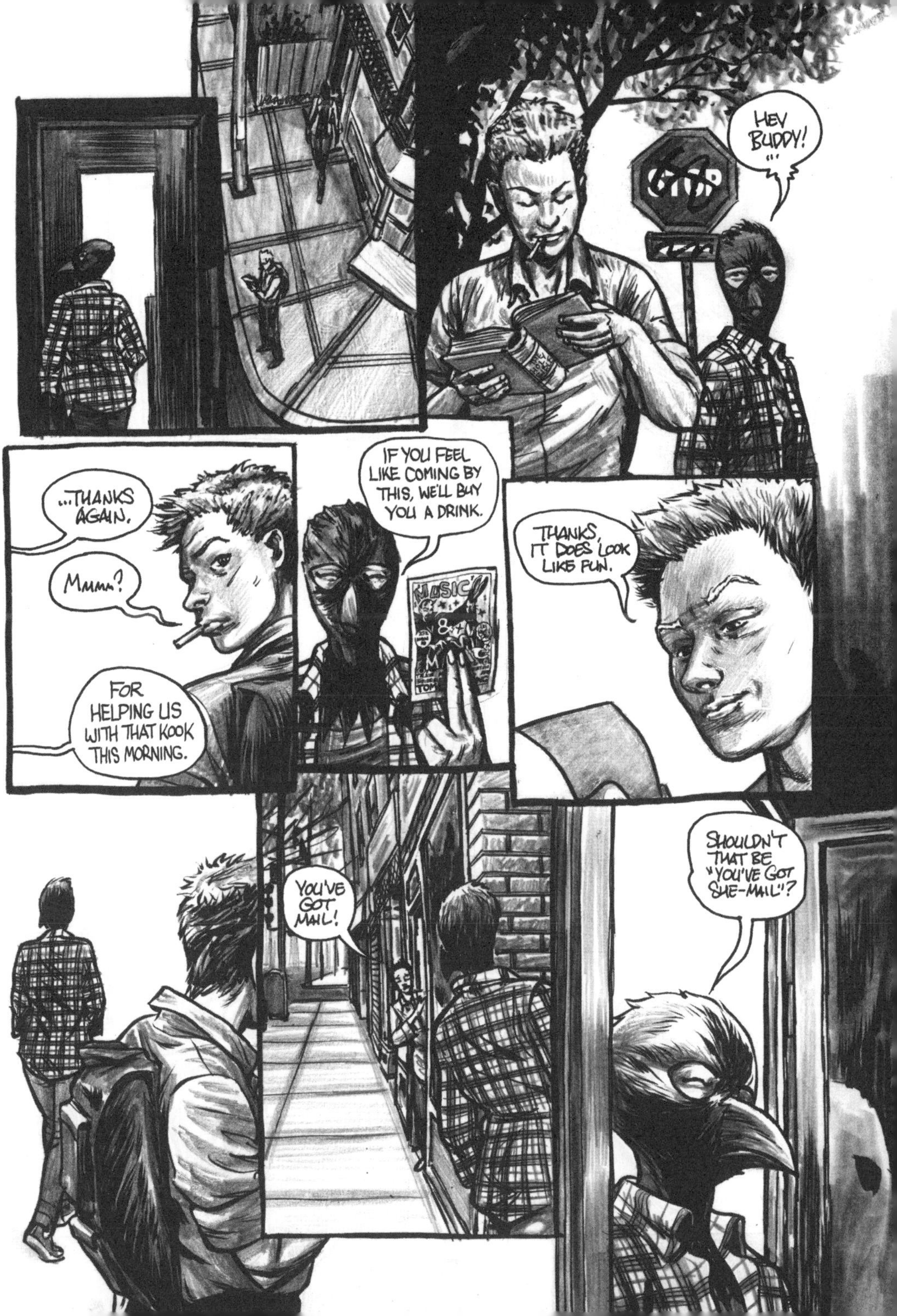
HEY BUDDY!
...THANKS AGAIN.
MMMM?
FOR HELPING US WITH THAT KOOK THIS MORNING.
IF YOU FEEL LIKE COMING BY THIS, WE'LL BUY YOU A DRINK.
MUSIC
THANKS, IT DOES LOOK LIKE FUN.
YOU'VE GOT MAIL!
SHOULDN'T THAT BE "YOU'VE GOT SHE-MAIL"?

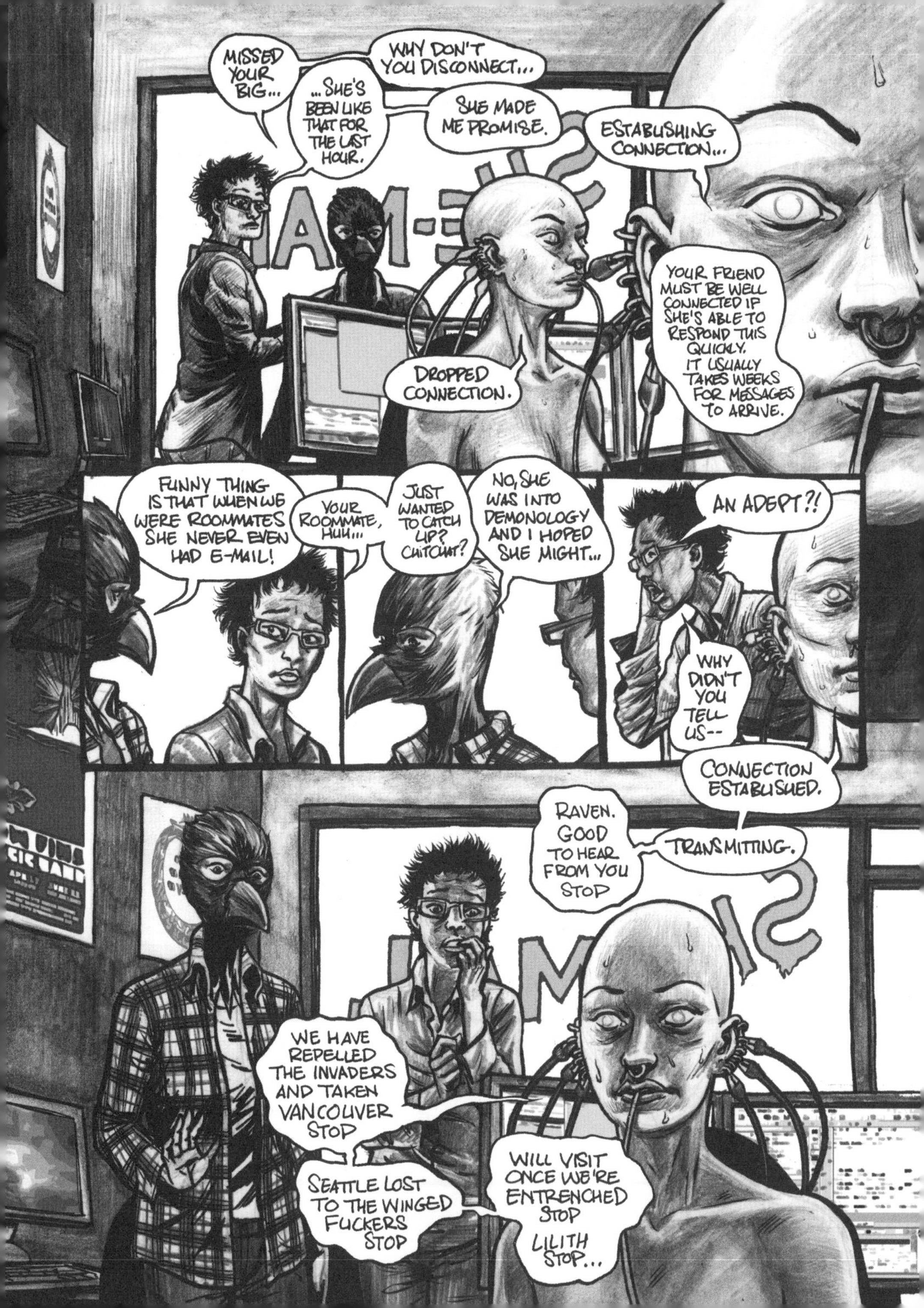
MISSED YOUR BIG...
WHY DON'T YOU DISCONNECT...
...SHE'S BEEN LIKE THAT FOR THE LAST HOUR.
SHE MADE ME PROMISE.
ESTABLISHING CONNECTION...
YOUR FRIEND MUST BE WELL CONNECTED IF SHE'S ABLE TO RESPOND THIS QUICKLY. IT USUALLY TAKES WEEKS FOR MESSAGES TO ARRIVE.
DROPPED CONNECTION.
FUNNY THING IS THAT WHEN WE WERE ROOMMATES SHE NEVER EVEN HAD E-MAIL!
YOUR ROOMMATE, HUH...
JUST WANTED TO CATCH UP? CHITCHAT?
NO, SHE WAS INTO DEMONOLOGY AND I HOPED SHE MIGHT...
AN ADEPT?!
WHY DIDN'T YOU TELL US--
CONNECTION ESTABLISHED.
TRANSMITTING.
RAVEN. GOOD TO HEAR FROM YOU STOP
WE HAVE REPELLED THE INVADERS AND TAKEN VANCOUVER STOP
SEATTLE LOST TO THE WINGED FUCKERS STOP
WILL VISIT ONCE WE'RE ENTRENCHED STOP
LILITH STOP...

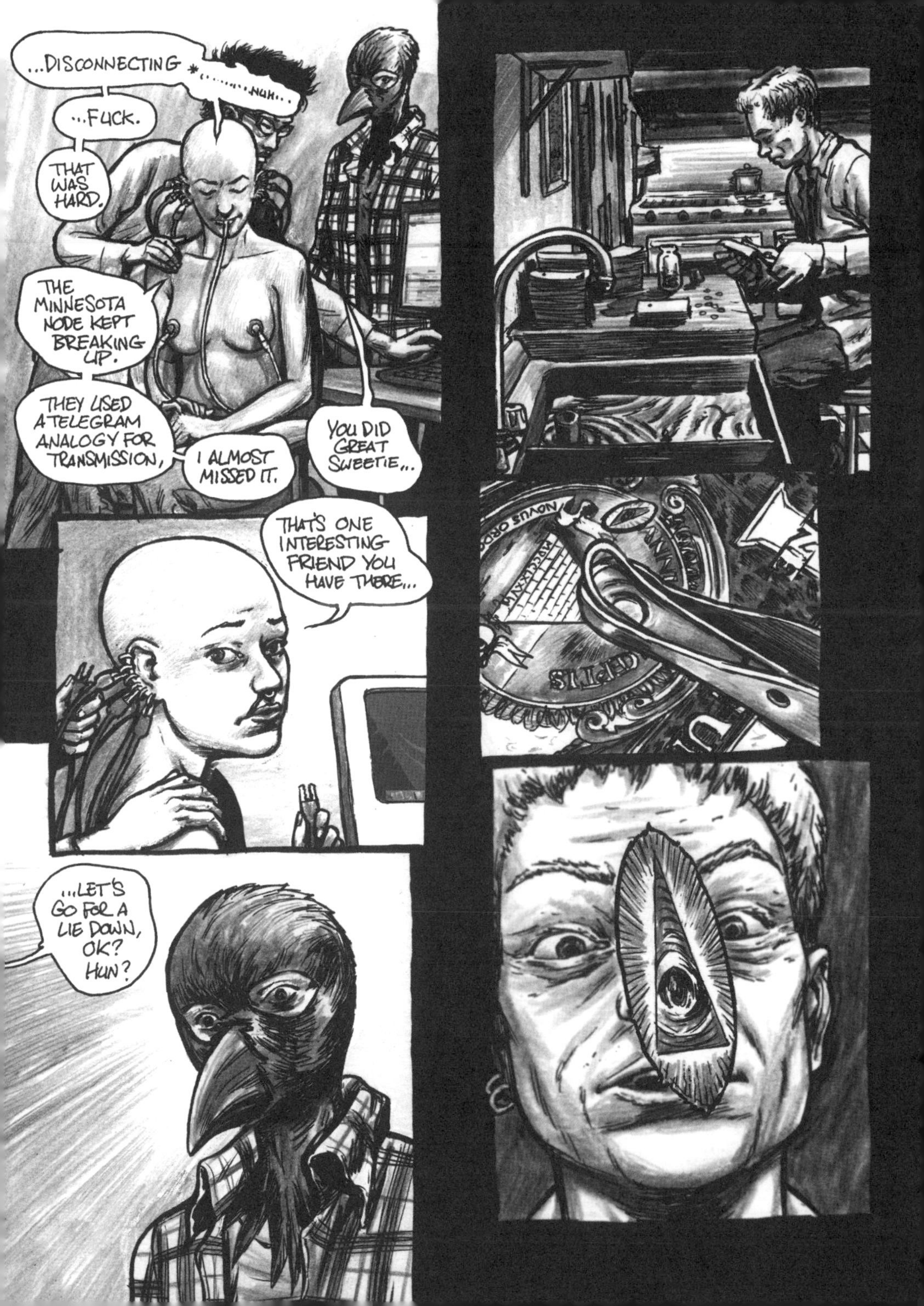
...DISCONNECTING *...........NUH...
...FUCK.
THAT WAS HARD.
THE MINNESOTA NODE KEPT BREAKING UP.
THEY USED A TELEGRAM ANALOGY FOR TRANSMISSION,
I ALMOST MISSED IT.
YOU DID GREAT SWEETIE...
THAT'S ONE INTERESTING FRIEND YOU HAVE THERE...
...LET'S GO FOR A LIE DOWN, OK? HUN?
NOVUS ORDO

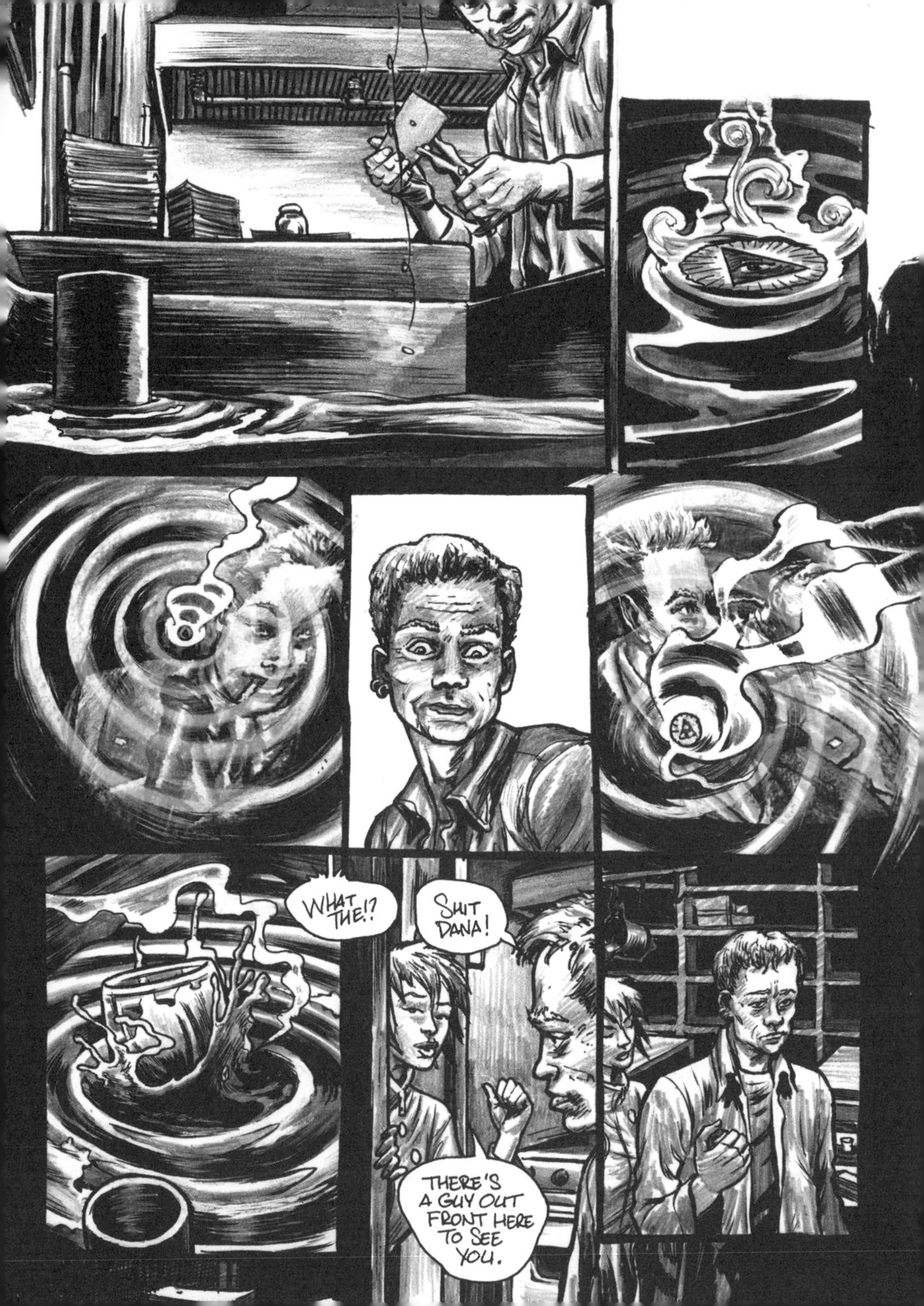
WHAT THE!?
SHIT DANA!
THERE'S A GUY OUT FRONT HERE TO SEE YOU.

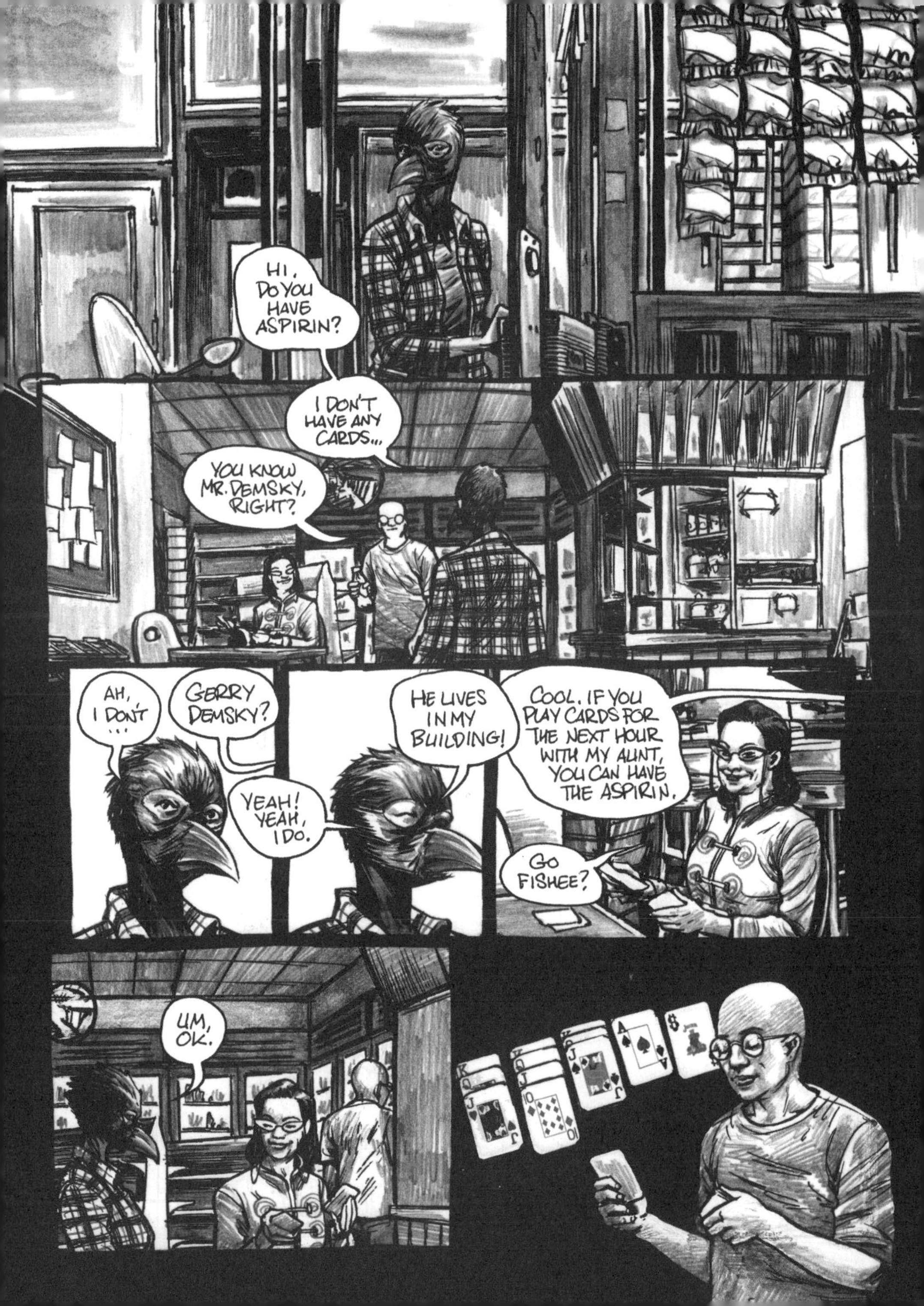
HI, DO YOU HAVE ASPIRIN?
I DON'T HAVE ANY CARDS...
YOU KNOW MR. DEMSKY, RIGHT?
AH, I DON'T ...
GERRY DEMSKY?
YEAH! YEAH, I DO.
HE LIVES IN MY BUILDING!
COOL. IF YOU PLAY CARDS FOR THE NEXT HOUR WITH MY AUNT, YOU CAN HAVE THE ASPIRIN.
GO FISHEE?
UM, OK.

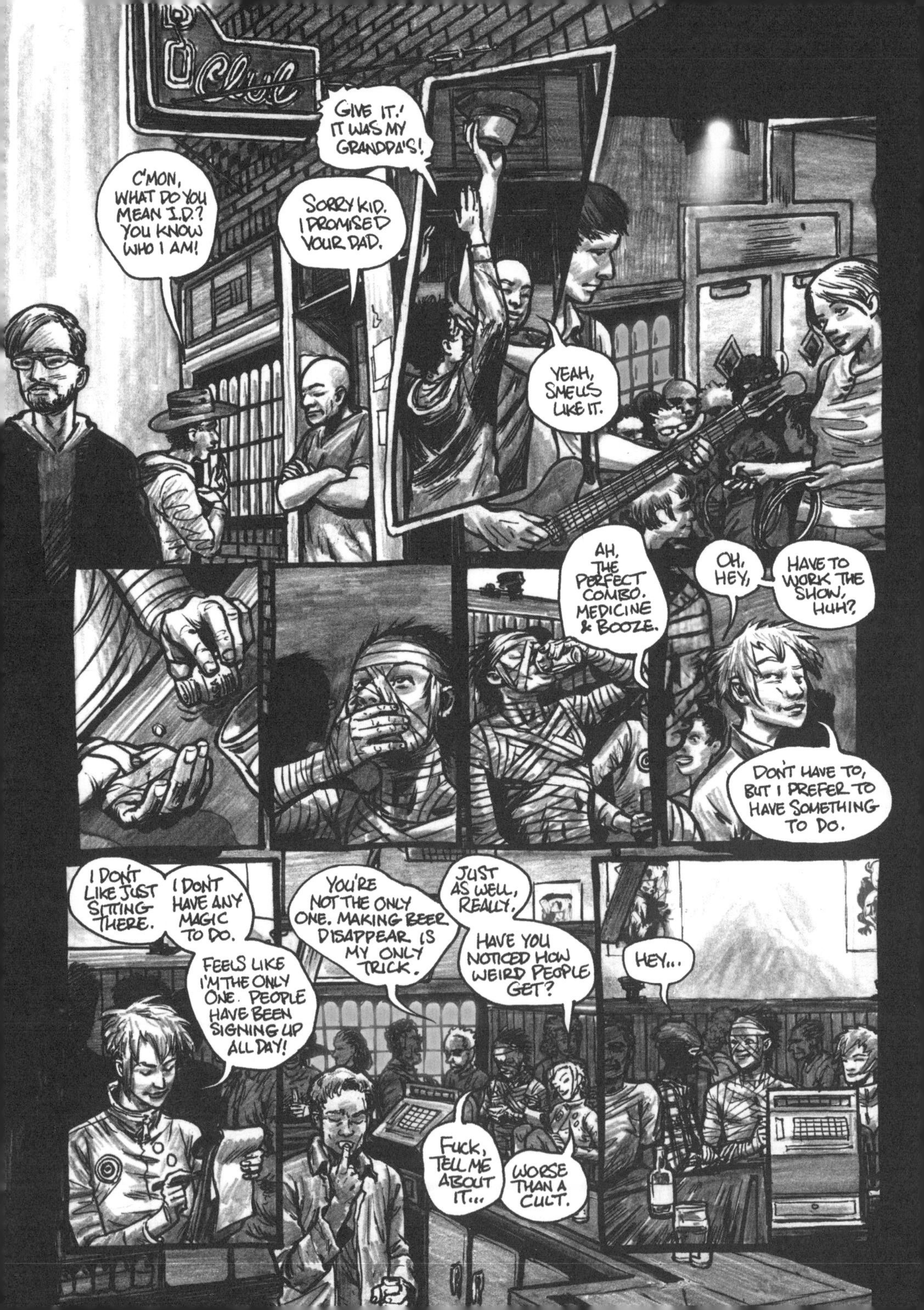
GIVE IT! IT WAS MY GRANDPA'S!
C'MON, WHAT DO YOU MEAN I.D.? YOU KNOW WHO I AM!
SORRY KID. I PROMISED YOUR DAD.
YEAH, SMELLS LIKE IT.
AH, THE PERFECT COMBO. MEDICINE & BOOZE.
OH, HEY,
HAVE TO WORK THE SHOW, HUH?
DON'T HAVE TO, BUT I PREFER TO HAVE SOMETHING TO DO.
I DON'T LIKE JUST SITTING THERE.
I DON'T HAVE ANY MAGIC TO DO.
FEELS LIKE I'M THE ONLY ONE. PEOPLE HAVE BEEN SIGNING UP ALL DAY!
YOU'RE NOT THE ONLY ONE. MAKING BEER DISAPPEAR IS MY ONLY TRICK.
JUST AS WELL, REALLY.
HAVE YOU NOTICED HOW WEIRD PEOPLE GET?
FUCK, TELL ME ABOUT IT...
WORSE THAN A CULT.
HEY...

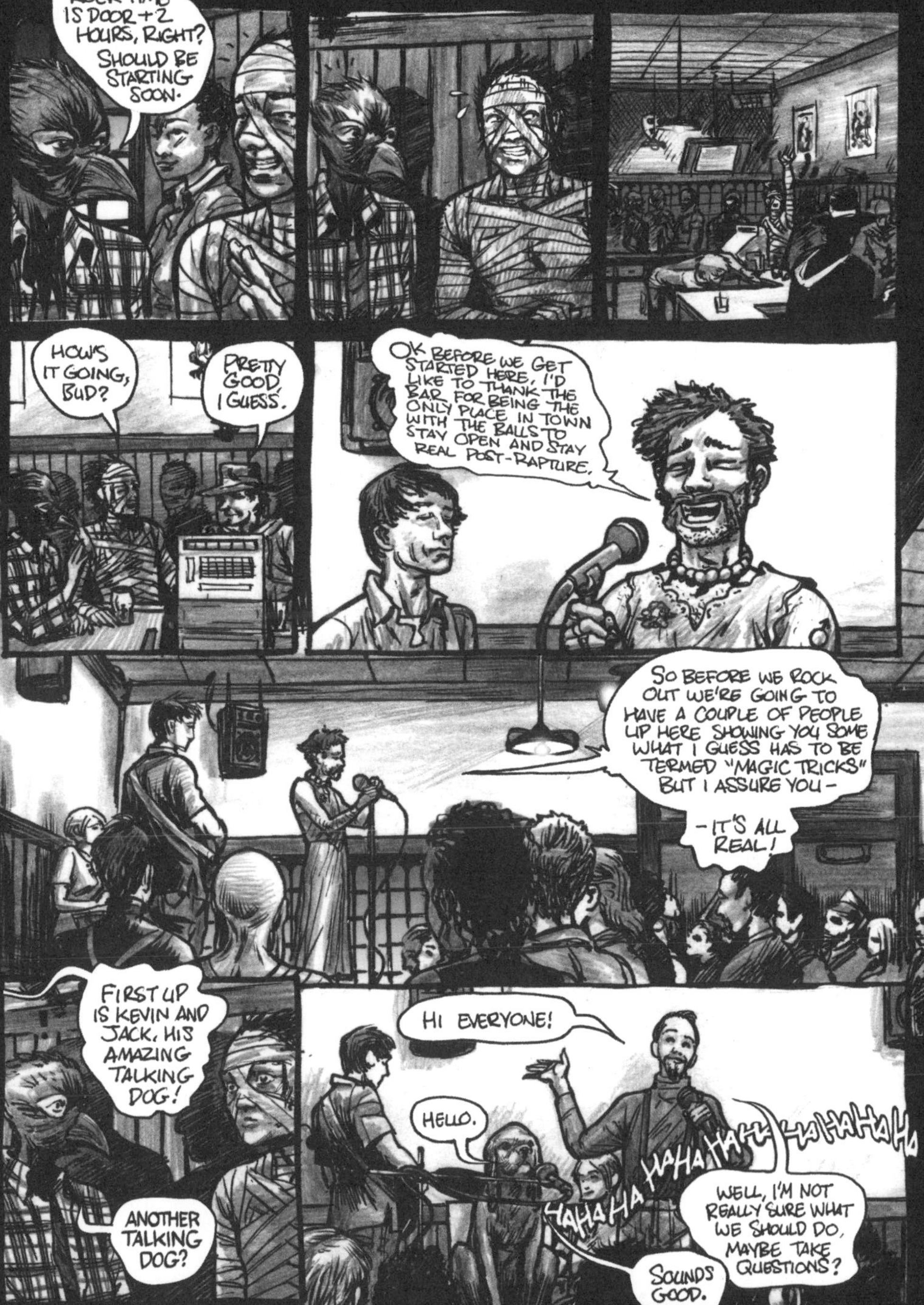
ROCK TIME IS DOOR + 2 HOURS, RIGHT? SHOULD BE STARTING SOON.
HOW'S IT GOING, BUD?
PRETTY GOOD, I GUESS.
OK BEFORE WE GET STARTED HERE, I'D LIKE TO THANK THE BAR FOR BEING THE ONLY PLACE IN TOWN WITH THE BALLS TO STAY OPEN AND STAY REAL POST-RAPTURE.
SO BEFORE WE ROCK OUT WE'RE GOING TO HAVE A COUPLE OF PEOPLE UP HERE SHOWING YOU SOME WHAT I GUESS HAS TO BE TERMED "MAGIC TRICKS" BUT I ASSURE YOU -
- IT'S ALL REAL!
FIRST UP IS KEVIN AND JACK, HIS AMAZING TALKING DOG!
ANOTHER TALKING DOG?
HI EVERYONE!
HELLO.
HAHAHAHAHAHAHAHAHAHAHAHAHA
WELL, I'M NOT REALLY SURE WHAT WE SHOULD DO, MAYBE TAKE QUESTIONS?
SOUNDS GOOD.

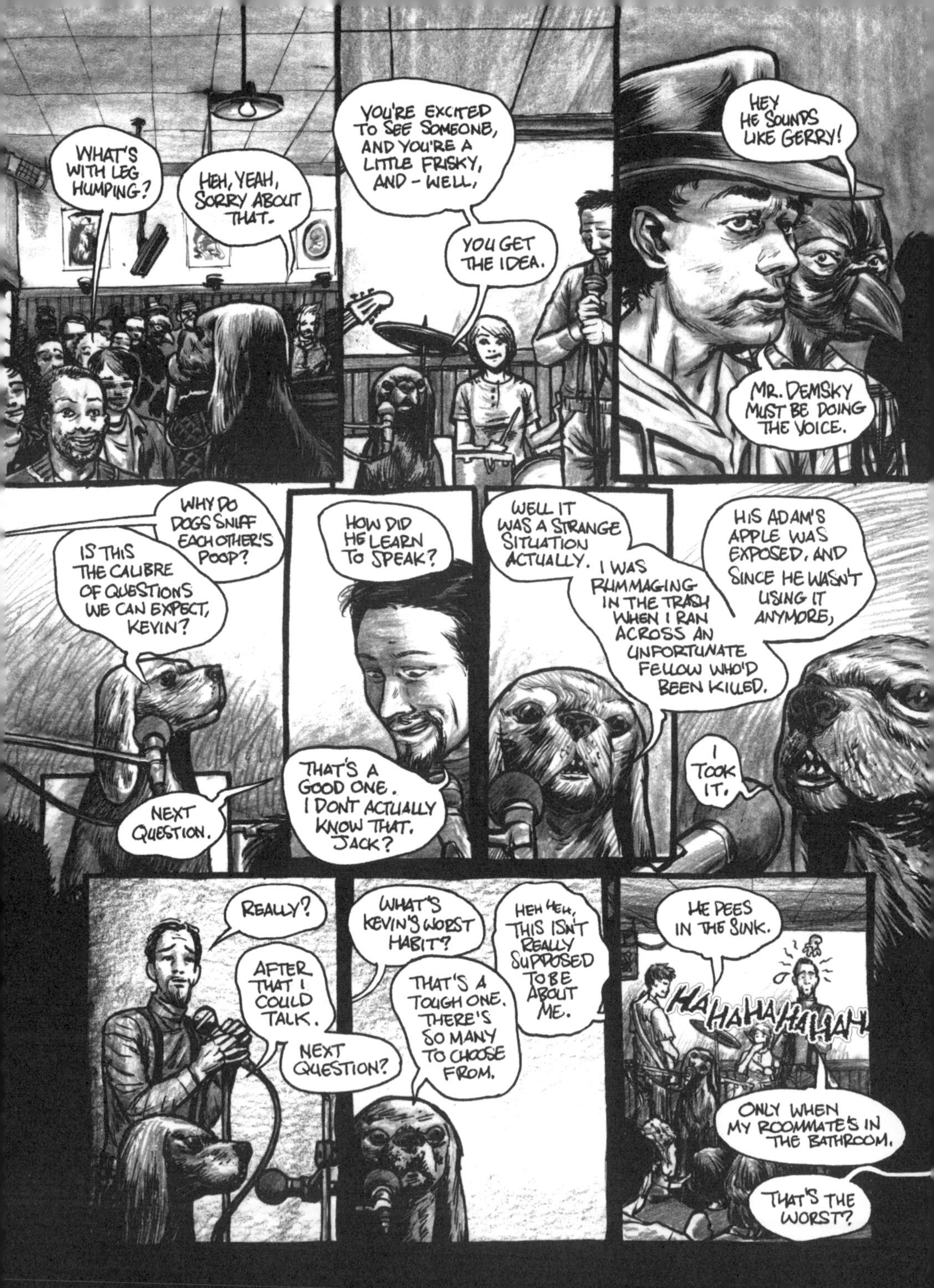
WHAT'S WITH LEG HUMPING?
HEH, YEAH, SORRY ABOUT THAT.
YOU'RE EXCITED TO SEE SOMEONE, AND YOU'RE A LITTLE FRISKY, AND - WELL,
YOU GET THE IDEA.
HEY HE SOUNDS LIKE GERRY!
MR. DEMSKY MUST BE DOING THE VOICE.
WHY DO DOGS SNIFF EACH OTHER'S POOP?
IS THIS THE CALIBRE OF QUESTIONS WE CAN EXPECT, KEVIN?
NEXT QUESTION.
HOW DID HE LEARN TO SPEAK?
THAT'S A GOOD ONE. I DONT ACTUALLY KNOW THAT. JACK?
WELL IT WAS A STRANGE SITUATION ACTUALLY.
I WAS RUMMAGING IN THE TRASH WHEN I RAN ACROSS AN UNFORTUNATE FELLOW WHO'D BEEN KILLED.
HIS ADAM'S APPLE WAS EXPOSED, AND SINCE HE WASN'T USING IT ANYMORE,
I TOOK IT.
REALLY?
AFTER THAT I COULD TALK.
NEXT QUESTION?
WHAT'S KEVIN'S WORST HABIT?
HEH HEH, THIS ISN'T REALLY SUPPOSED TO BE ABOUT ME.
THAT'S A TOUGH ONE. THERE'S SO MANY TO CHOOSE FROM.
HE PEES IN THE SINK.
HAHAHAHAHAH
ONLY WHEN MY ROOMMATE'S IN THE BATHROOM.
THAT'S THE WORST?

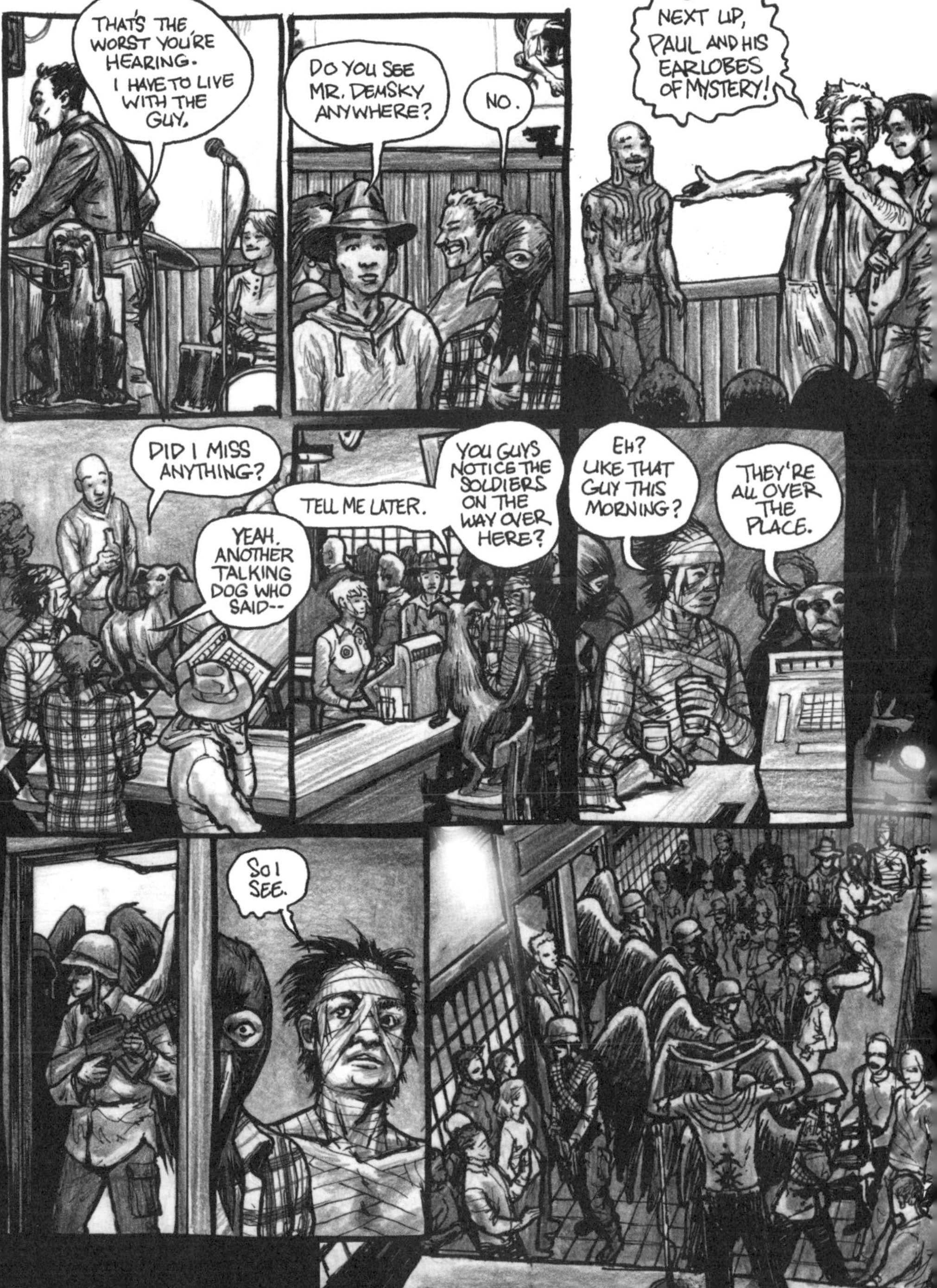
THAT'S THE WORST YOU'RE HEARING. I HAVE TO LIVE WITH THE GUY.
DO YOU SEE MR. DEMSKY ANYWHERE?
NO.
NEXT UP, PAUL AND HIS EARLOBES OF MYSTERY!
DID I MISS ANYTHING?
YEAH. ANOTHER TALKING DOG WHO SAID--
TELL ME LATER.
YOU GUYS NOTICE THE SOLDIERS ON THE WAY OVER HERE?
EH? LIKE THAT GUY THIS MORNING?
THEY'RE ALL OVER THE PLACE.
So I SEE.

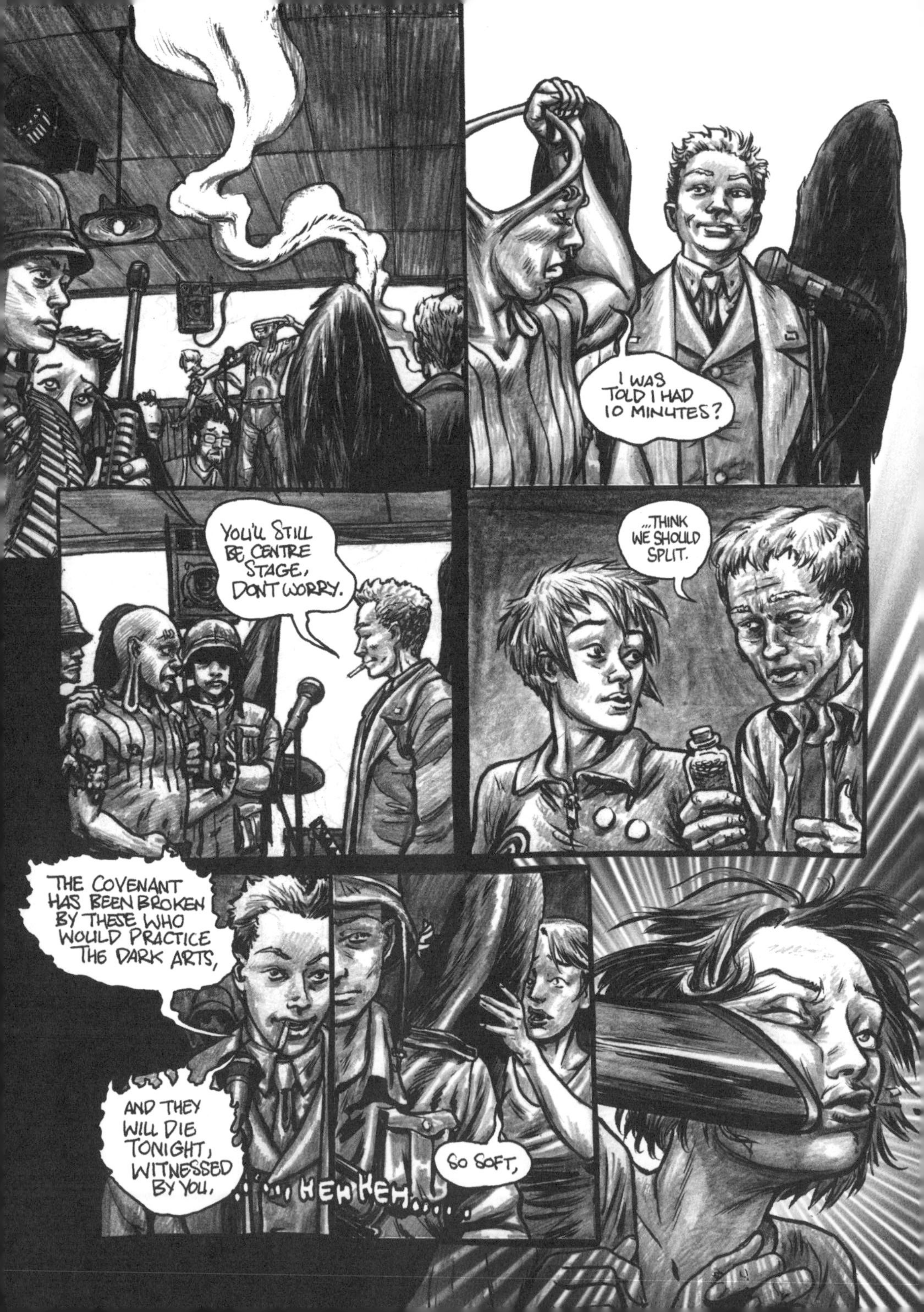
I WAS TOLD I HAD 10 MINUTES?
YOU'LL STILL BE CENTRE STAGE, DON'T WORRY.
...THINK WE SHOULD SPLIT.
THE COVENANT HAS BEEN BROKEN BY THESE WHO WOULD PRACTICE THE DARK ARTS,
AND THEY WILL DIE TONIGHT, WITNESSED BY YOU.
...HEH HEH.....
SO SOFT,

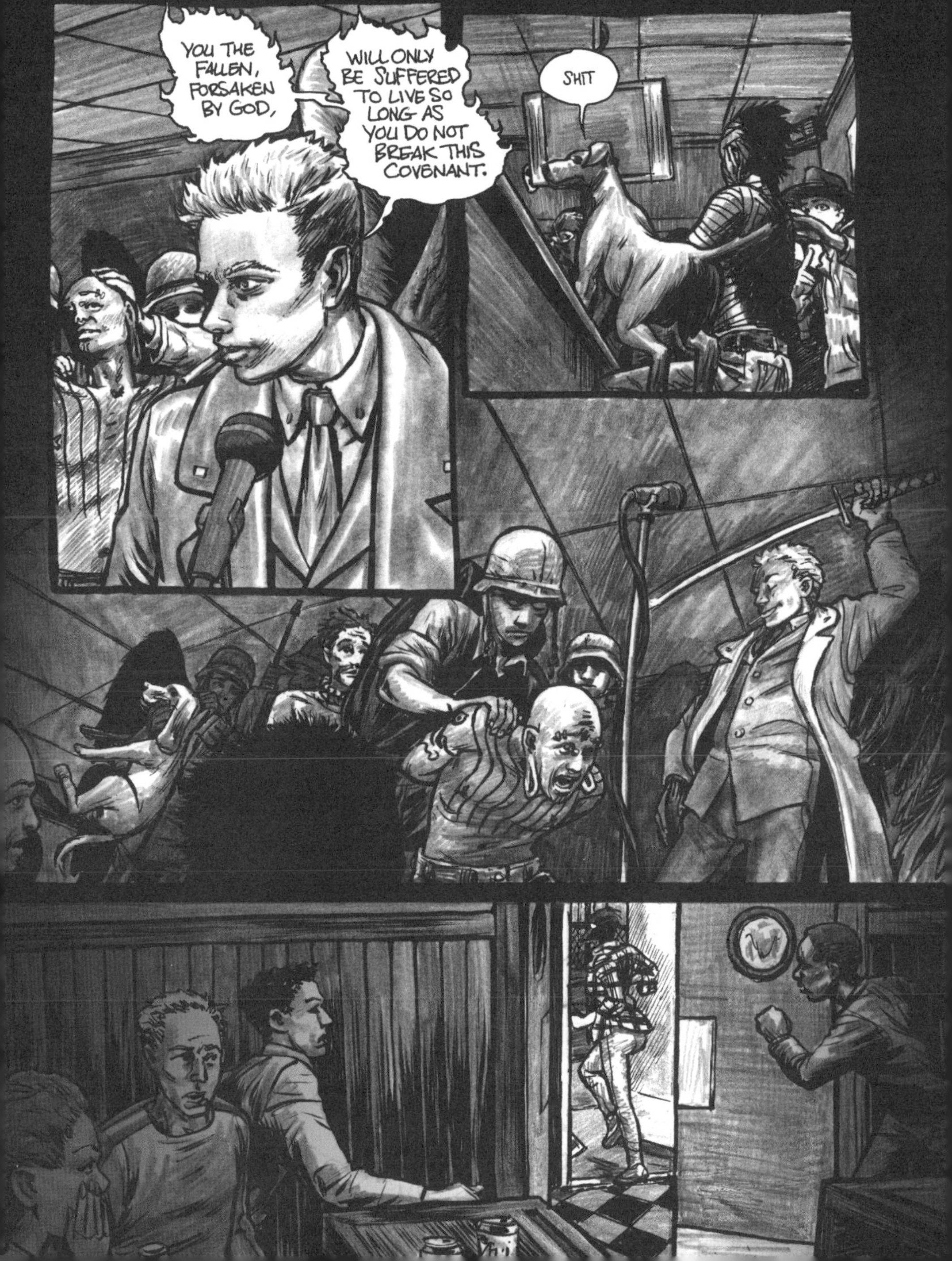

YOU THE FALLEN, FORSAKEN BY GOD,
WILL ONLY BE SUFFERED TO LIVE SO LONG AS YOU DO NOT BREAK THIS COVENANT.
SHIT

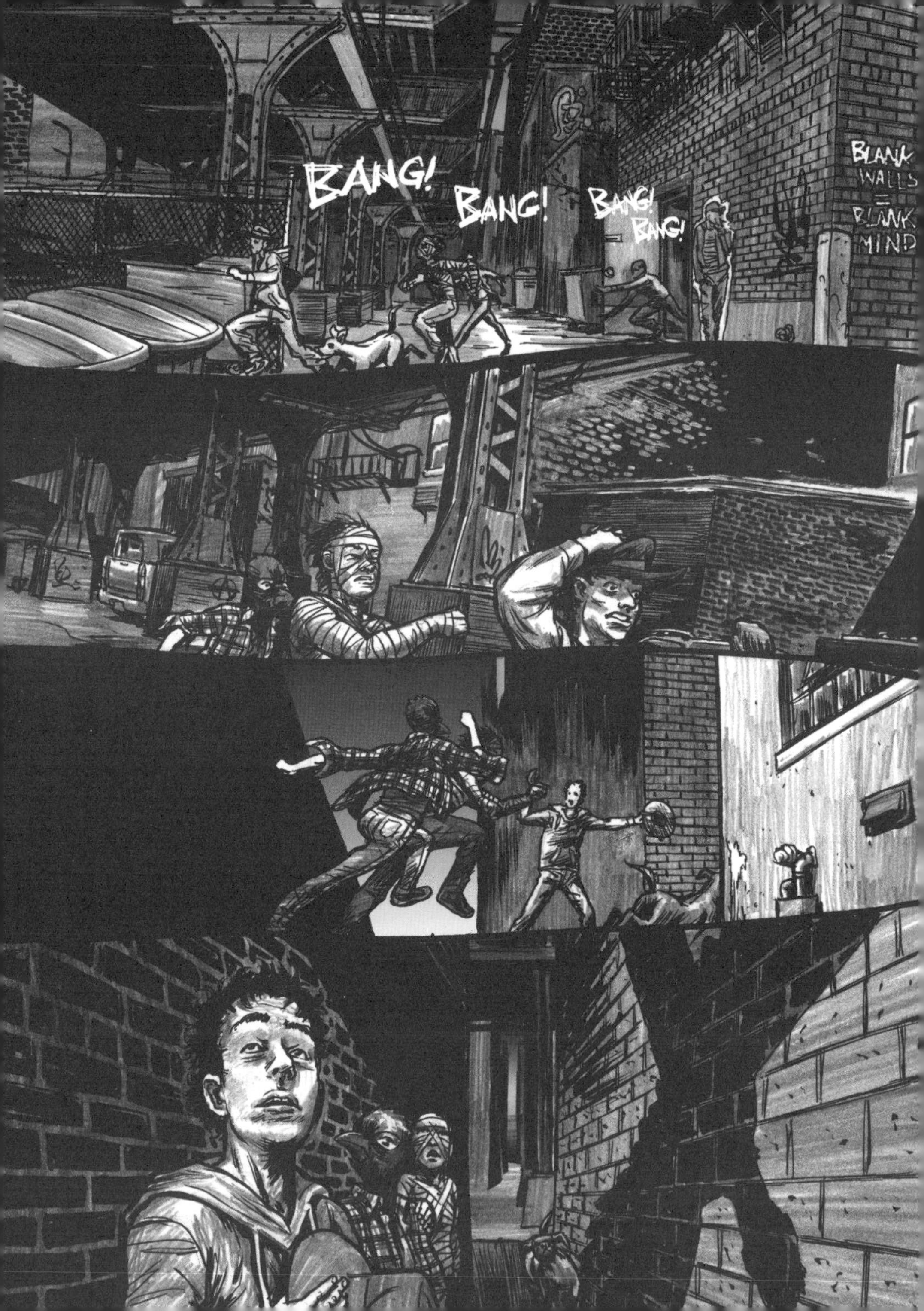
BANG!
BANG!
BANG!
BANG!
BLANK WALLS = BLANK MIND

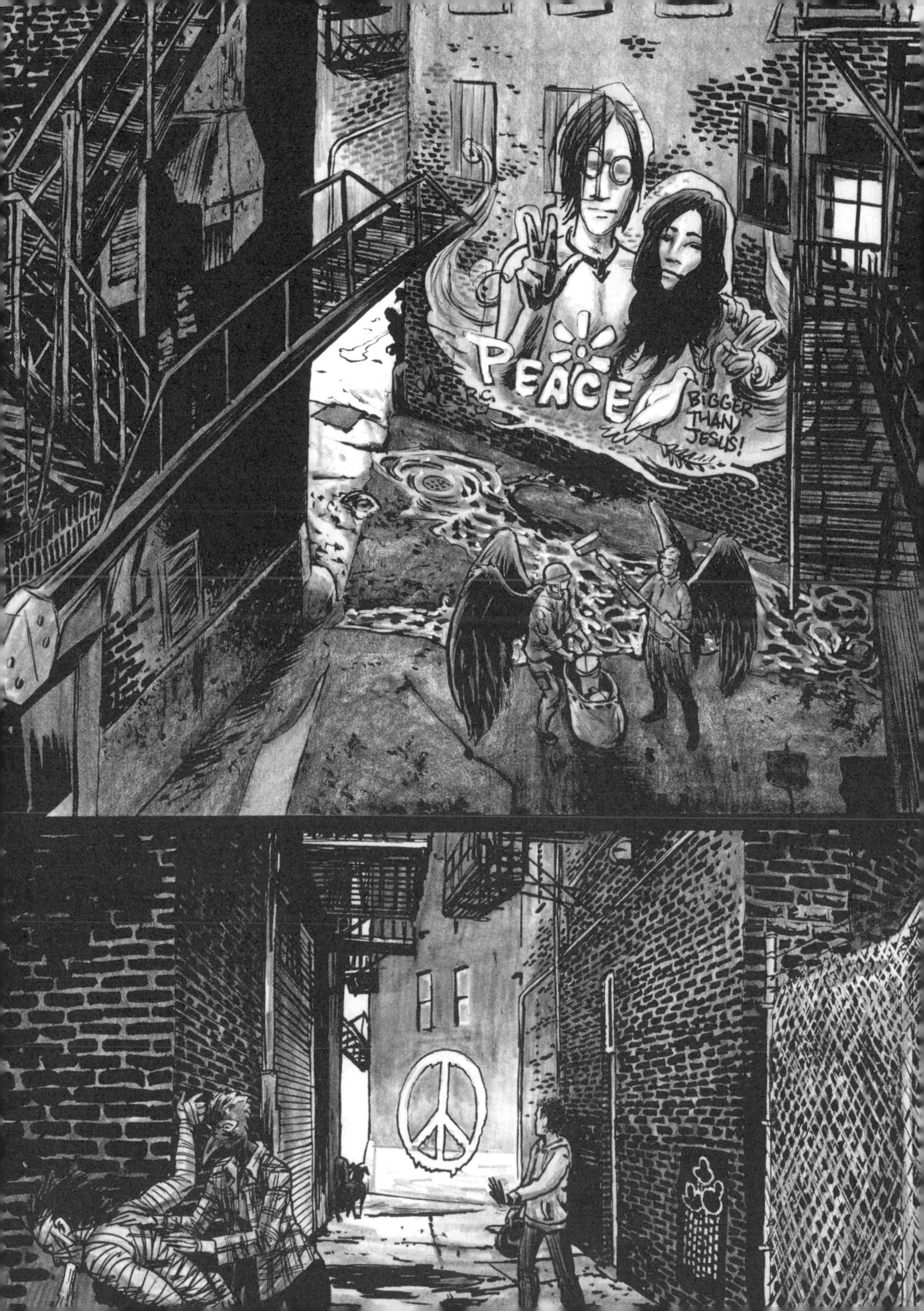
PEACE
BIGGER THAN JESUS!

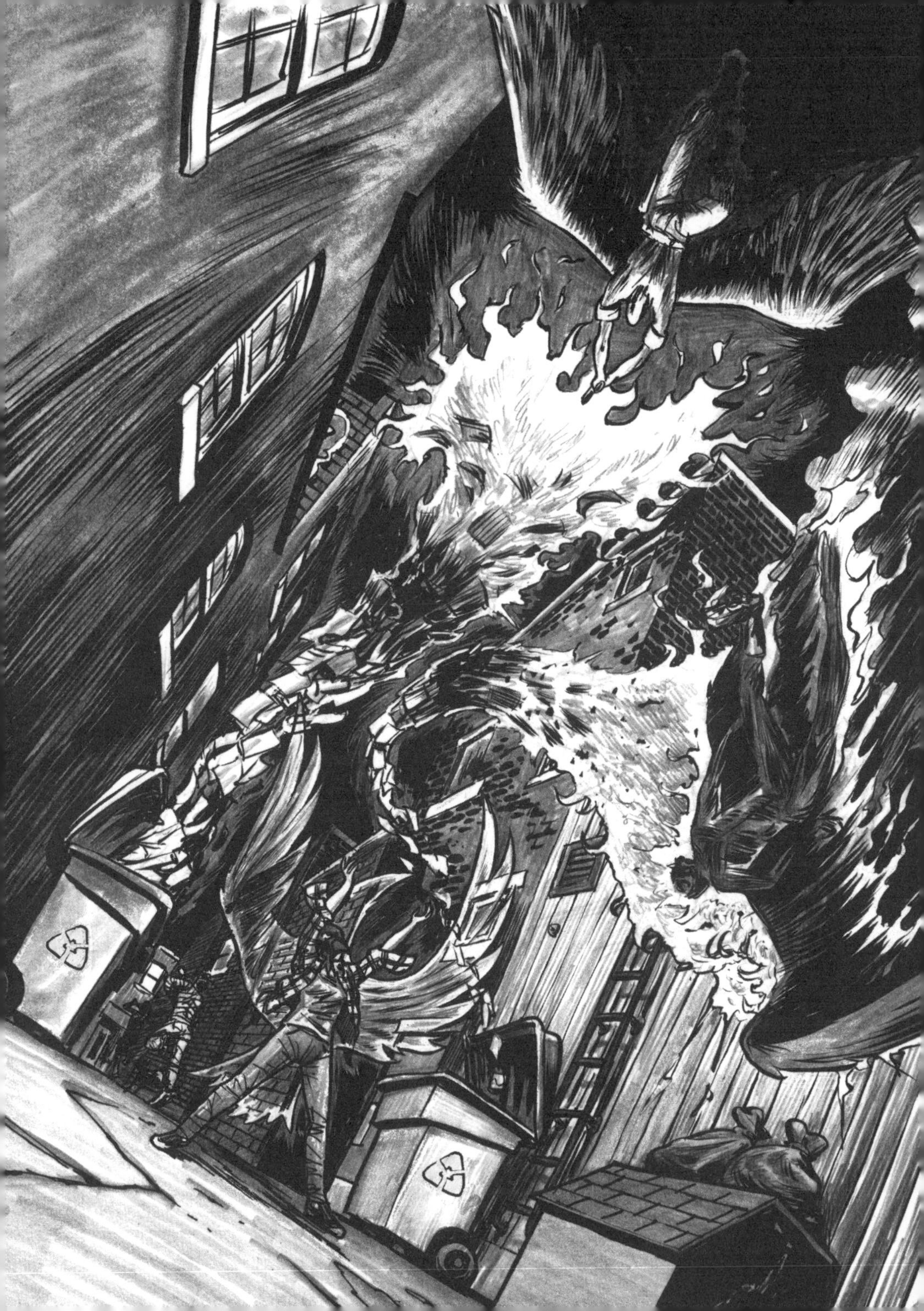

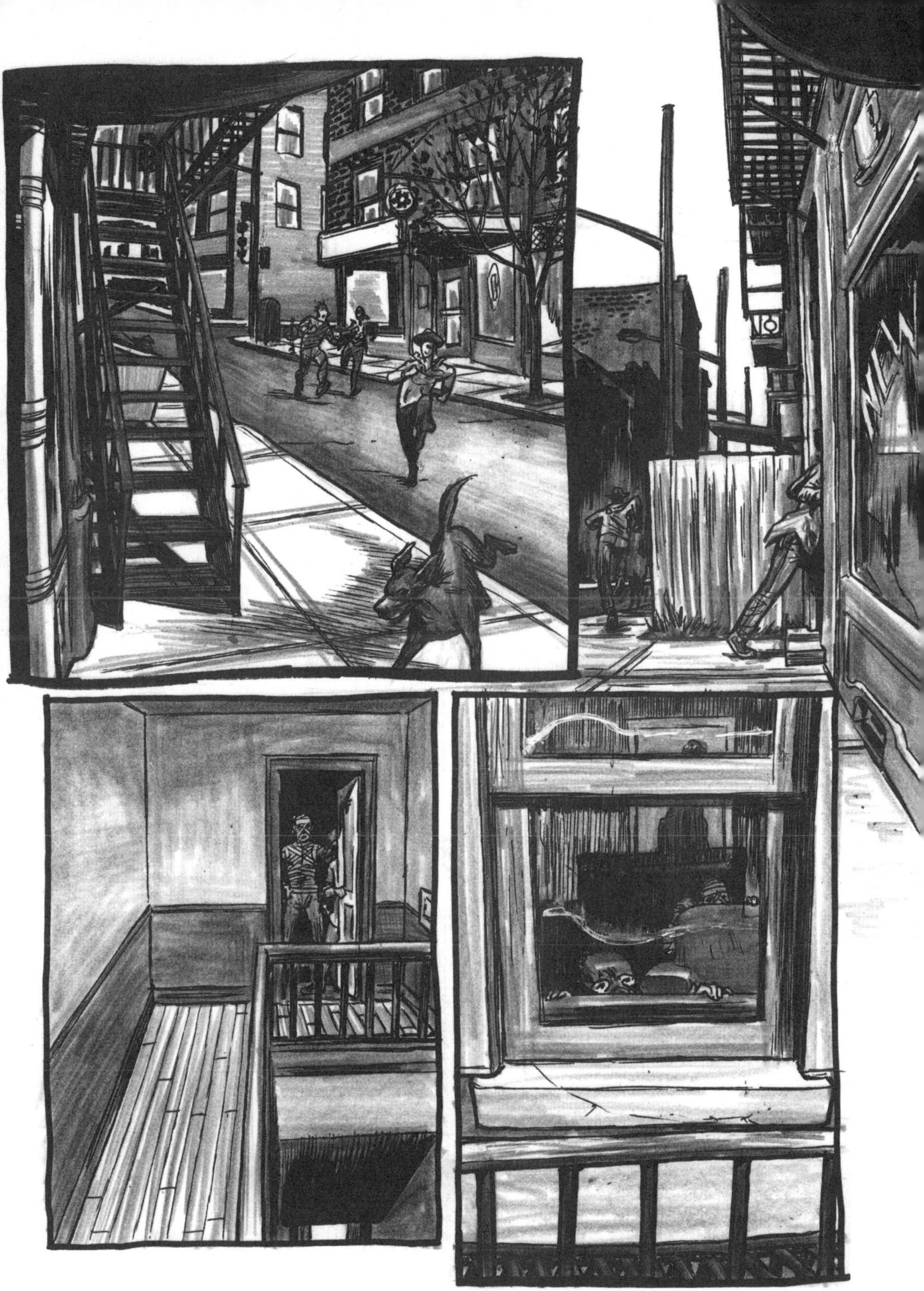

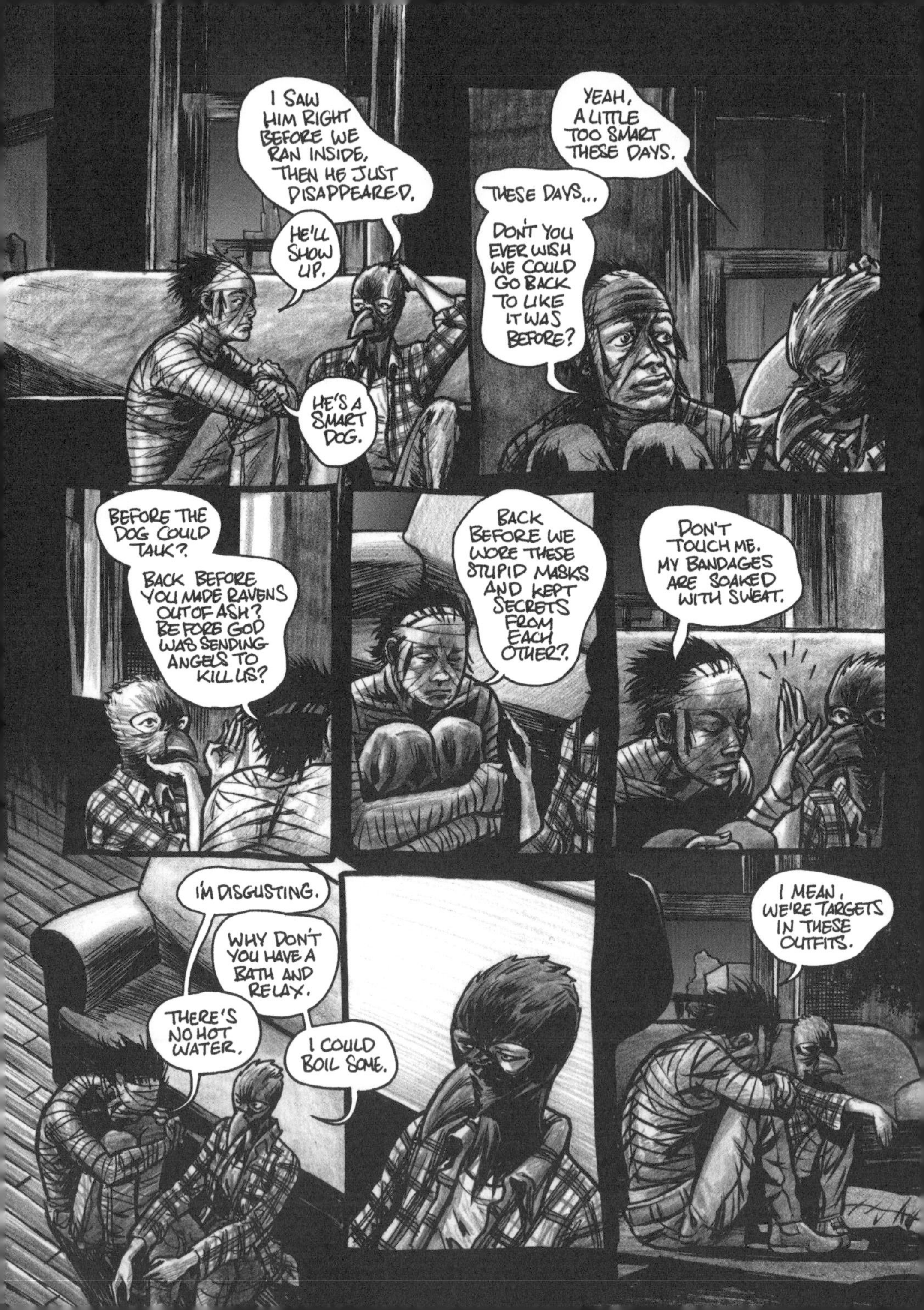
I SAW HIM RIGHT BEFORE WE RAN INSIDE, THEN HE JUST DISAPPEARED.
HE'LL SHOW UP.
HE'S A SMART DOG.
YEAH, A LITTLE TOO SMART THESE DAYS.
THESE DAYS...
DON'T YOU EVER WISH WE COULD GO BACK TO LIKE IT WAS BEFORE?
BEFORE THE DOG COULD TALK?
BACK BEFORE YOU MADE RAVENS OUT OF ASH? BEFORE GOD WAS SENDING ANGELS TO KILL US?
BACK BEFORE WE WORE THESE STUPID MASKS AND KEPT SECRETS FROM EACH OTHER?
DON'T TOUCH ME. MY BANDAGES ARE SOAKED WITH SWEAT.
I'M DISGUSTING.
WHY DON'T YOU HAVE A BATH AND RELAX.
THERE'S NO HOT WATER.
I COULD BOIL SOME.
I MEAN, WE'RE TARGETS IN THESE OUTFITS.

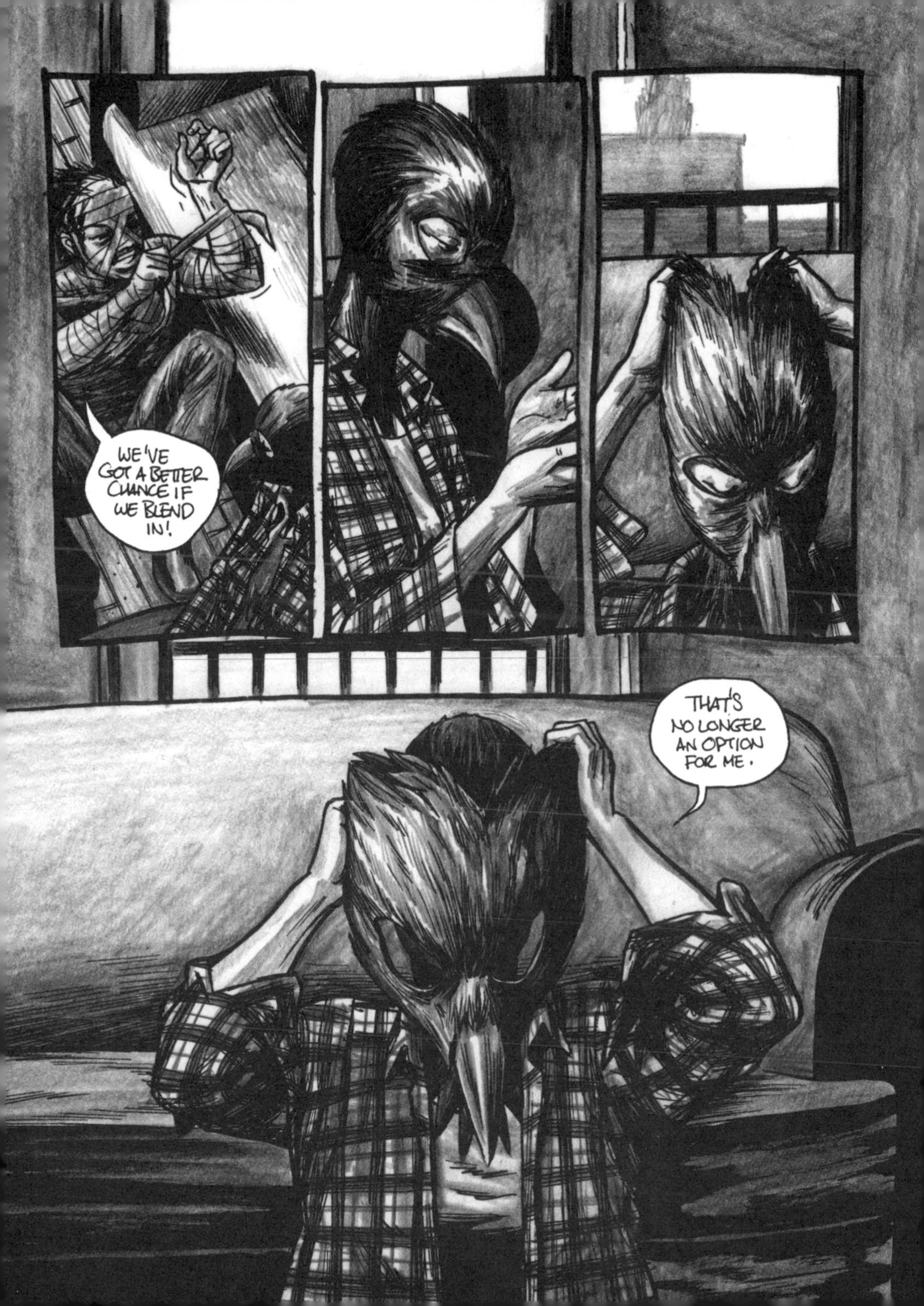
WE'VE GOT A BETTER CHANCE IF WE BLEND IN!
THAT'S NO LONGER AN OPTION FOR ME.

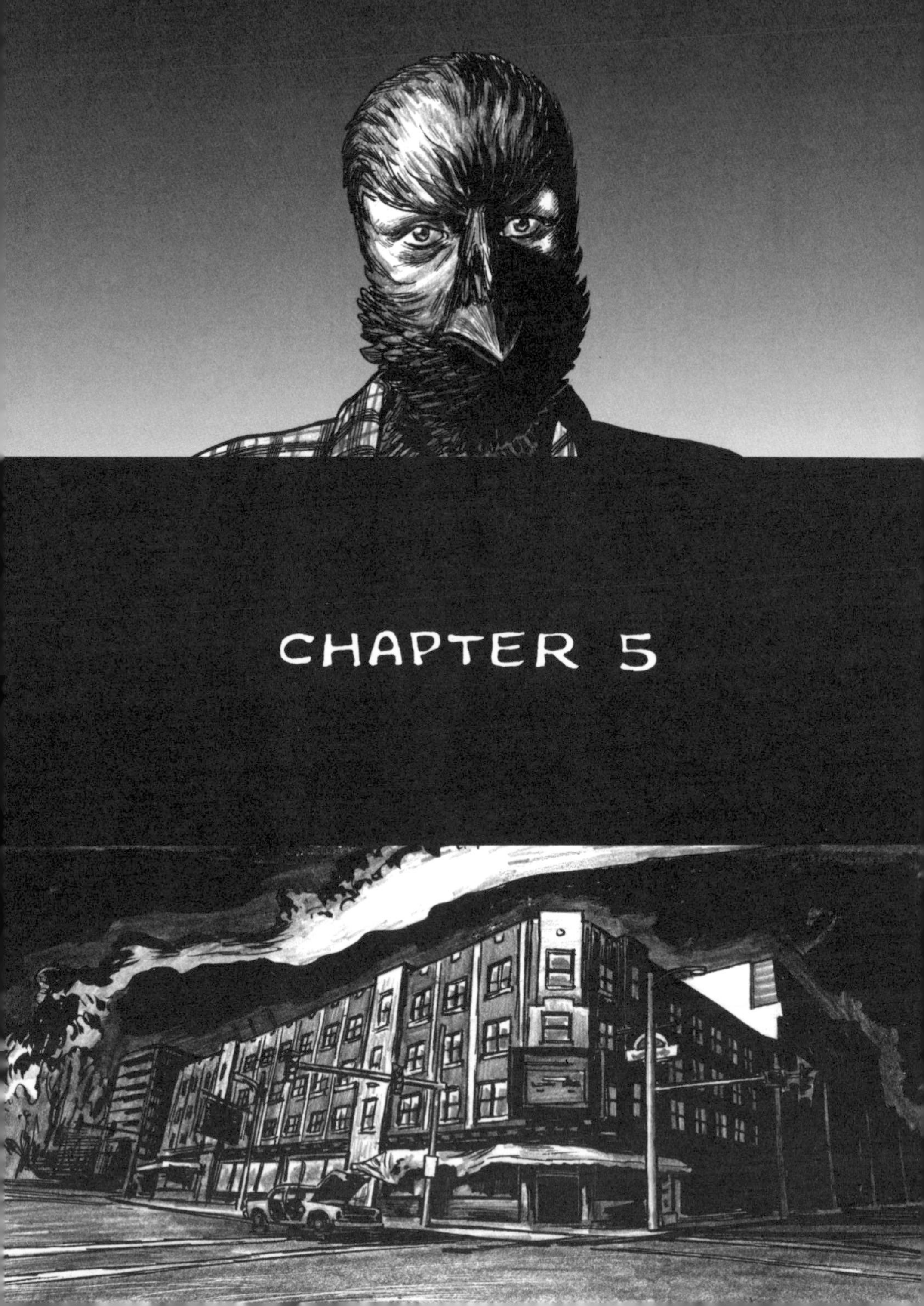
CHAPTER 5

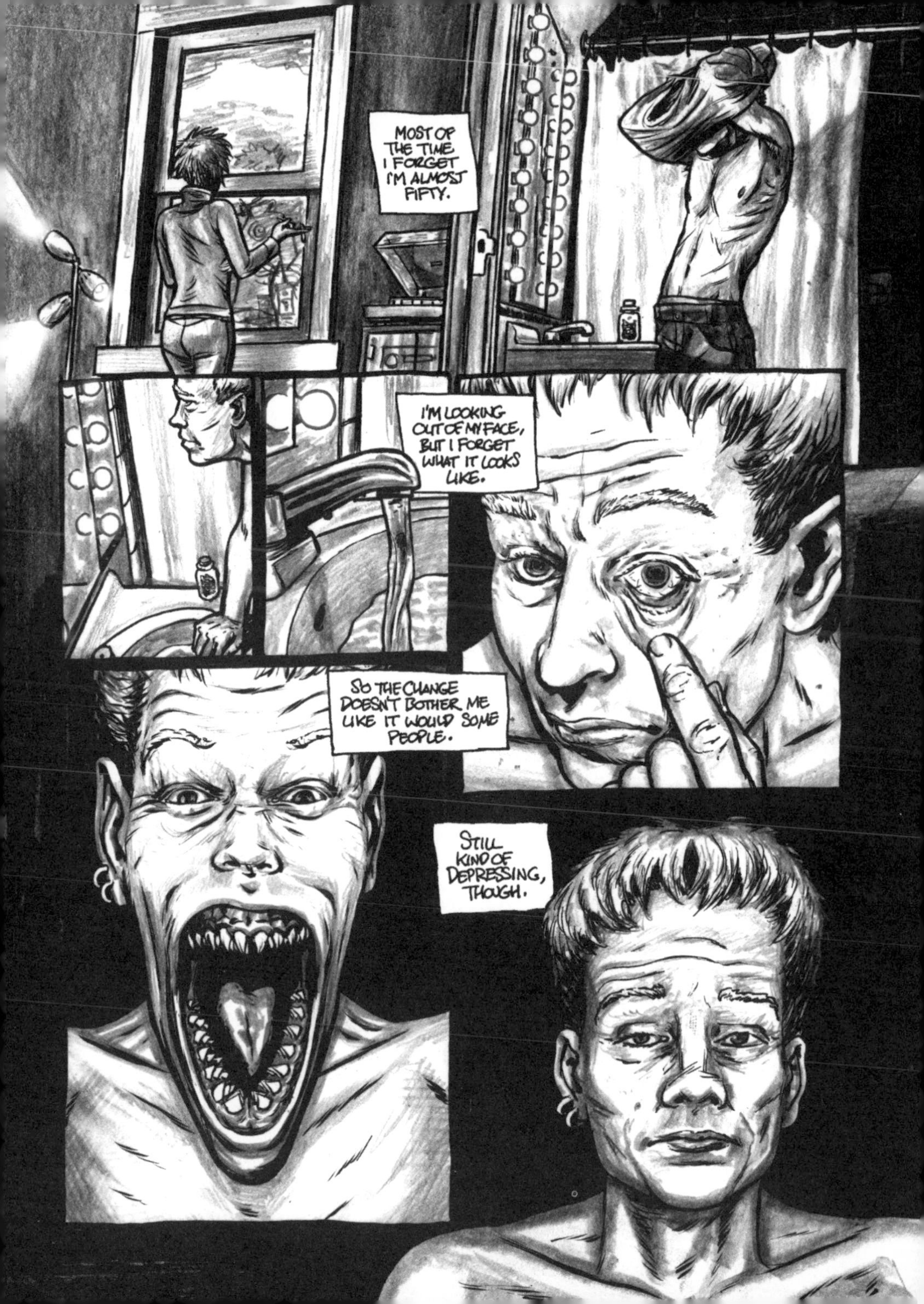
MOST OF THE TIME I FORGET I'M ALMOST FIFTY.
I'M LOOKING OUT OF MY FACE, BUT I FORGET WHAT IT LOOKS LIKE.
SO THE CHANGE DOESN'T BOTHER ME LIKE IT WOULD SOME PEOPLE.
STILL KIND OF DEPRESSING, THOUGH.

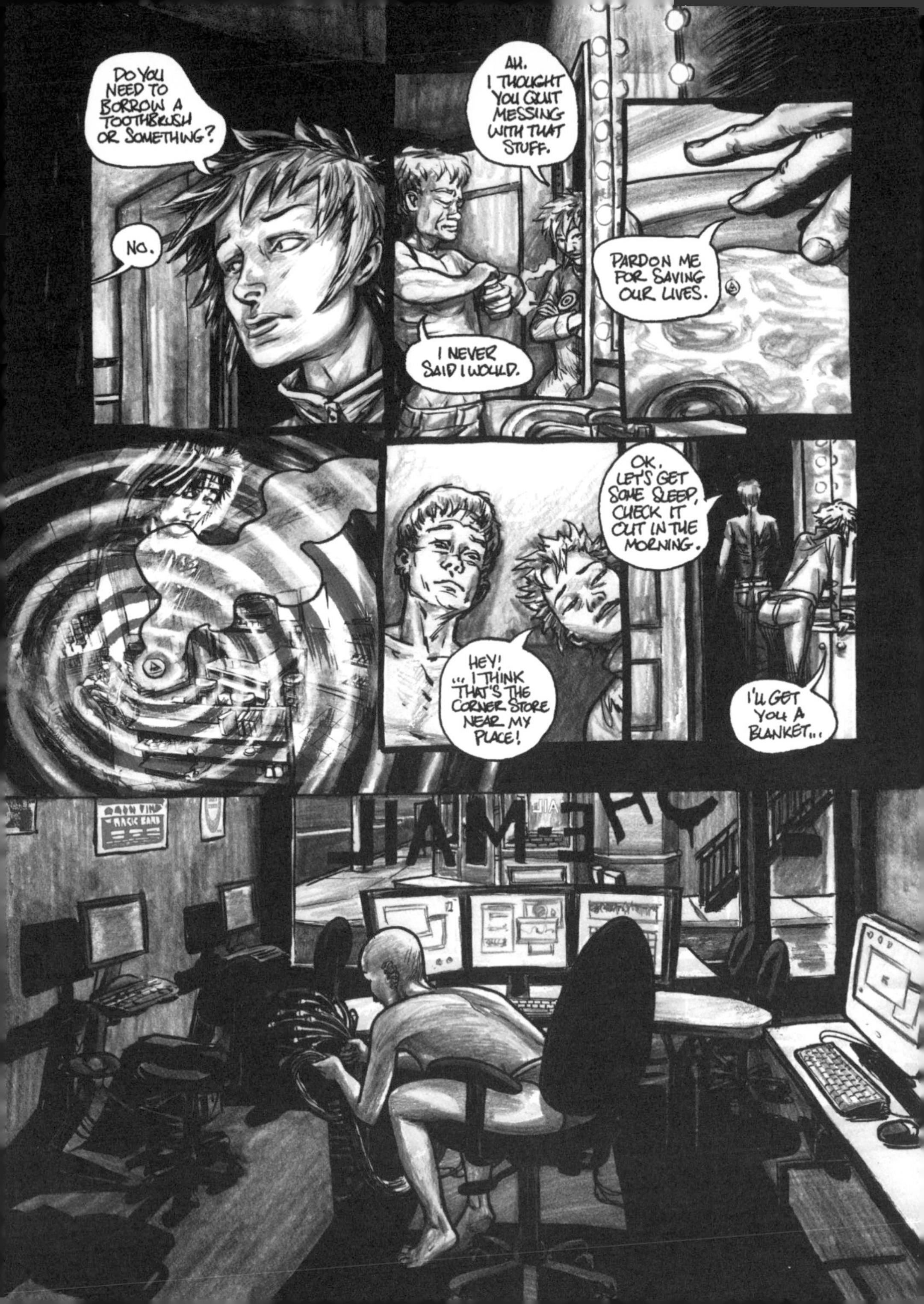
DO YOU NEED TO BORROW A TOOTHBRUSH OR SOMETHING?
NO.
AH. I THOUGHT YOU QUIT MESSING WITH THAT STUFF.
I NEVER SAID I WOULD.
PARDON ME FOR SAVING OUR LIVES.
OK. LET'S GET SOME SLEEP, CHECK IT OUT IN THE MORNING.
HEY! ... I THINK THAT'S THE CORNER STORE NEAR MY PLACE!
I'LL GET YOU A BLANKET...

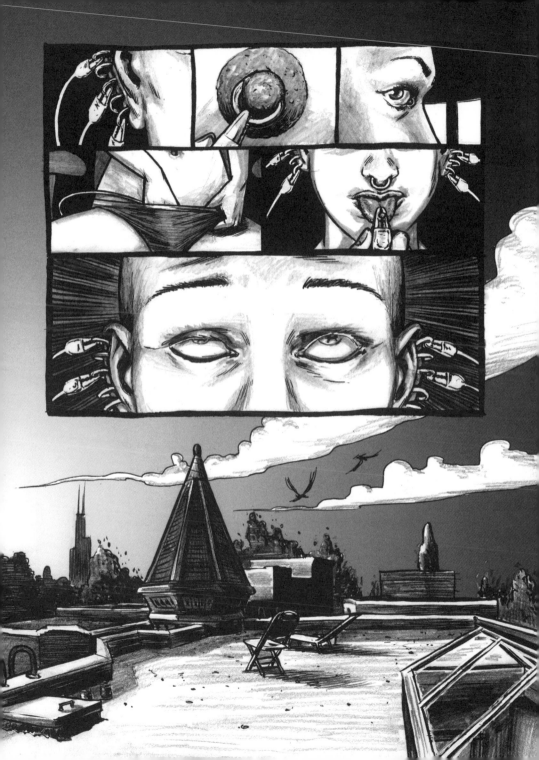

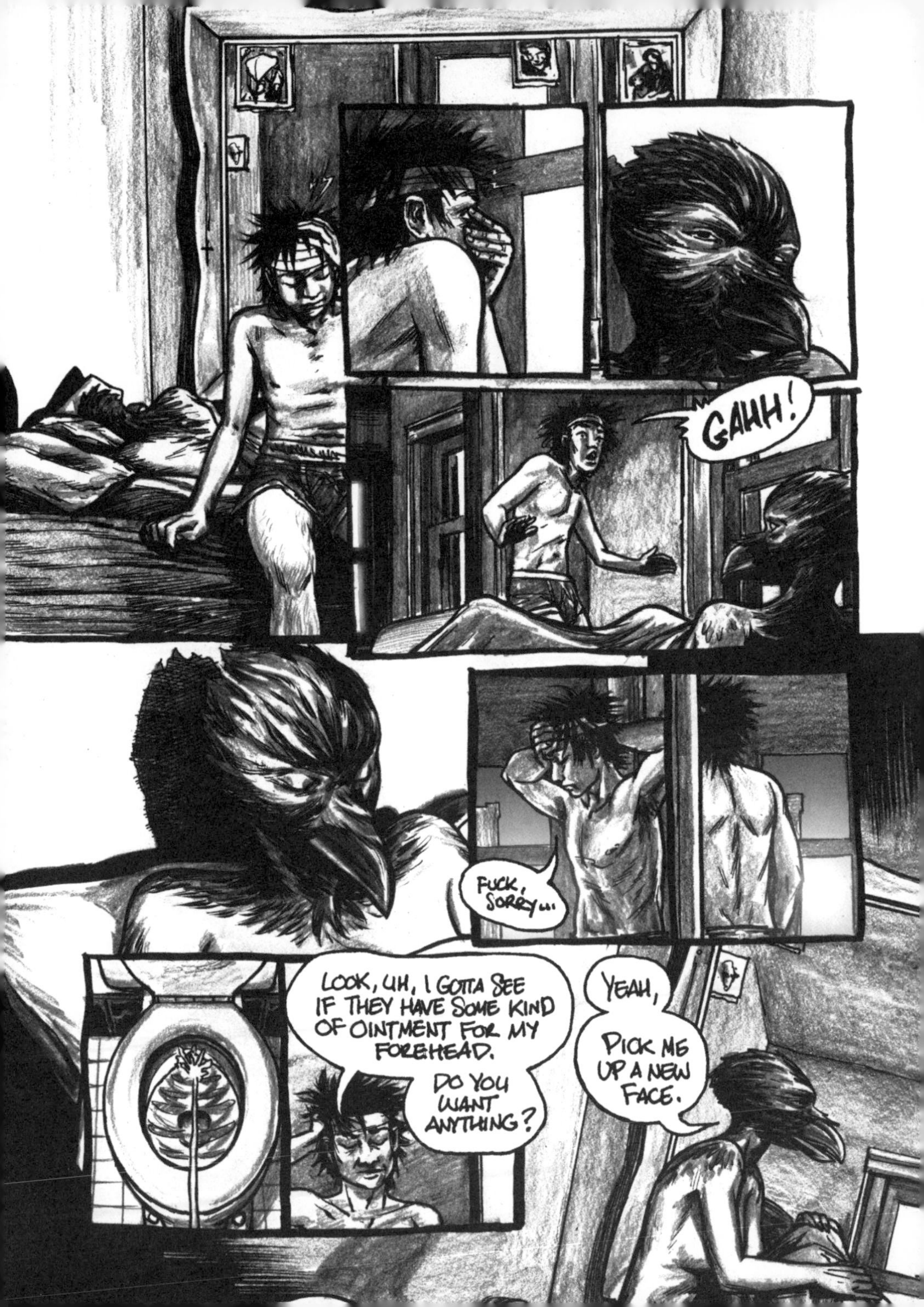
GAHH!
FUCK, SORRY...
LOOK, UH, I GOTTA SEE IF THEY HAVE SOME KIND OF OINTMENT FOR MY FOREHEAD.
DO YOU WANT ANYTHING?
YEAH,
PICK ME UP A NEW FACE.

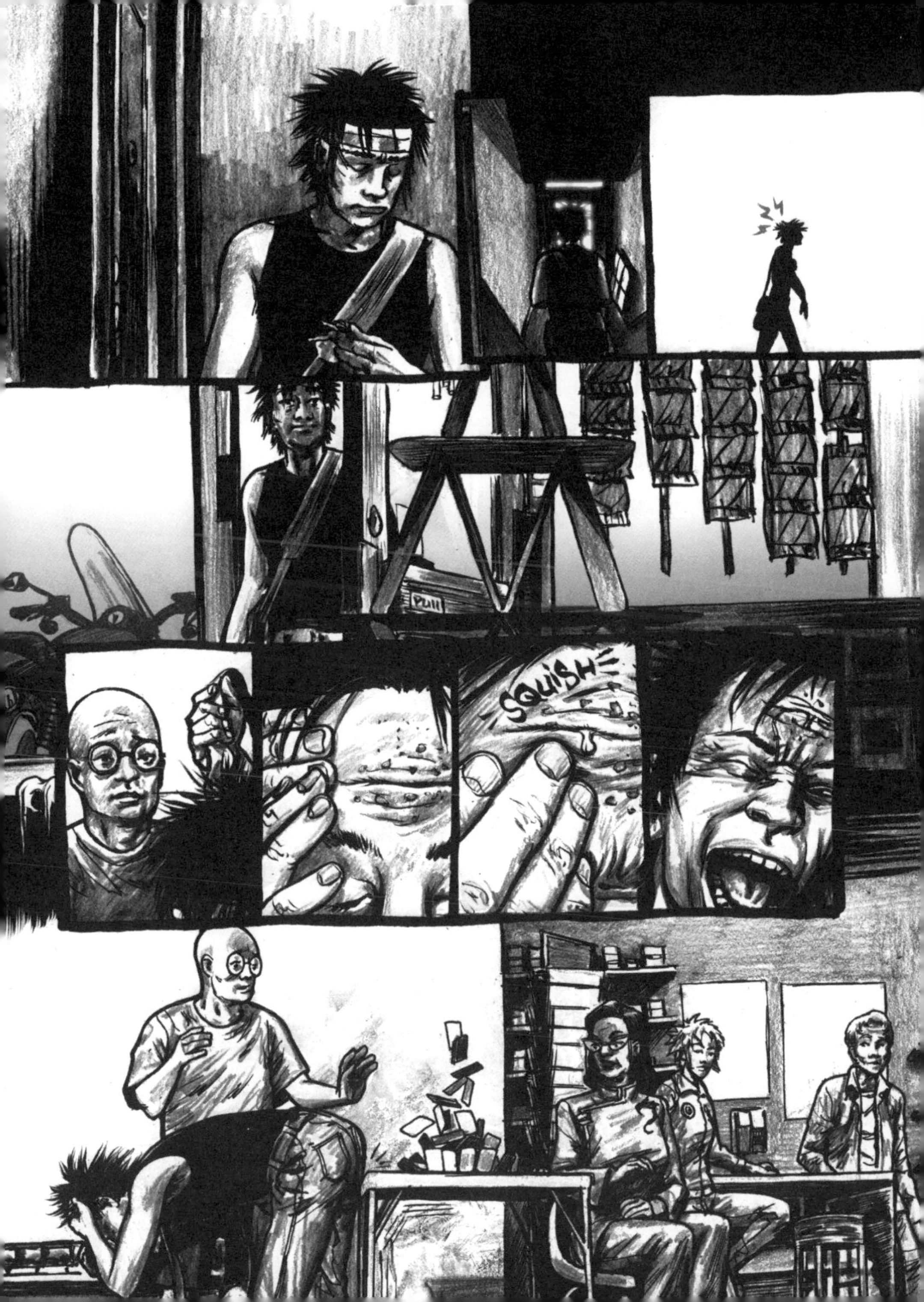
PULL
SQUISH

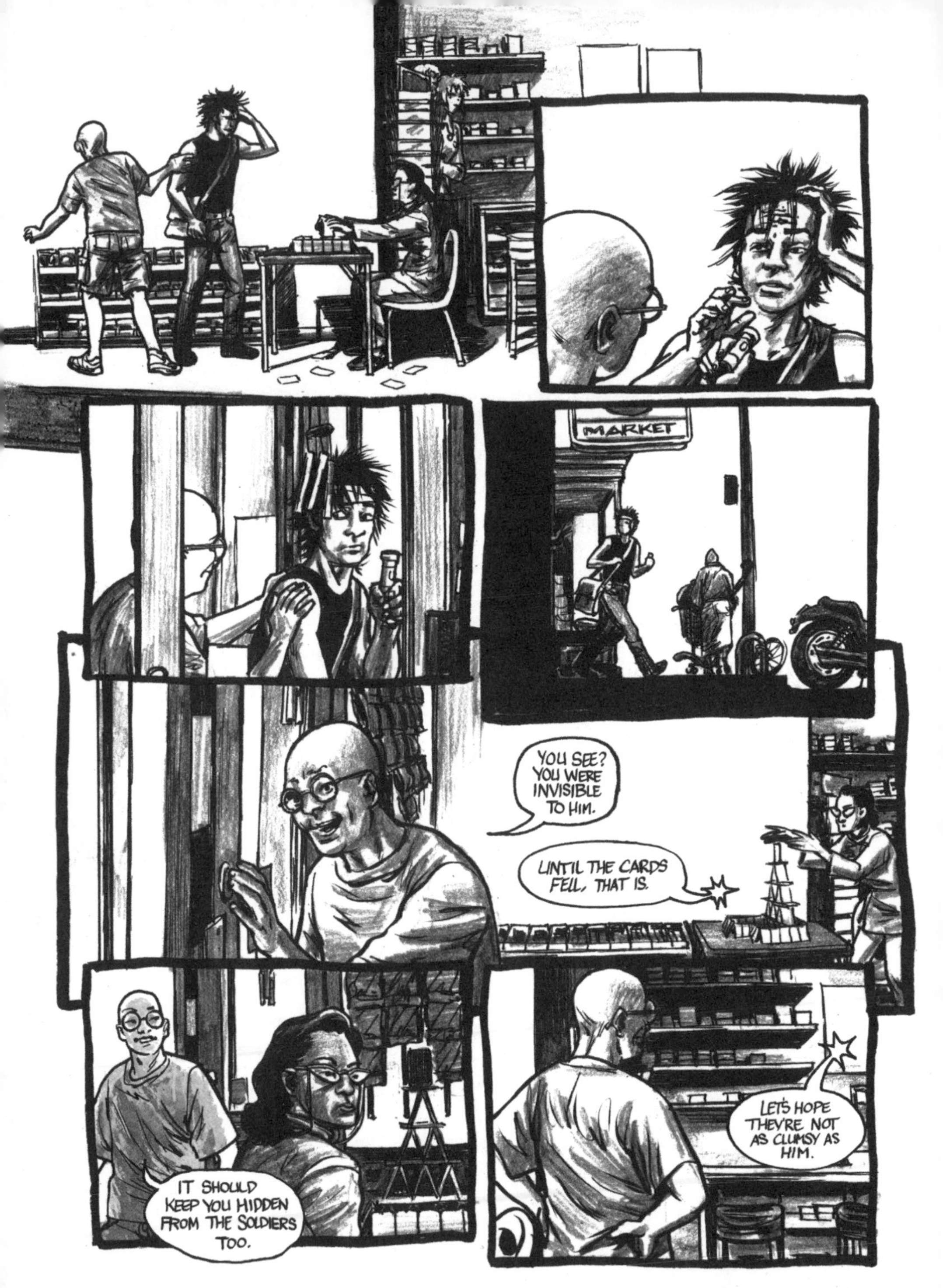
MARKET
YOU SEE? YOU WERE INVISIBLE TO HIM.
UNTIL THE CARDS FELL, THAT IS.
IT SHOULD KEEP YOU HIDDEN FROM THE SOLDIERS TOO.
LET'S HOPE THEY'RE NOT AS CLUMSY AS HIM.

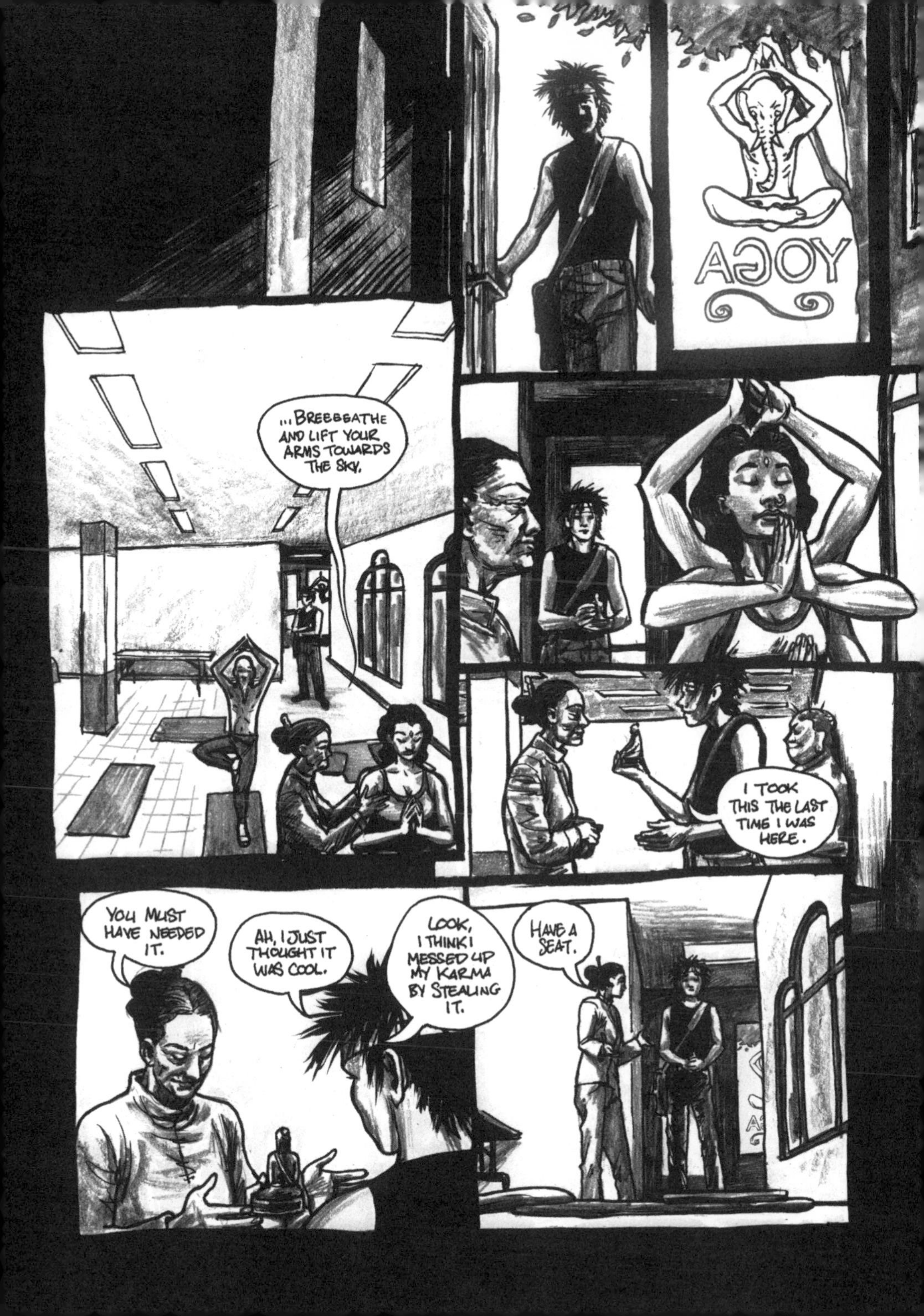
AYOG
YOGA
...BREEEEATHE AND LIFT YOUR ARMS TOWARDS THE SKY.
I TOOK THIS THE LAST TIME I WAS HERE.
YOU MUST HAVE NEEDED IT.
AH, I JUST THOUGHT IT WAS COOL.
LOOK, I THINK I MESSED UP MY KARMA BY STEALING IT.
HAVE A SEAT.

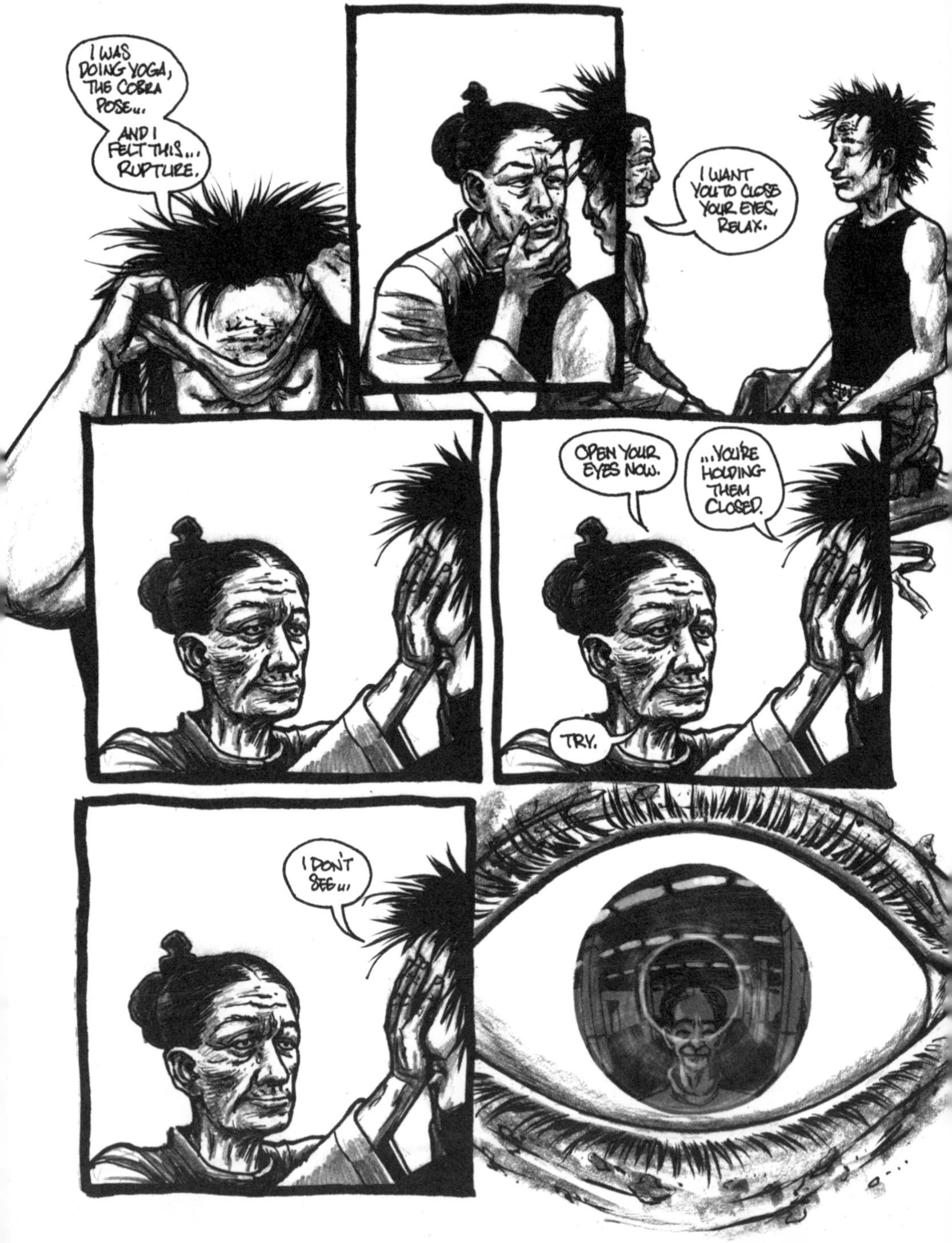
I WAS DOING YOGA, THE COBRA POSE...
AND I FELT THIS... RUPTURE.
I WANT YOU TO CLOSE YOUR EYES. RELAX.
OPEN YOUR EYES NOW.
...YOU'RE HOLDING THEM CLOSED.
TRY.
I DON'T SEE...

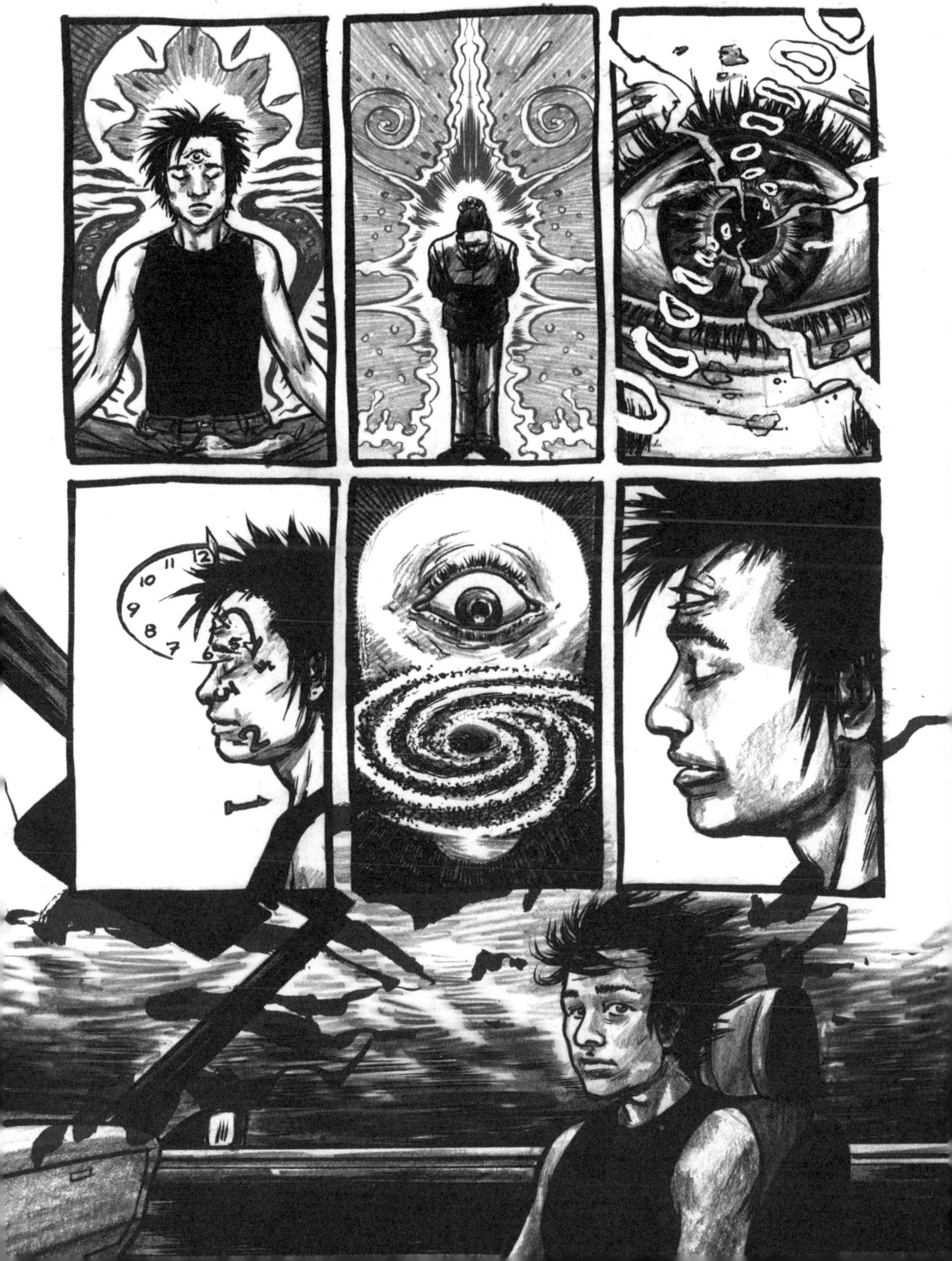

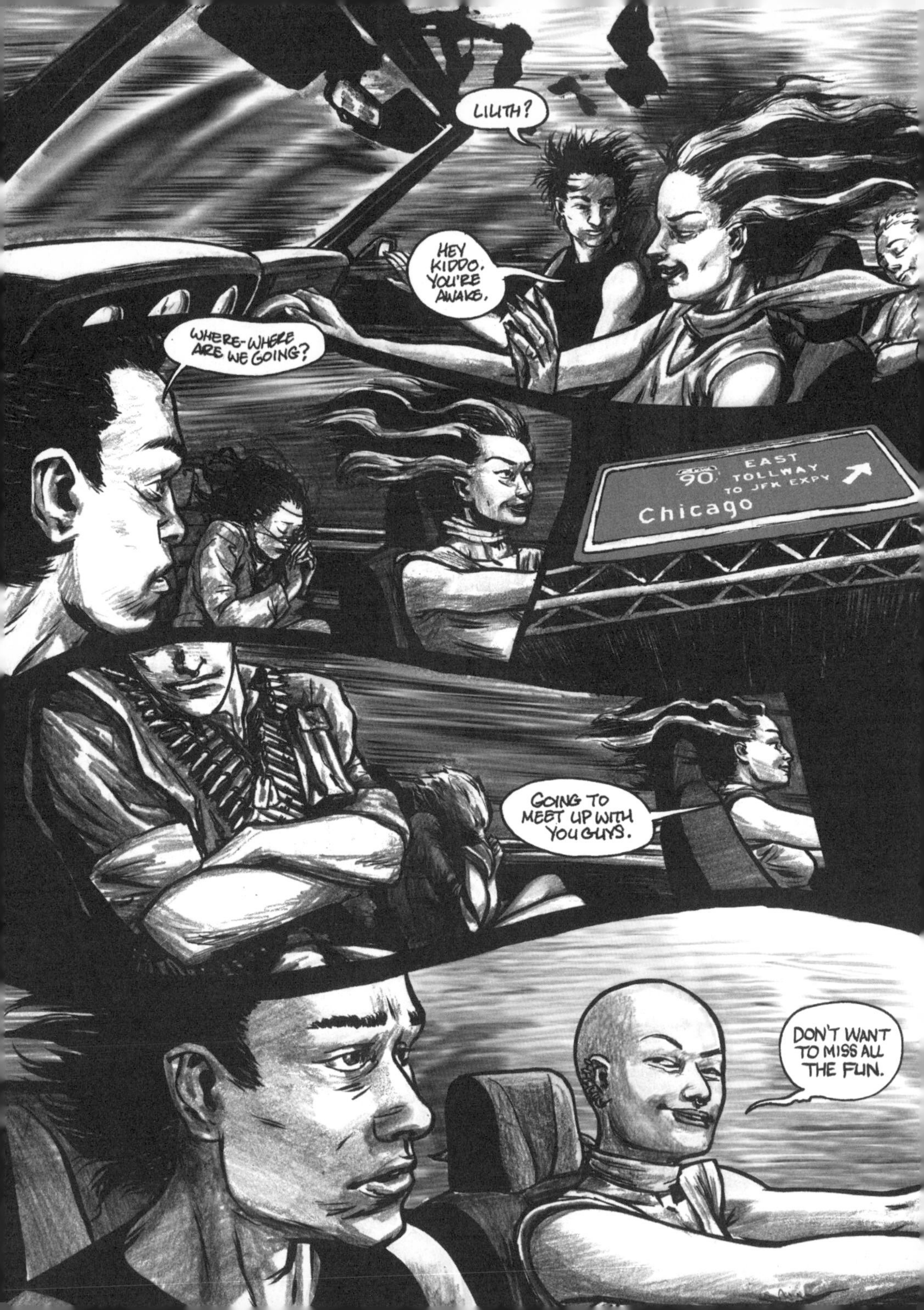

LILITH?
HEY KIDDO. YOU'RE AWAKE.
WHERE-WHERE ARE WE GOING?
EAST
90
TOLLWAY
TO JFK EXPY
Chicago
GOING TO MEET UP WITH YOU GUYS.
DON'T WANT TO MISS ALL THE FUN.

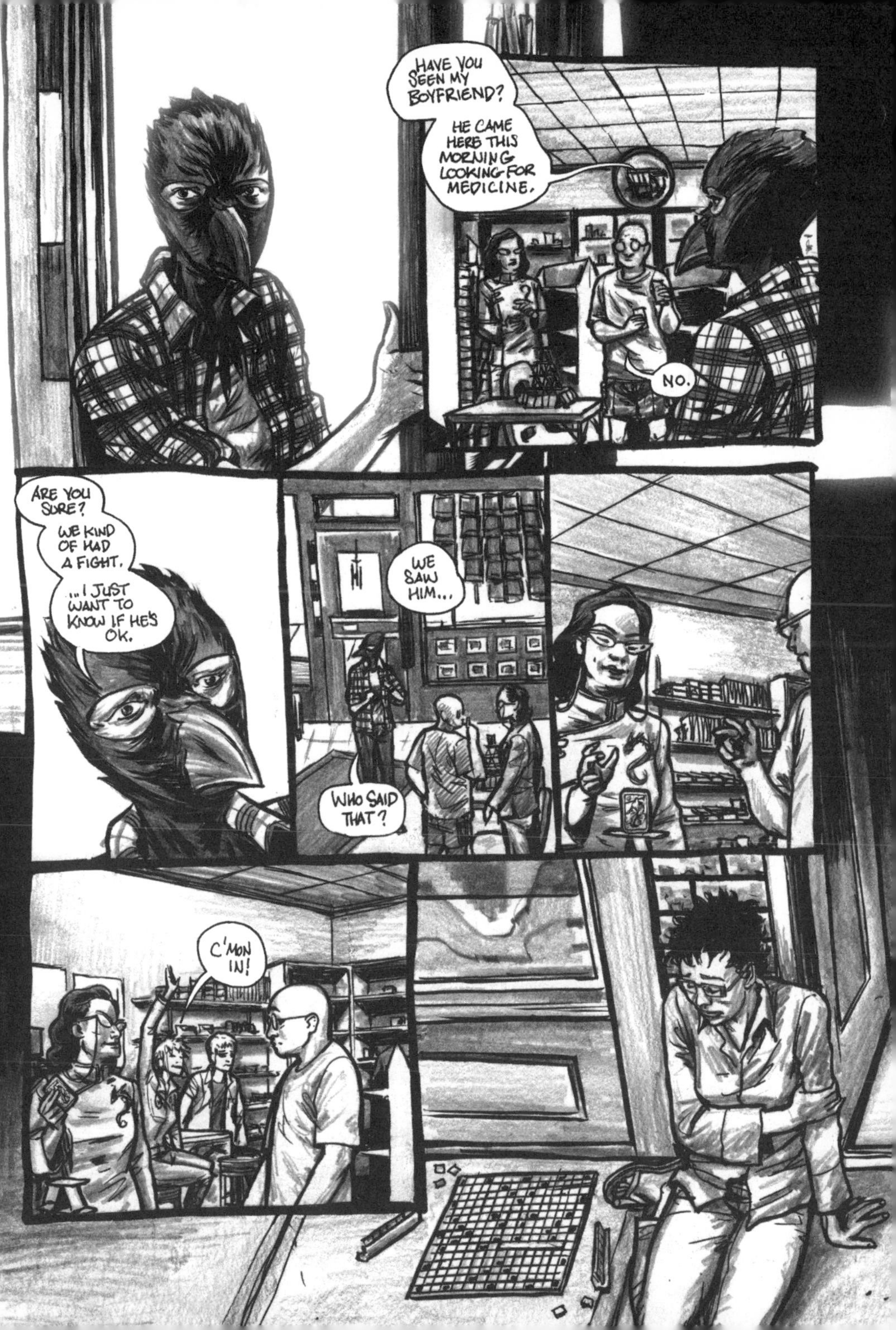
HAVE YOU SEEN MY BOYFRIEND?
HE CAME HERE THIS MORNING LOOKING FOR MEDICINE.
NO.
ARE YOU SURE?
WE KIND OF HAD A FIGHT.
...I JUST WANT TO KNOW IF HE'S OK.
WE SAW HIM...
WHO SAID THAT?
C'MON IN!

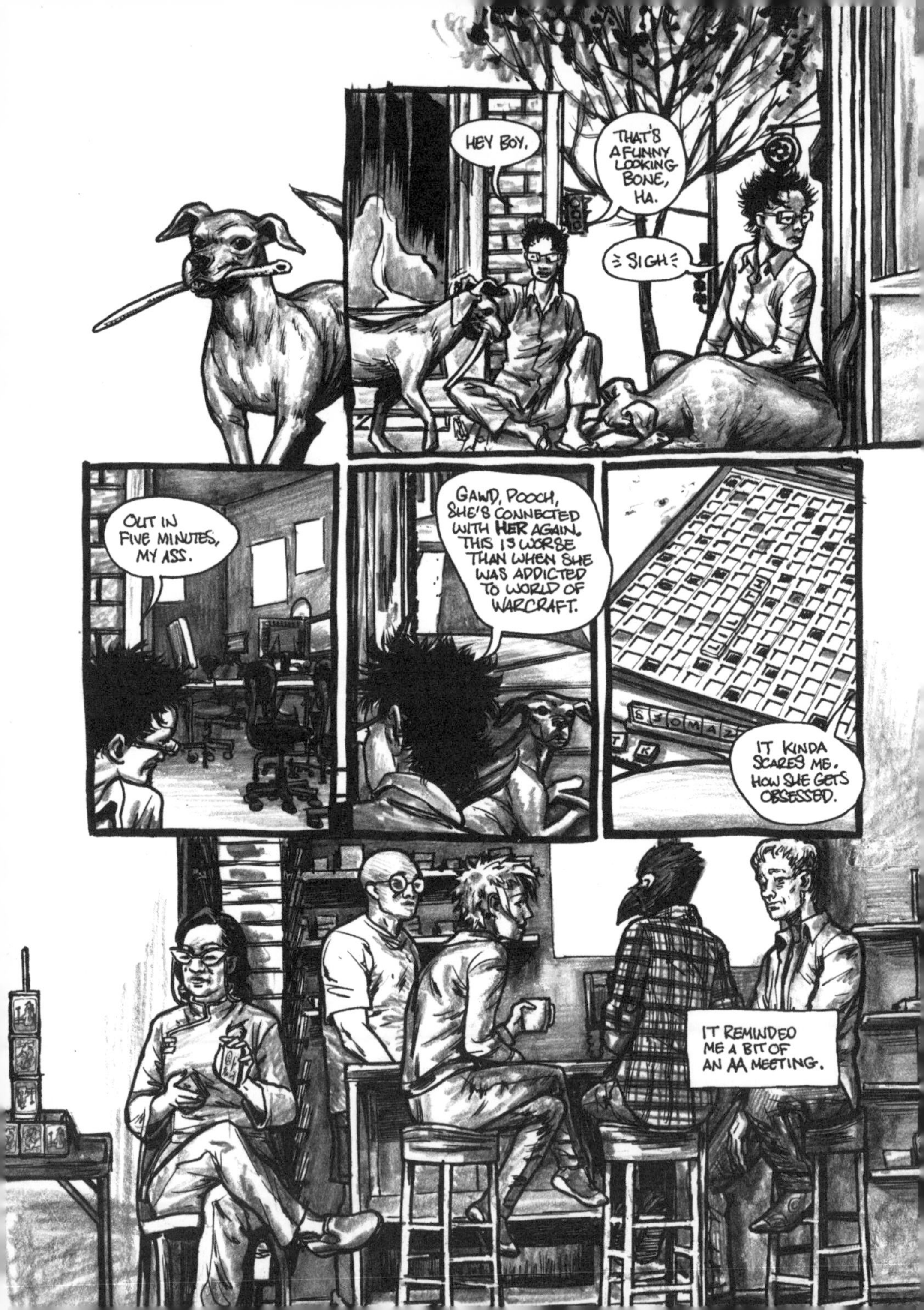
HEY BOY.
THAT'S A FUNNY LOOKING BONE, HA.
SIGH
OUT IN FIVE MINUTES, MY ASS.
GAWD, POOCH, SHE'S CONNECTED WITH HER AGAIN. THIS IS WORSE THAN WHEN SHE WAS ADDICTED TO WORLD OF WARCRAFT.
IT KINDA SCARES ME. HOW SHE GETS OBSESSED.
IT REMINDED ME A BIT OF AN AA MEETING.

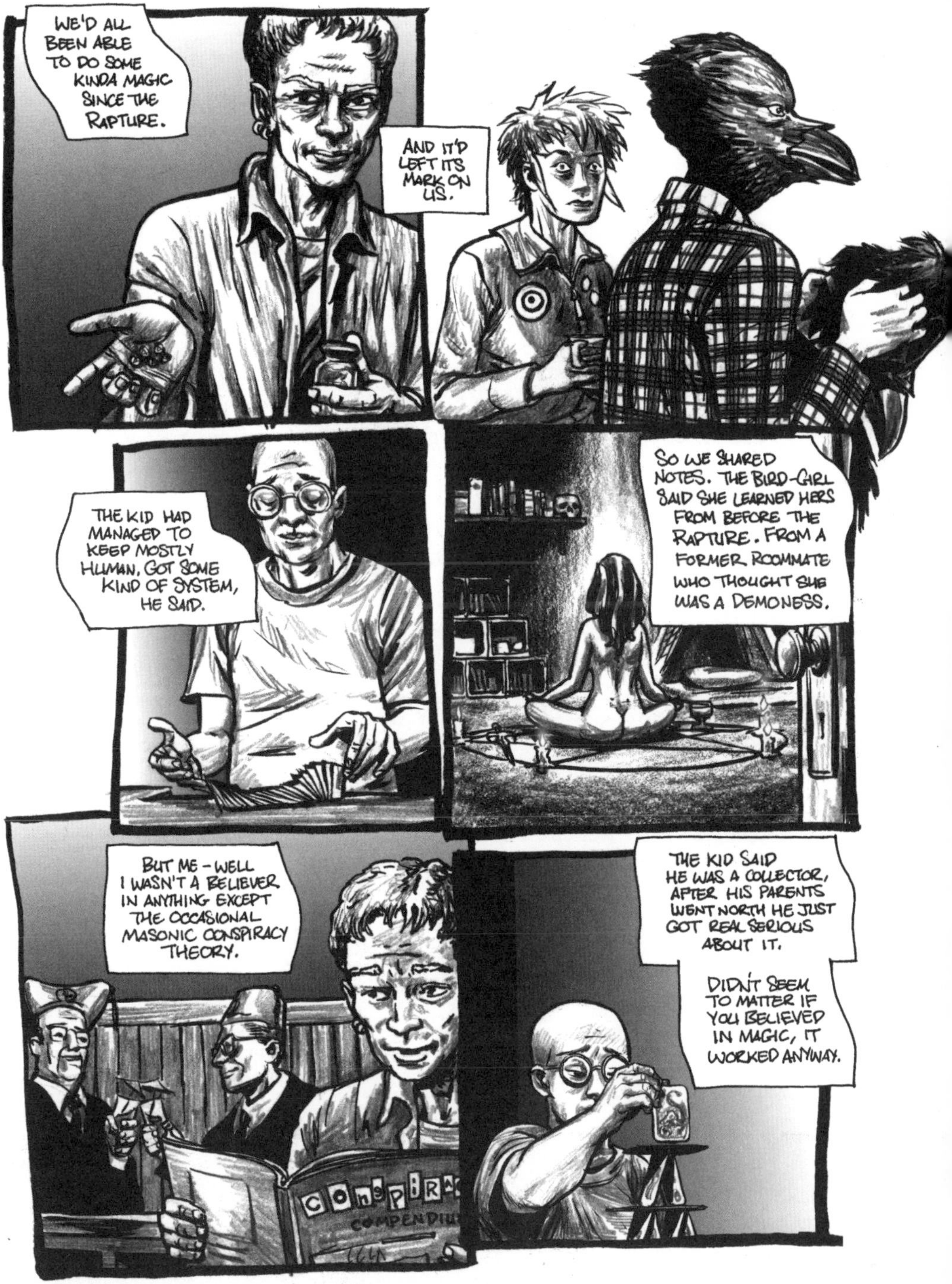
WE'D ALL BEEN ABLE TO DO SOME KINDA MAGIC SINCE THE RAPTURE.
AND IT'D LEFT ITS MARK ON US.
THE KID HAD MANAGED TO KEEP MOSTLY HUMAN, GOT SOME KIND OF SYSTEM, HE SAID.
SO WE SHARED NOTES. THE BIRD-GIRL SAID SHE LEARNED HERS FROM BEFORE THE RAPTURE. FROM A FORMER ROOMMATE WHO THOUGHT SHE WAS A DEMONESS.
BUT ME - WELL I WASN'T A BELIEVER IN ANYTHING EXCEPT THE OCCASIONAL MASONIC CONSPIRACY THEORY.
CONSPIRA
COMPENDIU
THE KID SAID HE WAS A COLLECTOR, AFTER HIS PARENTS WENT NORTH HE JUST GOT REAL SERIOUS ABOUT IT.
DIDN'T SEEM TO MATTER IF YOU BELIEVED IN MAGIC, IT WORKED ANYWAY.

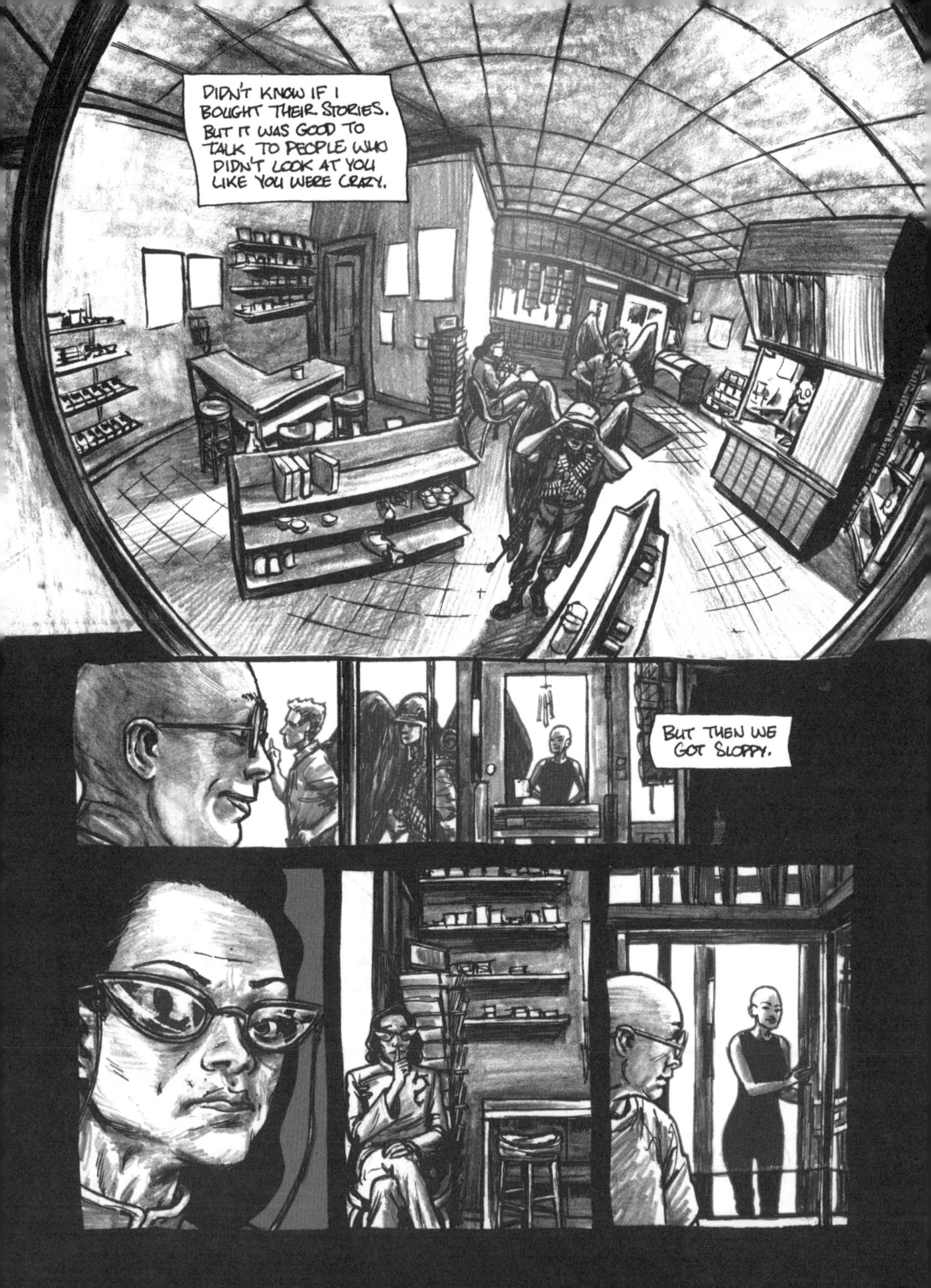
DIDN'T KNOW IF I BOUGHT THEIR STORIES. BUT IT WAS GOOD TO TALK TO PEOPLE WHO DIDN'T LOOK AT YOU LIKE YOU WERE CRAZY.
BUT THEN WE GOT SLOPPY.

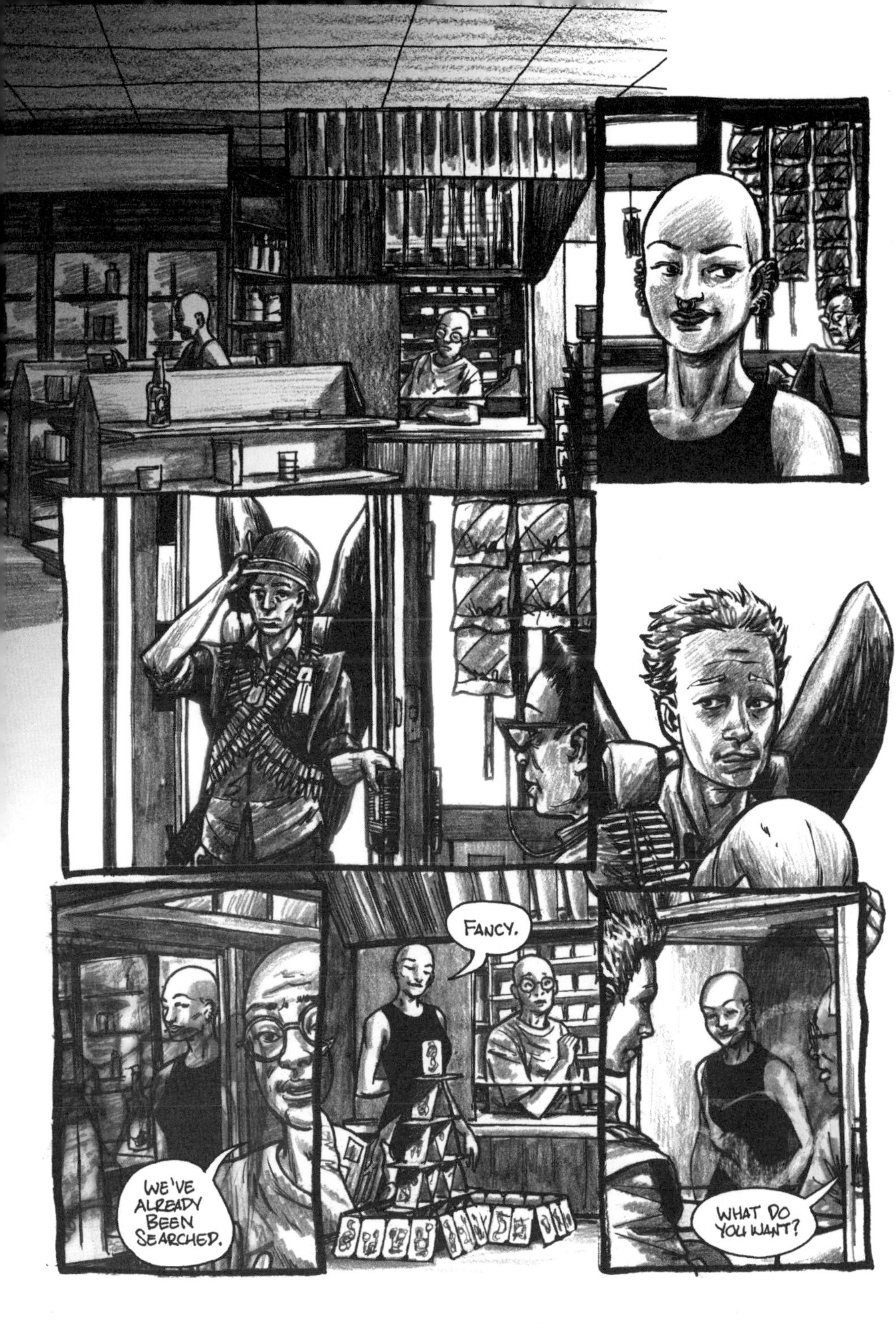
We've already been searched.
Fancy.
What do you want?

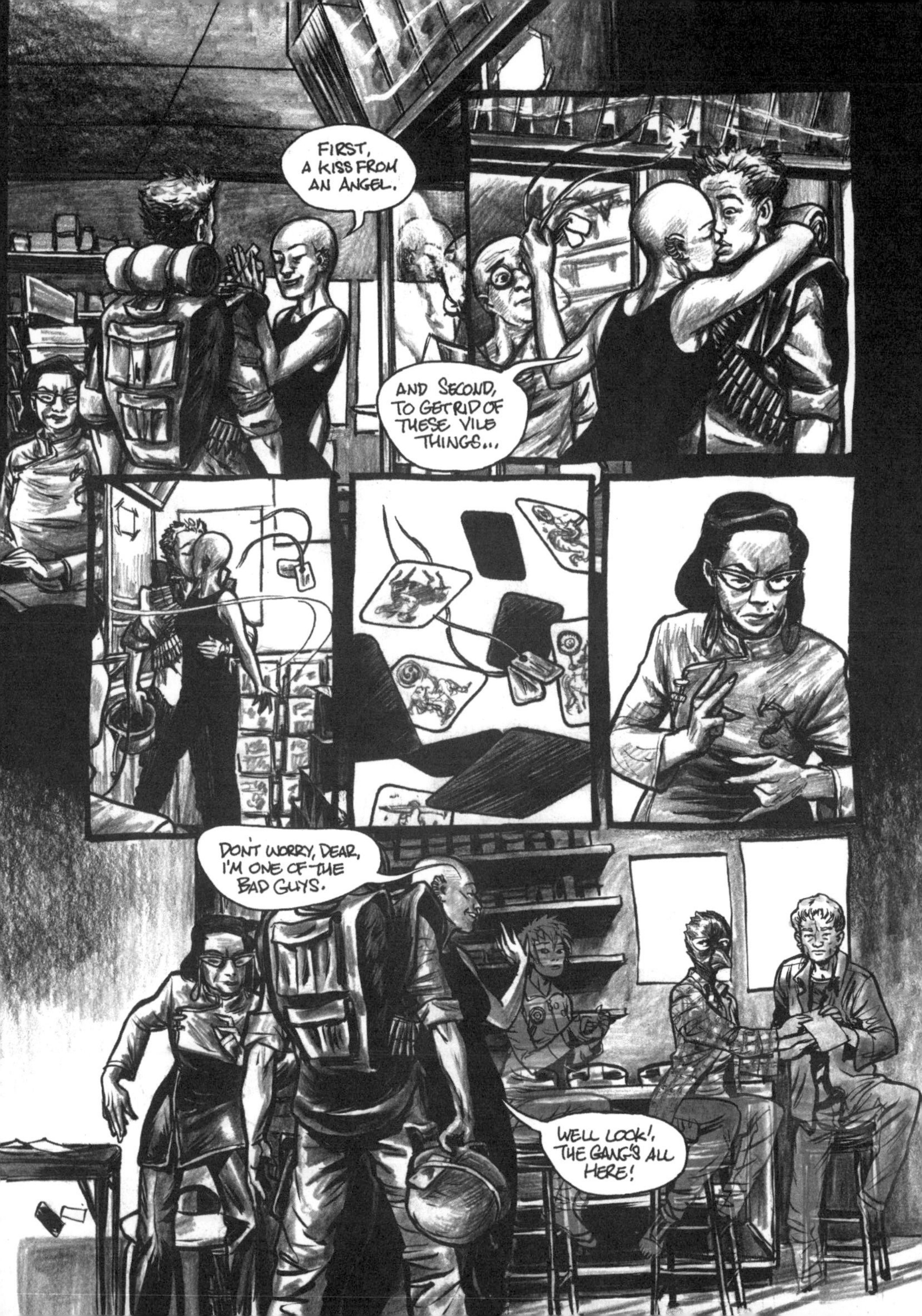
FIRST, A KISS FROM AN ANGEL.
AND SECOND, TO GET RID OF THESE VILE THINGS...
DON'T WORRY, DEAR, I'M ONE OF THE BAD GUYS.
WELL LOOK!, THE GANG'S ALL HERE!

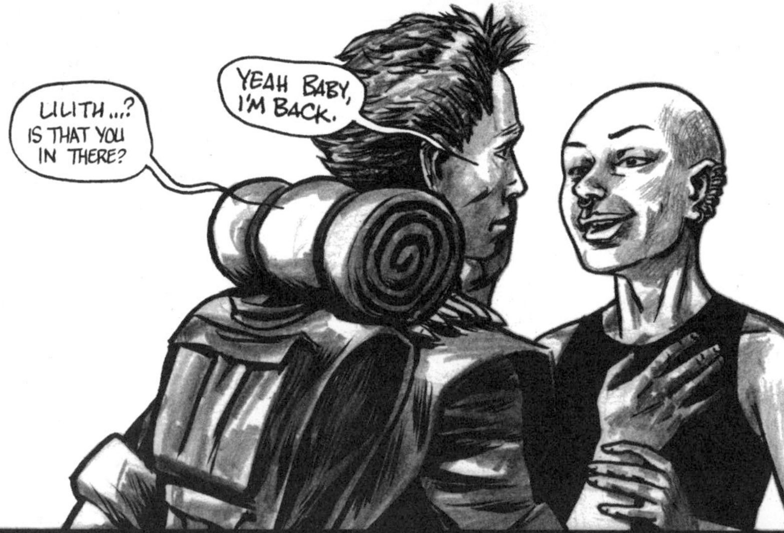
LILITH...?
IS THAT YOU
IN THERE?
YEAH BABY,
I'M BACK.

CHAPTER 6

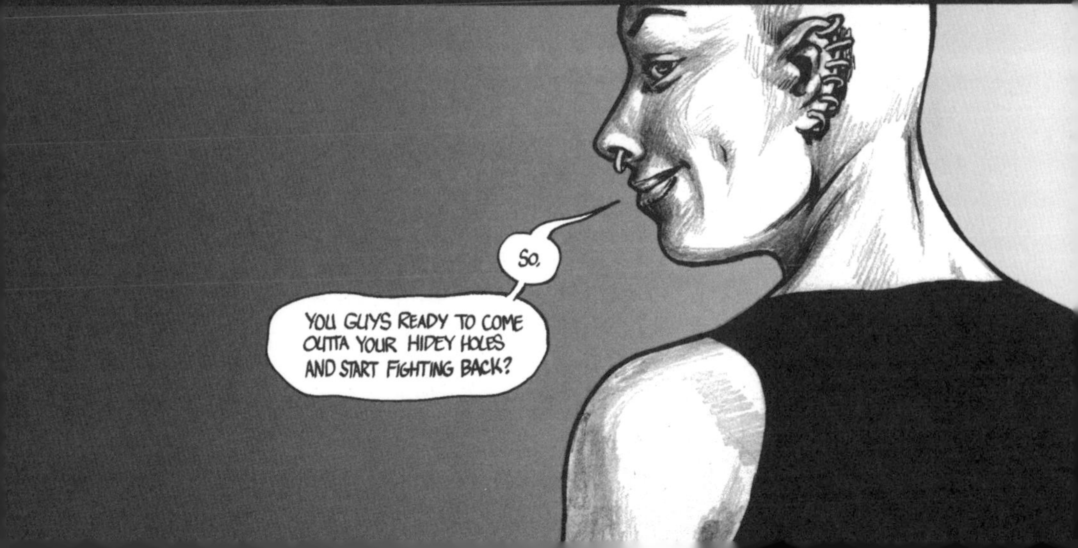
SO,
YOU GUYS READY TO COME
OUTTA YOUR HIDEY HOLES
AND START FIGHTING BACK?

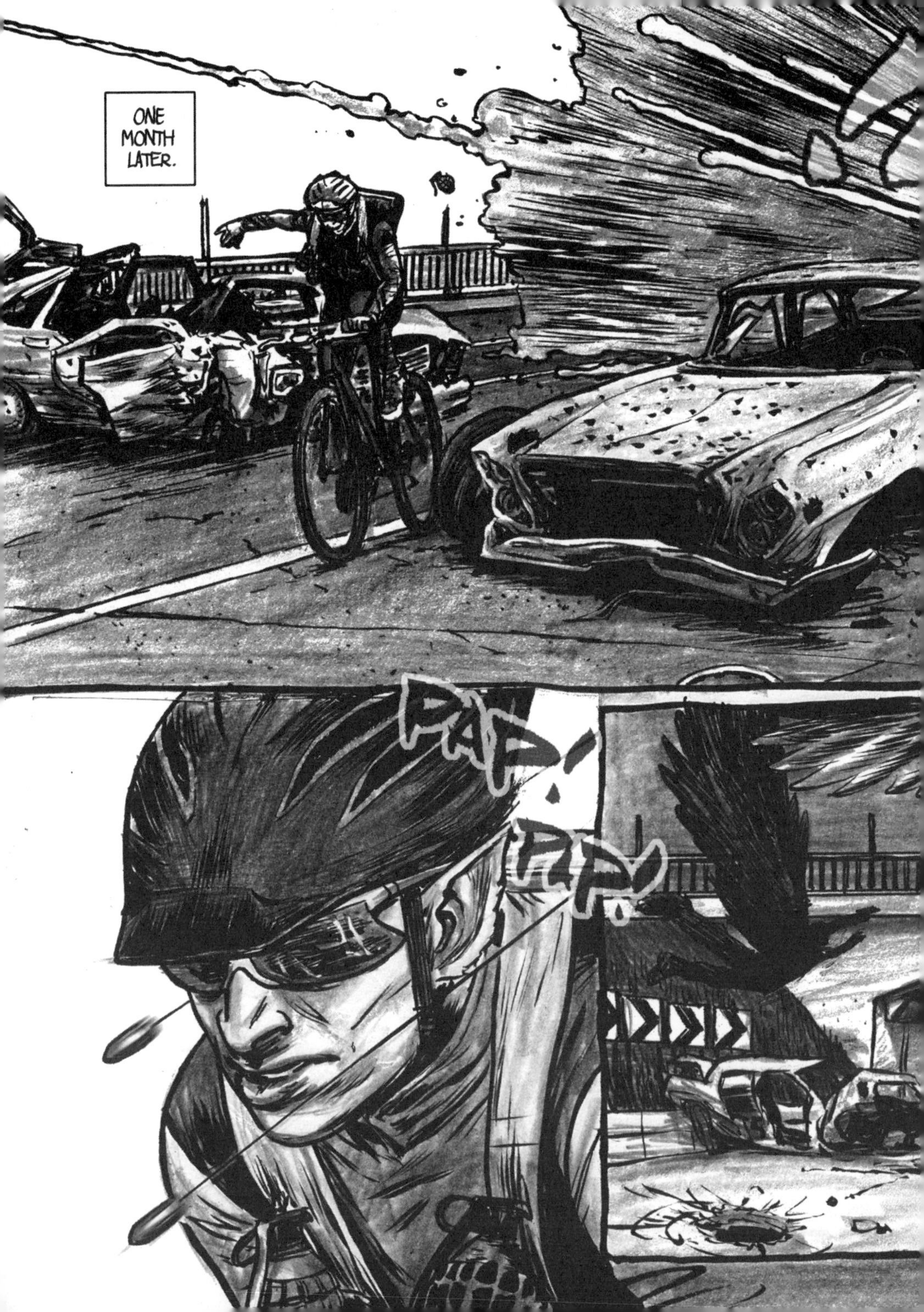
ONE MONTH LATER.
PAP!
PIP!

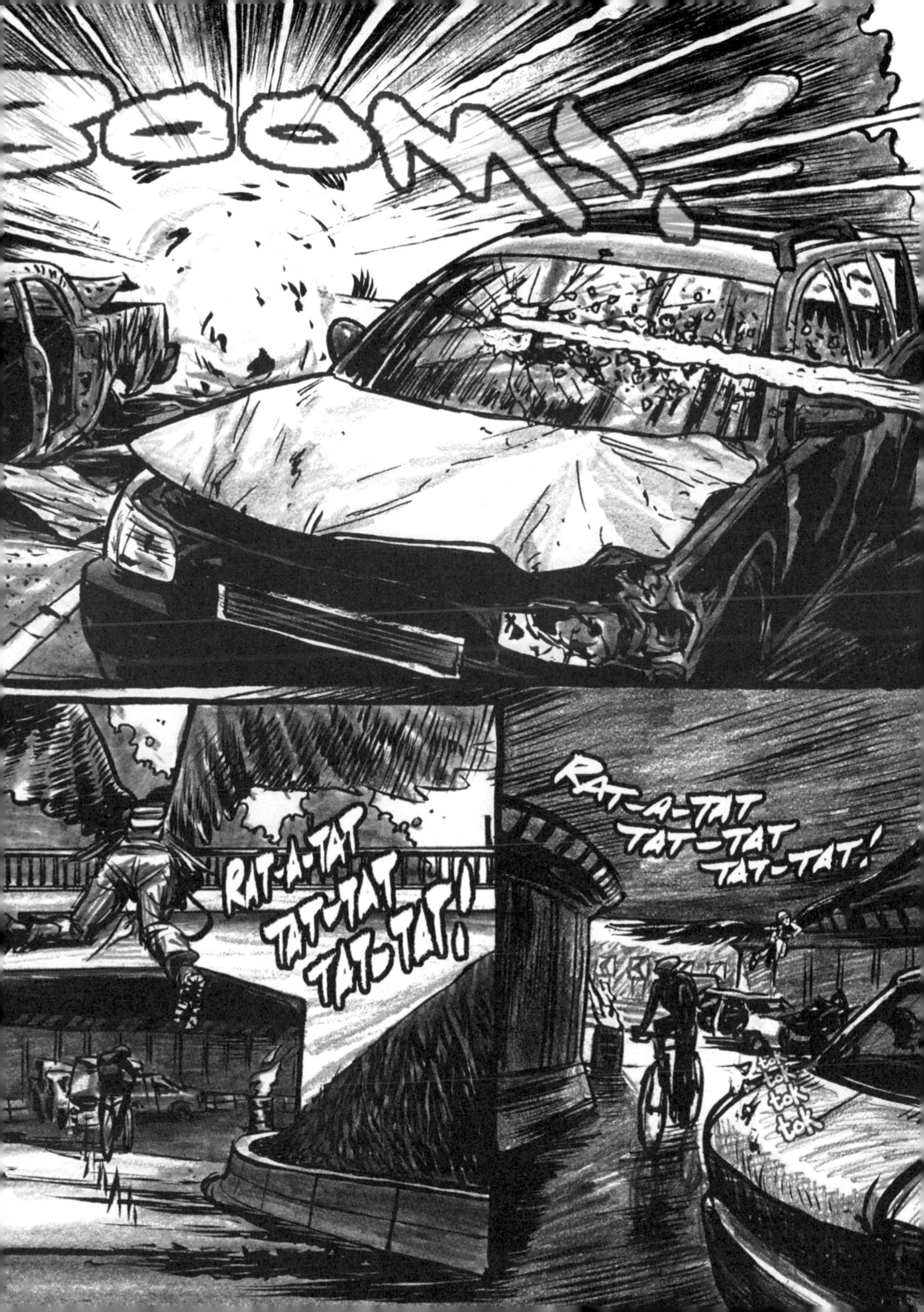
BOOOM!
RAT-A-TAT
TAT-TAT
TAT-TAT!
RAT-A-TAT
TAT-TAT
TAT-TAT!
tok
tok
tok
tok

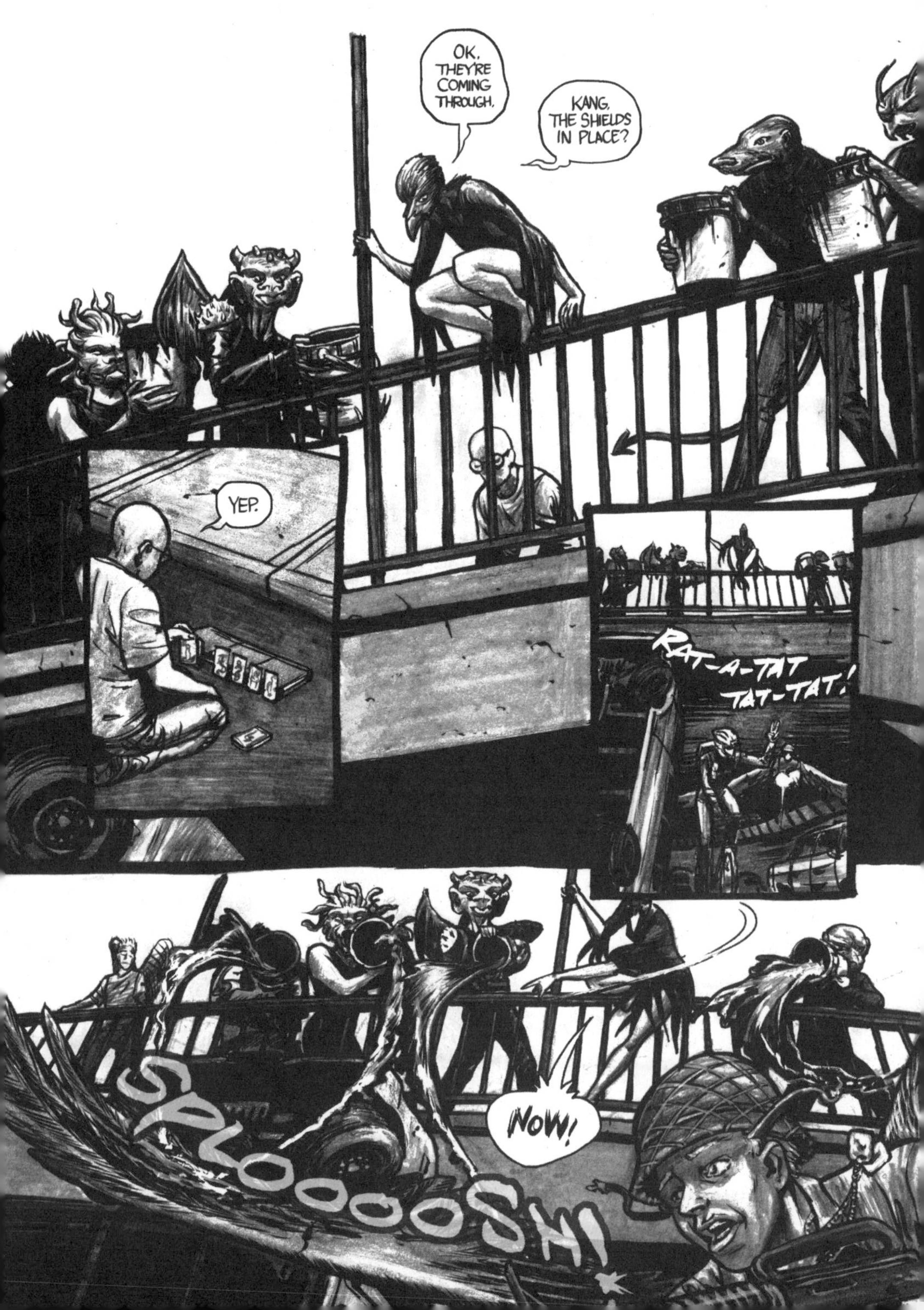
OK, THEY'RE COMING THROUGH.
KANG, THE SHIELDS IN PLACE?
YEP.
RAT-A-TAT TAT-TAT!
NOW!
SPLOOOOSH!

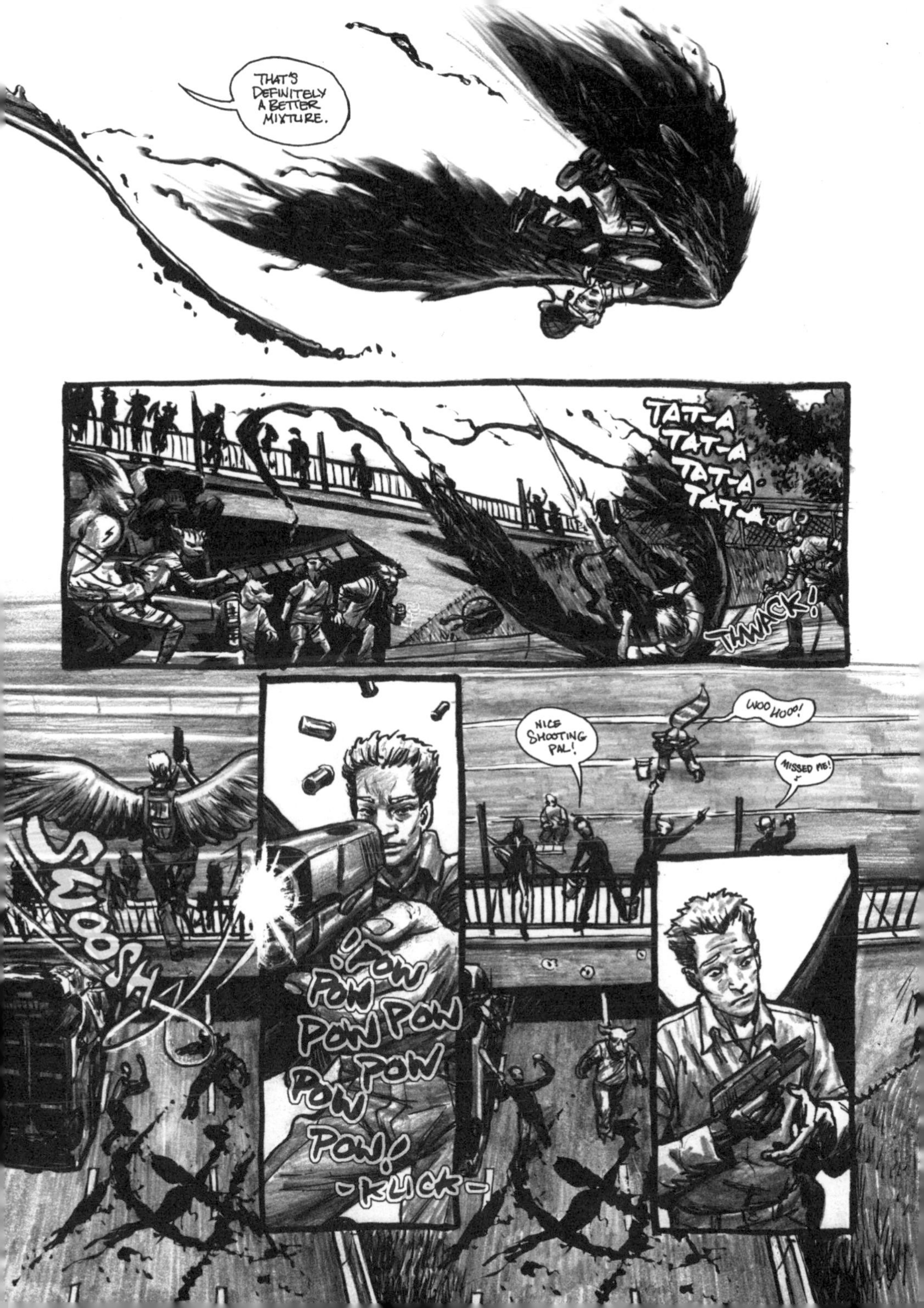
THAT'S DEFINITELY A BETTER MIXTURE.
TAT-A TAT-A TAT-A TAT-A
THWACK!
SWOOSH
POW POW POW POW POW POW POW POW!
-KLICK-
NICE SHOOTING PAL!
WOO HOO!
MISSED ME!

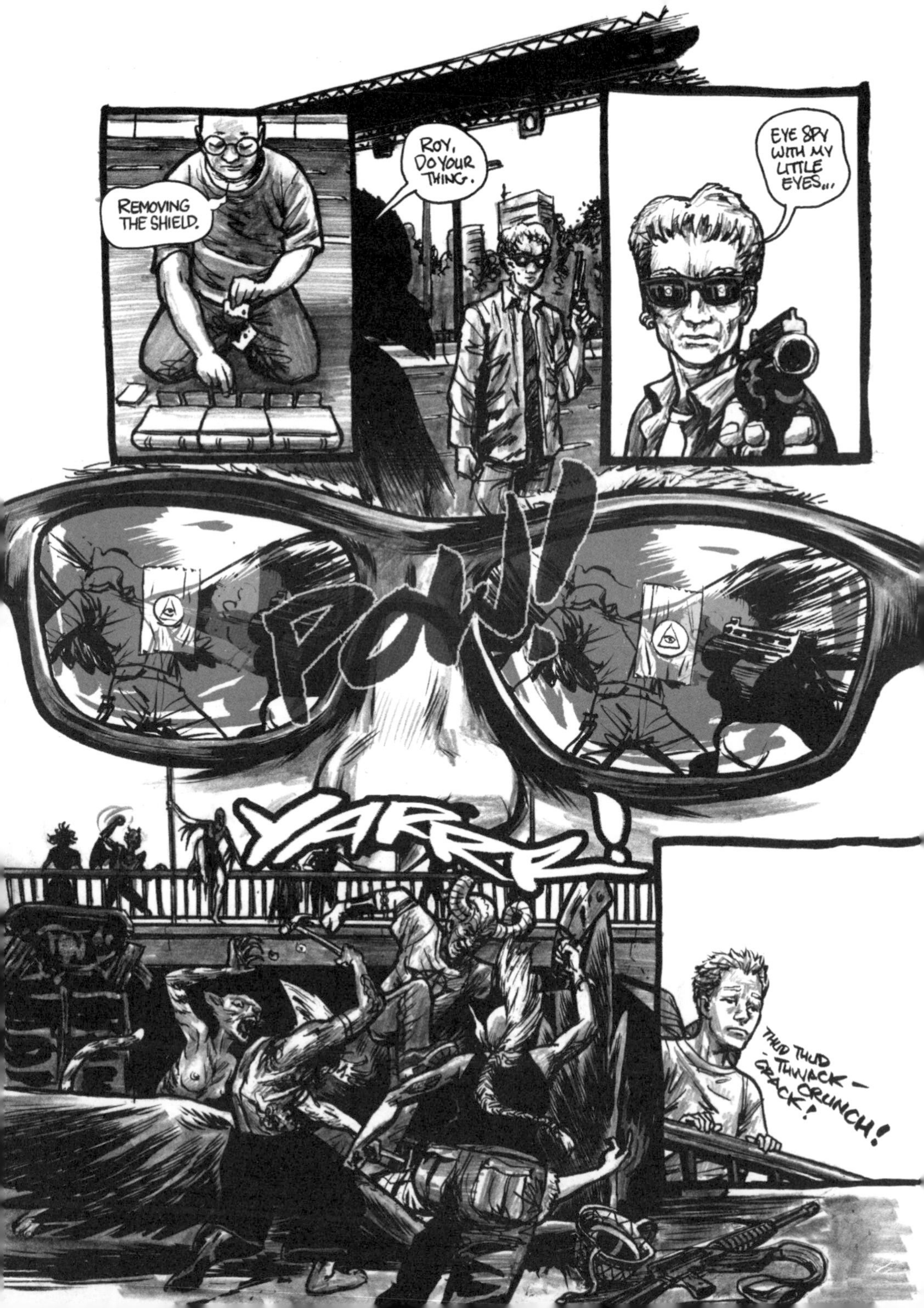
REMOVING THE SHIELD.
ROY, DO YOUR THING.
EYE SPY WITH MY LITTLE EYES...
POW!
YARRR!
THUD THUD THWACK - CRUNCH! CRACK!

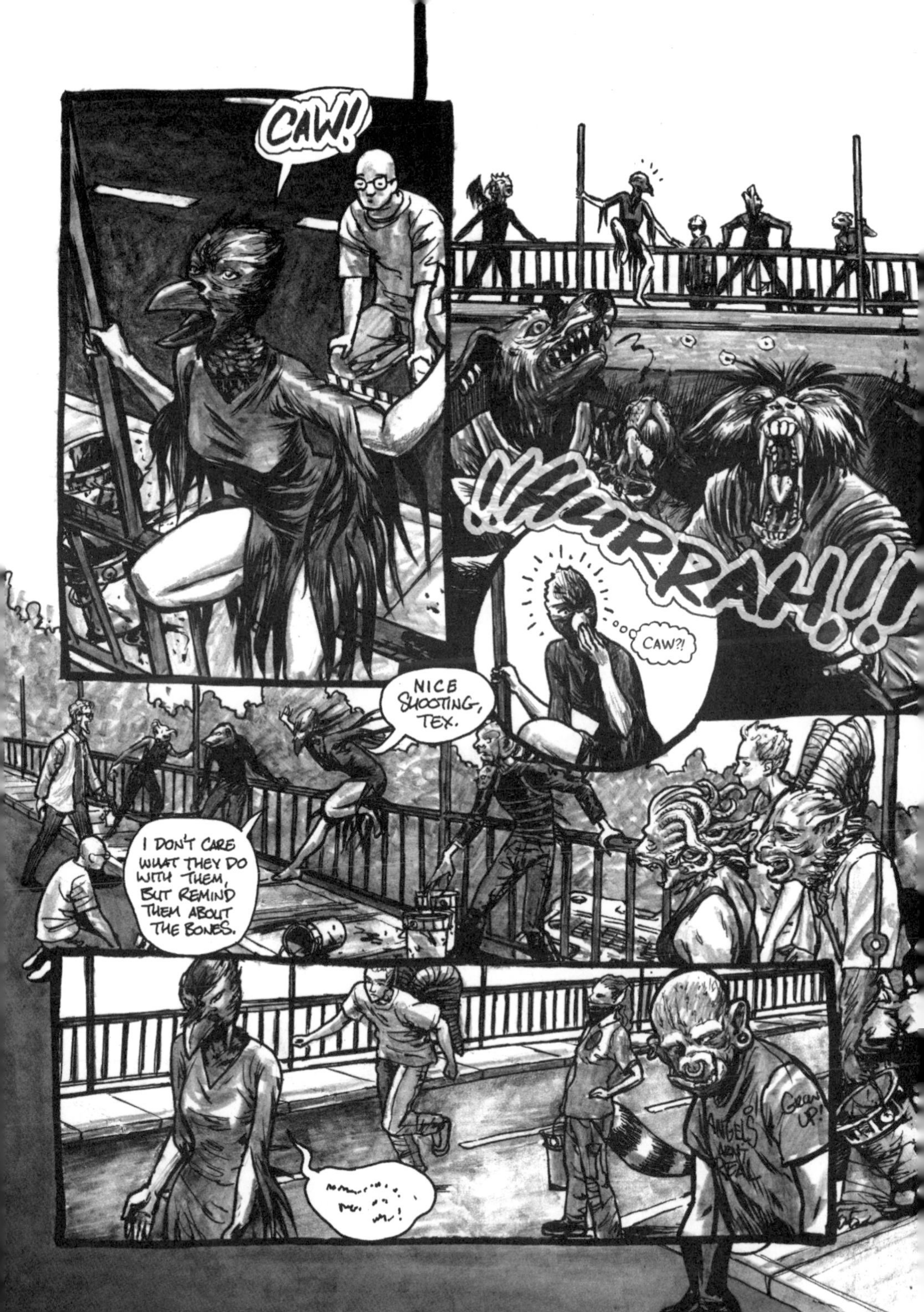
CAW!
!!WURRAH!!
CAW?!
NICE SHOOTING, TEX.
I DON'T CARE WHAT THEY DO WITH THEM, BUT REMIND THEM ABOUT THE BONES.
GROW UP!

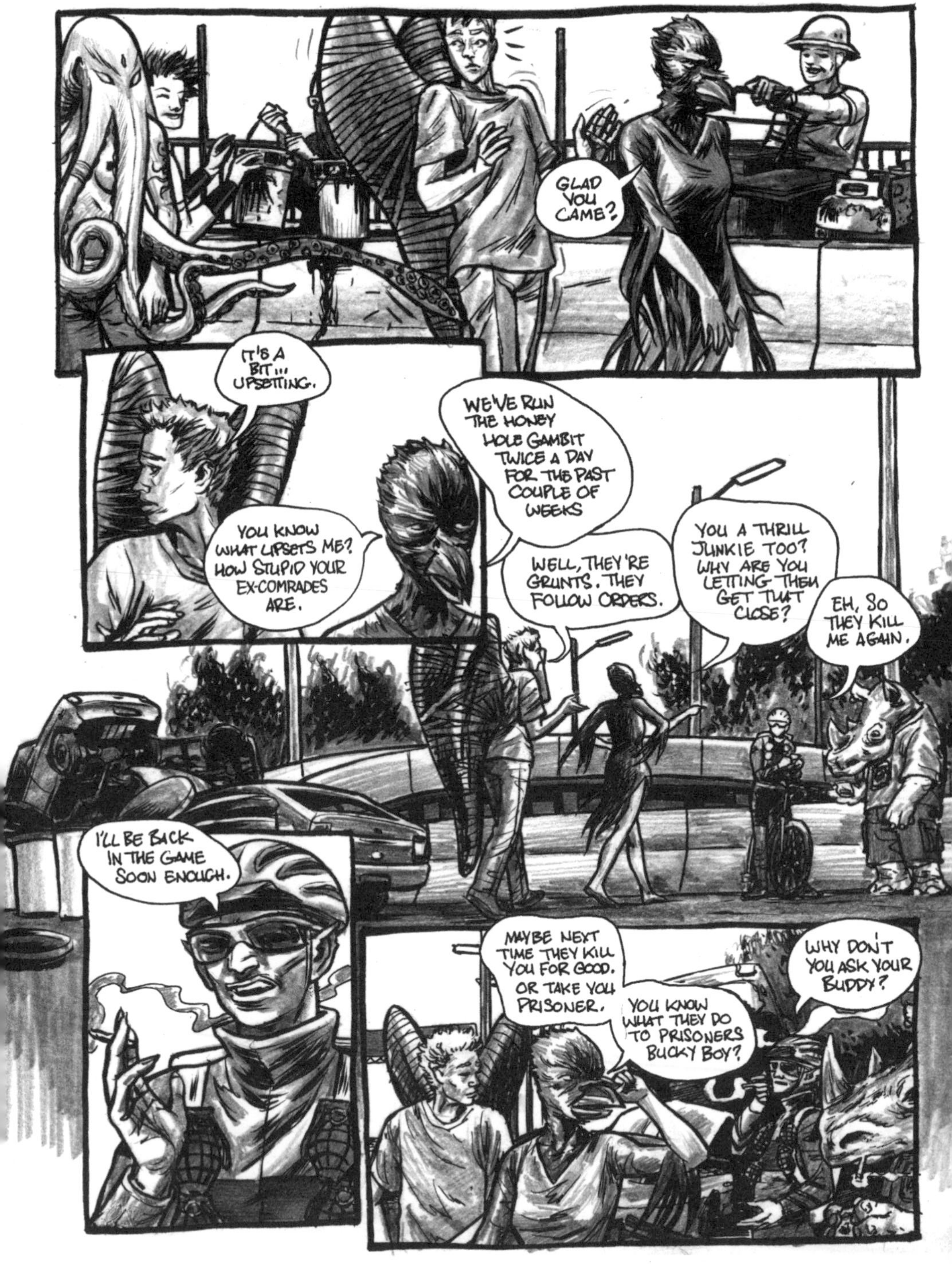
GLAD YOU CAME?
IT'S A BIT... UPSETTING.
YOU KNOW WHAT UPSETS ME? HOW STUPID YOUR EX-COMRADES ARE.
WE'VE RUN THE HONEY HOLE GAMBIT TWICE A DAY FOR THE PAST COUPLE OF WEEKS
WELL, THEY'RE GRUNTS. THEY FOLLOW ORDERS.
YOU A THRILL JUNKIE TOO? WHY ARE YOU LETTING THEM GET THAT CLOSE?
EH, SO THEY KILL ME AGAIN.
I'LL BE BACK IN THE GAME SOON ENOUGH.
MAYBE NEXT TIME THEY KILL YOU FOR GOOD. OR TAKE YOU PRISONER.
YOU KNOW WHAT THEY DO TO PRISONERS BUCKY BOY?
WHY DON'T YOU ASK YOUR BUDDY?

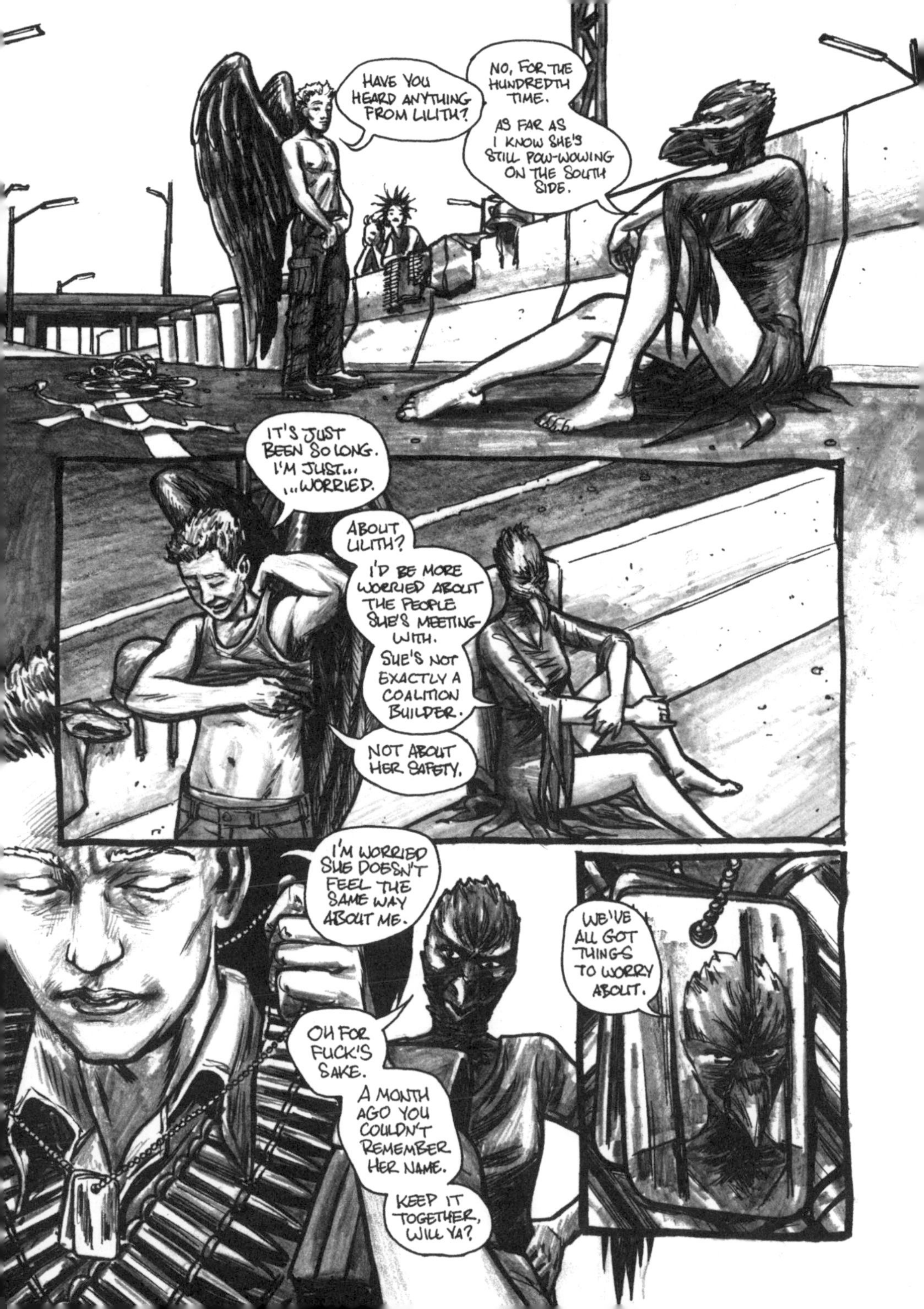
HAVE YOU HEARD ANYTHING FROM LILITH?
NO, FOR THE HUNDREDTH TIME.
AS FAR AS I KNOW SHE'S STILL POW-WOWING ON THE SOUTH SIDE.
IT'S JUST BEEN SO LONG. I'M JUST... ...WORRIED.
ABOUT LILITH?
I'D BE MORE WORRIED ABOUT THE PEOPLE SHE'S MEETING WITH.
SHE'S NOT EXACTLY A COALITION BUILDER.
NOT ABOUT HER SAFETY.
I'M WORRIED SHE DOESN'T FEEL THE SAME WAY ABOUT ME.
WE'VE ALL GOT THINGS TO WORRY ABOUT.
OH FOR FUCK'S SAKE.
A MONTH AGO YOU COULDN'T REMEMBER HER NAME.
KEEP IT TOGETHER, WILL YA?

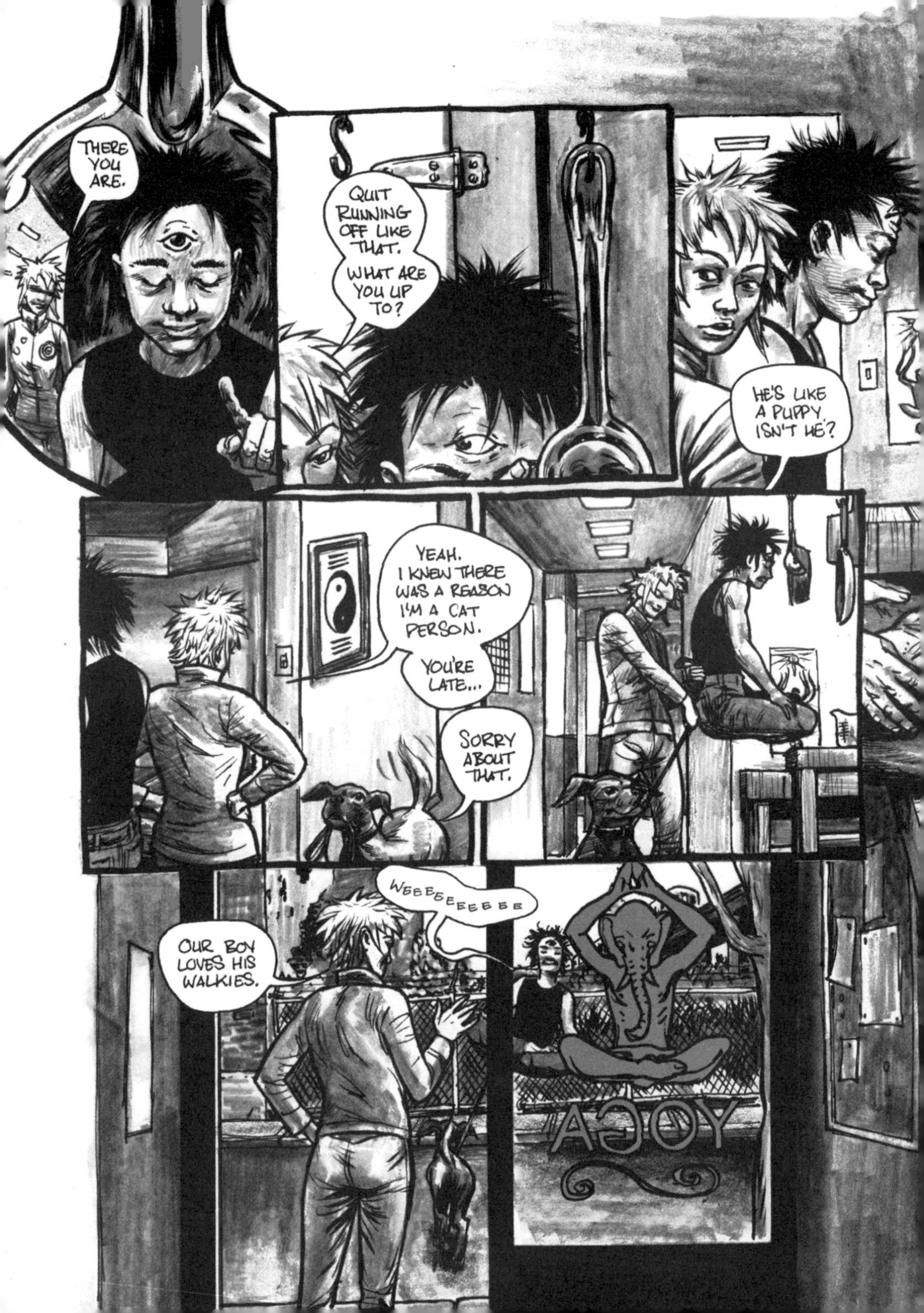
THERE YOU ARE.
QUIT RUNNING OFF LIKE THAT.
WHAT ARE YOU UP TO?
HE'S LIKE A PUPPY, ISN'T HE?
YEAH. I KNEW THERE WAS A REASON I'M A CAT PERSON.
YOU'RE LATE...
SORRY ABOUT THAT.
OUR BOY LOVES HIS WALKIES.
WEEEEEEEEEEEE
YOGA

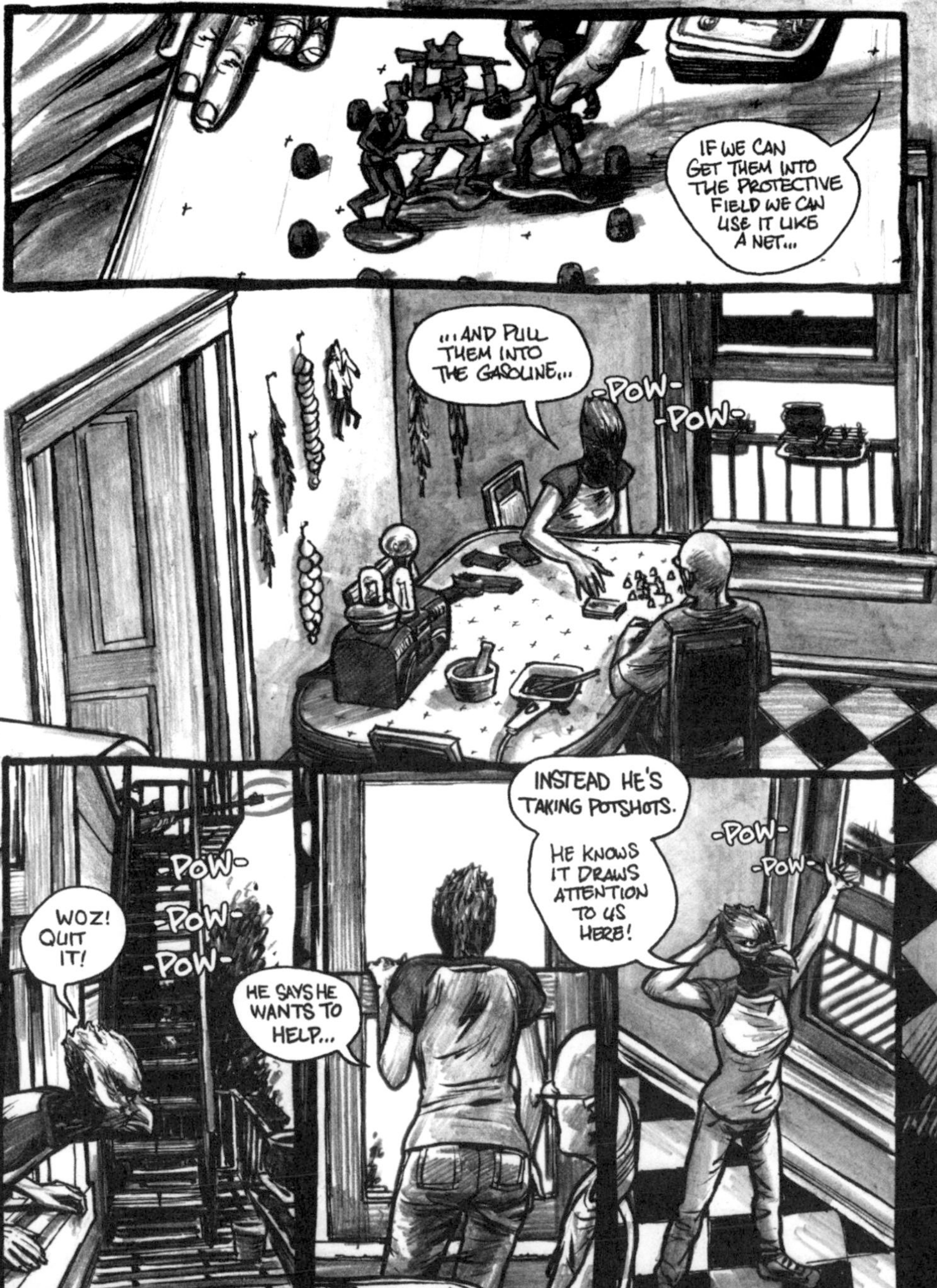
IF WE CAN GET THEM INTO THE PROTECTIVE FIELD WE CAN USE IT LIKE A NET...
...AND PULL THEM INTO THE GASOLINE...
-POW-
-POW-
-POW-
-POW-
-POW-
WOZ! QUIT IT!
HE SAYS HE WANTS TO HELP...
INSTEAD HE'S TAKING POTSHOTS.
HE KNOWS IT DRAWS ATTENTION TO US HERE!
-POW-
-POW-

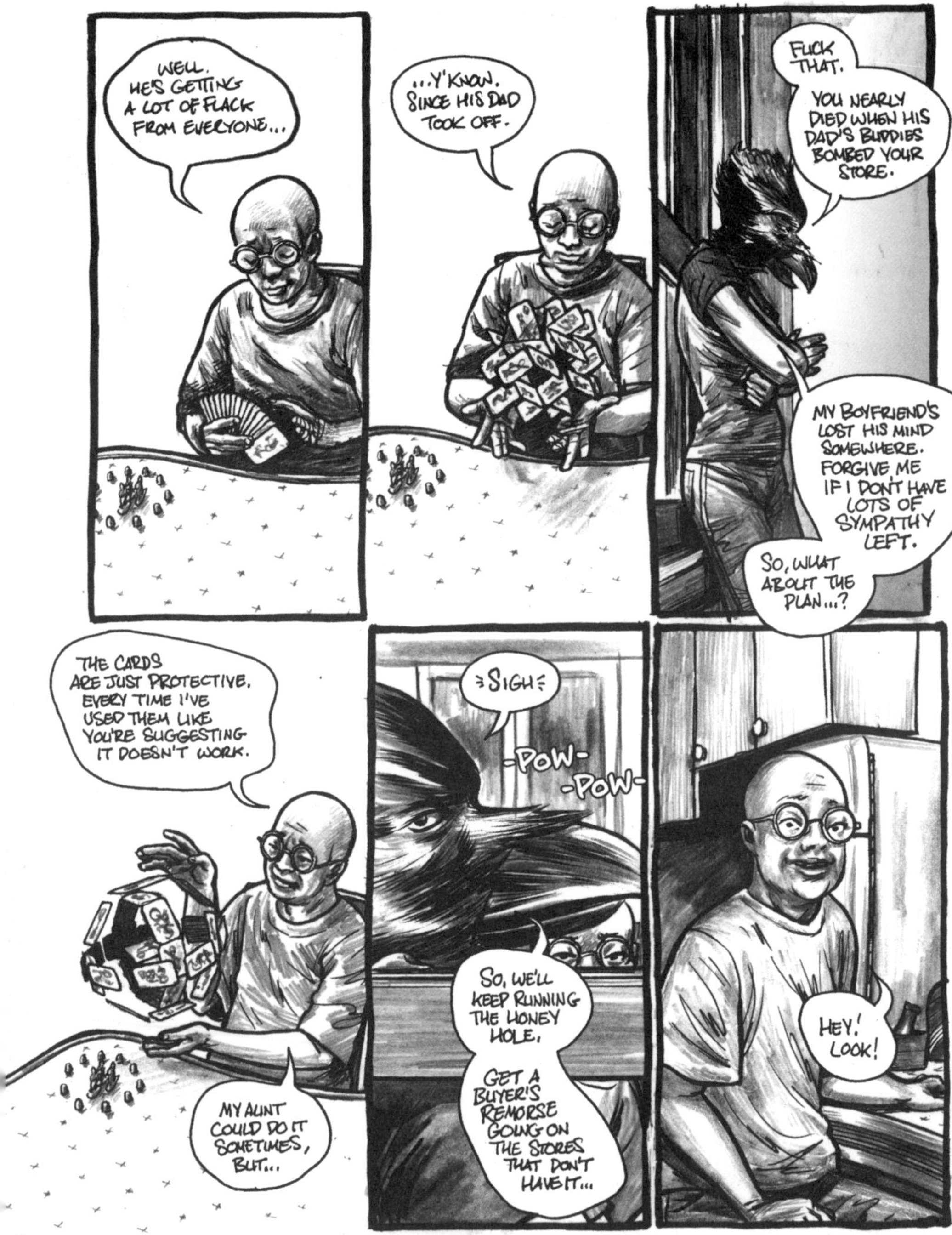
WELL. HE'S GETTING A LOT OF FLACK FROM EVERYONE...
...Y'KNOW. SINCE HIS DAD TOOK OFF.
FUCK THAT.
YOU NEARLY DIED WHEN HIS DAD'S BUDDIES BOMBED YOUR STORE.
MY BOYFRIEND'S LOST HIS MIND SOMEWHERE. FORGIVE ME IF I DON'T HAVE LOTS OF SYMPATHY LEFT.
SO, WHAT ABOUT THE PLAN...?
THE CARDS ARE JUST PROTECTIVE. EVERY TIME I'VE USED THEM LIKE YOU'RE SUGGESTING IT DOESN'T WORK.
MY AUNT COULD DO IT SOMETIMES, BUT...
SIGH
-POW-
-POW-
SO, WE'LL KEEP RUNNING THE HONEY HOLE.
GET A BUYER'S REMORSE GOING ON THE STORES THAT DON'T HAVE IT...
HEY! LOOK!

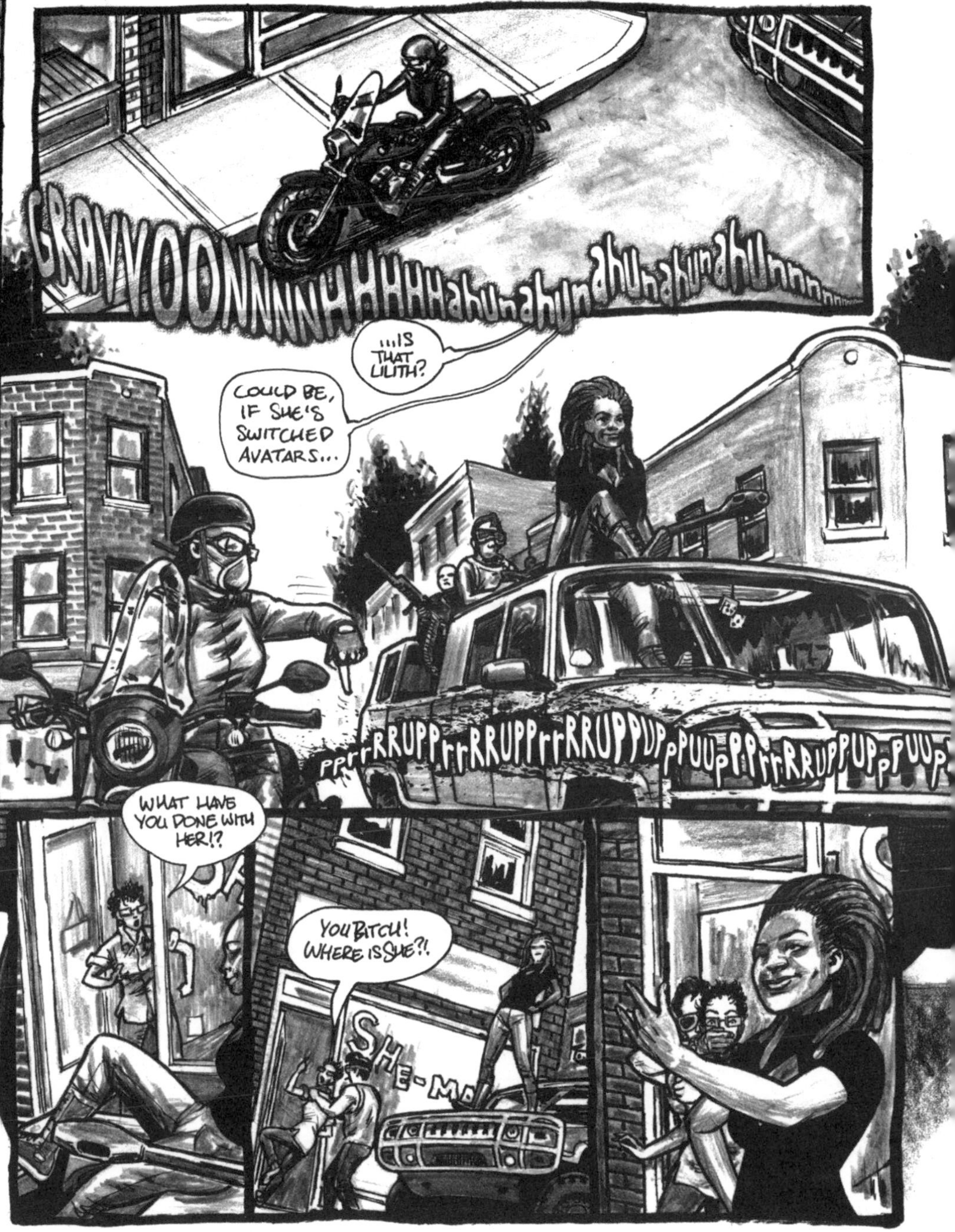
GRAVVOONNNNHHHHahunahunahunahunahunnnn
...IS THAT LILITH?
COULD BE, IF SHE'S SWITCHED AVATARS...
pprrRRUPPrrRRUPPrrRRUPPUPpPUUpPPrrRRUPPUPpPUUP
WHAT HAVE YOU DONE WITH HER!?
YOU BITCH! WHERE IS SHE?!
SHE-M

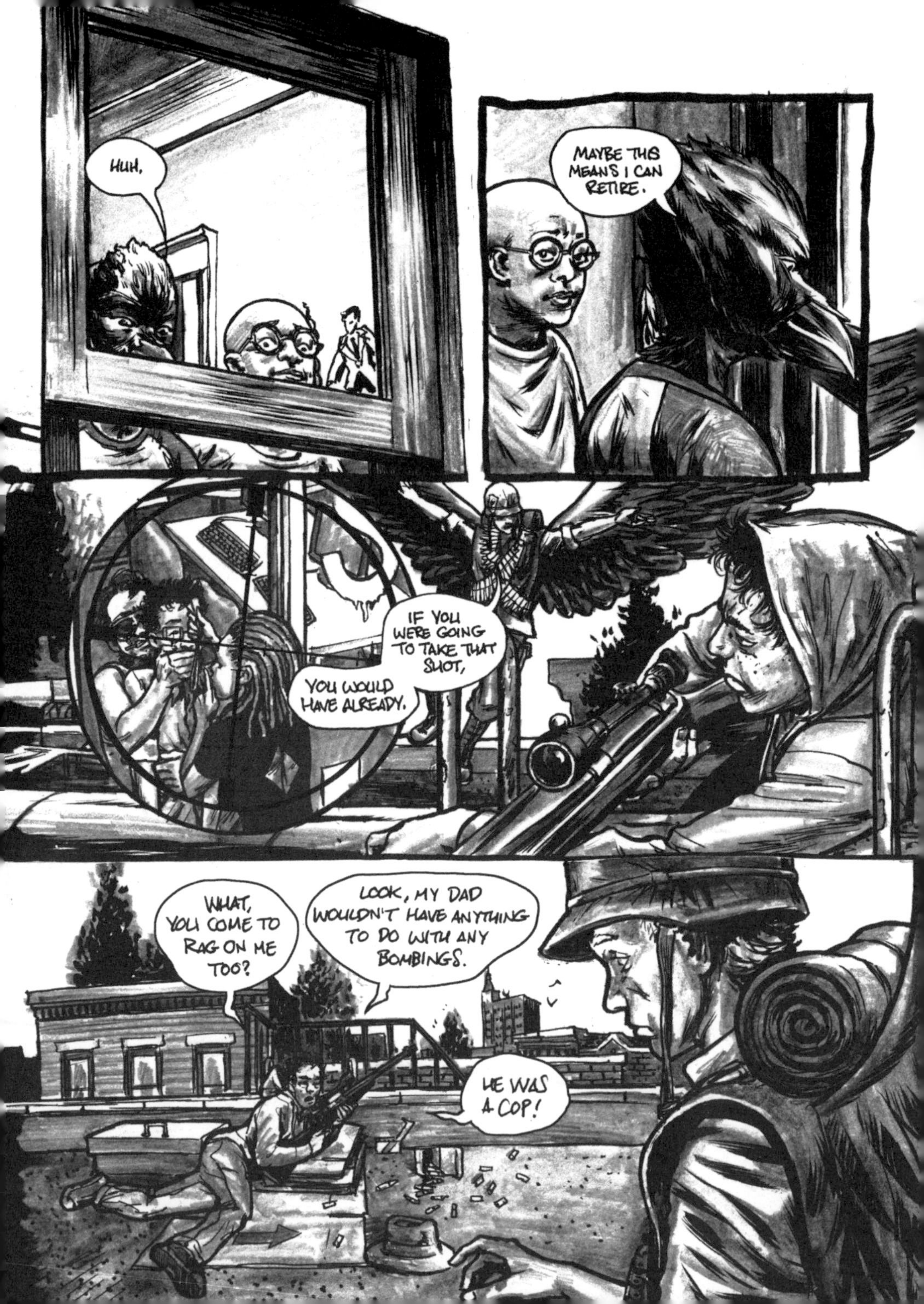
HUH.
MAYBE THIS MEANS I CAN RETIRE.
IF YOU WERE GOING TO TAKE THAT SHOT,
YOU WOULD HAVE ALREADY.
WHAT, YOU COME TO RAG ON ME TOO?
LOOK, MY DAD WOULDN'T HAVE ANYTHING TO DO WITH ANY BOMBINGS.
HE WAS A COP!

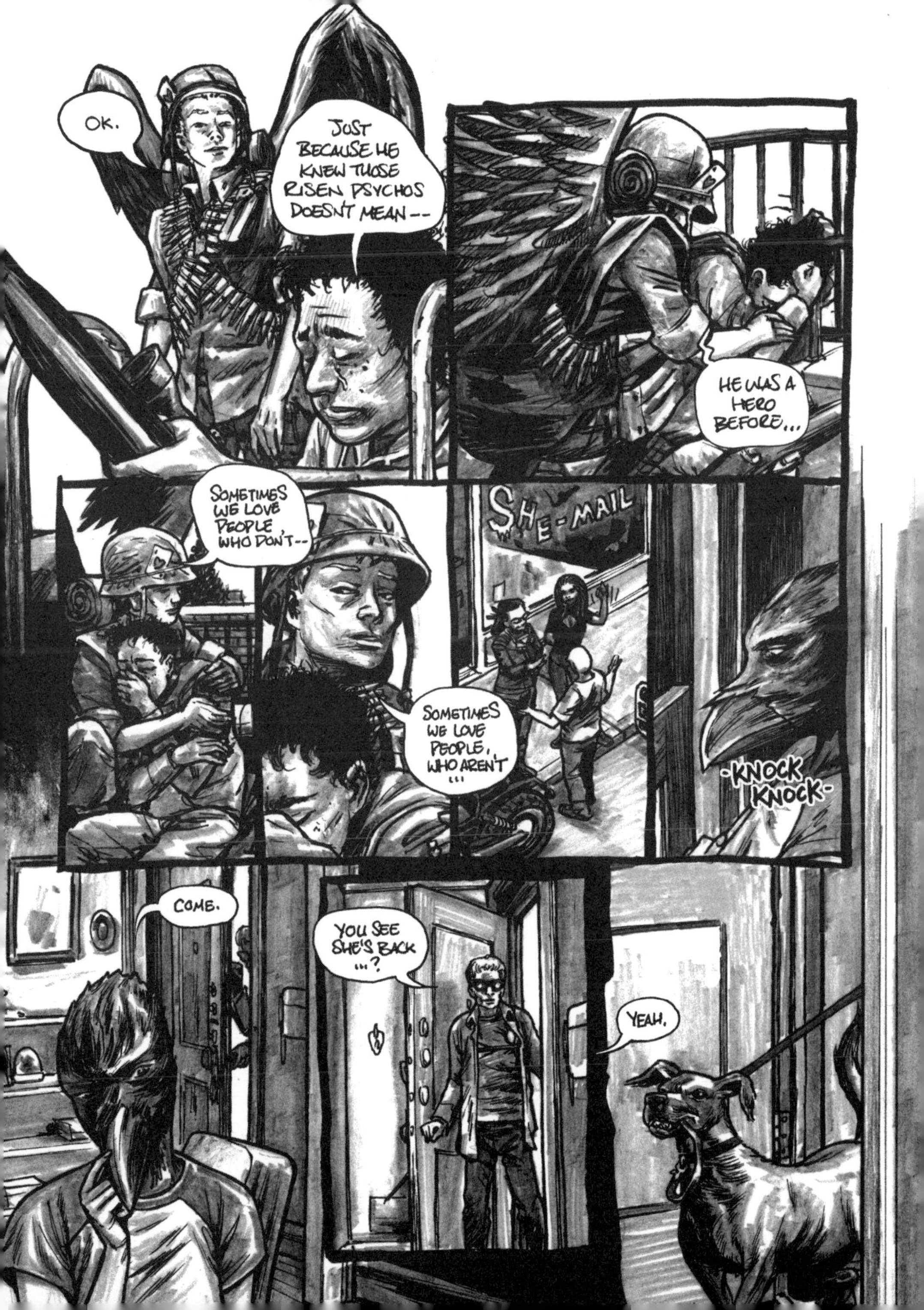
OK.
JUST BECAUSE HE KNEW THOSE RISEN PSYCHOS DOESN'T MEAN --
HE WAS A HERO BEFORE...
SOMETIMES WE LOVE PEOPLE, WHO DON'T--
SOMETIMES WE LOVE PEOPLE, WHO AREN'T ...
SHE-MAIL
-KNOCK KNOCK-
COME.
YOU SEE SHE'S BACK ...?
YEAH.

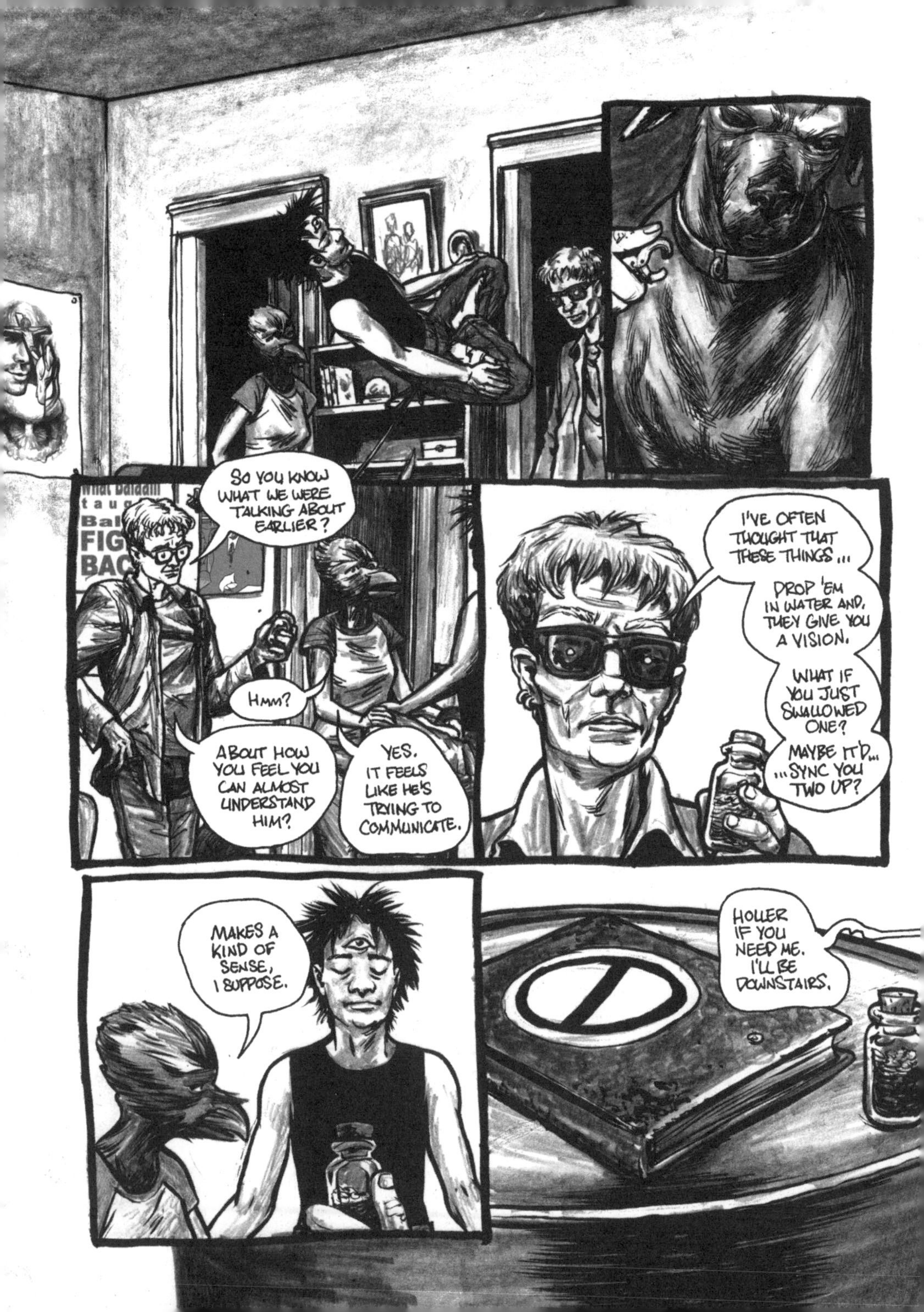
SO YOU KNOW WHAT WE WERE TALKING ABOUT EARLIER?
HMM?
ABOUT HOW YOU FEEL YOU CAN ALMOST UNDERSTAND HIM?
YES. IT FEELS LIKE HE'S TRYING TO COMMUNICATE.
I'VE OFTEN THOUGHT THAT THESE THINGS...
PROP 'EM IN WATER AND, THEY GIVE YOU A VISION.
WHAT IF YOU JUST SWALLOWED ONE?
MAYBE IT'D... ...SYNC YOU TWO UP?
MAKES A KIND OF SENSE, I SUPPOSE.
HOLLER IF YOU NEED ME. I'LL BE DOWNSTAIRS.

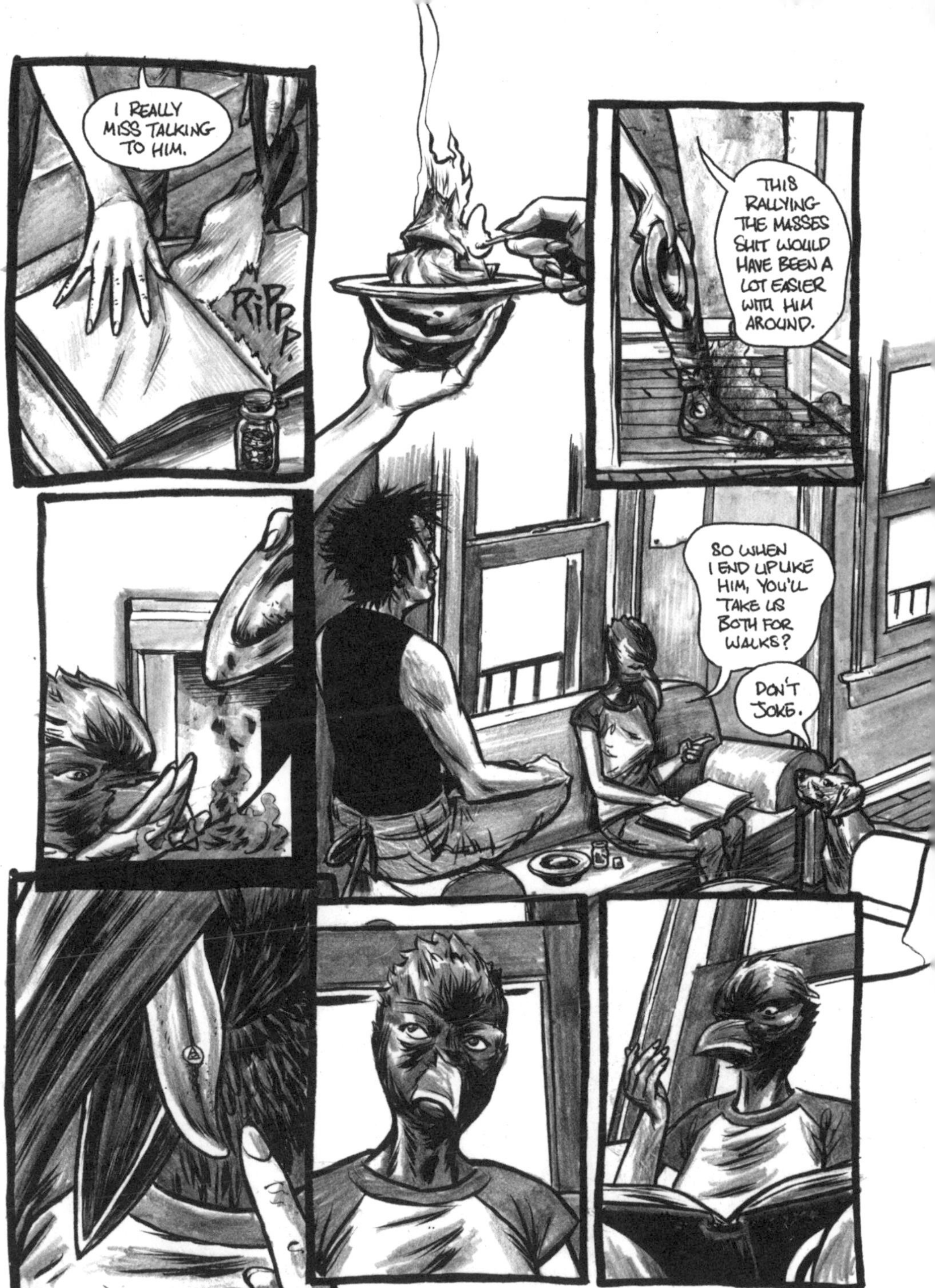
I REALLY MISS TALKING TO HIM.
RIPPP.
THIS RALLYING THE MASSES SHIT WOULD HAVE BEEN A LOT EASIER WITH HIM AROUND.
SO WHEN I END UP LIKE HIM, YOU'LL TAKE US BOTH FOR WALKS?
DON'T JOKE.

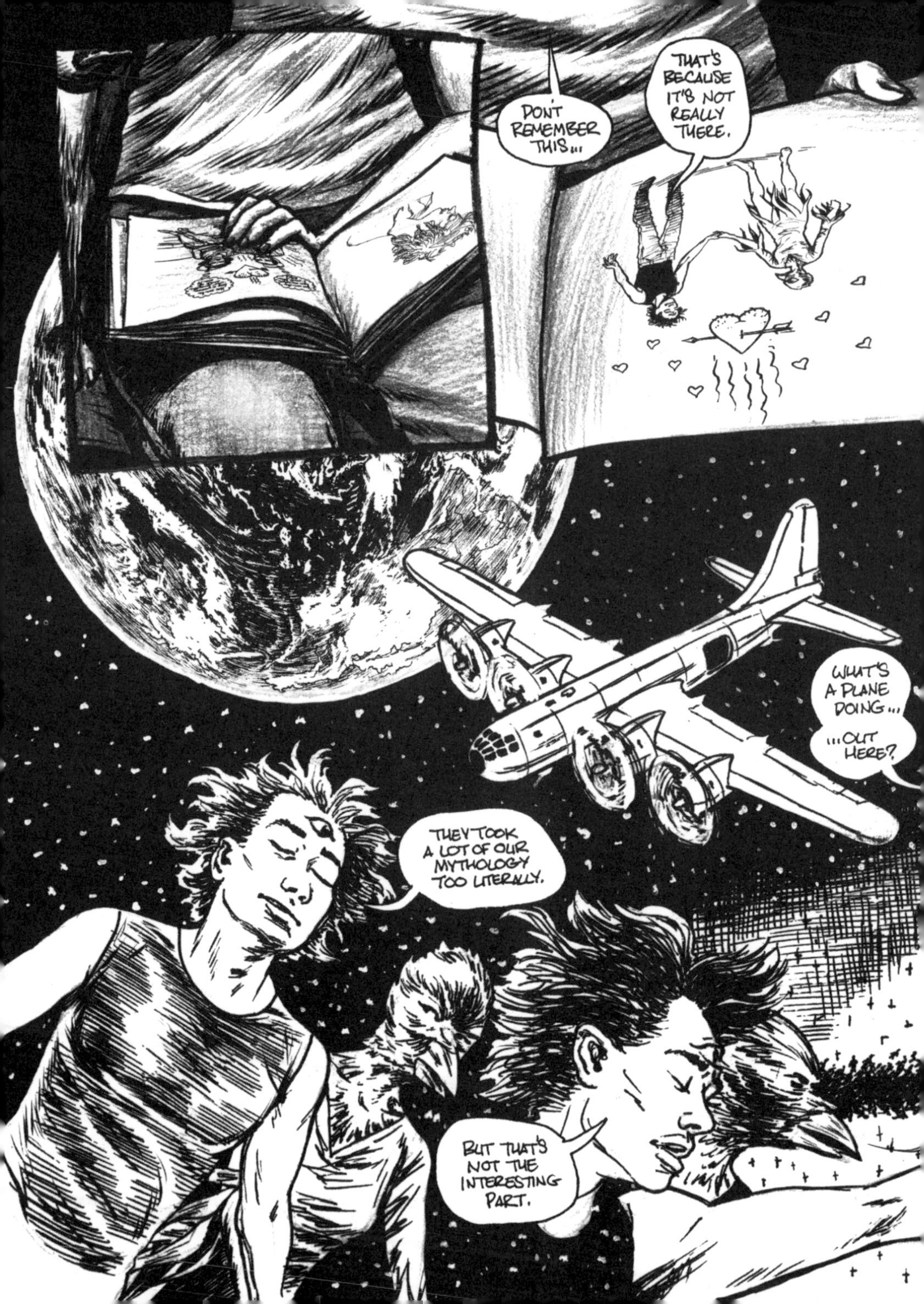
DON'T REMEMBER THIS...
THAT'S BECAUSE IT'S NOT REALLY THERE.
WHAT'S A PLANE DOING...
...OUT HERE?
THEY TOOK A LOT OF OUR MYTHOLOGY TOO LITERALLY.
BUT THAT'S NOT THE INTERESTING PART.

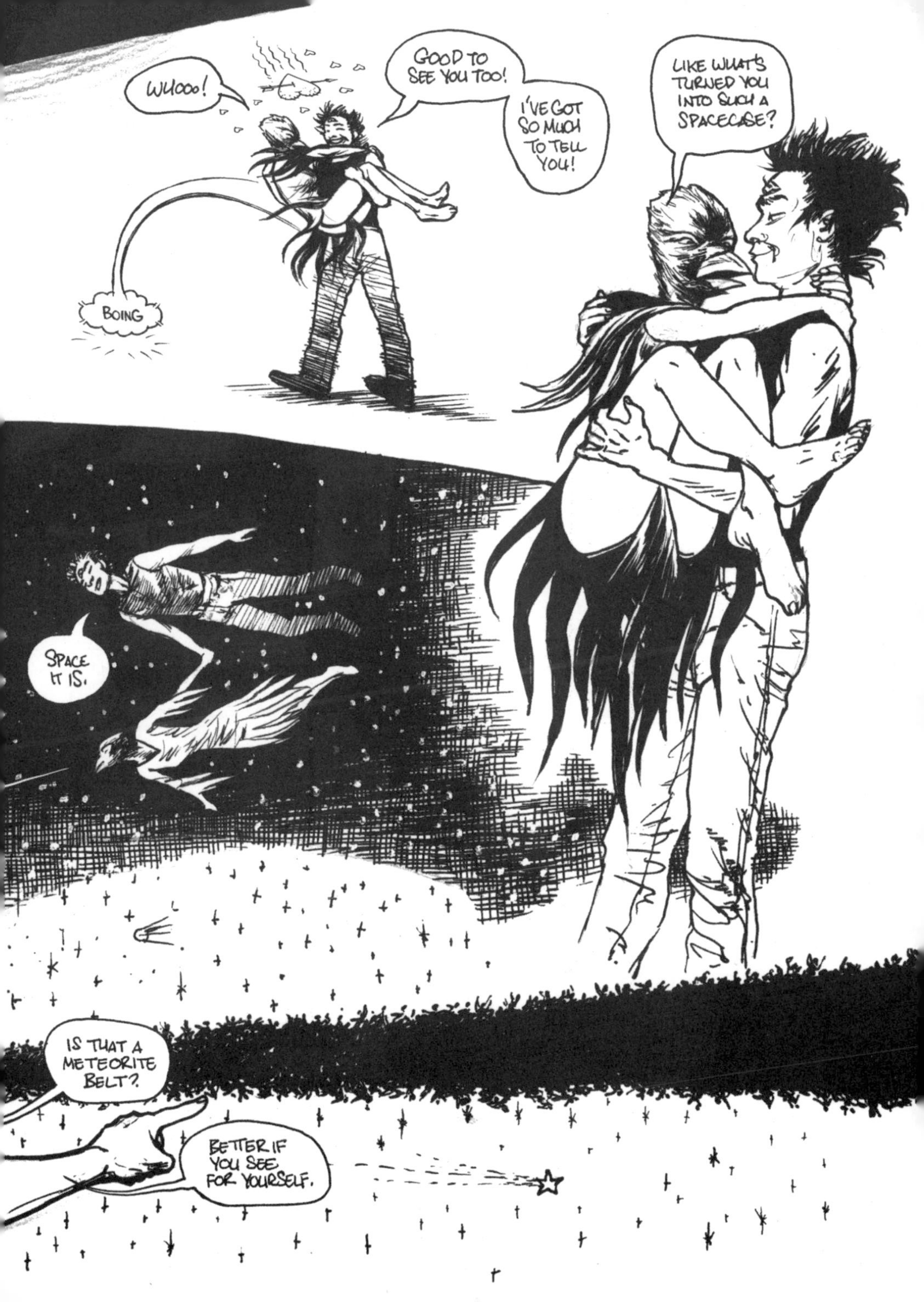
WHOOO!
GOOD TO SEE YOU TOO!
I'VE GOT SO MUCH TO TELL YOU!
BOING
LIKE WHAT'S TURNED YOU INTO SUCH A SPACECASE?
SPACE IT IS.
IS THAT A METEORITE BELT?
BETTER IF YOU SEE FOR YOURSELF.

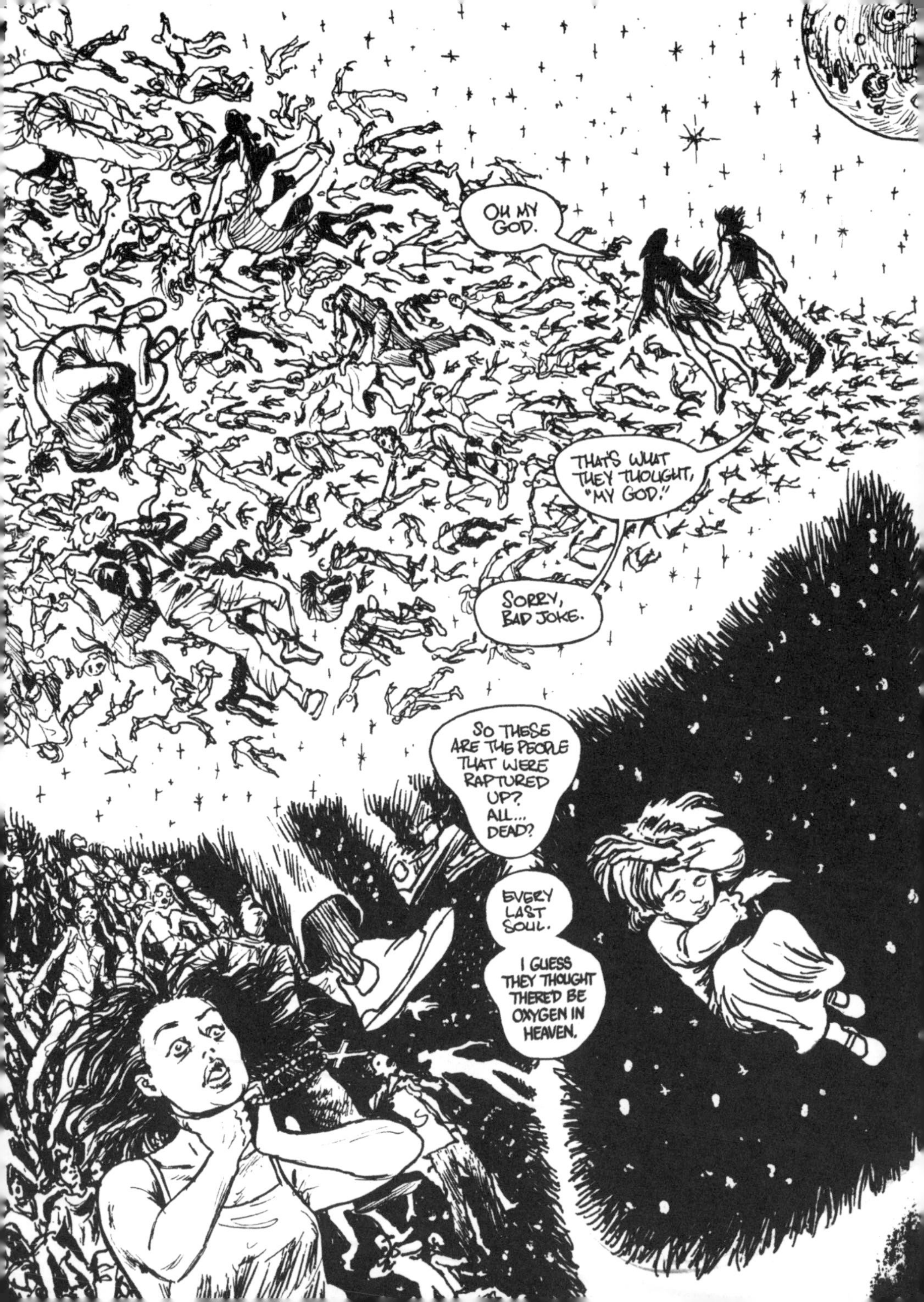
OH MY GOD.
THAT'S WHAT THEY THOUGHT, "MY GOD."
SORRY, BAD JOKE.
SO THESE ARE THE PEOPLE THAT WERE RAPTURED UP? ALL... DEAD?
EVERY LAST SOUL.
I GUESS THEY THOUGHT THERE'D BE OXYGEN IN HEAVEN.

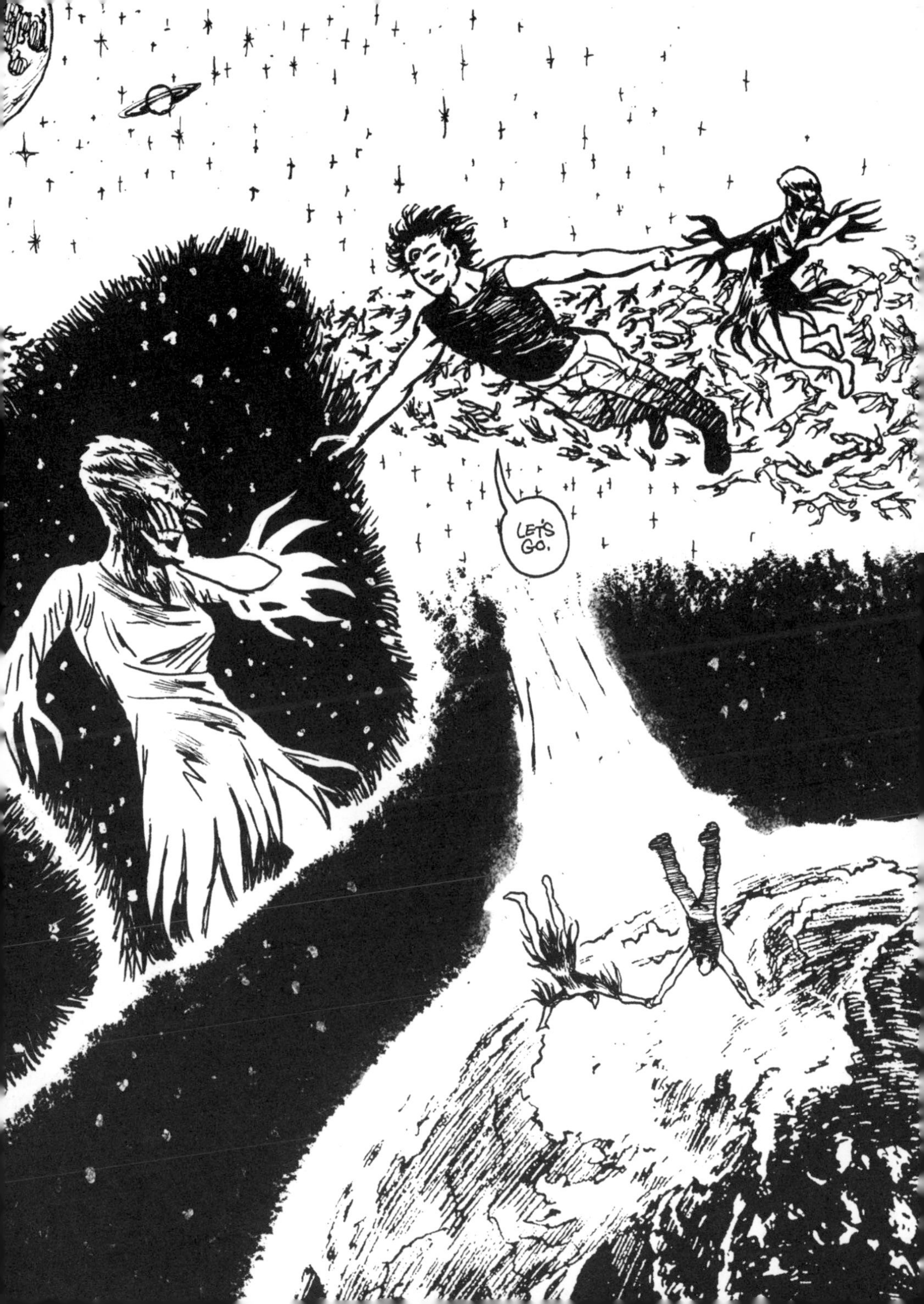
LET'S GO.

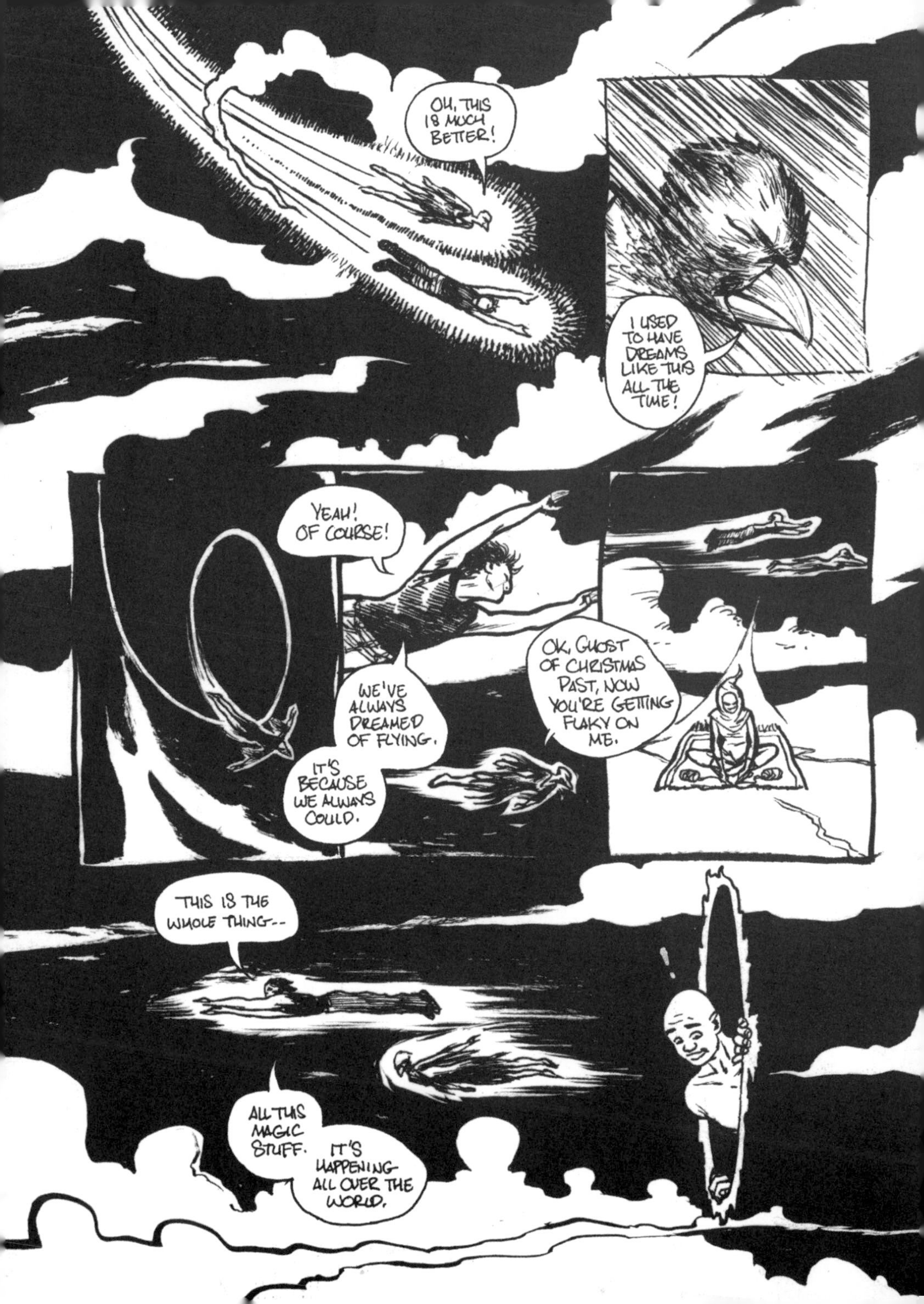
OH, THIS IS MUCH BETTER!
I USED TO HAVE DREAMS LIKE THIS ALL THE TIME!
YEAH! OF COURSE!
WE'VE ALWAYS DREAMED OF FLYING.
IT'S BECAUSE WE ALWAYS COULD.
OK, GHOST OF CHRISTMAS PAST, NOW YOU'RE GETTING FLAKY ON ME.
THIS IS THE WHOLE THING--
!
ALL THIS MAGIC STUFF.
IT'S HAPPENING ALL OVER THE WORLD.

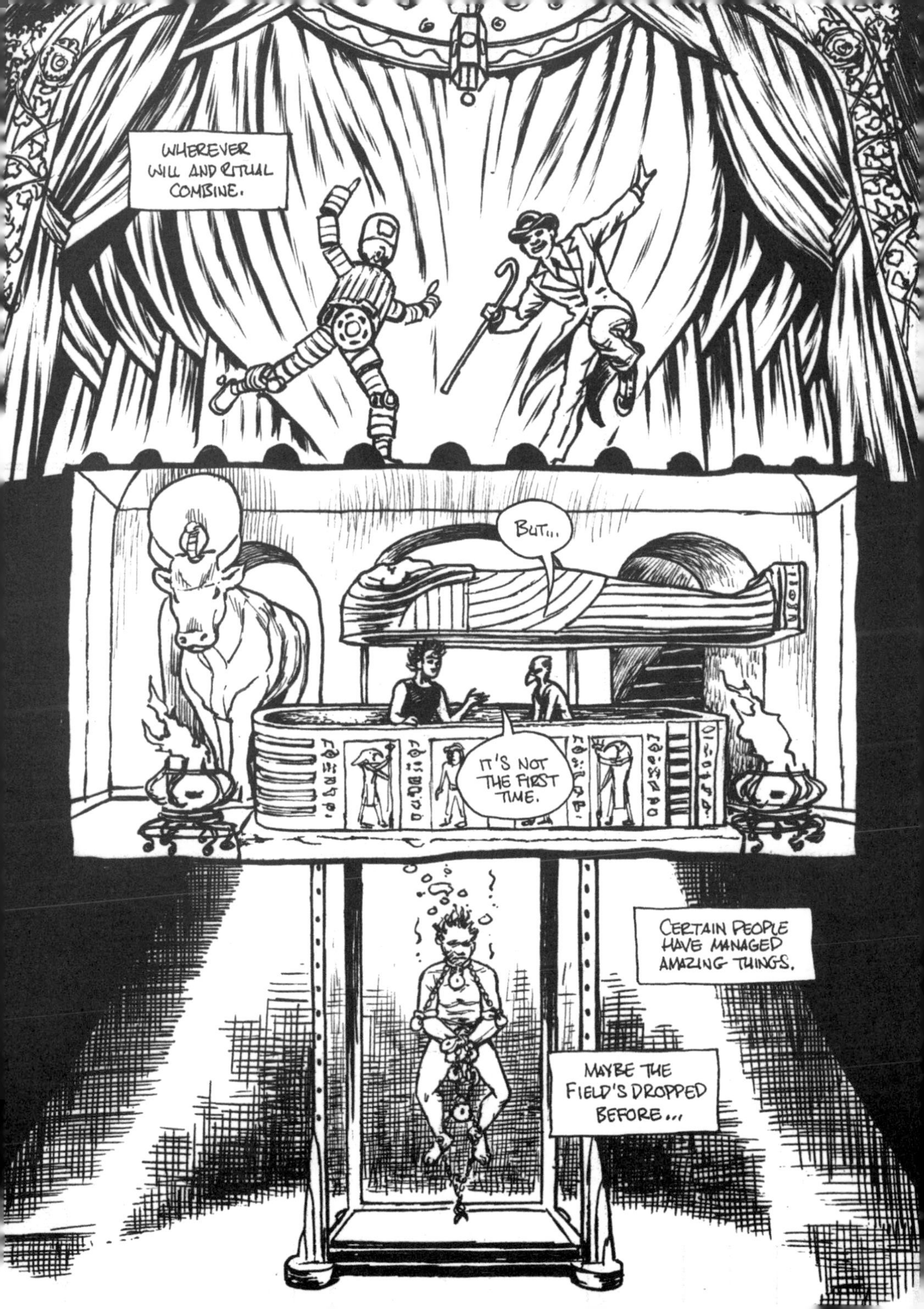
WHEREVER WILL AND RITUAL COMBINE.
BUT...
IT'S NOT THE FIRST TIME.
CERTAIN PEOPLE HAVE MANAGED AMAZING THINGS.
MAYBE THE FIELD'S DROPPED BEFORE...

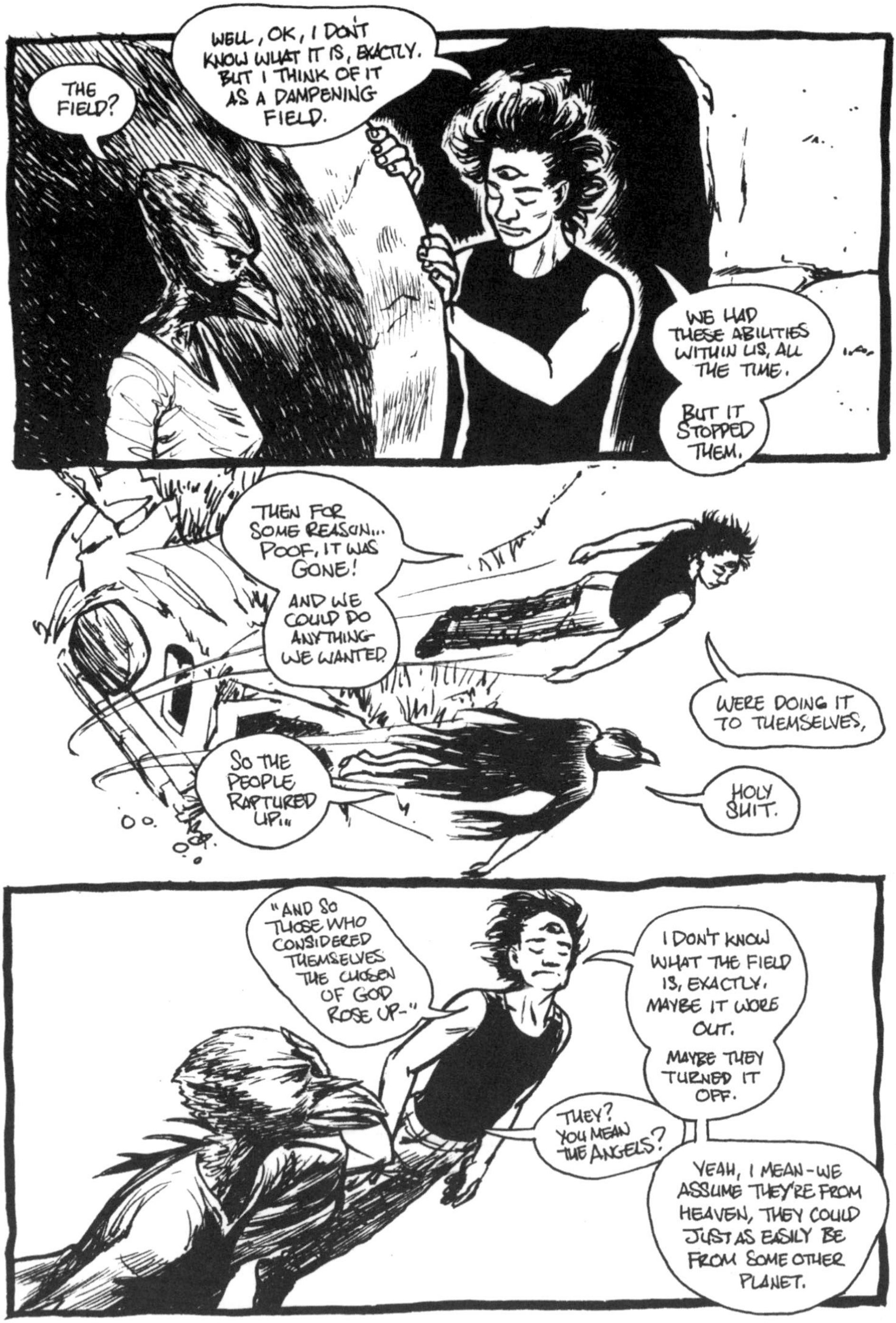
THE FIELD?
WELL, OK, I DON'T KNOW WHAT IT IS, EXACTLY. BUT I THINK OF IT AS A DAMPENING FIELD.
WE HAD THESE ABILITIES WITHIN US, ALL THE TIME.
BUT IT STOPPED THEM.
THEN FOR SOME REASON... POOF, IT WAS GONE!
AND WE COULD DO ANYTHING WE WANTED.
SO THE PEOPLE RAPTURED UP...
WERE DOING IT TO THEMSELVES,
HOLY SHIT.
"AND SO THOSE WHO CONSIDERED THEMSELVES THE CHOSEN OF GOD ROSE UP-"
I DON'T KNOW WHAT THE FIELD IS, EXACTLY. MAYBE IT WORE OUT.
MAYBE THEY TURNED IT OFF.
THEY? YOU MEAN THE ANGELS?
YEAH, I MEAN-WE ASSUME THEY'RE FROM HEAVEN, THEY COULD JUST AS EASILY BE FROM SOME OTHER PLANET.

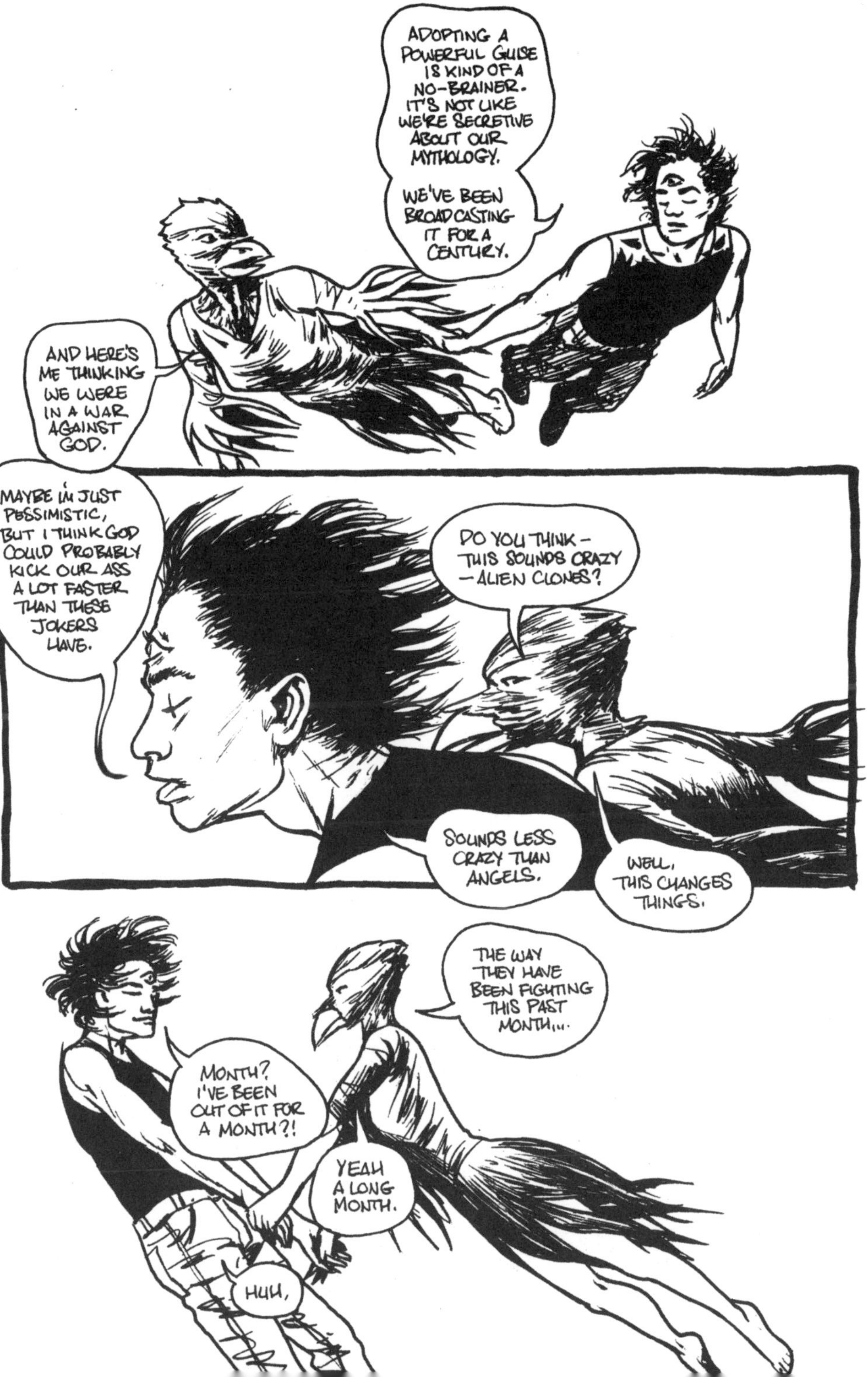
ADOPTING A POWERFUL GUISE IS KIND OF A NO-BRAINER. IT'S NOT LIKE WE'RE SECRETIVE ABOUT OUR MYTHOLOGY.
WE'VE BEEN BROADCASTING IT FOR A CENTURY.
AND HERE'S ME THINKING WE WERE IN A WAR AGAINST GOD.
MAYBE I'M JUST PESSIMISTIC, BUT I THINK GOD COULD PROBABLY KICK OUR ASS A LOT FASTER THAN THESE JOKERS HAVE.
DO YOU THINK - THIS SOUNDS CRAZY - ALIEN CLONES?
SOUNDS LESS CRAZY THAN ANGELS.
WELL, THIS CHANGES THINGS.
THE WAY THEY HAVE BEEN FIGHTING THIS PAST MONTH...
MONTH? I'VE BEEN OUT OF IT FOR A MONTH?!
YEAH A LONG MONTH.
HUH.

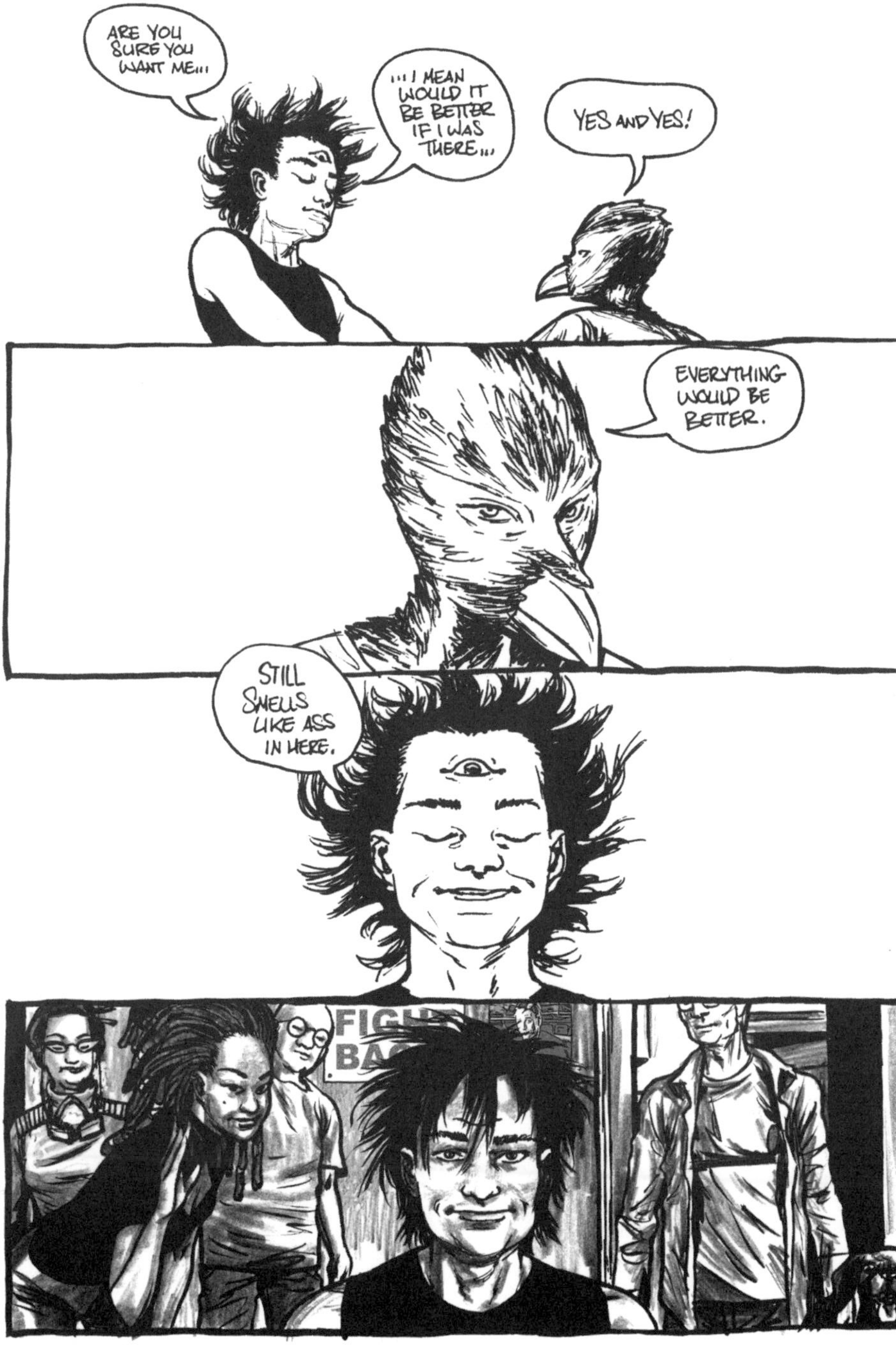
ARE YOU SURE YOU WANT ME...
...I MEAN WOULD IT BE BETTER IF I WAS THERE...
YES AND YES!
EVERYTHING WOULD BE BETTER.
STILL SMELLS LIKE ASS IN HERE.
FIGH
BA

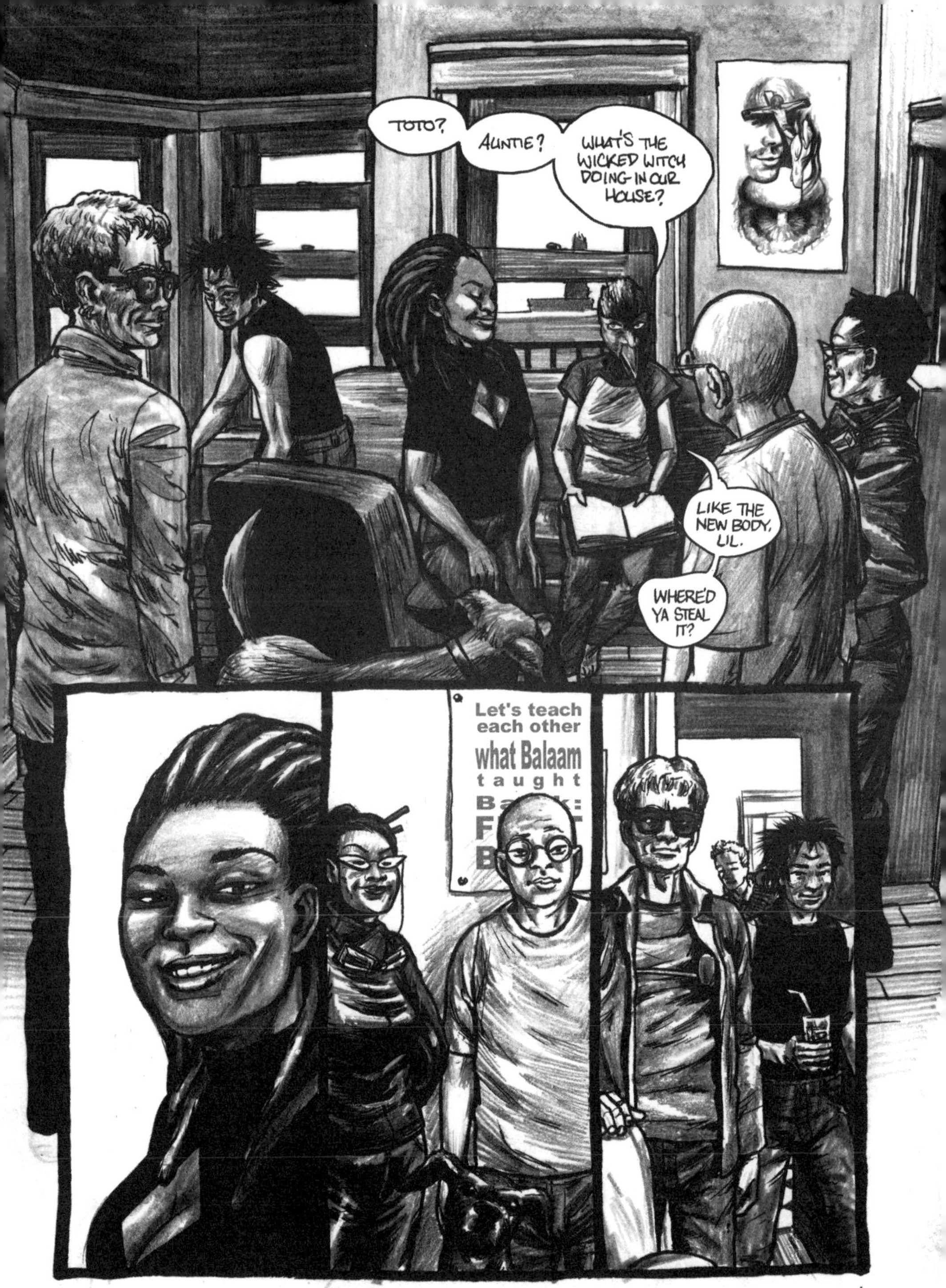
TOTO?
AUNTIE?
WHAT'S THE WICKED WITCH DOING IN OUR HOUSE?
LIKE THE NEW BODY, LIL.
WHERE'D YA STEAL IT?
Let's teach each other
what Balaam
taught

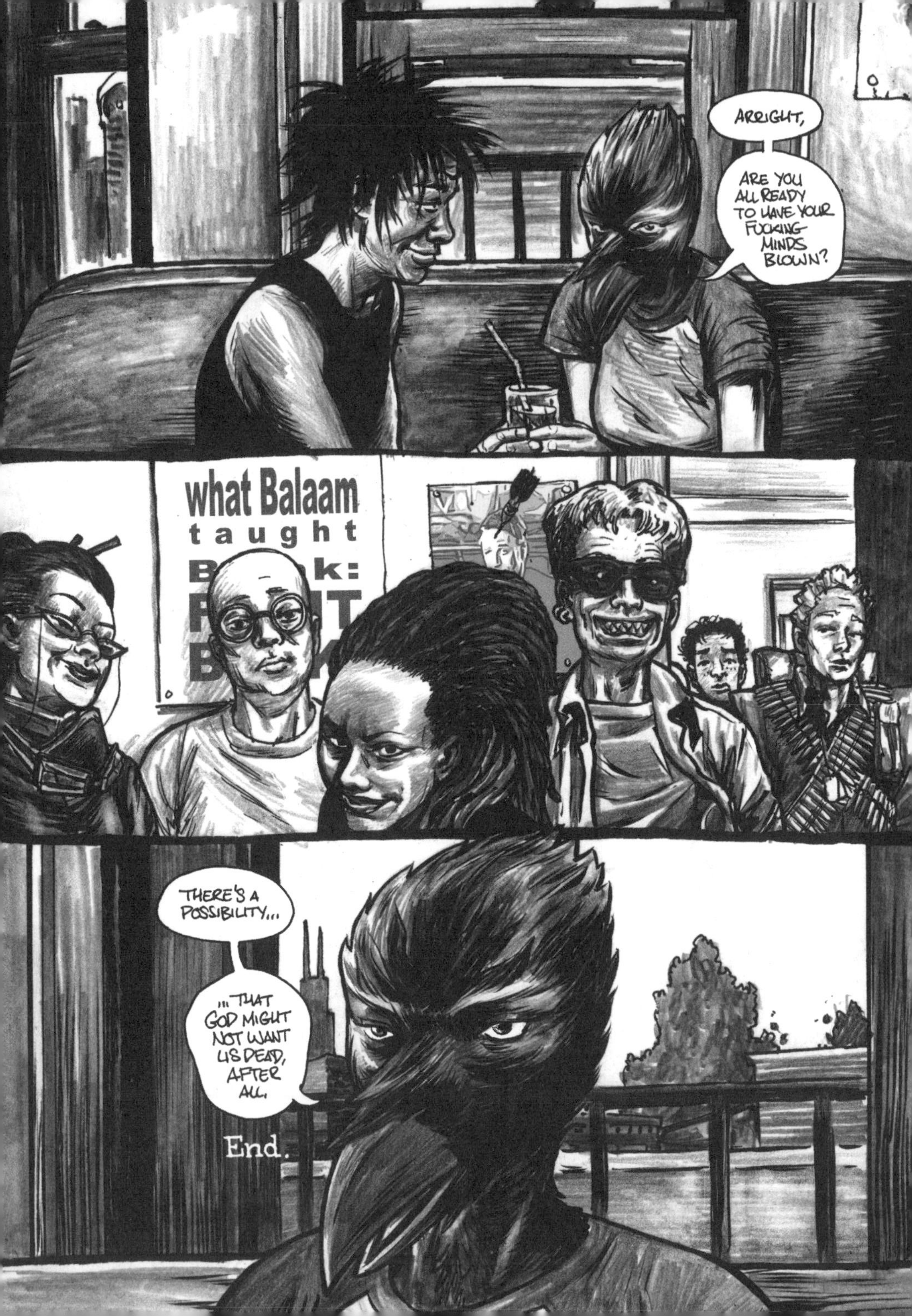

ARRIGHT,
ARE YOU ALL READY TO HAVE YOUR FUCKING MINDS BLOWN?
what Balaam
taught
THERE'S A POSSIBILITY...
...THAT GOD MIGHT NOT WANT US DEAD, AFTER ALL.
End.